EMS Finance

Dennis Mitterer, MS, BSN, EMT-P

Board of Certified Safety Professionals

American Society of Safety Engineers

American Insurance Institute–Risk Management

Pennsylvania Nurses Association

American Nurses Association

EMS Management Series

SERIES EDITOR, *Jeffrey T. Lindsey, PhD, PM, EFO, CFO*
Distance Education Coordinator
for the Fire and Emergency Services Programs
University of Florida
Gainesville, Florida

PEARSON

Boston   Columbus   Indianapolis   New York   San Francisco   Upper Saddle River
Amsterdam   Cape Town   Dubai   London   Madrid   Milan   Munich   Paris   Montreal   Toronto
Delhi   Mexico City   São Paulo   Sydney   Hong Kong   Seoul   Singapore   Taipei   Tokyo

Publisher: Julie Levin Alexander
Publisher's Assistant: Regina Bruno
Editor-in-Chief: Marlene McHugh Pratt
Product Manager: Sladjana Repic
Program Manager: Monica Moosang
Development Editor: Julie M. Vitale, iD8-TripleSSS
Editorial Assistant: Kelly Clark
Director of Marketing: David Gesell
Executive Marketing Manager: Brian Hoehl
Marketing Specialist: Michael Sirinides
Project Management Lead: Cynthia Zonneveld

Project Manager: Julie Boddorf
Full-Service Project Manager: Munesh Kumar, Aptara®, Inc.
Editorial Media Manager: Amy Peltier
Media Project Manager: Ellen Martino
Creative Director: Jayne Conte
Cover Designer: Suzanne Behnke
Cover Image: Shutterstock/B Calkins
Composition: Aptara®, Inc.
Text Font: Times Ten LT Std

Credits and acknowledgments borrowed from other sources and reproduced, with permission, in this textbook appear on the appropriate pages within text.

Library of Congress Cataloging-in-Publication Data

Mitterer, Dennis M.
 EMS finance/Dennis M. Mitterer, EMT & Jeffrey Lindsey, Ph.D., EMT-P, CHS IV, EFO, CFO St. Petersburg College, St. Petersburg, Florida.
    pages cm
 Includes bibliographical references and index.
 ISBN-13: 978-0-13-507482-4 (alk. paper)
 ISBN-10: 0-13-507482-7 (alk. paper)
  1. Emergency medical services—Management. 2. Emergency medical technicians. 3. Emergency medicine—Management. I. Lindsey, Jeffrey. II. Title. III. Title: Emergency medical services finance.
 RA645.5.M58 2014
 362.18068'1—dc23   2012047594

PEARSON

ISBN 13: 978-0-13-507482-4
ISBN 10:   0-13-507482-7

Dedication

To my lovely wife, Heather, who guided me with her encouragement and wisdom as I struggled to fill the pages with my thoughts and ideas and her unwavering commitment to push me onward on a daily basis, I am forever grateful.
To Jeff Lindsey, for having the faith in me to write this book and his guidance in focusing my thoughts and challenging me with each chapter submitted, I am truly thankful.
To Dave Bradley, for giving of his time and expertise in providing honest feedback on the technical aspects of this book, his insight about contacts to talk with for additional information, and his friendship throughout, I am indebted.

Contents

Chapter 7

Purchasing   144

Chapter 8

Analysis of Activity   180

Chapter 9

Billing for Services   201

Chapter 10

Risk Financing   231

Chapter 11

Auditing   254

Preface

Writing a book is full of challenges. Deciding what is important to the reader, gathering facts, and constructing the words in a meaningful way led to many sleepless nights and restless days. In the case of writing a book on emergency medical services (EMS) and the ever-changing environment of finance, the goal was to provide timeless guidance for nonfinancial managers with ideas and concepts that could help improve their abilities to develop a successful organization. Some ideas are basic, some are radical. Some of the information may seem foreign, and some may seem like common sense. Certainly this text does not cover all the information needed by EMS managers on a topic as important as finance. Volumes can be written on financial concepts in general, health care finance more specifically, and EMS finance in particular. The purpose is to introduce the concepts of finance to nonfinancial EMS managers. As Ben Franklin stated, "Education is not about opening a closed mind, but expanding an already open mind."

The purpose of this book is to present valuable information to new or experienced EMS leaders who may have varying degrees of experience, formal and informal, and to stimulate their thinking. Not everyone who reads this will agree with all the information, and truly it may not apply in every EMS structure. The goal is to stimulate thinking in order to change the way things are done, to avoid mistakes of the past, and to encourage future growth of EMS as a profession.

As with any book of this nature, the information may change. EMS managers must stay abreast of changes and incorporate new information in the most appropriate manner. But first, a change must take place in the thinking of decision makers so that they are open to new ideas. If this book challenges their current belief systems, then I say "Great!" because that's my goal.

Finance is measured in relation to objective facts. The application is subjective, based on the EMS leader's values, goals, and personal beliefs. Running an EMS organization is serious business that affects individuals and the communities served. It is imperative for EMS leaders to recognize this huge responsibility and seek the knowledge that assists in fulfilling the goals of the profession.

ORGANIZATION OF THIS TEXT

This text is organized to provide the reader with an overview of management functions and the role of finance in decision making. Building on the concepts of managerial decision making, the text describes accepted financial conventions. By introducing how financial resources are accounted for, the text provides the EMS manager with the "whys" and "hows" and the "rights" and "wrongs" of tracking finances through an EMS organization.

Chapter 1 describes management practice in terms of financial accountability. The reader is led through a historical walk of management in order to orient to how finance fits into the process of guiding an EMS organization. Chapter 1 also establishes a foundation for understanding the importance of the mission of EMS and how managing financial resources can support and build upon this foundation. Quality and finance are discussed to demonstrate that interacting with the public is more than just running emergency and nonemergency calls and submitting a bill for reimbursement. The discussion continues by introducing how economic considerations are important when making financial decisions.

Chapter 2 introduces accounting conventions and concepts of financial reporting. Managers learn about financial statements, cash flow tracking, and analysis. It is through the analysis that managers begin to understand the importance of objective decision making when using community assets.

Chapter 3 discusses the discipline of accounting and introduces important principles that EMS managers should understand. Many of the principles are specific to the accounting process. EMS managers are ultimately responsible for the financial health of the organization and, thus, must understand the process. Further discussion covers inventory control and the concept of depreciation.

Chapter 4 provides an overview of the role of finance in the EMS organization and how knowledge of economic principles such as supply and demand, interest rates, and determining the value of money aids in making good financial decisions.

Chapter 5 explores how EMS managers can use what they have learned to develop a fiscally sound program for the organization. Managers must understand that a financially sound program is only as good as the corresponding analysis of business activity. This chapter also discusses how to collect data, evaluate the accuracy of the data, and analyze the data to shape decision making.

Chapter 6 introduces the important concept of budgeting. To help the reader understand how a program is developed, the budget process and purchasing considerations are presented. The EMS manager will learn the differences between revenue and expense types. Four types of budgets are also discussed.

A review of master, capital, flexible, zero-based, and operating budgeting complete this chapter.

Purchasing is an important concept discussed in Chapter 7. The text aligns purchasing with the mission of the organization and shows how financial decisions, relative to purchasing, can improve the overall financial position of the organization and become more socially responsible. The concept of proactive purchasing, inventory control, contract, and green purchasing are also discussed. The concept of risk management is introduced to describe how EMS managers can avoid contractual pitfalls that negatively affect the financial position of the organization.

Chapter 8 provides important information and exercises on analyzing the financial activity of the EMS organization. Managers make decisions based on available information. At times, these decisions are made objectively, but often they are made subjectively. There is more room for error and questioning with subjective decision making. This chapter discusses how to analyze, details specific methods for developing analysis tools, and provides methods to extract valuable feedback from tracked data. Specific tools—such as statistical process control, the Balanced Scorecard, and SWOT analysis are reviewed. The chapter concludes with a discussion of business ratios.

Getting paid for services is an important management function, and Chapter 9 provides an overview of the billing process, history of payers, and the rules and regulations affecting EMS organizations. Patient care documentation is the foundation of submitting "clean" bills, and this chapter discusses the importance of educating EMTs and paramedics on the need to acquire complete patient information, document assessments very well, and complete treatment.

As with any decision making, there are risks. Managers risk the organization's finances and growth, and their personal reputation, especially with decisions that are made without a thorough review of the benefits to be had from important financial decisions. Chapter 10 discusses what risk is, how decisions are evaluated from a risk management perspective, and methods to use to evaluate financially important decisions. Even when decisions are made using tools that limit financial losses, audits are essential for ensuring that EMS managers are conducting business legally, ethically, and medically correctly.

Chapter 11 covers audits related to outside agencies, internal audits that evaluate operations, and the consequences of improper business activities. Developing checks and balances is an essential managerial function, and all EMS decision makers should embrace the stability that audits provide. This chapter discusses corporate governance, the concept of assurance, and types of audits.

Included in the appendix are values charts that assist EMS managers with calculating the effects of interest, annuity values, and determining the cost of money in the present and future. These graphs are important in determining the cost of an investment into a project, the cost of investing in short-term notes, and how interest rates affect decision making.

FEATURES

Chapter Objectives: Objectives are identified at the beginning of each chapter and outline the material the reader should understand upon completion of the chapter.

Key Terms: Key terms are listed at the beginning of each chapter and are highlighted in bold type at a key point within the chapter. Each chapter's terms are defined at the end of the chapter, and all terms are included in the comprehensive glossary at the end of the book.

What Would You Do? Case Study: Every chapter starts with an EMS manager tackling some issue related to public information and education that is related to the content of the chapter. How the EMS manager resolved the issue based on information in the chapter is presented at the end in the What Would You Do? Reflection section.

Best Practice: Every chapter includes a real-world example that illustrates information from the chapter having been used successfully.

Sidebars: This feature relates interesting information that corresponds very closely to text discussion.

Review Questions: Students are required to draw on the knowledge presented in the chapter to answer the questions.

References: A list of references and other useful source material appears at the end of each chapter.

ROAD MAP/HOW TO USE THIS TEXT

This text is designed to be used as a resource for the application of finance principles in a managerial context. As with any book, specific information (rules and regulations) can change. The text was written for nonfinancial managers, new managers, and professionals who aspire to become better managers by utilizing knowledge of finance that is easily incorporated into management processes. The text can be used in a formal collegiate setting or as a reference for managers needing to refresh their knowledge of the financial activities of EMS. To be of any value, the information must be implemented as the underlying premise is based on sound financial philosophies and time-tested managerial activities.

TEACHING AND LEARNING RESOURCES

For information on instructor resources, including PowerPoint presentations and assessment tools, please contact your Brady sales representative.

ACKNOWLEDGMENTS

I would like to thank Bryan Smith, of First Aid and Safety Patrol (FASP), Lebanon, Pennsylvania, for meeting with me to discuss finance issues, for the use of FASP's facilities for photo work, and for access to his staff. I also would like to thank Kelly and Bill Lamkin for creating photographs that helped capture the essence of why EMS is in the people business. Thank you to Skip Kirkwood for providing his insight and expertise gained from years of leading EMS organizations.

Finally, I owe a debt of gratitude to the staff at Pearson, especially Monica Moosang, as well as to my editors Julie M. Vitale , Tracy Grenier, and Heath Lynn Silberfeld for their encouragement, faith, and professionalism throughout this project. I could not have done this without you.

Reviewers

David A. Bradley, B.S., NREMT-P
David is an Education and Training Specialist for VFIS, a subsidiary of the Glatfelter Insurance Group. His responsibilities include national delivery of education and training programs, consulting services, curriculum development, and information analysis for VFIS.

Dave has more than 35 years of experience in EMS. He has served in many roles during his career, from volunteer EMT to Career EMS Chief. He is a Nationally Registered Paramedic and holds a bachelor's degree in safety engineering.

Heather Mitterer, EMT
Heather is an account manager at Echo Data Group managing international accounts for product fulfillment. She is a past production supervisor handling millions of dollars of products for large multinational customers. Her business and finance experience has helped improve the success of many volunteer, nonprofit, and for-profit companies. Heather has over 15 years of EMS experience and has functioned in many roles in EMS organizations. She holds an associate's degree in business administration from Harrisburg Area Community College and is studying business and organizational behavior at Pennsylvania State University.

John L. Beckman, FF, EMT-PP
Instructor
Technology Center of DuPage
Deerfield, IL

Diane Flint
Program Director
EHS Undergraduate Management
University of Maryland
Baltimore, MD

Steven E. Lynn
Paramedic, Firefighter, Adjunct Instructor
Southwestern Illinois College
Belleville, IL

John Vastano, CPA
Pittsgrove, NJ

Michael Vastano
EMT Program Director
Captain James A. Lovell Federal Health Care Center
Kenosha, WI

About the Author

DENNIS MITTERER, MS, BSN, EMT-P

Dennis Mitterer has more than 30 years experience in EMS and health care. Starting as a first responder and earning his EMT and then paramedic credentials, he worked for years honing his clinical knowledge. He became an instructor for EMTs and paramedics, and eventually his aspirations led him back to college to study business administration with a concentration in health care. After graduating from Elizabethtown College, he enrolled and graduated from Pennsylvania State University, Smeal Business School, with a master's degree in management with a concentration in health care.

Mr. Mitterer has worked as the director of health and safety in a privately held manufacturing organization, director of industrial medicine at a hospital, and administrator of two multiphysician offices. He has earned the designation of Certified Safety Professional (CSP) and Associate in Risk Management (ARM). He is also a registered nurse and earned his bachelor's in that field from Pennsylvania State University.

Mr. Mitterer's management guidance has improved many organizations' financial positions by his adherence to the basic principles of financial management. He has also successfully guided financial improvement efforts at a credit union and has led initiatives to develop and rebuild a local community center.

Mr. Mitterer teaches business and finance classes at three colleges and universities. He has lectured nationally on business and EMS topics and continues to develop programs to enhance EMS development and learning for seasoned and upcoming managers. He is currently pursuing his doctoral degree in leadership and organizational behavior.

About the Series Editor

JEFFREY T. LINDSEY, PhD, PM, EFO, CFO

Dr. Jeffrey Lindsey has served in a variety of roles in the fire and EMS arena for the past 30 years. He has held positions of firefighter, paramedic, dispatcher, educator, coordinator, deputy chief, and chief. He started his career in Carlisle, Pennsylvania, as a volunteer firefighter/EMT. In 1985 Dr. Lindsey pioneered the first advanced life support service in Cumberland County, Pennsylvania. He is retired as the Fire/EMS Chief for Estero Fire Rescue, where he served as the South Division Incident Commander during major events. He was also part of the Area Command for Lee County EOC. Currently he is the Distance Education Coordinator for the Fire and Emergency Services Programs at the University of Florida.

He has served as an inaugural member on the National EMS Advisory Council, representing fire-based EMS, and is a past member of the State of Florida EMS Advisory Council, where he served as the firefighter/paramedic representative. He currently serves as representative to the Fire and Emergency Services Higher Education EMS degree committee. He has been active in the IAFC, serving as liaison to ACEP and attending various meetings representing fire-based EMS, and as the inaugural chair of the Community Paramedic committee, and he is an associate member of the Prehospital Research Forum.

He was a monthly columnist on product reviews for 3 years for *The Journal of Emergency Medical Services (JEMS),* a national EMS journal. He is a columnist for Firerehab.com and has authored numerous fire and EMS texts for Brady/Pearson. He is currently the Chief Learning Officer for the Health and Safety Institute, which produces *24-7 EMS* and *24-7* Fire videos. He also was an EMS professor for St. Petersburg College (Florida).

Dr. Lindsey has been involved in a number of large events and has served within the incident command system at the upper level, including during a number of wildland fires and Hurricane Charley. He has also been involved in the preparations for a number of other hurricanes and tropical storms.

He holds an associate's degree in paramedicine from Harrisburg Area Community College, a bachelor's degree in Fire and Safety from the University of Cincinnati, a master's degree in Instructional Technology from the University of South Florida, and a Ph.D. in Instructional Technology/Adult Education from the University of South Florida.

In addition, Dr. Lindsey has completed the Executive Fire Officer Program at the National Fire Academy. He has designed and developed various courses in fire and EMS. Dr. Lindsey is accredited with the Chief Fire Officer Designation. He also is a certified Fire Officer II, Fire Instructor III, and paramedic in the state of Florida; holds a paramedic certificate for the state of Pennsylvania; and is a certified instructor in these and a variety of other courses.

Dr. Lindsey has an innate interest in alternative health. He is a certified nutritional counselor, a master herbalist, and a holistic health practitioner.

About FESHE

FESHE (Fire and Emergency Services Higher Education) is a dedicated group of individuals from around the country. It is hosted by the United States Fire Administration through the National Fire Academy. The mission of this group is to develop a uniform model curriculum for associate's, bachelor's, and master's degrees. In December 2006, a group of EMS educators convened as the inaugural EMS committee for FESHE. The mission was to develop a model curriculum in EMS management at the bachelor's level. It was the consensus of the leaders across the United States that the committee focus on the management issues of EMS. The clinical portion of the industry is addressed through the National EMS Education Standards and is mainly focused at the associate's level.

This text is written to meet the needs of the national model curriculum for EMS management at the bachelor's level. The EMS management curriculum includes six core courses and seven elective courses. Following are titles in Brady's *EMS Management Series,* designed to meet the FESHE curriculum.

CORE

- Foundations of EMS Systems
- Management of EMS
- EMS Community Risk Reduction
- EMS Quality Management and Research
- Legal, Political and Regulatory Environment in EMS
- EMS Safety and Risk Management

ELECTIVE

- Management of Ambulance Services
- Foundations for the Practice of EMS Education
- EMS Special Operations
- EMS Public Information and Community Relations
- EMS Communications and Information Technology
- EMS Finance
- Analytical Approaches to EMS

Management Philosophy: Traditional and Contemporary

Objectives

After reading this chapter, the student should be able to:

1.1 Describe the difference between traditional management and contemporary thinking.
1.2 Discuss how finance fits into management decision making.
1.3 Review why the EMS manager should learn the language of finance to better prepare for discussions regarding the organization's financial needs and viability.
1.4 Discuss how quality is integrated into operations and how quality impacts the financial success of the organization.
1.5 Understand the basics of how the economy affects the daily operations of the EMS organization.

Overview

The purpose of this text is to introduce the concepts of finance to nonfinancial EMS managers. The chapters present valuable information to both new and experienced EMS leaders who may have varying degrees of experience, formal and informal. The goal is to stimulate thinking in order to change the way things are done, to avoid mistakes of the past, and to encourage future growth of EMS as a profession.

Key Terms

budget	dissemination	leading (commanding)	relevant
controlling	ethical	moral	risk
coordinating	ethics	organizing	strategy
delegating	integrity	planning	variance
disseminator			

WHAT WOULD YOU DO?

You have recently received a promotion from street EMS provider to a supervisor on the day shift. As you reflect back on your days on the street, you remember good supervisors, and supervisors whose management style you would not copy. However, you have had little mentoring or formal education in dealing with people at this new level. "Learning management" encompasses understanding the intricacies of the organization, including financial decision making. As a new manager your decisions have an effect on the financial success of the organization. The board of directors (BOD) volunteers time to provide guidance with reaching the organization's goals. No one on the BOD has formal financial education, nor does anyone have time to teach you about EMS finance.

Questions

1. How will you learn what decisions to make and how to gauge the success of those decisions on daily outcomes?
2. What education is required to gain an understanding of how management and finance are used to guide an EMS organization to success?
3. How does a new or experienced EMS manager balance the needs of management and finance without emphasizing or prioritizing one over the other?

The concepts presented in this chapter will provide information on where to start seeking answers to the roles of the EMS manager relative to management and finance.

INTRODUCTION

Managing an EMS organization is a challenging, yet rewarding experience. Whatever the title—manager, operations chief, administrator, chief executive officer, director of operations—the person in charge of the EMS organization has a lot of responsibility. Ensuring the smooth operations is an ongoing process that requires input from multiple disciplines: finance, human resources, supervisory, legal, government, insurance, and individuals both inside and outside the organization. Small or large, the manager needs to understand the inner workings and nuances and allocate the necessary resources in order to guide the organization in reaching its goals.

Many individuals obtain the position of manager through attrition or longevity. Many have very little exposure to intimate knowledge of business operations. Most know prehospital medicine. Knowledge of human resource law, insurance requirements, actual business functions, and finance is limited at best. The reader must first understand management and business basics before understanding finance. Let's start by defining the organization.

MANAGEMENT OF AN ORGANIZATION

First let's establish what an organization is: An organization is a place where people come together and work to achieve a common goal. The organization, by its mere existence, has a purpose. Within the framework of conducting business, the organization acquires assets (buildings, vehicles, intellectual property, and so on). Without people, these assets are worthless. It is the people who give the organization life.

Management's role within the organization is to understand the organization. Why does it exist? What is its purpose? What is the organization trying to accomplish? How do we best accomplish the purpose? Where does the organization want to be in 5 years? 10 years? How will we get there? Running an EMS organization is not about the people in charge. The organization does not exist to fulfill individual goals as its primary purpose. Individuals assist the organization in fulfilling the organization's purpose. The individuals use their talents and available resources to further the goals of the organization; it is not the other way around. Managers should understand the concept that the organization is its own entity and must exist on its own. The organization is built on a foundation by individuals who adopt this belief. When people begin to believe the organization is there for them or, worse yet, that they are the organization, it is a sign that the manager is no longer effective.

When we look at management's role relative to finance, we begin to understand that the financial aspect of running an organization is a means to accomplish the goals. The financial success of any organization is an objective way of measuring the ability of the manager to grow the organization. Growth does not necessarily mean buying more ambulances or paying higher salaries. Growth refers to the organization's ability to achieve the goals and objectives established by individuals. Having the financial means to accomplish growth is a fundamental ingredient, but not the sole measurement, of success.

Since many managers have not had any formal education on finance or any related disciplines, this book helps describe how finance is important to any business, what finance can do to help build a business, and how finance can be used to measure whether or not the business is meeting its goals. One thing to stress is this critical point: *Finance does not run the business.* Managers make decisions with the input of finance, much as they use input from the human resources department when making decisions on hiring and firing. When managers cross the line and allow decisions to be made based on money, then the decision making is reduced to looking at numbers.

Many successful companies have been reduced to rubble as a result of managers being influenced by the bottom line or just numbers. Running an EMS organization should not be about profiting from the sicknesses or injuries of others. The purpose of the discussion in this book focuses on the genuine and original intention of EMS: to help others, not to generate finances or money at their expense.

Management should not be swayed to increase profitability by not buying the best equipment or forcing EMS providers to take another call just so the next due ambulance does not respond. Managers of EMS organizations who generate profit to satisfy personal living standards sacrifice the essence of the work in order to maximize profit.

Running an EMS organization based on competition and acquiring more territory with the intention of growing does little but cause ill feelings. This behavior undermines the professionalism of EMS. When individuals use the organization to satisfy their individual needs, the underlying purpose of the organization suffers. Managers can say they are successful and the organization is growing. They can even argue they are improving the opportunity for jobs. However, these arguments are a smoke screen around the intention of the individual to use finance as a justification to achieve personal goals.

Management's role in finance within the organization is to establish plans for achieving the goals and objectives developed through the strategic planning process and to implement plans to ensure that the organization's resources are used appropriately. For the organizational plans to succeed, people need a road map—objectives. Objectives are guidelines prepared by the top management of the organization. The objectives must align with the mission or purpose of the organization. One obvious objective in every organization is to make more money than is spent. The organization must have the ability to pay employees, creditors, and other businesses that provide goods or services to the organization. Again, obviously, if the organization is unable to meet its financial obligation to any business or individual to whom it owes money, it risks shutting down the organization.

Each organization must establish its own set of goals and objectives that serve as a guide for management's decisions. During the execu-

tion of their duties, managers make decisions based on the goals of the organization and are guided by **moral** and **ethical** belief systems. This statement is so important in organizations these days. One can find many examples where the financial success of the organization has led to personal greed and the ultimate downfall of the organization. When managers control not only the financial resources but also decision making, the opportunity for abuse increases. Managers must act in alignment with the highest **integrity** and moral character.

Side Bar

The goal of accounting is to provide useful information for making decisions. For information to be useful, it must be trusted. This demands ethical behavior from managers who control, evaluate, and report the financial condition of the EMS organization.

This book is not a management book. However, those who specialize in finance or management, who are responsible for managing the organization and for overseeing its financial aspects, must have a clear idea of the manager's role. For this reason, we discuss aspects of management that are relevant to the EMS manager in charge of finance.

Indeed, managers of both profit and nonprofit organizations can establish a mission that maximizes profits at the expense of quality equipment, personnel, or services. In both types of organizations, managers can decide to divert operational monies to the coffers or pockets of select individuals. Likewise, individuals in both organizations can forgo enhancing their economic position in society and work diligently to adhere to the broader goal of EMS and spend money on delivering the best health care available. These options are choices made by the administration and management.

Finance is not a science of deciding where resources are spent. Rather, it is about measuring the success of management operations. It is the people in organizations who can either abuse the power to control the resources or develop a philosophy of building a strong organization of service, providing the best care to people who need that service and striving to equip those working on the street with the tools to help those in need.

Both types of organizations will have the same financial constraints, problems, and rewards. These activities are going to occur both internally and externally. The responsibilities may be divided up and given to two or more folks in the organization, or one person may handle them all. It is the understanding of the basic concepts of economics and accounting concepts that will prove invaluable to the manager (Figure 1.1).

As stated earlier, every business entity, including EMS organizations, requires the knowledge and skills of a manager and leadership team that understand the complexity of the business function. This is the essence of management. Under the umbrella of management, in order to make smart decisions, the EMS manager and leadership team must understand how to use financial resources to deliver or improve the service or product of prehospital medical care.

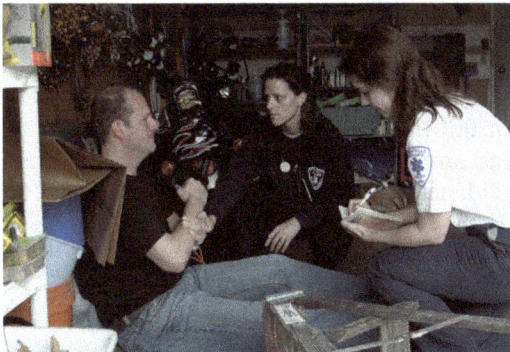

FIGURE 1.1 ■ EMS personnel evaluating a patient. *Courtesy of Dennis Mitterer.*

Often, people will attend college to learn management or finance. During formal learning, some classes discuss the science of each specialty. Management teaches how to work with people, and finance teaches how to fund a business. Integrating the two disciplines is often left to experience. Gaining experience by watching others and by determining what did and did not work is helpful, but not definitive. Managing others depends on the EMS manager's internal belief systems and personality. In addition, there are some theories that can help develop administrators into skilled managers who can integrate the science of finance into the activities of management without tipping the scales toward one or the other.

In this chapter, an overview of traditional and nontraditional management theory is discussed. Also discussed are how management can use finance to make decisions and where the science of finance fits into the function of management. The chapter will close with an overview of key financial concepts used by managers to make appropriate financial decisions.

■ TRADITIONAL MANAGEMENT THEORY

Henri Fayol introduced the concept of traditional management process in 1916, and he believed that management had five basic functions (Wren et al., 2002):

1. **Planning**
2. **Organizing**
3. **Coordinating**
4. **Controlling**
5. **Leading (commanding)**

PLANNING

Planning can mean many things to many managers. It can include scheduling crews for the next month, determining if a crew is available for a standby, scheduling meetings, or more complex tasks such as determining the strategic direction of the organization. Planning is the process of identifying alternative courses of action, evaluating the alternatives, and choosing the best actions that will take the organization closer to its goals. This process includes understanding the vision and mission of the organization (Figure 1.2). Strategic planning continues with developing goals and objectives. It concludes by establishing responsibilities and providing feedback. Within this context, all plans involve finance in some meaningful way.

Strategic planning can be short term or long term. During the planning process, mangers should include what the organization will look like next year and in 5 years. Obviously, any plans involve having the money to fund any projects.

Planning also includes budgeting. Budgeting is the quantification of plans to guide future operations and measure performance. A **budget** is a document that communicates management's plan for the organization. It establishes the standard that the organization will use to measure performance.

ORGANIZING

Another function of management is organizing. This process allows managers to determine the

FIGURE 1.2 ■ Construction project for a new building. *Courtesy of Dennis Mitterer.*

best method to achieve the goals of the organization. Managers identify the proper resources and responsibilities for using all of the organization's resources. When organizing, the manager, with the help of others, determines the priorities and establishes the process to achieve the objectives. The manager determines what resources are available and moves those resources to the appropriate areas. The manager also must monitor the activities of the organization and make adjustments that appropriately reflect the current state and what is needed to achieve future goals. Moving resources, for example, can include many areas that encompass personnel, equipment, finance, and other resources. The key to organizing is to ensure that jobs or activities make sense in the overall plan. Organizing can be as simple as putting the inventory in logical order and as complex as ensuring different maturity dates for payments or investments. Moving resources around just for the sake of doing things differently may seem like a legitimate management function, but the cost could be great to the budget, lower staff morale, or increase expenses.

COORDINATING

Coordinating involves determining the timing of activities so they mesh properly. The belief is that a manager should plan the structure of the jobs performed and make sure that the work supports all aspects of the organization in order for the organization to do well. Under classical management theory, the manager should ensure that employees understand their role and are able to complete their job with direct guidance and use of available resources. The manager coordinates these activities to reach the objectives of the organization.

CONTROLLING

Controlling is the process of ensuring successful implementation of the plan. Accounting plays a crucial role by providing feedback on how well operations carry out the daily activities. The act of developing reports that compare the organization's actual revenue with the budget, expenses with anticipated costs, and what money remains for growth is an example of a control mechanism. In a report, a comparison of the difference between the expected and the actual is called the **variance**. Variances tell management whether operations are under control. During the controlling process, management's emphasis is on keeping the actual financial results in line with planned financial goals.

Controlling the organization is ongoing—it never stops. After discussion, agreement, and implementation of the operational plans, management observes the results and compares them to the plan. Changes are made as necessary, and the recent results are compared with the adjusted plan. It is the accounting department and/or the manager who is responsible for the financial health of the organization.

The EMS manager's ability to control decisions based on the numbers is an essential skill. Since revenues and expenses are real, the manager must make decisions based on objective evaluation of the financial picture of the organization.

Controlling is not meant to be negative. Control outlines who makes the decisions within the organization and who is responsible for the outcomes. Using a cruise liner as a metaphor, controlling is like operating a ship. One person, the captain (the manager), must set the course and subsequently steer the ship. It takes hundreds of people to get the ship to its destination. If we scale back the size of the operation to a 23-foot pleasure boat, the number of people needed is greatly reduced, but one person must set the course and steer the ship. In this way, controlling is about setting a course and maneuvering toward a goal, as opposed to a

personality trait that reflects a person's need to be the boss.

LEADING

Leading is about understanding the interrelationship of business and people. It is an art, a science, and a style. According to Fayol (Wren et al., 2002), a leader looks beyond the numbers and sets the direction for the organization. He or she integrates the business of doing business with the why's, how's, and when's of the organization and its people. Many books have been written on the subject of leadership, but for the purposes of this discussion, leadership is about guiding people toward a common goal.

CONTEMPORARY MANAGEMENT THEORY

There are multiple views of management: who a manager is and what his or her role is in an organization. One thing is certain: The manager cannot be packaged neatly in a box with only a few responsibilities. Mintzberg (Andrews, 1976) believed management was much broader than what Henri Fayol postulated. Mintzberg studied many roles of management and determined that management can be described as "calculated chaos" or "controlled disorder."

One can agree there are many routine tasks a manager performs. Study after study indicates, on a daily basis, that these routines are just the string keeping the organization running and that most duties of a manager are unplanned. To understand the organization, managers require information to process and decide on the current state of affairs. This information does not come from periodicals, news reports, or government agencies. The information comes from soft sources that are timelier, such as the staff, discussions with peers, and "odds and ends of tangible details," according to Narayanan and Nath (1993). Managers require good interpersonal relationships with many individuals, but they must maintain the respect of many individuals as the figurehead of the organization. The formal management role provides authority and potentially enormous power, but the leadership role determines how successful managers are within the organization.

The manager deals with information. The manager coordinates the flow of information between peers and staff. He becomes the center of the flow of information to others. Managers must not only monitor the information that is flowing through the organization and what current trends are occurring outside the organization, but they must also synthesize the information and share the information appropriately. As the **disseminator**, the manager also provides tools for others to make decisions.

As the decision maker, the manager commits valuable resources to designated projects or goals. In this role, the manager must determine what resources are necessary to achieve the established goals or, in an emergent situation, must be capable of allocating resources appropriately while maintaining stability and future success. No organization is so standardized that it has considered every contingency in advance. As Peter Drucker (1973) wrote:

> The manager has the task of creating a true whole that is larger than the sum of its parts, a productive entity that turns out more than the sum of the resources put into it. One analogy is the conductor of a symphony orchestra, through whose effort, vision and leadership individual instrumental parts that are so much noise by themselves become the living whole of music. The conductor has the composer's score; he is the only interpreter. The manager is both composer and conductor. (p. 398)

Managers must continuously make decisions. These decisions cannot be arbitrary or based on emotion. Each decision should consider the effect on the organization and on other decisions. Managers should consider the costs and benefits of each decision and its effect on people, the community, and the organization.

Ultimately, the manager is neither as rigid as Fayol theorized, nor as carefree as many imagine, with the manager out golfing and meeting with others in social situations. Certainly, many managers have turned their jobs into such roles, but these individuals do not last long as managers, nor do their organizations thrive. The role of the manager is complex. Each function within the organization must become integrated with all other functions. According to Mintzberg (Andrews, 1976), "The manager's effectiveness is significantly influenced by their insight into their own work." Managers who are swayed by financial numbers, exclusively, will work to maximize the bottom line at the expense of other critical areas. If the manager desires to or finds more satisfaction in external contacts and socialization, building external power, or seeming important in the eyes of others, then he will lose touch with the internal workings of the organization. The manager will become unaware of the underlying daily issues and will be ill prepared when an internal conflict occurs.

If the manager spends more time focusing on the clinical aspect of the EMS organization because that is where he is most comfortable, then formal monitoring and regulation adherence flounder. The contemporary manager must grow and mature into a well-rounded communicator seeking to improve not only the organization but also the people within the organization, without seeking to consciously increase his power and influence.

Best Practice

Managers' values and beliefs bleed into the EMS culture whether intended or not. What they know, how they act, and the types of decisions they make influence how employees make decisions, and ultimately determine the success of the organization. Ben Cohen and Jerry Greenfield (better known as the founders of Ben & Jerry's Ice Cream) realized early on in their zeal to create a successful company that business was more than making a profit. Greenfield said, "It is not about money made, but improving the quality of life." He said that implementing a socially responsible business model was a "process of innovation" (Rogers, 2012). Cohen was prepared to demonstrate his willingness to fly in the face of traditional corporate culture in many endeavors. Both Cohen and Greenfield displayed irreverence

for traditional procedure and bureaucracy, and thus their "new" corporate culture gained respectability, even though their style was not based on traditional laws of business.

As the company grew, Cohen and Greenfield hired more senior-level "traditional businesspeople" who demonstrated they were more into profit-making than philanthropy. Cohen watched as the once "big happy family" culture begin to erode in an environment of money making over all else. They eventually came to terms with the balance needed to run a large organization; however, at the same time Cohen and Greenfield did not succumb to the profit mentality and many of the traditionally minded managers left (Entrepreneur, 2008).

■ THE ROLE OF FINANCE IN MANAGEMENT

Though financial measurements can guide short-term decisions, the EMS manager is responsible for the success of the organization. Managers must remember that finance looks at short-term results with a long-term view.

For the EMS manager, an understanding of the activities encompassing the financial function has become necessary for the successful discharge of managerial responsibility in most organizational settings. The personality, education, and background of managers and financial professionals must be in alignment with financial principles, although procedures and applications may vary according to customs.

During the performance of business activities, EMS managers employ the theoretical

constructs of business economics and utilize accounting principles to make appropriate decisions. Orientation to future and long-term survival of the organization is necessary. Managers allocate today's resources to benefit tomorrow. Managers must maintain responsibility to ensure adherence to strategic plans and the pursuit of organizational objectives. With the long-term view established, EMS managers must realize that finance touches on the activities of almost all functional areas of the organization.

In many organizations, there is no division of labor in management. In many circumstances the CEO, COO, or board president may be the individual who handles all the financial functions and at reporting time contracts with an accountant to review the yearly activity. Other organizations are large enough to employ both a manager and finance professional. Some variation of any of these scenarios is possible. The organization's management should understand that managerial finance is important to the survivability of any EMS organization. The important thing to remember is that the success of an organization is not dependent on to whom responsibilities are assigned, but rather that someone addresses these responsibilities in a timely and effective fashion (Narayanan and Nath, 1993).

The functions of finance should be handled in accordance with the basic goal of the organization. In for-profit enterprises, this goal is to maximize the wealth of the organization's stockholders. Although this may seem appropriate to Wall Street, this single philosophy will cause collateral damage and result in many casualties in the service world. The EMS organization that puts profits above customer service or employee growth may find itself reducing the quality of training or equipment, accepting the results of a production mentality, and taking shortcuts that result in personnel injuries or adverse patient outcomes. Focusing on a philosophy that encompasses the very nature of what EMS is will guide financial decisions.

Let's look at a philosophical EMS goal: *To deliver medical services to the maximum number of customers within the constraints of the resources available to the organization under a spirit of cooperation with others.* This goal can easily encompass many areas of decision making. It guides management to find ways to evaluate its services and programs. Compare that philosophy with this one: *It is the goal of XYZ EMS organization to deliver consistently superior medical care in the most effective manner while maintaining financial strength.* If the organization's management team focuses on medical care and also financial strength, eventually these two concepts will clash and compete for resources. A governmental EMS agency may have a goal to deliver the service at a cost that is reasonable for the constituents. Either way, the philosophy

of an EMS organization must match the goals that are established.

Side Bar
"Business has a responsibility to give back to the community." —Ben Cohen

EMS organizations acquire funds through ordinary business activities. Management allocates resources and tracks financial performance. When money is a common factor in almost every activity, finance often becomes the focal point of managerial attention and decisions. Because of the strong influence that finance has on the success of an organization, it sometimes takes an unbalanced role in leading the organization. Decisions are made because of finance or the input of the financial officers, whereas executives and managers should make decisions based, as appropriate, on the input of finance as well as operations, risk management, and human resources. In other words, finance should be the scorekeeper, not the coach on the sideline.

Managers sometimes make decisions based on financial considerations as a means of reducing their responsibility for making tough choices. It is easy to say "We can't do such and such because it's not in the budget" or "We didn't make any money, so such and such can't happen." Although this may be true at times, often it is just an easy way for managers to deflect responsibility for not fulfilling their role or responsibility regarding planning or controlling. Finance is objective in nature, and managers tend to lean toward financial decision making because it is an unemotional decision-making tool.

How many organizations base their future on the bottom line? CEOs, executives, and managers who concentrate on the bottom line by always trying to maximize it as if it is the only goal may miss the positive achievement of using the bottom line as a measurement of their success. Finance is just one of the focal points for information on which to make decisions regarding the current organization's position. It is not intended to be the only focal point. It is the measuring stick used to show how well managers are fulfilling their obligations to the organization; it is not the force driving the organization. In the book, *Why Smart Executives Fail*, Sidney Finkelstein (2003) points out that there are no guarantees in business. When executives and managers focus on the essentials of their core business, using financial results as a measurement of success instead of establishing the ultimate goal of making the most money, they are much better equipped to succeed.

EMS managers must use finance for its intended purpose. Not all benefits of the organization can be expressed in quantitative terms or in monetary measurements. Managers must realize that finance is a tool to be used to guide decisions and plan for the future. Every community has a stake in the viability of its emergency service organizations. Good scorekeeping systems, rational procedures for the allocation of capital, and appropriate **dissemination** of financial information are needed to avoid the excessive waste of valuable and often limited community resources.

The role of finance, particularly in the area of scorekeeping and capital allocation, impacts managerial decision making even in nonfinance activities. All managers must develop an understanding of the objectives, tools, and functions of finance. Conversely, financial folks should familiarize themselves with the absolute role of management and broaden the view of success: It is not all about dollars and cents. Lack of such understanding of the roles and responsibilities of management and finance will stunt the growth of the organization—especially if the manager is also responsible for finance. For the new EMS

manager or one who has had the responsibility without the formal education, management and finance are two different specialties, and each must be learned to be successful.

With much of the responsibility of the success of the organization placed on the finance people, it is no wonder they have a strong voice in the operations of the organization. Often the CEOs, chiefs, or managers do not understand the intricacies of the financial piece of the organization. They ultimately rely on the finance "expert" to provide guidance on their organization's operations. After all, "that's what we pay them for." The downside of allowing one person or a department unfettered control of operations because of managerial naïveté can cause many problems, especially if the compensation of the manager and/or the finance staff is tied to the profitability of the organization. Based on salary, in whole or in part, on the bottom line, creates the potential for manipulating numbers for personal benefit.

For organizations that have a separate financial department, management must utilize the financial folks as a resource for decision making. Management must establish the perimeters and constraints of the finance department. EMS managers must adhere to the notion that it is management's responsibility to learn and overcome any knowledge deficit or weakness in understanding the financial position of the organization; they must not rely on finance to take an active or leading role in operational decisions.

Unfortunately, in many medium and smaller EMS organizations, the CEOs, chiefs, or managers have moved up the ladder of responsibility with little, if any, knowledge of management or finance. Thus, they may hire an expert, resulting over time in the lure of power, control, and/or personal situations that may cause the person in charge of money to take liberties, while the manager has little clue or is complicit in the activity. If the responsibility of finance falls on the shoulders of the chief or EMS manager, the same temptations of money can lead to poorly executed decision making.

Side Bar

"A minor addiction to money may not always be hurtful to business; but when taken to excess it is nearly always bad."
—Clarence Day

THE LANGUAGE OF FINANCE

Managers must learn the language of finance. Finance is the language of business. All managers, in either nonprofit or for-profit organizations, have a vested interest in understanding the language of finance to communicate effectively to organizations or persons with a stake in the organization's success. It is direct and clear communication that allows the manager to discuss the business plan and financial position with those in the organization and the public. In the absence of firsthand familiarity of the language of finance, the manager is at a disadvantage related to communication. In an EMS organization, trying to convey the need for a budget to fund yearly operations becomes problematic if the manager is financially illiterate, unable to present a case for a budget, and incapable of discussing it with the organization's board of directors or paid accountant.

The manager must realize, in the language of finance, that any major allocation of the organization's financial resources will require forecasts of benefits over the life of the project. Good management practice dictates that all projects are analyzed for appropriateness and approved. Familiarity with the theory and practice of capital budgeting will accomplish this. Major allocation is all relative, however. In a small EMS organization whose budget is

only $35,000 per year, buying a $3,500 ambulance stretcher is a significant purchase. In this case, as well as in organizations ten times this size, the decision makers must determine if the purchase is necessary, reasonable, and possible. The decision to buy a new stretcher should not be made based on the desire of the crew. This is not to say that the crew is not correct in needing a new stretcher but, rather, the point is that management must analyze the financial implications of the purchase.

The language of finance imposes a quantifiable discipline on all parts of the organization. It forces the expression of the organization's plans and goals in terms that can be understood by everyone, even if the assumptions underlying the plans are incomplete. Managers who understand the language can speak intelligently to lenders and business professionals. This same language requires managers to interpret and communicate the financial language to staff may not understand the terms or concepts. As stated earlier, the complex role of management in the organization requires excellent communication skills. When discussing budgets or the financial state of the organization, acceptance can only be expected if the staff understands the financial position or decisions when the numbers are translated into language the staff understands. One function of management is to communicate information effectively. Presenting the financial picture to a banker or a grant evaluator should look different from presenting the same information to the community or the staff. The manager must gain the needed skills to take the same information and present it in different and meaningful ways depending on the audience.

To gain a working knowledge of the language of management and finance, the EMS manager must proactively enroll in college classes or a financial curriculum, critically read professional journals or articles related to these topics, or research terms found in contracts or agreements. Finding a mentor who can guide this learning is also an effective route to learning.

■ QUALITY AND FINANCE ————

The most effective organizations, in terms of quality and financial results, are led by senior teams with a shared sense of purpose and a collective vision of how to achieve planned goals. They understand the link between cost and quality, and they manage both as unified goals. When financial goals of the organization are integrated with outcomes and quality, EMS organizations are far more likely to achieve improvements in patient care and financial position.

Linking quality and financial results can reduce waste and improve efficiency. In some health care institutions (e.g., hospitals, long-term-care facilities), reducing waste reduces the risk of having to raise prices. In EMS, waste reduction and increased efficiency allow for the development of programs that will improve services, purchase better equipment, or improve benefits to staff.

By looking at quality, EMS organizations can reduce costs and improve the financial position. Three key areas, based on the work of Japanese quality scholar Noriaki Kano and applied to EMS, define the linkages between costs and quality can be used as a baseline for an integrated approach:

1. *Quality problems arise because of unmet customer expectations.* Often the consumer is unaware of what EMS care should look like. However, providers know what proper care is. Attempting four IV starts is not what patients expect. If providers are not evaluated (i.e., tested on competencies), then what tracking mechanisms exist to evaluate the quality of care? Does the organization care that a provider is lacking in basic skills?

2. *Costs should be reduced while maintaining quality.* This concept needs defining because people may believe that buying poorer equipment that adequately addresses the need is the way to go. Does the organization save money if a piece of equipment, of poor quality, is purchased to save money but is constantly in need of repair?

3. *Customer expectations can be exceeded by providing services perceived as universally high in value.* EMS professionals are expected to deliver quality EMS care during every single call. Time and again, we see providers do only as much as is needed to get by. A patient drop, a provider injury, an ambulance crash, an airway problem not identified and now a liability, for example, fully demonstrate situations that show EMS providers are not quality conscious. EMS organization should understand the relationship between high quality and improved financial position.

Experience has shown that when finances align with high-quality goals, organizations improve. When management teams establish a common understandable language and share information with staff, organizations excel. When the financial people take an active role in quality improvements, the organization grows. Ensuring financial viability and improving care for patients should not be separate, compartmentalized responsibilities. They should be integrated parts of the overall **strategy**: to improve the delivery of care.

Effective financial management must take into account the needs and concerns of those who supply capital to the organization (Narayanan and Nath, 1993). When assessing the desirability of a loan or a grant application, the lender evaluates the viability of the project. Analysis of the past financial statements, current financial plans, and control procedures is performed. Similarly, suppliers will look for the strength and creditworthiness of the EMS organization. All outsiders have a vested interest in understanding the financial position of the organization.

Contributors to nonprofit organizations have a similar interest. These contributors can be individuals or heads of households, small businesses, large corporations, or local and state governmental agencies. Knowledge of financial control procedures permits them to judge the worthiness of their contribution. Trustees of public money have a responsibility to their constituents in interpreting and assessing how the money is going to be used. This person is often the one who has moved up the ranks of the EMS organization, who accepts the responsibility to run the organization, and who has no formal education in the world of finance. Therefore, the newly promoted EMT or paramedic may not understand the relationship between contributors of revenue and the expectations that come along with the contribution. The newly promoted EMS manager may believe any money received may be spent as he or she sees fit. The new EMS manager may not understand the role of trustee of public money.

> ## Side Bar
>
> "Surplus wealth is a sacred trust which its possessor is bound to administer in his lifetime for the good of the community."
> —Andrew Carnegie

Any applied science—for example, engineering, medicine, and law—is built on a basic body of knowledge. It employs certain common tools of analysis and practices within an accepted framework. Finance follows this pattern. It is based on economic theory, employs specialized tools, and operates within a well-defined set of perimeters. The vocabulary of finance utilizes concepts and communicates with others within this sphere of science. A number of basic concepts and vocabulary must be mastered. The study and understanding of economics, math, and law are also required. The person who moves from being a street provider, to being a supervisor, and further aspires to higher levels of management and administration must grow into those positions by learning the intricacies of the science of management, leadership, and finance. The administrator who does not see the value of learning to be a good leader and believes in just being the "boss" may be successful to a certain degree. However, in most cases the success is limited and short lived.

Many members of the managerial team perform financial functions. Regardless of title—CEO, chief officer, chief, director of operations, marketing manager, supervisor, and so on—everyone contributes to the control of organizational assets.

Any person who is responsible for and reports on the financial position of an organization must **relevant** and timely information for planning and controlling decisions. Financial managers or managers who wear multiple hats must exercise sound judgment in determining the information reported. EMS managers should not arbitrarily withhold information because they personally believe such information is theirs. In fact, the information belongs to the organization. Individuals who are responsible for making any organizational decisions may need the financial numbers to make the best decision. The manager's role regarding finance is to collect, analyze, and report information, not necessarily to determine its use. Managers who perform financial tasks must understand that the information is not a secret and should be shared with everyone who has a stake in the organization.

One of the objectives of the managerial financing specialist is to assist other operational managers in increasing revenue and decreasing the expenses. The key word is *assist*. Often, the financial people or manager, by virtue of controlling the money, becomes a major decision maker regarding management of the organization. Accountants working for an EMS organization have the responsibility to ensure the integrity of the data so that ethical decisions are made. Managers who are responsible for the finances have the responsibility to use these resources for the betterment of the organization.

The manager should become familiar with many concepts. It is within these concepts that the manger develops his or her decision-making process or personal value system. Many of these concepts touch on other sciences within the management field, including sociology, ethics, and, of course, finance. The EMS manager can make decisions about the direction of the organization that fall outside the daily medical operations or fall into other categories of business. These other areas will still have a financial impact on the success of the organization.

FIGURE 1.3 ▇ Medical waste disposed of improperly. *Courtesy of Dennis Mitterer.*

▇ SOCIAL RESPONSIBILITY

The concept that businesses should be actively concerned with the welfare of society is extremely valuable today. Many articles and books suggest how business fits into society. Are businesses members of society, stewards of the community, or just economic entities? For example, Main Street EMS management must decide how to dispose of its medical waste. One option is to dispose of it properly as established by the Medical Waste Tracking Act (MWTA) of 1988 and subsequently by the Resource Conservation and Recovery Act (U.S. Environmental Protection Agency, 2012). However, doing this significantly increases the costs to the organization. Management can choose to pay the cost to dispose of the medical waste appropriately or save the cost and spend the money on a program or new equipment (Figure 1.3). Some managers may try to justify not spending the money on proper disposal as a way to feel good about throwing the medical waste in regular trash and using the money to pay higher salaries or purchase equipment, using the reasoning that it cannot afford to do both and the community needs it to respond.

The cost of social responsibility may seem high in the short term, but an EMS manager who avoids catastrophic costs over the long term is a valuable asset to the organization. By building the costs of social responsibility into the EMS budget, the organization is better prepared to identify needed financial resources preemptively as opposed to trying to find money to fix and repair the mistakes of bad social decisions. The cost to the organization—through publicity, lost contracts, reputation, and fines—due to throwing its medical waste into the regular trash will always exceed the cost of doing things right the first time.

▇ BUSINESS ETHICS

Ethics is a study of the standard of conduct or moral behavior of a person or a society. It can be thought of as a company's attitude and conduct toward its personnel, customers, community, and end users (Drucker, 1954). High standards of ethical behavior demand that

EMS organizations treat each of these constituents in a consistent and principled manner. Obviously, it is not the organization, but the people who represent the organization, who treat people one way or another. All people who wear the organization's patch or, going one step further, who represent the EMS profession should maintain an exemplary degree of ethical behavior.

An EMS organization's commitment to business ethics is measured by the firm and by its personnel's adherence to laws and regulations relating to safety and quality, employment practices, use of confidential information, community involvement, and adherence to professional and organizational goals. All top executives must be committed to ethical behavior and continually communicate this commitment through their personal actions as well as through company policies, directives, and activities.

The manager without an ethical backbone, who experiences ethical lapses, will cost the organization money, and the manager who develops a strong code of ethics within the organization will reduce the risk and the liability of ethical lapses.

There is a certain degree of danger in reducing ethics into simple dictates or simplifying decision making, because there is so much variability in daily activities and people. There is also a danger of ethical lapses if the message is not kept simple and short. Managers must understand that serious consequences follow poor ethical decisions, and many poor decisions have significant financial consequences.

The point is this: The manager must identify ethical issues and allocate resources to ensure that staff adheres to a preestablished expectation. During a training session, simply saying, "Do not take a bribe or gift" is not sufficient, but on the flip side spending $10,000 dollars on a speaker or ethics program designed for the manufacturing world or, more broadly, for medicine and not EMS may waste organizational money. The key to ethics is hiring good people with a strong orientation to do the right thing or what is called "value based ethics." Values are critical where rules do not provide enough guidance. Thus, honesty, respect, and responsibility are three fundamental values that staff should possess.

From a financial perspective, the organization must commit resources to ensure an acceptable level of ethical behavior. This can take the form of identifying staff in the prehire stage who have high values and ethical behavior. Annual training, establishing policies that outline ethical behavior, and responding to ethical infractions quickly but systematically are also very important. As pointed out, the investment in a good ethical program before an incident is less expensive than dealing with the financial consequences of an ethical lapse.

All programs are going to cost money, so the manager must allocate a degree of financial resources to ethical training. If managers do not believe or are unaware of the need for proactive ethical training, they should allocate financial resources to ensure payment for ethical lapses by purchasing insurance. Either way, there is a cost that must be accounted for by the organization.

■ EFFECT ON PROGRAMS

Another concept the manager should become familiar with is the cost of money. Every dollar earned costs the organization something. That something could be the work involved in writing a grant or the accountant's salary for tracking down nonpayers. If, for example, a person volunteers his or her time to write a grant, that time has a dollar value. Any capital realized or earned requires an outlay of resources. The four most fundamental factors affecting the cost of money are (1) production opportunities; (2) time preference for consumption; (3)

risk; and (4) inflation, which this chapter does not address.

PRODUCTION OPPORTUNITIES

Business opportunities occur in every area of EMS. Revenues are the monetary returns that are available from the investment of the organization in cash-generating activities. Production creates revenue. When a manager determines how many financial resources should be spent on a project, he or she is hoping the project will generate opportunities that may lead to revenue. There are beneficial opportunities, and there are lost opportunities. Managers must understand that money spent on one project reduces the money available to spend on another project.

Production is a descriptor used for the actual daily activities that an EMS organization conducts to fulfill its goals. Each 9-1-1 call received and responded to by a provider would be considered production. When that call comes in, whether the crew arrives at the scene and treats the patient or not, money is spent. Every CPR class taught is production. Every piece of paper filed is production. Thus, EMS managers must determine what production activities provide the greatest value for the use of resources.

Keeping information is required by many agencies. If, for example, investing in a computer system eliminates the cost of gathering, collating, copying, and filing, then allocating financial resources may not only improve costs but results in **delegating** other job duties to important personnel. The take-home point is that every activity will cost something, and each activity takes away from another activity. The opportunity to improve the EMS organization is directly related to the manager's ability to determine which production activity increases value and what amount of financial resources will be allocated to support production.

TIME PREFERENCE FOR CONSUMPTION

A preference of a consumer for current consumption, as opposed to saving for future consumption, is the time preference for consumption.

Consumers do not plan when an emergency occurs. Therefore, the consumer does not decide when to utilize EMS services. People do not plan for the emergency to occur at a later, more convenient time. When an emergency does occur, the consumer loses, even for the short term, the ability to make or spend money. The time preference for consumption is a concept that people have choices about how or when to make or spend financial resources, in most situations. In the situation of a consumer requiring the services of the local EMS unit, the consumer does not have a choice. In short, the time preference for consumption occurs when a consumer has the choice to buy something now or later.

The EMS manager should understand that the consumer values his or her time, and his or her time can have a dollar amount assigned to it. The EMS organization has a time value of money as well. When the EMS organization is constantly going to one address, only to have the patient sign off, each response costs the EMS organization money. The EMS manager must be careful not to rationalize accepting these calls as "part of doing business." The manager should look at other options for this situation. Contacting a community social service organization for assistance in determining the needs of the caller relative to medical care is a proactive option. In this situation, the time preference for consumption for the EMS organization is proactive rather than reactive. In any case, there is a cost either way. The proactive costs may include the manager's time contacting the community organization, meeting to discuss the situation, meeting the patient, and working out a plan. The reactive costs may include the wear and tear on the EMS vehicle, the cost of the crew to respond, and intangible costs such as frustration and another missed call. The proactive process allows the EMS organization to control the costs, as opposed to responding to the caller any time of day or night and absorbing the cost.

RISK

Another example of the time preference of consumption is seen in the **risk** inherent in initiating a new project and the eventual return on invested capital. When looking at risk, the manager determines that the higher the perceived risk of an endeavor, the higher the rate of return should be. In emergency services, the risk is weighed against the potential gain from the services provided to the community. For example, an EMS organization determines that it undoubtedly needs to invest in high-angle rescue equipment because there is a mountain nearby. Management should determine the risk versus the benefit of the investment. If the equipment and training costs are $50,000 for the initial investment and $5,000 per year, management must look at the return on this investment and determine whether the risk is appropriate. If the EMS organization has responded twice for a rescue in the mountains in the past 3 years, one may argue against the justification for the expense.

Objective decision making would look at the overall strategic plan, the reasons why the investment is required, the actual risk of performing the service, the additional hidden costs that may be associated with the service, and the perceived public response. If the return on investment is simply the publicity that results when a rescue occurs, objective decision making would determine if the return is worth the investment. If the decision to invest in this new line of service is emotional—"Just because I want it"—then the decision is subjective and based on the degree of influence and the control of finances that the manager has. It may sound like a glory-filled activity that could

gain a lot of publicity and support, but is this endeavor financially viable and needed given the limited responses? The EMS manager must evaluate whether the consumption of money, now, for a questionable program is better than waiting for a better opportunity in the future.

■ MANAGERS AND THE ECONOMY

How does the broader concept of the economy affect the operations of an EMS organization? This is just one area that impacts how an EMS manager will either save or cost the organization money based on decisions he or she makes during operational activities. The EMS manager should recognize that every decision made within the organization can and will affect other economic factors that impact the EMS organization in the long term.

ECONOMIC EFFECTS OF DECISIONS

EMS leaders must be aware of the relationship between supply and demand relative to the availability of money. Outside economics plays a large role in the success of organizations, far and above what many people believe.

Let's use the example of disposing of medical waste. Management decides to throw medical waste in the regular trash and continues to practice this for five years. Through orientation and on-the-job exposure, new personnel are shown (directly or indirectly) this practice. To fulfill their role as an EMS provider, all responders adopt this practice, not knowing whether it is right or wrong. At some point, a provider questions the practice and management responds that it is nothing to worry about: "We have it under control and are aware of what can be disposed of." The responder is uncomfortable with the answer and reports management to the state environmental protection agency. An investigation is initiated, and the organization is found to be liable for all past dumping and any subsequent damage.

The organization goes through nasty publicity and pays huge fines, well above the money saved by the illegal disposal. Four years later, the organization applies for a loan for a new building. The bank perceives the organization to be a high risk, and society's current demand for money is high (i.e., a lot of growth, borrowing, etc. are happening). Due to the high risk, the EMS organization may pay a higher interest rate if it wants to expand or purchase equipment. (Borrowers who qualify for money may have the opportunity to receive funds at a lower cost if they are not perceived to be a high risk.) Even if society's

demand for money is low, the organization's past practice has placed it in a high-risk category, and the cost of money may still be higher than what it could have been if the rules were followed years before.

Let's consider another scenario. The EMS organization is in good standing, and management has established sound financial policies. If the demand for funds in the market declines, as in a recession, interest rates will decline. The EMS organization may be a better risk for receiving a loan at a very attractive rate, which benefits not only the organization but also the people in the community because the project being funded may improve services at a lower cost while the money saved can be used to expand other projects or services.

CHAPTER REVIEW

Summary

Management is a complex job that requires a person to be knowledgeable about many aspects of business. EMS managers should be familiar with the clinical requirements to provide high levels of patient care, the implications of various management theories on success, how finance factors into decision making, and what costs are related to organizational decision making. EMS managers should understand that every decision has a cost and that each cost has an effect on the organization. By learning how to balance the management aspect of the job and the financial constraints of running the organization, the EMS manager inches closer to reaching the goals of the organization. Tipping the scales dominantly in one direction or another will negatively affect the growth of the organization. This is not to say the organization is not successful, but that the organization will not maximize its potential success.

Management and finance are very different sciences that should function in tandem. If the manager of the organization is also responsible for the financial aspects of running the organization, then an objective scorecard is necessary to ensure that the organization is strong financially. There must be checks and balances built in so the manager/financial person does not have unfettered control of incoming money and of deciding how the money is spent.

Organizations that are sufficiently large enough to have a finance person and a management team should understand their respective roles and develop a relationship that seeks to grow the organization through quality decision making and accurate measurements of financial success. Management is ultimately responsible for the success of the organization, and EMS managers must understand how financial decisions guide the organization.

WHAT WOULD YOU DO? Reflection

In your new management role, you may have certain preconceived notions of what management is about. Management is a specific science, yet it is not an exact science. As a supervisor, you will learn that you must work with people in order to be successful, not boss them around. You will learn that management requires a completely different set of skills than is required for working with people at an accident scene. You must have an open mind in order to have a greater vision, different priorities, and an expanded responsibility to people and the organization. As a member of the management team, you will be making (or should

begin to assist in making) decisions that affect the organization for the long term, not just for a particular call. Your desire to learn about management will help you be successful in your new role.

To be successful, you should seek learning opportunities that expand your knowledge. This includes the financial position of the organization. Remember, businesses grow and fail based on decisions. A good understanding about what goes into the organization from a financial perspective is required in order for you to gain an understanding of good decision making, organizational success, and personal growth.

Review Questions

1. In the classic approach to management, what are the primary functions of a manager according to Henri Fayol?
2. How would you compare the classical approach of management with the more contemporary approach postulated by Mintzberg?
3. Why is it possible that some organizations lose their focus on developing needed resources for responding to the community during a medical emergency to ensuring a positive bottom line?
4. Describe how the language of management and finance can assist the EMS professional in becoming more successful.
5. How does quality in operations affect the financial outlook of the organization?
6. How can operational decisions affect the future availability or cost of money to the organization?
7. Where does a person who has recently been given the responsibility to grow an organization learn how to accomplish the goal?
8. How does the manager of an EMS organization measure his or her success?
9. Why is learning about management so important?
10. How important is the integration of finance and management to an EMS organization?

References

Andrews, F. (1976, October 29). "Management: How a Boss Works in Calculated Chaos." *New York Times,* pp. D1, D12.

Drucker, P. (1973). *Management: Tasks, Responsibilities, Practices.* New York: Harper & Row.

Entrepreneur. (2008, October 10). "Ben Cohen & Jerry Greenfield: Caring Capitalists." *Entrepreneur.* See the organization website.

Finkelstein, S. (2003). *Why Smart Executives Fail and What You Can Learn from Their Mistakes.* New York: Penguin Group.

Harcourt College Publishers. (2002). "Chapter 1: An Overview of Financial Management." Fort Worth, TX: Author. Accessed August 2, 2012, at www.business.auburn.edu/%7Epagedan/ch1sol.pdf

Kano, N. (n.d.). "Discovering the Kano Model." Accessed August 12, 2012, at www.kanomodel.com

Kolata, G. (1988, July 12). "A Low Risk of Disease Seen from Syringes on Beaches." *New York Times*. Accessed August 18, 2012 at www.nytimes.com/1988/07/12/nyregion/a-low-risk-of-disease-seen-from-syringes-on-beaches.html

Maverick, S. M. (2004, May 16). *Financial Management & Project Cost Management*. Retrieved from Project Management Demystified: http://projectmanagementysm.blogspot.com/2004/05/financial-management-project-cost.html

Moorhead, G., and R. Griffin. (2001) *Organizational Behavior: Managing People and Organizations*, 6th ed. Boston: Houghton Mifflin Company.

Narayanan, V. K., and R. Nath. (1993). *Organization Theory: A Strategic Approach*. New York: McGraw-Hill.

Parkin, M. (2010). *Microeconomics*, 9th ed. Boston: Pearson.

Rogers, S. (2012, March 12). "Ben & Jerry's Co-founder Emphasizes Spirituality in Business." *Western Kentucky University Herald*. Accessed August 18, 2012 at http://wkuherald.com/news/article_ac1fd44e-7243-11e1-b2e0-0019bb30f31a.html

SEC Info. (n.d.). "US Treasury Money Fund of America–N-30D–For 9/30/02." Accessed August 27, 2012, at from www.secinfo.com/dQyd4.35.htm

Spiro, H. (1996). *Finance for the Non-Financial Manager*. New York: John Wiley & Sons.

U.S. Environmental Protection Agency (EPA). (2012, July). "Medical Waste Frequent Questions." Accessed August 12, 2012, at www.epa.gov/wastes/nonhaz/industrial/medical/mwfaqs.htm

Weston, F., and E. Brigham. (1990). *Introduction to Management Finance*, 9th ed. Orlando, FL: The Dryden Press.

Wren, D. A., A. G. Bedeian, and J. D. Breeze. (2002). "The Foundations of Henri Fayol's Administrative Theory." *Management Decision 40*(9), 906–918.

Key Terms

budget Inclusive list of proposed expenditures and expected receipts of any person, enterprise, or government for a specified period, usually 1 year. Budget estimates are based on the expenditures and receipts of a similar previous period, modified by any expected changes.

controlling Authority or ability to manage or direct.

coordinating Determining the timing of activities so they mesh properly.

delegating Committing or entrusting to another or giving or committing (duties, powers, etc.) to another as agent or representative.

dissemination Circulation: causing to become widely known; spreading information.

disseminator The manager who provides tools for others to make decisions.

ethical Being in accordance with the accepted principles of right and wrong that govern the conduct of a profession.

ethics A branch of philosophy that seeks to address questions about morality—that is, about concepts such as good and bad, right and wrong, justice, and virtue; the standards that govern the conduct of a person, especially a member of a profession.

integrity Steadfast adherence to a strict moral or ethical code.

leading (commanding) The process by which a person influences others to accomplish an objective and directs the organization in a way that makes it more cohesive and coherent.

moral Concerned with principles of right and wrong or conforming to standards of behavior and character based on those principles.

organizing Assembling required resources to attain organizational objectives.

planning: Establishing goals and objectives to pursue during a future period; the process of setting goals, developing strategies, and outlining tasks and schedules to accomplish the goals of an organization.

relevant How pertinent, connected, or applicable something is to a given matter.

risk The expected value of one or more results of one or more future events; technically, the value of those results may be positive or negative.

strategy A plan of action designed to achieve a particular goal.

variance The difference between a budgeted, planned, or standard amount and the actual amount incurred/sold; variances can be computed for both costs and revenues.

Accounting Conventions

Objectives

After reading this chapter, the student should be able to:

2.1   Describe what an accounting convention is and how it will apply in EMS.
2.2   List the accounting conventions that apply to a business.
2.3   Review and discuss financial statements, balance sheets, and income and cash flow statements.
2.4   Discuss the importance of financial reports.
2.5   Introduce how to analyze the finances of an EMS organization to determine if goals have been met.

Overview

The purpose of this text is to introduce the concepts of finance to nonfinancial EMS managers. The chapters present valuable information to both new and experienced EMS leaders who may have varying degrees of experience, formal and informal. The goal is to stimulate thinking in order to change the way things are done, to avoid mistakes of the past, and to encourage future growth of EMS as a profession.

Key Terms

accounting conventions	assets	cost basis
accounting equation	balance sheet	current assets
accounting period	cash flow	current liabilities
accruals concept	cash flow cycle	current ratio
annual report	cash flow statement	entity
	consistency concept	fixed assets

flow	market value	quick ratio	tangible assets
full disclosure	matching	Securities and	total assets
going concern	materiality	Exchange	total liabilities
income statement	net income	Commission (SEC)	working capital
liabilities	net working capital	stock	working capital policy
long-term liabilities	prudence concept		

WHAT WOULD YOU DO?

A new board of directors has asked to review the business activity of the last few years. He has recently joined the organization due to his expertise in accounting and business development. He informs you about people in the community raising concerns that money received through fund-raising was not used in the manner intended.

Questions

1. Why are the organization's finances tracked in a formal manner?

2. How are financial results used to measure the success of organization?
3. Why are decisions made based on financial results in a specific accounting period?
4. Why does the organization have a process for reporting the financial results?
5. What reports can you provide to the board member that demonstrate the accuracy of your financial tracking?
6. What other business concerns must you consider based on the inquiry?

■ INTRODUCTION

This chapter introduces standardized accounting conventions. EMS business managers, unless they are accountants, will have minimal knowledge of the intricacies of accounting. However, the lack of knowledge is a call to EMS managers to learn about accounting to better prepare for the financial questions that will arise. EMS managers should be motivated to become more familiar with many aspects of finances and accounting processes. This is not to say that the EMS manager is required to be an accountant, but by virtue of the responsibility of the position, the EMS manager must understand where financial resources are going and how to report activity and justify spending. If

an independent professional audits the financial position of the EMS organization and submits a report, the manager must be capable of interpreting the information.

■ ACCOUNTING CONVENTIONS

Accounting conventions are loosely defined as methods or procedures used by accounting practitioners. They are based on customary practices and are subject to change as developments arise. For example, a new accounting or tax requirement mandated by the **Securities and Exchange Commission (SEC)** may make a convention inappropriate. EMS managers must realize that ongoing communication with the person who performs accounting functions for the EMS

TABLE 2.1 ■ Accounting Concepts

Accruals concept	To allocate revenue and expenses appropriately. The accrual takes into account when a transaction occurs and not when the cash is received or paid out.
Consistency concept	Once an entity has chosen an accounting method, it should continue to use the same method, unless there is a sound reason to do otherwise. Any change in the accounting method must be disclosed in a method that allows someone who is evaluating the organization to readily see when and why the accounting process changed.
Going concern	An organization for which accounts are being prepared is solvent and viable, and will continue to be in business in the foreseeable future.
Prudence concept	In a report, revenue and profits are included in the balance sheet only when they are realized (or there is reasonable "certainty" of realizing them). Liabilities are included when there is a reasonable "possibility" of incurring them. This is also called the conservation concept.

organization is essential. As rules change, the manager must evaluate the change relative to the effect on the operations of the organization. Accounting changes affecting EMS can be identified through organizations such as the American Institute of Certified Public Accountants or in publications that delineate the current Statement of Financial Accounting Standards.

The EMS manager must understand that there are certain ground rules of accounting that are (or should be) followed for preparation of all accounting and financial statements.

The board of directors and the EMS manager should ensure that the person who is monitoring and reporting on the finances is not only qualified but is also knowledgeable about the intricacies of accounting conventions and is able to discuss them when necessary (Table 2.1).

The EMS manager also should be familiar with other accounting terms. A working knowledge of these terms helps develop comfort with the language of accounting in order to discuss the financial position of the EMS organization (Table 2.2).

TABLE 2.2 ■ Accounting Terms

Accounting equation	TA = TL + OE. The total assets (TA) of an entity are equal to the total liabilities (TL) plus owners' equity (OE). In nonprofits there is no owners' equity, so generally the accounting equation will be TA = TL.
Accounting period	An accounting period is the specific time period that is considered when preparing accounts.
Cost basis	When an asset value is recorded in the organization's financial books, it should be the actual cost paid for the asset, not the asset's current market value.
Entity	Any accounting record that reflects the financial activities of a specific business or organization, and not of its owners or employees.

(Continued)

TABLE 2.2 ■ *(Continued)*	
Full disclosure	The financial statements and their notes (footnotes) should contain all pertinent data relevant to the activities of the entity.
Lower of cost or market value	Inventory is valued either at cost or the market value (whichever is lower) to reflect the effects of obsolescence.
Maintenance of capital	In a for-profit organization, any profit can be realized only after capital of the firm has been restored to its original level, or is maintained at a predetermined level. For the nonprofit organization, any balance of revenue after expenses are paid is considered revenue over expenses.
Matching	Transactions affecting both revenues and expenses should be recognized in the same accounting period.
Materiality	Relatively minor events may be ignored, but the major ones should be fully disclosed. The question to ask is "Does an event greatly affect the operations of the organization?"
Money measurement	Accounting process that records only those activities that can be expressed in monetary terms (with some exceptions, as in cost accounting).
Monetary measurement	Only the activities measurable in terms of money should be recorded.
Objectivity	Financial statements should be based only on verifiable evidence, comprising an audit trail.
Realization	Any change in the market value of an asset or liability is not recognized as a profit or loss until the asset is sold or the liability is paid off (discharged).
Unit of measurement	Financial data should be recorded with a common unit of measure (dollar, pound sterling, yen, etc.).

The manager must begin to understand the terms and then determine where the concepts are applied to the financial aspect of operations. Most disciplines use specific terminology. Often the terminology of finance has substantially different meanings to accountants than to the general public. A high degree of confusion arises when attempting to understand these terms and concepts.

■ FINANCIAL STATEMENTS AND REPORTS ────────

Financial decisions are routinely formulated on the basis of information generated by the accounting department or financial manager. Proper interpretation of the data requires an understanding of the assumptions underlying the reports. Fundamental to understanding the accounting system is the differentiation between **stock** and **flow**. A stock, in this context, refers to wealth in dollars or other assets (buildings, land, and accounts receivable) available to the organization at a given point in time. Similarly, it refers to obligations due the organization at the same point in time. A flow refers to the receipt or disbursement of wealth occurring between any two points in time.

Accounting systems recognize the differences between stock and flow. The basic statement of the stock of wealth is termed the **balance sheet**; the flow of wealth is presented in the **income statement**. The balance sheet reflects the position (wealth) of the organization at a point in time; the income statement presents the flow of wealth between two stated points in time.

The balance sheet and the income statement are key documents of financial accounting. The recording and portrayal of historical financial events occurs on these reports. Conventions have evolved that require tracking of financial activities of the organization. Accountants track entries based on a column system. Accountants refer to entries made on the left side as debits and those made on the right side as credits. On the balance sheet, the **assets** of the organization are presented on the left side (debt side) and **liabilities** and ownership are presented on the right side (credit side).

Adding to the asset is referred to as "debiting" the asset, whereas adding to liabilities is termed "crediting" the account. As discussed previously, the balance sheet portrays the stock of wealth at any given point. In nonprofit organizations, it is the entity to which the wealth belongs that requires tracking.

A word of caution: The highest-level administrator may believe the organization's wealth is his wealth. People read in the newspaper how a treasurer or CEO took money from an organization to benefit himself, often to the surprise of others. The excuses for this behavior run the gamut from "It was owed to me," to "I put this place on the map," to "If it was not for me this organization would not be where it is." Other statements about this include "It was easy" and "I needed it to pay my bills." The underlying theme voiced by perpetrators is that they believed the money was theirs to take or use. It is not. The money belongs to the organization, but in a broader sense the money belongs to the community.

In a for-profit organization, the wealth belongs to the legal entity and describes the net wealth of the owners. The responsibility for management is that the wealth must be delineated, defined, tracked, and reported appropriately.

When looking at the physical report, whether on paper or on-screen, the assets to which the entity has primary claim are listed on the left side (debit side). The following are all examples of assets:

Cash on hand or in the bank

Accounts receivable

Investments

Land

Buildings

Equipment

Prepaid expenses

All of these examples are **tangible assets**, which can be identified as physical objects or documentable claims. The balance sheet also lists intangible assets, such as goodwill.

The right side of the balance sheet (credit side) contains outsiders' claims on the assets of the entity. Outsiders fall into two categories: lenders and owners. The accounting term for what is owed to lenders is **liabilities**, and the claims of owners are equity or net worth. The following are examples of liabilities:

* Accounts payable—accounts that the organization is required to pay in a future period. These costs are incurred during the normal course of business activity and the payment for goods and services are postponed.

* Mortgages—a transfer of interest of a property as security for the payment of money borrowed on the property.

* Deferred revenue—where the receipts are booked until the membership year begins (Many EMS agencies have membership or fund drives that can be considered deferred revenue.)

The following are examples of equity accounts:

* Preferred stock
* Common stock
* Retained earnings
* Paid in surplus

The following formula is used to determine the wealth of the organization:

Assets = Liabilities + Equity (for-profit organizations)

Assets = Liabilities (for nonprofit or municipal-based organizations)

Side Bar

The accounting system reflects two basic aspects of a company: what it owns and what it owes. Assets are resources with future benefits that are owned or controlled by the company. Liabilities are what a company owes its creditors.

Two categories comprise the asset group: **current assets** and **fixed assets**. Current assets consist of cash or claims against external organizations or people that are expected to be converted into cash in less than a year. Fixed assets have a longer life expectancy. An example of a long-term asset would be the building that houses the ambulances and staff.

Liabilities are also grouped into two main categories. **current liabilities**, those expected to be discharged in less than a year, and **long-term liabilities**, those not due within the coming year. Current liabilities would include accounts payable. Mortgages and large loans are examples of long-term liabilities. (For the purposes of this book, equity accounts will not be discussed. The complexity of stocks and stock ownership can become overwhelming with the huge variations that can be developed to take money out of operations to pay back owners for their investment.)

The **annual report** is one of the most important documents generated in an organization. The report contains basic information on both the financial and operational activities from the preceding year's operations. The EMS manager summarizes the operational activities and the future developments of the organization. The report should review the challenges of the organization as well as highlights.

The report should include the financial statements: the income statement, the balance sheet, and the statement of cash flows. The information should include two of the most recent years along with a historical summary of key operational statistics for the previous 5 to 10 years. The financial reports provide information on what happened during the previous 12 months.

BALANCE SHEET

The balance sheet is a statement that reports the financial position during a defined period of time. Items included on the balance sheet are cash and other assets, liabilities, inventory accounting systems, and depreciation methods. (This chapter does not intend to review and discuss the intricacies of the balance sheet—that is, how to record entries in each category, develop T accounts, complete journal entries or develop a comprehensive balance sheet.) The discussion in this chapter introduces the concepts and gives the EMS manager the opportunity to educate himself on the concepts. It offers a basic understanding of what a balance sheet is, what it is used for, and how to extrapolate information to make operational decisions.

The balance sheet is divided into two sides. The left side reflects the assets of the organization, and the right side reflects the liabilities of the organization. In a for-profit organization, or publicly held company, the shareholders' equity provides an accounting of the value of the shareholders' claims on a company and is included on the balance sheet (Figure 2.1). For the nonprofit or governmental EMS organization, this section would be omitted from the balance sheet.

Side Bar

Management must understand accounting data to set financial goals, make financing decisions, and evaluate operating performance.

Balance Sheet			

[Date]
(all numbers in $000)

ASSETS		LIABILITIES	
Current Assets		**Current Liabilities**	
Cash		Accounts payable	
Accounts receivable		Short-term notes	
(less doubtful accounts)		Current portion of long-term notes	
Inventory		Interest payable	
Temporary investment		Taxes payable	
Prepaid expenses		Accrued payroll	
Total Current Assets		**Total Current Liabilities**	
Fixed Assets		**Long-term Liabilities**	
Long-term investments		Mortgage	
Land		Other long-term liabilities	
Buildings		**Total Long-Term Liabilities**	
(less accumulated depreciation)			
Plant and equipment			
(less accumulated depreciation)		**Shareholders' Equity**	
Furniture and fixtures		Capital stock	
(less accumulated depreciation)		Retained earnings	
Total Net Fixed Assets		**Total Shareholders' Equity**	
TOTAL ASSETS		**TOTAL LIABILITIES & EQUITY**	

FIGURE 2.1 ■ Balance Sheet.

The managerial accountant is sometimes considered the controller because he deals with the right side of the balance sheet. By looking at the right side of the balance sheet or liabilities of the organization, the controller determines how the company is performing relative to expenses. Nonetheless, the manager must understand the impact of expenses or liabilities on the organization.

INCOME STATEMENT

The income statement is also referred to as the profit and loss (P&L) statement, earnings statement, operating statement, or state-ment of operations. It is a company report that indicates how revenue converts to net income. **Net income** is the result after all revenues and expenses have been accounted for, also known as the bottom line. The income statement displays the revenues for a defined accounting period, and the cost and expenses charged against these revenues. The purpose of the income statement is to show managers, the board of directors, municipal government officials, and other affected persons whether the organization made or lost money during the reporting period. The important thing to remember about an income statement is that

Income Statement Main Street EMS For Month Ended June 30, xx10	
Revenues	
Net sales	$5,000.00
Training revenue	1,000.00
Total revenues	**$6,000.00**
Expenses	
Wages expense	$1,500.00
Cost of marketing	1,000.00
Utilities expense	250.00
Supplies expense	250.00
Total operating expenses	3,000.00
Net income/loss	**$3,000.00**

FIGURE 2.2 ▪ Income Statement, Main Street EMS.

it represents a defined accounting period. This contrasts with the balance sheet, which represents a single point in time. When payments for services are rendered, the flow of wealth is involved. If the organization pays salaries, buys supplies, or pays interest on loans (which most organizations do), a summary of these transactions appears on the income statement.

In Figure 2.2, an example of a basic income statement, we see that the EMS organization had revenues of $6,000 minus expenses of $3,000, which resulted in a net income of $3,000.

The income statement in Figure 2.2 indicates how gross revenue is recorded as net income. In the first section, revenue generation occurs from services provided. For EMS organizations, gross revenue is money received from individuals, insurance companies, or other payers. The EMS manager must determine the amount of write-offs or bad debt that will not be collected. By subtracting bad debt from gross revenue, the EMS manager can determine the net revenue available to the organization.

The second category is the cost of doing business or **cost of operations**. The organization must consider all aspects of the costs of performing medical services. However, many EMS managers do not consider some of the relevant subcategories. To arrive at a clear and accurate picture of the organization's strengths and determine areas of improvement, these areas should be included in the evaluation.

Expenses are the third area included in the income statement (Figure 2.3). The detail provided is an example of the information included under expenses. The reader should see that each of these categories can be tracked and trended to determine areas of improvements.

Because the income statement is prepared using the accrual basis of accounting, the revenue reported may not have been collected. Similarly, the expenses reported on the income statement might not have been paid during the period that is being reported.

Two formats are commonly used to prepare income statements: the single-step and the multiple-step income statement. The example in Figure 2.3 is a single-step income statement. It consists of just two sections: revenues and expenses. Expenses are deducted from revenues to find net income or loss.

In a multiple-step income statement, the results of transactions are shown in sections separating operating activities from non-operating activities. In addition, it classifies expenses by function. For example, operational expenses are shown separately from administrative expenses.

CASH FLOW

EMS mangers should familiarize themselves with various reports that relate information on the organization's financial standing. The **cash flow statement** examines the flow of funds within the entity and between the entity and suppliers of capital. The cash flow statement

Income Statement _____
[Name]
[Time Period]
Financial Statements in U.S. Dollars

Revenue

Gross Revenue
Less: Write-offs for bad debt
Net Revenue

Cost of Operations

Beginning Inventory	
Add:	Purchases
	Freight-in
	Direct Labor
	Indirect Expenses
Inventory Available	
Less: Ending Inventory	
Cost of Goods Sold	
Gross Profit (Loss)	

Expenses

Advertising
Amortization
Bad Debts
Bank Charges
Charitable Contributions
Contract Labor
Depreciation
Dues and Subscriptions
Employee Benefit Programs
Insurance
Interest
Legal and Professional Fees
Licenses and Fees
Miscellaneous
Office Expense
Payroll Taxes
Postage
Rent
Repairs and Maintenance
Supplies
Telephone
Travel
Utilities
Vehicle Expenses
Wages
Total Expenses
Net Operating Income

Other Income

Gain (Loss) on Sale of Assets
Interest Income
Total Other Income
Net Income (Loss)

FIGURE 2.3 ■ Income Statement.

reports the cash generated and used during a predetermined period of time. This statement is used to reconcile past flows of capital and, probably more importantly, to help plan for future flows. With information from the cash flow statement, managers can monitor the change in long-term debt, determine liquidity of assets, and prepare for capital purchases. This statement typically is generated to compare changes from one year to the next. It organizes and reports the cash generated and used in the following categories:

1. *Operating activities.* Converts the items reported on the income statement from the accrual basis of accounting to cash.
2. *Investing activities.* Reports the purchase and sale of long-term investments and property, plant and equipment.
3. *Financing activities.* For EMS organizations who are organized as a for-profit, this activity reports the issuance and repurchase of the company's bonds and stocks and the payment of dividends.

For most EMS organizations, stock and dividends do not affect the financial operations of the reporting. Figure 2.4 shows the statement of cash flow used as a tool for the EMS manager.

This example illustrates a for-profit view of cash flow. The cash flow statement should be modified to reflect the EMS organization's needs. For example, as stated earlier, most non-profit or governmental EMS agencies do not report cash for stock or cash paid in dividends. However, several of the other categories are essential for the EMS manager to determine the net effect of the movement of cash in a given period in the organization.

This cash flow statement reports the impact of the organization's operating, investing, and financing activities on cash flows over an accounting period. The statement's design is to show the effect EMS operations have on the use of cash and to show the relationship of cash

	[Name]	[Time Period]
Cash flow from operating activities		
Cash received from patients, insurance, or government		
Cash paid for inventory		
Cash paid for wages and other operating expenses		
Cash paid for interest		
Cash paid for taxes		
Other		
Net cash provided (used) by operating activities		
Cash flow from investing activities		
Cash received from sale of capital assets (plant and equipment, etc.)		
Cash received from collection of notes receivable		
Cash paid for purchase of capital assets		
Cash paid to acquire businesses		
Other		
Net cash provided (used) by investing activities		
Cash flow from financing activities		
Cash received from issuing stock		
Cash received from long-term borrowings		
Cash paid to repurchase stock		
Cash paid to retire long-term debt		
Cash paid for dividends		
Other		
Net cash provided (used) in financing activities		
Increase (decrease) in cash during the period		
Cash balance at the beginning of the period		
Cash balance at the end of the period		

FIGURE 2.4 ■ Statement of Cash Flow.

flow among operations, investing, and financing activities. It helps to answer questions such as these: Is the organization meeting the goals of growth? Is the organization generating enough cash to purchase additional fixed assets for growth? Does the organization have too much excess cash that can be used to pay down exist-

ing debt or to invest in other projects that benefit the community?

ACCRUAL ACCOUNTING

Accrual is the adding together or the act of accumulating something during a predetermined period of time. In accounting, accrual describes the method whereby revenues and expenses are recognized when they are occurring, regardless of when the actual cash is received or paid out.

Accrual accounting measures the performance and position of a company's economic events regardless of when the cash transaction occurred. Recognition of the event (e.g., a CPR class or an emergency call) occurs by matching revenues to expenses when the transaction occurs rather than when the payment is received. It is essential for the EMS manager to recognize the event and record it in order to determine how much money is expected during a future period, typically 30 to 90 days in the future. "Accrual" of future revenue allows the manager to plan cash flow through the organization.

Of the many supporting budgeting activities, none is as important to management as the cash budget. The reason is simple; regardless of the future potential income of an organization, unless cash is available now to meet near-term obligations, such as payroll, power, gas, telephone, notes due, and such, the organization is essentially out of business. By knowing what revenue is expected in the future, the manager can budget what bills are paid, inventory purchased, or debt reduced.

Budgeting systems, for long-term planning and control purposes, follow accepted accounting principles. For example, revenue generated by an emergency call, transport, or CPR class is recorded at the time the activity is billed, not at the time payment is received. Since these transactions reflect a credit to accounts receivable, they do not automatically increase the availability of cash. As most organizations require cash to handle the day-to-day operations, increasing the accounts receivable reduces the cash balances available to the organization. Performance reports will reflect higher accounts receivable totals, but available cash may be reduced. Financial management should be guided by the long-term goal of revenue generation subject to the availability of cash. It should be apparent, by running emergency calls, transports, conducting training, receiving grants, or any other revenue-generating activity, that receiving payment will probably occur in the future. The key to successful financial management is to continuously examine processes that generate and accrue income for future use by the organization, but also, and more important, which ensure that the organization is receiving what is owed in a timely manner.

Best Practices

PopCap, a startup company founded by Jason Kapalka, John Vechey, and Brian Feite, illustrates the value of understanding accounting concepts. These entrepreneurs met and started an online game company. The young trio developed a system to account for everything, including cash, revenues, receivables, and payables. They also adjusted to the deferral and accrual of revenues and expenses. Kapalka states, "We were trying to keep a very simple business model. The team fine-tunes their accounting system as they remain focused on revenues, income, assets, and liabilities. They insist on timely and accurate accounting, so they took time to understand accounting adjustments and the effect on their company."

Sources: PopCap.com, January 2009; *Entrepreneur*, February 2008; *Wired*, March 2008; *2o2p Magazine*, September 2006; *Washington Post*, March 2008.

CASH FLOW CYCLE

The **cash flow cycle** is the way in which actual cash flows into or out of the organization during predetermined periods. Accounts receivable and accounts payable affect the cash flow cycle. Accounts receivable are those accounts in which an outside entity owes the organization money for services already performed. For example, an EMS organization responds to 300 calls in a month. The emergency responder documents each call, and each call is coded by the billing department. The codes are "collected" or collated and sent in batches to the payer. Income, expected by the EMS organization for services already performed, is recorded in accounts receivable. When the money is received, the cash account is debited, and the accounts receivable account is adjusted appropriately.

Similarly, when a bill comes into the organization—say, an insurance premium that is due in 90 days—the manager or the person responsible for receiving or paying bills would record the dollar value in accounts payable. When the bill is paid, the money is debited from the cash account, and accounts payable is credited to reflect the payment.

Decision makers must understand their cash flow processes to avoid being cash short in times of need, which can force the organization to take on debt or reduce services. Accurate cash flow forecasting is a critical element in good financial planning for an organization.

One method for tracking cash flow is through the statement of cash flow. This statement reports the impact of the organization's operating, investing, and financing activities on cash flows over an accounting period. The statement is designed to show the effect EMS operations have on the use of cash and to show the relationship of cash flow between operations, investing, and financing activities. It helps to answer questions like these: Is the organization meeting the goals of growth? Is the organization generating enough cash to purchase additional fixed assets for growth? Does the organization have too much excess cash, which could be used to pay down existing debt or invested in other projects that benefit the community?

CASH FLOW ANALYSIS

Cash flow is the actual net cash, as opposed to net income, that flows into a company during a specified period and allows the organization to provide services. Cash flow is related to profits, which are simply net income as reported on the income statement. Again, the intention of this discussion is to help the EMS manager understand finance and learn how to use reports to track the success of and grow the organization for the benefit of the community. The information is not intended to teach managers to make excess profits, especially if executive compensation is based on the bottom line.

EMS organizations can be thought of as having two separate but related bases of value: *existing assets* (provide revenue over expenses) and *growth opportunities* (represent opportunities to make new investments) that will increase revenue and cash flow. The ability to take advantage of growth opportunities often depends on the availability of cash to buy new assets or develop new programs. The cash flow from existing assets is often the primary source for funding any new venture.

There are two classes of cash flow: (1) operating cash flow and (2) other cash flows. Operating cash flow arises from normal operations and is the difference between revenue and expenses. Other cash flows arise from borrowing, grants, and fund-raising activities. To a lesser extent, cash flow can be raised from investment income.

■ PROCESS FOR MANAGING FINANCES

To get an understanding of financial processes, a review of terminology is important (Table 2.3).

It is important to have a working capital management process in place for several reasons. Much of a manager's time is spent on the day-to-day operations that require working with finance. The manager balances the needs of operations with the availability of financial resources. In most EMS organizations, current assets represent a large portion of **total assets**. Managing current assets is a dynamic process, and it requires the financial manager or operations manager to monitor revenues and ensure that assets are available in sufficient quantity to meet operational needs. Revenue can be used for short-term or long-term needs, whereas working capital allows the EMS organization to pay for its current obligations. Working capital is important in many EMS organizations because of the dynamic and ever-changing environment. Small EMS organizations have limited access to long-term capital. They must often rely on savings accounts or short-term loans to meet organizational needs. Therefore, having a defined financial process allows the manager to accomplish daily oversight of operational activities while maintaining a big picture view of the organization related to business activity.

TABLE 2.3 ■ Finance Terminology

Working capital	Current assets
Net working capital	Current assets minus current liabilities
Current ratio	Current assets divided by current liabilities (This ratio provides information on the firm's liquidity.)
Quick ratio	Current assets minus inventories divided by current liabilities (This ratio measures the organization's ability to meet current obligations.)
Working capital policy	The organization's basic policies regarding the target level for cash in each category of current assets and how current assets will be financed

CHAPTER REVIEW

Summary

The discussion in this chapter exemplifies the complexity of EMS managers' work relative to running the operations and ensuring the financial viability of the organization. Some of the tools introduced help take the guesswork out of knowing if the company is doing well and simplifies tracking of the financial results. By understanding some of the financial conventions, the EMS manager can understand financial reports and the information they contain. The more familiar the EMS manager is with financial reports, the better prepared he will be to deliver financial news to the board of directors or to governmental agencies.

WHAT WOULD YOU DO? Reflection

The board member has raised appropriate, yet difficult, questions. As the EMS manager, you should generate a balance sheet, an income statement, and a statement of cash flow. A recent audit of the financial position of the organization would provide comforting information for the board of directors. Ongoing reports you should share include the immediate, short-term, and long-term goals of the organization and how the finances align with the stated goals; purchases that reflect goal achievement; and adjustments made to either the goals or finances relative to current trends. You should request ongoing feedback from the experts on the board to ensure that the communication is appropriate and adequate.

Review Questions

1. What is meant by *accounting conventions*?
2. Why must the EMS manager understand accounting conventions?
3. How does the balance sheet reflect the financial position of the EMS organization?
4. What information is critical on the balance sheet for reporting purposes?
5. What two comparisons are made on the balance sheet?
6. What is the important difference between the income statement and the balance sheet?
7. When looking at the cash flow statement, what information helps determine how the organization is performing?
8. Why should the EMS manager establish financial policies for tracking financing and for analyzing the organization's finances?
9. What ratios are important to incorporate in reporting the EMS organization's finances?
10. Overall, how does the accounting process affect the success of an organization?

References

Spiro, H. (1996). *Finance for the Nonfinancial Manager*. New York: John Wiley & Sons, Inc.

Weston, F., and E. Brigham. (1990). *Introduction to Management Finance,* 9th ed. Orlando, FL: The Dryden Press.

Key Terms

accounting conventions Methods or procedures used by accounting practitioners. They are based on custom (past practices) and are subject to change as new developments arise.

accounting equation In nonprofits, the accounting equation will read TA = TL.

accounting period A recording of the financial transactions pertaining only to a specific period that are considered when preparing accounts for that period.

accrual concept Takes into account when a transaction occurs and not when the cash is received or paid out.

annual report Contains basic information on both the financial and operational activities both from the preceding year's operations.

assets A resource with economic value that an individual, corporation or country owns or controls with the expectation that it will provide future benefit.

balance sheet Report that tracks the assets and the liabilities and ownership of the organization.

cash flow Actual net cash, as opposed to net income, that flows into a company during a specified period and allows the organization to provide services.

cash flow cycle Way in which actual cash flows into or out of the organization during predetermined periods.

cash flow statement Examines the flow of funds within the entity and between the entity and suppliers of capital.

consistency concept An accounting method used the same way every time.

cost basis An asset's value is recorded in the organization's financial books they should be actual cost paid.

current assets A balance sheet account that represents the value of all assets that are expected to be converted into cash within one year in the normal course of business. Current assets include cash, accounts receivable, inventory, marketable securities, prepaid expenses and other liquid assets that can be readily converted to cash.

current liabilities A company's debts or obligations that are due within one year. Current liabilities appear on the company's balance sheet and include short term debt, accounts payable, accrued liabilities and other debts.

current ratio A financial ratio that measures whether or not a firm has enough resources to pay its debts over the next 12 months.

entity Accounting records that reflects the financial activities of a specific business.

fixed assets A long-term tangible piece of property that a firm owns and uses in the production of its income and is not expected to be consumed or converted into cash any sooner than at least one year's time.

flow Process by which inputs and outputs move in an organization.

full disclosure The financial statements and their notes (footnotes) that contain all pertinent data relevant to the activities of the entity.

going concern An organization for which accounts are being prepared is solvent and viable,

and will continue to be in business in the foreseeable future.

income statement A summary of a management's performance as reflected in the profitability (or lack of it) of an organization over a certain period. It itemizes the revenues and expenses of past that led to the current profit or loss, and indicates what may be done to improve the results.

liabilities An obligation of an entity arising from past transactions or events.

long-term liabilities Obligations payable at a future period more than 12 months away from today or the date of the balance sheet.

market value Inventory valued either at cost or the market value (whichever is lower).

matching Transactions that affect both revenues and expenses in the same accounting period.

materiality Events that should be fully disclosed if they make a significant difference in the finances of an organization.

net income Income after all revenues and expenses have been accounted for; also known as the bottom line.

net working capital The difference between current assets and current liabilities.

prudence concept Revenue and profits are recorded on the balance sheet only when they are realized.

quick ratio Measures the ability of a company to use its near cash or quick assets; Current assets less inventory divided by current liabilities.

Securities and Exchange Commission (SEC) An independent agency which holds primary responsibility for enforcing the federal securities laws and regulating the securities industry.

stock Refers to wealth in monetary (dollars) or other forms (buildings, land, accounts receivable) available to owners at a given point in time.

tangible assets Physical assets represents property, plant, and equipment.

total assets All current assets, fixed assets, and other assets.

total liabilities All current liabilities and long-term debt.

working capital A measure of current assets of a business that exceeds its liabilities and can be applied to its operation.

working capital policy The organization's basic policies regarding the target level for cash in each category of current assets and how current assets will be financed.

Generally Accepted Accounting Principles

Objectives

After reading this chapter, the student should be able to:

3.1 Describe what GAAP is and how it applies to EMS management.
3.2 List the different principles with which the EMS manager should be familiar.
3.3 Review and discuss inventory control and depreciation.
3.4 Discuss the importance of preparing an equipment replacement program and its effect on business operations.
3.5 Introduce how inventory control and depreciation affect the finances of an EMS organization.

Overview

The purpose of this text is to introduce the concepts of finance to nonfinancial EMS managers. The chapters present valuable information to both new and experienced EMS leaders who may have varying degrees of experience, formal and informal. The goal is to stimulate thinking in order to change the way things are done, to avoid mistakes of the past, and to encourage future growth of EMS as a profession.

Key Terms

accrual	credibility	Generally Accepted	matching
accrued expense	deferred expense	Accounting	materiality
audit	depreciation	Principles (GAAP)	opinion
carrying costs	economic ordering	marginal	prepaid expenses
coherence	quantity (EOQ)	marginalism	standards
conformity			

WHAT WOULD YOU DO?

You and the board of directors have decided to implement a vehicle replacement program. In this program the board has agreed to replace the organization's vehicles every 7 years. The board suggests that each vehicle should be purchased with a combination of cash from operations and low-interest loans. Your accountant has suggested that the organization use the sum-of-the-years depreciation method on each subsequent new vehicle purchased.

Questions

1. How would you prepare for the implementation of the program knowing that the first vehicle will be replaced in 2 years and that each vehicle will be replaced every 3 years after that?
2. What is your understanding of Generally Accepted Accounting Principles?
3. Why should an organization's finances be audited by an objective professional?
4. Why are the audit results reviewed by the board of directors or other advisory body?
5. What is the purpose of having an inventory control program?
6. What methods do organizations use for recognizing depreciation?

■ INTRODUCTION

Generally Accepted Accounting Principles (GAAP) is a term referring to the standard framework of guidelines for financial accounting. GAAP includes the **standards**, conventions, and rules that accountants follow in recording and summarizing transactions, and in preparing financial statements.

Why is it important for the EMS manager to know this information? We present two scenarios. First, if the manager outsources the function of finance, or the organization employs a specialist to track the financial activities, the board of directors (BOD) and/or the manager must understand the process—whether it is appropriate or not. If the process is not legal, or is at best questionable, the manager cannot plead ignorance to regulators, auditors, or any other legal investigator.

Second, if the manager of a small EMS organization performs the financial activities, he must realize the long-term implications if the process is not performed within the parameters of accepted accounting principles. **Conformity** to accounting standards is essential in order to ensure reliability of the information.

THE ACCOUNTING DISCIPLINE——

Accounting is comprised of several specialty areas that are defined in a variety of ways. The three broad areas of accounting include public accounting, governmental accounting, and management accounting. These specialty areas are illustrated in Figure 3.1 and discussed individually below.

PUBLIC ACCOUNTING

Public accounting, although the area of accounting most familiar to the general public, is a relatively narrow part of accounting that places a major emphasis on auditing general-purpose financial statements: income statements, balance sheets, and cash statements. Certified public accountants (CPAs) also provide tax and other types of advisory services to their clients, but this is still rather narrow when compared to the whole range of activities performed in the accounting discipline. Some may ask, "Do we need a CPA to sit on the board or track the financial aspects of the organization?" The answer is no. A CPA and an accountant can perform the same duties. Accountants look after the financial records of an organization. They are also responsible for issuing financial reports. A CPA has passed a rigorous exam issued by a state, and it is the CPA that has the final say in financial matters. Both professionals are capable of offering an **opinion** of an organization's financial activity, but it is the CPA who can advise and **audit** the financial aspects of an organization.

GOVERNMENTAL ACCOUNTING

Governmental accounting is nonaccrual accounting used by governmental agencies as well as by nonprofit organizations such as state universities. It is completely different from the material studied in financial and management accounting courses.

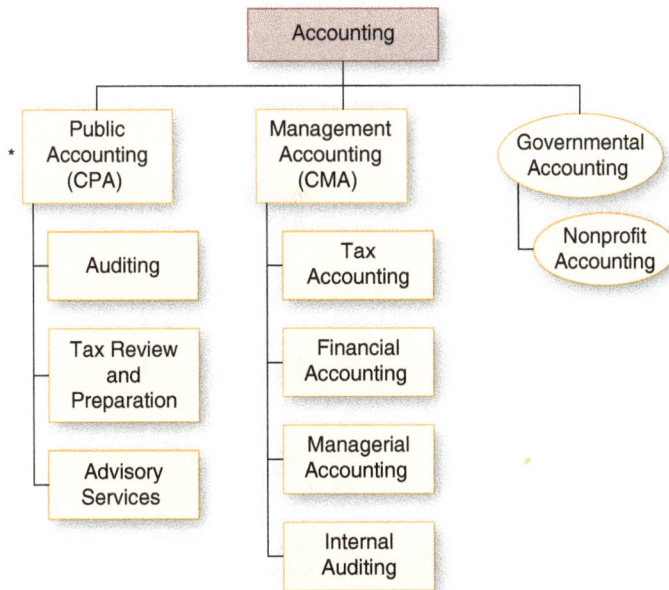

FIGURE 3.1 ■ The accounting discipline.

MANAGEMENT ACCOUNTING

Management accounting includes tax accounting, financial accounting, managerial accounting, and internal auditing. The concept definitions and relationships among the branches of management accounting are discussed below. The CMA designation that appears in Figure 3.2 represents "certified management accountant."

Management accounting and the connecting branches shown on Figure 3.2 provide the focus of this discussion. As indicated in the diagram, managerial accounting is linked to cost accounting, cost management, operational management, and investment management. Managerial accounting involves generating information for internal users including all levels of management and others within the organization. Some of the same information reported appears in external financial statements. Most of the information in managerial reports provides internal users more detail, more often, and in many differ-ent forms, depending on how the information is to be used. A significant difference between financial accounting and managerial accounting is that managerial accounting reports are not directly constrained by GAAP.

Tax and Financial Accounting

Tax accounting and financial accounting both involve generating financial reports for external users, although the two reports may be very different. Tax returns are required for reporting to the Internal Revenue Service (IRS) and must conform to a specific set of rules. Financial accounting, on the other hand, involves preparing general-purpose financial statements for managers, boards of directors, and creditors. Financial accounting statements must conform to GAAP. This requirement causes external financial statements to be of limited usefulness for internal purposes. Internal statement users tend to need more timely, less aggregated information than external statement users.

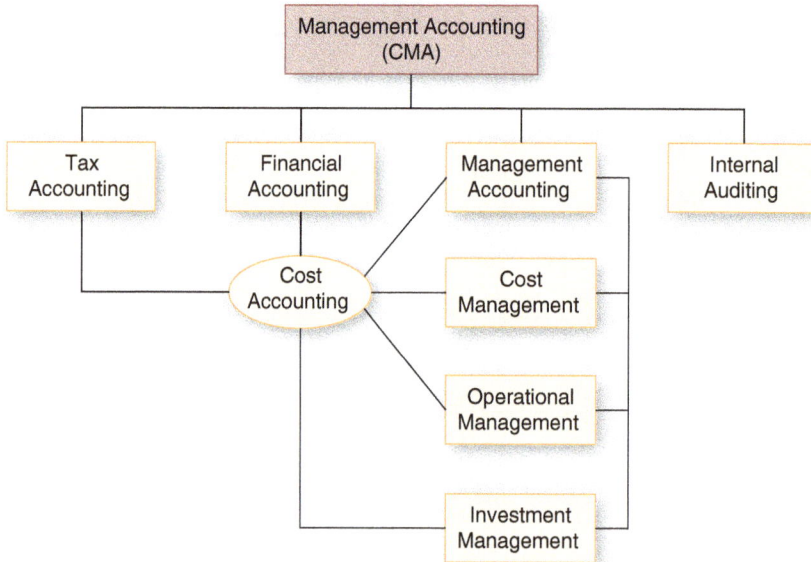

FIGURE 3.2 ■ Concepts of managerial accounting.

Cost Accounting

Cost accounting is linked to tax accounting, financial accounting, and managerial accounting (Figure 3.2) because it is an important component of each discipline. Why? Cost accounting involves determining the cost of a product, service, activity, or some other cost activity. These costs are needed for several purposes. For example, the costs of providing EMS services are needed for both tax and external financial statements. In other words, tax accounting and financial accounting both depend on cost accounting to provide information. Information about costs is also needed for a variety of management decisions. For example, cost estimates are needed to determine the feasibility of adding a training program or whether a new line of service can support itself and add to the overall revenue of the EMS organization, or whether to discontinue a service. Unit costs of a service are also needed to determine pricing. From this perspective, cost accounting is perhaps underrated as a discipline since none of the other disciplines, including tax accounting, financial accounting, and managerial accounting, could exist without cost accounting.

Cost Management. Cost management is a more comprehensive concept than cost accounting in that the emphasis is on managing and reducing costs rather than reporting costs. In other words, it is a long-run, proactive approach rather than a short-run, reactive approach. James Brimson (1991), who originally served as CAM-I's Cost Management Systems (CMS) project director, defines cost management as "the management and control of activities to determine an accurate cost, improve business processes, eliminate waste, identify cost drivers, plan operations, and set business strategies" (p. 205). Based on Brimson's definition, the concept of activity management is part of the cost management discipline originally defined, although the term cost management might be interpreted differently.

Best Practice

A joint survey conducted by Ernst & Young (E&Y) and the Institute of Management Accountants (IMA) had the goal of understanding how roles have evolved within the finance function, what tools and solutions are most commonly adopted, and what best practices are being adopted. Based on the interviews, E&Y and IMA identified best practices that they believed began to set the framework for a successful foundation in cost management.

Best-practice companies typically manage by information—that is, "they base important decisions on systematically generated, accurate, and timely collected facts as opposed to managing through a combination of intuition, tradition, and output from ad hoc reports." Finance professionals fulfill a unique role in that they are able to serve as a bridge between operations, IT, and top management. The drive toward betterment is the goal of all activities. Best practitioners are rarely satisfied with what they have achieved to date. Instead, they strive for continuous improvement, realigning systems with changes in business processes and market needs.

Garg, A., D. Ghosh, and H. Halper. (2004). "Best Practices in Management Accounting." *Cost Management* 18(2), 21–25.

Operational Management. According to Martin (n.d.), operational management, or activity based management, places emphasis on continuously improving the activities and tasks, or work that people perform in an organization. The main idea is to find and eliminate waste.

Conceptually, operational management is somewhat different from cost management in that it focuses on the waste itself, not the cost of waste. It is a process oriented approach rather than an accounting results-oriented approach. Operational management also has a long-run, rather than a short-run emphasis. Although activity management is part of the cost management system (CMS), it is important to make a distinction between managing costs (accounting results) and managing activities (processes or work). This distinction is important because placing too much emphasis on costs (or any other short run, results-oriented measurement) may cause managers to make decisions that reduce costs but are not in the best interest of the organization's long-run performance and competitiveness. A few examples include a manager's decision to reduce employee training, and preventive maintenance just to improve short-term accounting results.

■ ACCOUNTING PRINCIPLES————

Accounting principles are the rules and guidelines of accounting. They determine such matters as the measurement of assets, the timing of revenue recognition, and the **accrual** of expenses. To be accepted as part of GAAP, an accounting principle must have "substantial authoritative support" such as by promulgation of a Financial Accounting Standards Board (FASB) pronouncement. Accounting principles are based on the necessary objectives of financial reporting. Accrual is an example of an accounting principle.

Financial information must be assembled and reported objectively. Outside agencies, organizations, or people who rely on the information have a right to be assured that the data are free from bias and inconsistency, whether deliberate or not. These entities include the local municipal government, banks, and boards of directors. Those persons who report financial information must establish **credibility** with those receiving the information. Conforming to acceptable standards provides the basis for trust and credibility.

In any report of financial statements (audit, compilation, review), the preparer/auditor must indicate to the reader whether or not the information contained within the statements complies with GAAP. If the EMS manager prepares a balance sheet, he must provide, in writing, an assurance that the balance sheet complies with the appropriate standards. The general rules and concepts that govern the field of accounting form the groundwork on which accounting rules are based.

GAAP consists of three important sets of rules:

1. Accounting principles and guidelines
2. Detailed rules and standards issued by FASB (FASB uses basic principles and guidelines for its own detailed and comprehensive set of accounting standards.)
3. Generally accepted industry practices

GAAP is exceedingly useful because it attempts to standardize and regulate accounting definitions and assumptions. EMS managers should be familiar with GAAP principles and accounting language. The following economic concepts provide an overview of accounting principles for general knowledge:

Principle of regularity—Define conformity to enforced rules and laws.

Principle of consistency—Require accountants to apply the same methods and procedures from period to period.

Principle of sincerity—States that the accounting unit should reflect in good faith the reality of the company's financial status.

Principle of the permanence of methods—Aims to allow the **coherence** and comparison of financial information published by the company.

Principle of noncompensation—Requires disclosure of the full details of the financial information and not compensating debt with an asset, a revenue with an expense.

Principle of prudence—Shows the situation "as is." The EMS manager should not try to make things look better than they are. Typically, revenue is recorded only when it is certain, and a provision should be entered only for an expense that is probable.

Principle of continuity—One should assume that the business will not be interrupted. This principle mitigates the principle of prudence: Assets do not have to be accounted for at their disposal value, but it is accepted that they are at their historical value.

The introduction of a few more economic concepts provides a deeper understanding of how decision making occurs and how finance affects decisions. These concepts have their bases in the historical development of overall economic concepts. The EMS manager should understand that these concepts do not impact the daily operations of the organization. These concepts are better used to understand how economic concepts work when making business decisions.

MARGINALISM

This concept defines the use of marginal concepts within economics. **Marginal** concepts are associated with a change in the quantity used of a good or a service, as opposed to the overall significance of the good or service. For example, a local high school requests the EMS service to stand by at a low-risk fundraising

event that occurs annually. The EMS organization owns one ambulance; thus, when they cover this event, they must go out of service for the entire day. By going out of service, historically, the organization misses, on average three emergency calls. Proactively, the organization alerts the neighboring ambulance organization, which covers the calls and receives the reimbursement. The local ambulance receives a token donation for the standby at the fundraising event.

The marginal concept maintains that the value for using the local ambulance to stand by is low relative to the community's need to have a local ambulance respond to 9-1-1 calls. In other words, the community has a greater need for the local ambulance than does the high school. The concept of **marginalism** would dictate that the ambulance should stay in service for the community because a greater good is served versus attending the fundraiser, unless the donation made by the high school is greater than the combined reimbursement the EMS organization receives from submitting claims from the 9-1-1 responses.

PRINCIPLE OF CONSISTENCY

This principle is a basic accounting concept which states that, once an accounting method is adopted, it should be followed consistently from one accounting period to another. If for any reason the accounting method changes, a full disclosure of the change and an explanation of its effects on the financial statements must be given in the accompanying notes. One of the duties of the auditor is to make sure the consistency principle is followed because, otherwise, any changes might make interpretation of the financial data a futile effort.

MATCHING PRINCIPLE

This is a cornerstone of accrual accounting. The **matching** principle is the combination of accrual accounting and the revenue recognition principle. Together they determine the accounting period. According to the revenue recognition principle, expenses are recognized when obligations are (1) incurred—usually when goods are transferred, or services rendered, and (2) offset against recognized revenues, which were generated from those expenses, no matter when cash is paid. The matching principle requires that expenses be matched with revenues.

Managers should become familiar with accounting concepts and be capable of understanding how they become operational concepts. Cash accounting is the operational extension of the matching principle.

In cash accounting, expenses are recognized when cash is paid. Once the service is rendered (a 9-1-1 call or CPR class is completed) and cash is paid by the recipient of the service, the recording of the transaction is completed. In cash accounting, costs are recognized as expenses in the accounting period they are used or consumed.

Prepaid expenses are not recognized as expenses. An organization will make payments for goods or services that will be received or used in the future. The value of the service will be expensed when the good or service is received. An example of a prepaid expense would be a payment for insurance.

Lastly, if no connection with revenues can be established, costs are recognized immediately as expenses. The matching principle allows better evaluation of actual profitability and performance and reduces noise, or discrepancies, from timing mismatches between when costs are incurred and when revenue is realized.

EXPENSE VERSUS CASH TIMING—

Two types of accounts exist to avoid the appearance that an EMS organization either profited or lost money in a specific accounting period.

This could occur when cash is used to pay a bill in a different accounting period than the one in which expenses are recognized. Expenses are recognized when obligations are incurred regardless of when cash is paid out according to the matching principle. Cash can be paid out in an earlier or later period than obligations are incurred and related expenses are recognized, but the EMS manager must record the transactions using one of the following two categories:

Accrued expense—expense recognized before cash is paid out.

Deferred expense—expense is recognized after cash is paid out.

An accrued expense is a liability. It is an obligation to pay for goods or services received from another entity. Cash is paid for the good or service in a later period. The amount paid is deducted from accrued expenses. For example, an EMS organization has contracted with the local coffee company to supply coffee on a weekly basis, and the coffee is used on an ongoing basis, but the payment is not made to the supplier each time an individual cup of coffee is consumed; rather, it is paid monthly. If the payment in the future is based on the number of pounds of coffee, the expense could change from month to month.

The manager would accrue the expense in the budget, and, as each month passes, he would credit the expense from this category. Simultaneously, the manager would debit the cash account. In our example, the manager budgets $1,200 for coffee per year in the accrued expense account. Every month he subtracts $100 from the account and writes a check for the monthly payment. At the end of the budget year, the coffee account is $0, and the cash account records a total of $1,200 in payments for coffee.

Deferred expenses are an asset. Cash is paid to another entity for goods or services that will be received in a later accounting period.

For example, insurance is paid either quarterly, semiannually, or annually. A portion of the insurance is used per month. The dollar value of the insurance used is added to prepaid expense, which is decreased by a fractional amount. In an EMS organization, the entire insurance bill is paid at the beginning of the budget year. The organization reports expenses to the board of directors on a quarterly basis. Every 3 months, one-quarter of the expense is allocated to that accounting period under the deferred expenses accounting category, and the total of deferred expense is reduced by 25 percent.

▨ MATERIALITY

Materiality is based on management's decision to include or omit financial information on a report. The standard relates to a concept or convention within auditing and accounting relating to the importance or significance of an amount, transaction, or discrepancy. It is also defined as an omission or misstatement of accounting information that, in light of the surrounding circumstances, makes it probable that the judgment of a reasonable person relying on the information would have been changed or influenced by the omission or misstatement (FASB Statement of Financial Accounting Concepts No. 2, Qualitative Characteristics of Accounting Information).

The FASB standard explains that materiality is not a constant. It may vary between two entities of different size and types. The determination of materiality takes into account how users of the information could reasonably be expected to be influenced in making financial decisions. Users are assumed to:

1. have an appropriate knowledge of business and economic activities and accounting and a willingness to study the information in the financial statements.
2. understand that financial statements are audited to levels of materiality.
3. make appropriate economic decisions on the basis of the information in the financial statements. (FASB Statement on Auditing Standards No. 107)

Best Practice

Akebono Brake Industry is a $2 billion per year brake pad manufacturer. The organization uses conventional management techniques in a unique way to gather, analyze, and make decisions. Materials Resource Planning (MRP) was used to reorganize the entire management and reporting system. Managers have traditionally used MRP to perform many accounting functions like inventory control and creating balance sheets and income statements. The management team knew that MRP had capabilities that could provide additional cost management information.

Prior to implementation management identified employees who needed the advanced reporting system and matched their needs with business needs, creating a win-win solution. The redesigned MRP provided a high degree of analysis, which conventional MRP systems are unable to accomplish, allowing greater control over the data that measured company activity.

Adapted from Garg, A., D. Ghosh, and H. Halper. (2004). "Best Practices in Management Accounting." *Cost Management 18*(2), 21–25.

This operational concept influences how organizations conduct business and monitor their finances. It is important for the EMS manager to become familiar with accounting standards to ensure that all financial transactions are conducted and recorded appropriately. Trying to memorize and understand each concept can be overwhelming, but knowing standards exist can help establish methods to track the financial success of the organization.

Another operational concept that is important for EMS managers to understand is inventory control. Inventory control may seem to be a trivial matter in small EMS organizations. No matter the size of the EMS organization, inventory control and accounting are important aspects of an organization.

■ INVENTORY MANAGEMENT

Ideally, investments in any of the asset accounts on the balance sheet—whether land, equipment, inventory, or even cash—are made for the purpose of increasing the expected amounts of money available to provide services or improve quality. Capital budgeting provides an approach for determining the desirability of acquiring long-term assets once expected financial returns are determined by the management team. The responsibility of financial management, in these instances, is limited to determining the desirability of the financial goals.

In many organizations, financial management doubles as operational management. When the organization's hierarchy does not differentiate between the financial manager, inventory manager, or collections manager (all finance subspecialists), then one person has a voice in multiple functions within the organization. It is the financial voice that is held accountable for the cash flow of the organization. The person responsible for finance has a substantial stake in the appropriate levels of inventory, rate of collections, and budgets of departments. If, for example, inventory exceeds anticipated levels without corresponding increases in calls, funds are, in effect, tied up in nonproductive activities, and the overall profits or levels of service of the organization are diminished.

Some organizations believe more is better. In other words, they believe the more they have in inventory, the better able they are to serve patients. The "what-if scenarios" play into this mindset. For example, what if the winter is bad and the organization runs out of XYZ? The holding of inventory gives rise to a series of costs that would not be experienced without the inventory. Some of these costs are obvious, such as the costs of increased capital requirements needed to finance the additional inventory and the cost of increased facilities to store the additional inventory. To determine the additional cost of storage, the EMS manager associates square-foot cost in a ratio with overall costs. Suddenly, the additional space used becomes important. In addition, the extra space that is used becomes space that is not available for other operations. The old adage applies: Once the space is allocated, it will be hard to change its use. In addition, excess inventory can lead to an increased cost for obsolescence and spoilage (outdates). There will also be an increase in labor costs for monitoring and tracking of the additional inventory.

Although other costs are directly apparent, the indirect costs are also real. Some of the less obvious costs are increases in insurance costs to cover lost or damaged inventory. These financial costs must be taken into consideration when making straightforward management decisions.

Some of the costs of inventory decrease on a per unit basis with increasing levels of inventory. Ordering costs are one such decrease. As the quantity of each purchased item increases, the number of reorders decreases in any given period. However, each order also has associated costs ranging from taking of actual inventory to ascertaining shortages, to the time the manager takes in deciding how much to order, to the actual processing of the order. The costs of receiving, sorting, and stocking supplies and ultimately authorizing payments for the purchased supplies must be considered. The larger and less frequent the orders are, the less costly they are per unit.

Another significant aspect of inventory policies is cash flow. Investment in inventory absorbs cash that might be required in other aspects of the organization. The use of capital could constrain the expansion of fixed assets and accounts receivable. As in all situations, a balance must be maintained and consistent policies developed. Trade-offs among cash flow, inventory requirements, and other competing uses are resolved through management discretion. With a solid financial process that minimizes arbitrary decisions and allows management to view the organization globally, determining the best course of action becomes less stressful.

DETERMINING INVENTORY

Inventory management focuses on three basic questions:

1. How many of each inventory item should the organization hold in stock?
2. How many units should be ordered at any given time?
3. At what point should inventory be ordered?

Managing assets of all kinds can be viewed as an inventory problem because the same principles apply to cash and fixed assets as to inventories. First, working stock (e.g., IV catheters, oxygen tubing, and bandaging material) must be available to meet expected needs: The size of inventory depends on expected 9-1-1 call volume. Second, because demand for an item may be greater than expected, it is necessary to have safety stock available. The additional cost of holding the safety stock must be balanced against the revenue generated from 9-1-1 responses. Depletion of current medical inventory may occur if there is a high demand leading to an inventory shortage. The actual level of inventory carried will equal the sum of the working and safety stock.*

$$\text{Total Inventory} = \text{Working Stock} + \text{Safety Stock}$$

When buying inventory, it is often less expensive to buy larger quantities than it is to buy smaller quantities on a weekly or monthly basis. However, purchasing more inventory than needed increases the organization's carrying costs and exposes it to risks of obsolete or outdated stock if demand falls or there are fewer calls than expected. To avoid this situation, determining the economic ordering quantity can help determine the optimal levels.

The goal of inventory management is to provide the inventories necessary to sustain operations at a minimum cost. The first step is to identify all costs involved in purchasing and maintaining inventories. These costs are divided into three broad categories: costs associated with carrying inventories, costs associated with ordering and receiving inventories, and the cost of running short of inventories.

Carrying costs include such expenses as the cost of inventory that is not used, storage and handling, insurance, depreciation, and obsolescence. Storage and handling are determined by calculating the cost per square foot of the inventory storage area. When calculating carrying costs, the financial manager or operations manager should also consider the cost of storage for each piece of equipment in each of the responding EMS units.

---

*The following abbreviations are used in the equations in this chapter: C = percentage of carrying cost; P = purchase price per unit; A = average number of units; Q = quantity ordered; S = number of units used per year; F = fixed cost for placing an order; and U = annual usage.

Carrying costs rise in proportion to the average amount of inventory carried, which, in turn, depends on the frequency with which inventory is used for calls. Let's say that Main Street Ambulance wants to calculate its carrying costs. It uses S units of a product per year and orders Q units in equal size N times per year. The average inventory for X product would be:

$$\text{Average Inventory} = A = \frac{\text{Quantity Ordered}}{2} = \frac{Q}{2}$$

Note that quantity ordered Q, is equal to S divided by N. Substituting Q, we see the equation looks like this:

$$\text{Average Inventory} = A$$

$$= \frac{\text{Annual Unit Used/Number of Orders}}{2} = \frac{S/N}{2}$$

If for Main Street Ambulance S = 6,000 bags of normal saline used per year and N= orders made 4 times per year, its average inventory will be A = 750 bags:

$$A = \frac{Q}{2} = \frac{S/N}{2} = \frac{6000/4}{2} = \frac{1500}{2} = 750 \text{ units}$$

Inventory will range from a high of 1,500 units just after an order is received to 0 just before an order is placed and arrives. If the EMS organization purchases each bag for $2, the average inventory value is A × P = 750 × $2 = $1,500

If the cost of capital for Main Street Ambulance is 10 percent, it incurs $150 to carry the inventory of normal saline. Let's assume that the storage cost is $3.50 per square foot and storage space is 100 feet = $350, with $100 inventory insurance and $50 obsolescence cost. The total cost for carrying inventory and normal saline is, therefore, $150 + $350 + $100 + $50 = $650 per year. The percentage cost of carrying the inventory is $650/1500 = 0.433 =

43.3 percent. We can now determine the total carrying cost (TCC) as:

$$\text{TCC} = C \times P \times A = 0.4333 \times \$2 \times 750$$
$$= \$649.50 \text{ or } \$650$$

This cost is just for normal saline. To calculate the cost for lactated Ringer's solution, the number of units would be determined first. There would be no other costs (square foot costs, insurance costs, obsolescence cost) as these would encompass any inventory stored in the same area. The EMS manager would have to calculate the cost of capital and storage costs if inventory were stored in another area of the building.

TCC takes into account all costs associated with holding a particular item in stock for a period of time. Managers should review the different factors that make up the costs for inventory held and then determine how much the entire inventory is costing. By performing this review, managers can see how much money is allocated to holding inventory.

ORDERING COSTS

Ordering costs, unlike carrying costs, are fixed. The cost of placing and receiving orders, making phone calls, and taking delivery are essentially the same activity. The amount of time allocated for each order is consistent, so the fixed costs stay the same for each order. The formula for total ordering costs (TOC) is:

$$\text{TOC} = \text{Number of Orders} \times \text{Cost Per Order}$$

Using the previous example, if the organization uses 6,000 liters of normal saline per year, places four (4) orders per year, and ordering requires 1 hour, the TOC can be calculated as follows:

$$\text{TOC} = \frac{F(S)}{Q}$$

$$\text{TOC} = \frac{\$15\,(6000)}{750}$$

$$\text{TOC} = \$120/\text{order}$$

Total inventory costs (TIC) can be defined by the following equation:

$$TIC = TCC + TOC$$

$$= (C) \times (P) \times (A) + \frac{F(S)}{(Q)}$$

$$= (C) \times (P) \times \frac{(Q)}{2} + \frac{F(S)}{(Q)}$$

Therefore, we can determine the TIC for Main Street Ambulance as:

$$TIC = \$650 + \$120$$

$$TIC = \$770 \text{ for normal saline}$$

Analyzing Main Street Ambulance's inventory, the cost to carry just normal saline is very high, due to the fact that we assigned all the storage costs to this one item in the inventory. When an organization orders, the organization should identify vendors that can process multiple inventoried items, thus reducing the overall inventory costs for one item as shown in the example. The point to this exercise is merely to show EMS managers the costs associated with inventory and ordering. Having a basic understanding of costs allows the EMS manager to plan for, and build into the budget, a method to control costs and document inventory costs on the balance sheet. Controlling excess costs of, in this case, inventory is one function of finance. As stated earlier, the organization must survive on its own merits. The management team must utilize finite resources in order to achieve the goals of the organization. If the EMS manager takes for granted or does not think about the costs associated with every operational function, it is easy to see how expenses can and will increase without adding value to the organization.

If more responsibilities are added to the job duties of the person who performs all the ordering and additional functions, he could easily be overwhelmed. He may request an assistant to help; however, management could respond that there is no money for that. However, this may be true only in part. If, for example, inventory is controlled, as opposed to ordering being an ongoing process of doing business, the organization could save money and thereby afford the assistant.

Balancing competing needs is an ongoing issue confronting both the operations manager and the financial manager. Clearly, the business cannot exist without inventory. However, if all the inventory or best equipment that is needed or wanted is acquired all at once, resources may be so strained that other areas requiring financing, such as capital expenditures, acquisition of fixed assets, and money for personnel training, may be curtailed.

Economic theory provides guidelines for solving this dilemma. In general, output should be increased to the point where marginal revenues equal marginal costs. In this case, an additional item should be held in inventory as long as the increase in 9-1-1 call revenue equals the cost of holding that item. To arrive at a solution that is objective, estimates in terms of costs of inventory can be prepared while estimates of 9-1-1 call volumes can be reviewed. Although the analysis of the numbers will never be precise, the combined assessment will lead to identifying an appropriate range of acceptable inventory levels. This process may also help highlight costs that are frequently not visible to operations.

Management can exercise tight control over inventory levels by using computer technology and bar coding. Tracking information coupled with a mathematical formulation of inventory costs, storage capacity, and 9-1-1 call expectations permit a rapid calculation of reordering points and order quantities.

ECONOMIC ORDERING QUANTITY

EMS organizations must purchase inventory in order to operate. The organization must balance what it uses with what the potential need is or could be. If the organization has too much inventory, the holding costs will be high, and cash flow will be affected. Organizations can determine the best amount of inventory by utilizing the **economic ordering quantity (EOQ)**.

The following formula helps determine the number of units to be ordered each time an order is placed. As discussed, the fewer the orders placed, the more the cost of ordering decreases. On the other hand, when more units are received with each order, the storage and associated costs of holding inventory increase. The EOQ model attempts to quantify the number of units that should be ordered each time so that overall costs associated with inventory management are minimized.

F = Costs Associated with Placing One Order[*]

For the sake of this example, assume inventory purchases and usage during calls are consistent and predictable. The formula illustrates how an optimal number of units ordered each time will minimize the overall inventory costs.[*]

$$EOQ = \sqrt{\frac{2FU}{C}}$$

For example:

F = Fixed Costs Per Order $5
U = Units Used Per Year   5,000
C = Carrying Cost Per Unit/Per Year $0.80

Then:

$$EOQ = \sqrt{\frac{2 \times 5 \times 5,000}{0.80}} = 250 \text{ units}$$

---

[*]These include paperwork, time to make phone calls, making payments, and so on. These costs are independent of the size of the order.

[*]U = units used per year; C = costs per year associated with carrying one item in inventory (including storage costs, insurance, and labor).

This example shows that a good inventory management system calls for orders to be placed in lots of 250 units at a time. The best time for placing these orders will depend on the par levels required and the seasonality of the item.

One has to consider that inventory costs will fluctuate, especially if large inventories are held by the organization. The average investment in inventories depends on the frequency of orders. Larger orders mean larger inventories, increased holding costs, higher interest on funds, and higher insurance costs. However, ordering costs will decline on larger orders. The following example will demonstrate the order quantity that minimizes the total cost invested in inventory for Main Street Ambulance. The formula is a little different from the general formula presented above. Determining the EOQ is derived in a few ways; however, the manager must decide on and use a consistent formula when determining inventory levels.

$$EOQ = \sqrt{\frac{2(F)(S)}{(C)(P)}}$$

Some basic assumptions are made in this model:

> EMS calls are forecasted.

> EMS calls can be shown to be distributed throughout the year.

> Orders are received without delays.

> The factors listed above are all independent.

Main Street Ambulance's EOQ is found by inserting known (but hypothetical) values into the formula. EMS managers will need to determine individual numbers for their organizations.

> F = 1 person making $15.00/hour taking 1 hour to order the material

> S = 6,000 units/year

> C = 0.4333

> P = 2.00

$$EOQ = \sqrt{\frac{2\,(15.00/\text{hr})(6000\text{u}/\text{yr})}{(0.4333)(\$2.00)}}$$

$$EOQ = \sqrt{\frac{2\,(90,000)}{.8666}}$$

$$EOQ = \sqrt{\frac{180,000}{.8666}}$$

$$EOQ = \sqrt{207,708}$$

$$EOQ = 455.75 \text{ units}$$

What we have learned is that the EOQ for one person to order normal saline is calculated at a minimum of 455.75 units per order. To determine if the organization can do better than this, it could order more from the same vendor, reduce the carrying costs, search for a more competitive alternative, or reduce the amount ordered if there is a significant amount of leftover at the end of the year.

One of the newer concepts in inventory management is the Just in Time (JIT) delivery method. The primary focus of JIT delivery is to reduce ordering costs and the purchase price of goods. The JIT method reduces the need for the organization to carry inventories by passing the inventory holding costs back to the suppliers. The coordination between suppliers and users lessens the total inventory requirements and reduces overall organizational costs.

The management of inventory falls directly in the category of costs of doing business reflected on the balance sheet. Careful control of inventory costs can positively affect the implementation of new revenue-generating programs, improve existing equipment, or offer better employee benefits. The goal in this discussion is to place tools in the hands of the manager that affect the success of the organization. By understanding how accounting principles can be applied to inventory control and thus impact the operations of the organization, EMS managers can learn how to adjust current practices to improve their operations.

DEPRECIATION

Depreciation is the method of attributing the purchase cost of an asset across its useful life. It is another concept that should be understood by EMS managers. In this section, a discussion of the effects depreciation has on the operations of the EMS organization can provide valuable insight.

A widely held misconception regarding cash flow is how depreciation affects the cash budget. Depreciation charges are often alleged to generate cash flow. Depreciation is not a line item in the cash flow budget, either as a receipt or a disbursement of cash. The erroneous belief regarding the role of depreciation in cash flow projections emanates from adjustments that are made to the income statement. Depreciation expense reduces reported income from what otherwise would have been reported without entailing the actual outflow of cash from the organization. The addition of depreciation to accounting income compensates for this discrepancy. To use projected profits as a reliable indicator of cash flow, many other adjustments are required. Although the addition of depreciation to projected revenue may provide a quick estimate of cash flow, it is hardly a reliable estimate. This can only be achieved through the preparation of a cash budget.

This topic is important because depreciation influences the availability of cash, the reported income, and the tax liabilities of the organization (if tax liabilities exist). Recording depreciation is not only a concern for management but also the Internal Revenue Service (IRS). The involvement of the IRS stems from the effect that depreciation has on tax liabilities.

Side Bar
Depreciation does not necessarily indicate that an asset declined in market value.

Depreciation arises from the recognition that, with the exception of land, all capital assets have a finite life span. The cause of this could be technological and economic obsolescence, or simply wear and tear from routine use. In addition to labor costs, delivering a service must include an allowance for depreciation.

Depreciation deals mostly with assets with a short or fixed life, as introduced in the matching principle discussion. The recording of depreciation will cause an expense to be recognized which lowers the "profits" on the income statement. The same asset will decline on the balance sheet relative to its actual value (the portion of the purchase price that remains).

When purchasing an asset, the value is recorded on the balance sheet at the original cost. As the asset ages, the resultant effect is that it loses productive value to the organization;

thus, the organization can adjust the value of the asset downward.

There are many methods for recording depreciation, including straight line, declining balance, and sum of the years. These recordings are based on the observation that a reduction in market value of equipment is real. Some organizations may take more depreciation in the earlier years, affecting net profits reported and tax reporting, whereas others may spread the depreciation out consistently over many years.

STRAIGHT-LINE DEPRECIATION

This is the simplest and most often used method to account for the value of an asset. Estimating the value of an asset, say an ambulance or a cardiac monitor, at the end of its useful life provides the organization with a means to spread the cost of the asset over time.

For example, if an organization buys an ambulance for $100,000 and its useful life is 5 years, it will have a residual value of $15,000. How much can the organization depreciate its value for each year (Figure 3.3)?

Annual Depreciation Expense =

$$\frac{\text{Cost of the Asset} - \text{Residual Value}}{\text{Useful life of asset (years)}}$$

$$\text{Depreciation} = \frac{\$100,000 - \$15,000}{5 \text{ years}}$$

Depreciation = $17,000 per year

Residual value is the amount a company expects to sell a fixed asset for at the end of its useful life.

DECLINING BALANCE METHOD

Declining balance is a method that provides a higher depreciation charge during the first years of the asset's life and gradually decreases the depreciation over the last few years. This

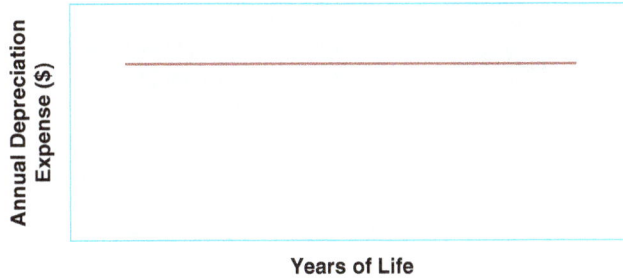

FIGURE 3.3 ■ Straight-line depreciation.

method reflects the assets' expected benefit over the use of the asset. Most assets have greater value when new as opposed to as they age. With this method, the EMS manager considers the value of the asset when it is new and then accelerates the depreciation. Each subsequent year, the percentage of depreciation reduces until the end of the fifth year when the scrap value of the asset is assessed.

With the purchase of the $100,000 ambulance and using straight-line depreciation, the organization records that a 17 percent decrease in the value of the vehicle occurs each year. In the accelerated depreciation method (Figure 3.4), the first year of depreciation may be 2 × 17 percent, or 34 percent. The resulting value would be:

Value New	New Value
Year 1: Depreciation = $100,000 − $34,000	$66,000
Year 2: Depreciation = $66,000 − $17,000	$49,000
Year 3: Depreciation = $49,000 − $17,000	$32,000
Year 4: Depreciation = $32,000 − $17,000	$15,000
Year 5: Depreciation = $ 15,000 − Book Value of $8,000, leaves a depreciation value of $7,000.	

The book value of an object is the value of an asset that is equal to its current cost minus any accumulated depreciation.

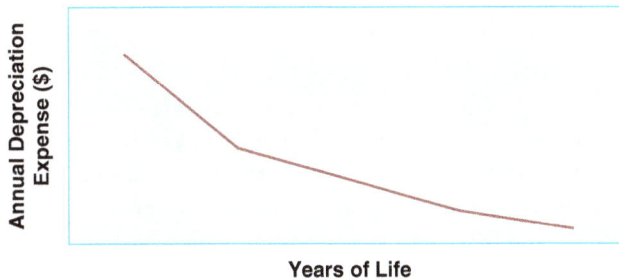

FIGURE 3.4 ■ Accelerated depreciation.

SUM-OF-THE-YEARS METHOD

Another approach to depreciation is the sum-of-the-years method. In this model, the depreciation occurs faster than with straight-line depreciation but slower than with the declining balance method.

Consider an asset valued at $100,000 with a useful life of 5 years and salvage value of $3,000. (The salvage value of an asset is the market value of a depreciable asset at the time sold or removed from use.) Calculate the rate of depreciation by determining the number of years of useful life of the asset. In this example, the ambulance has a 5-year life. The digits are 5, 4, 3, 2, and 1. Next we calculate the sum of the digits: $5 + 4 + 3 + 2 + 1 = 15$. The depreciation rate would then be 5/15 for the first year, 4/15 for the second year, 3/15 for the third year, 2/15 for the fourth year, and 1/15 for the last year.

Accounting for the value of the asset throughout its useful life is important for many reasons.

1. It provides a method for determining the actual value of an asset for the balance sheet.
2. Tracking the value of an asset can help management determine the useful life of an asset and develop a replacement plan.

3. Management can initiate ideas to increase the useful life of an asset, thus improving the financial position of the organization.
4. By calculating the mathematical value of an asset and comparing it to the actual value, management can determine the workload placed on an asset and determine if the asset should be replaced sooner, if staff should be reeducated on how to handle the equipment, or if working with the manufacturer might identify ways to improve the value of the asset.

Depreciation is another area that EMS managers should become familiar with. It provides an accurate assessment of the current value of the fleet or equipment in the ambulance and of furniture or equipment in the building (computers, office equipment, etc.). However, it is essential to seek an expert opinion from an accountant before any of these depreciation concepts are introduced into business practice. There are many financial and business implications to each method. The EMS manager would be wise to seek additional help to maximize the financial resources of the organization.

CHAPTER REVIEW

Summary

This chapter discussed how accounting concepts are based on Generally Accepted Accounting Principles (GAAP). These concepts guide the financial or EMS manager on tracking the organization's finances and how to establish a conventional method to track the financial assets of the organization. The EMS manager should understand the complexity of GAAP and accounting principles to which organizations must adhere. The goal of this chapter was to identify some commonly used concepts and to familiarize the EMS manager with methods to improve the operations of the organization.

WHAT WOULD YOU DO? Reflection

You first make sure you have a clear understanding of the instructions from the board of directors. You discuss what percentage of the purchase price should be generated from operations and what percentage should come from low-interest loans. Should part of the cost come from the sale of the replaced vehicle, or will that vehicle become a backup within the fleet?

Second, you determine the actual life of the vehicle and compare it to the accounting life suggested by the organization's accountant. Performing this exercise will provide a basic understanding of the residual value, both actual and financial. Third, you compare the current, available cash with what is expected in 2 years. Finally, you determine what amount of cash is necessary to offset the necessary balance. Calculate the dollar

amount needed, from operations, over each month, quarter, or other appropriate period. You research the cost of borrowing money and terms of the payback for the first vehicle and every subsequent vehicle. If the payback for each vehicle overlaps, the total fixed costs (loan payments) may exceed revenue that is available for other expenses or program development. You also evaluate the equipment on the ambulance. Does it need to be replaced? Just like the ambulance, the equipment has a useful life and should be replaced on a scheduled basis. Obviously, the equipment replacement program may differ from the ambulance replacement program, but each program is going to require careful consideration and implementation within the financial constraints of the organization.

Review Questions

1. How do GAAP principles affect decision making by the EMS manager, and why should the EMS manager become familiar with these concepts?

2. When looking at accounting principles, how does the EMS manager use concepts such as marginalism to decide what the organization should or should not do relative to providing service to the community?

3. When performing an assessment of the financial position of the organization, how does the EMS manager ensure that the measurement of revenue matches the actual cash in and cash out?

4. How important is inventory control to the success of the organization?

5. When determining inventory, how does the manager objectively look at all the incurred

expenses to determine the ultimate cost of ordering supplies for the organization?

6. Why is determining inventory costs important to negotiating reimbursement from payers?

7. How does depreciation affect the revenue of the organization in terms of cash flow and determining asset value?

8. Why is the distinction between concept definitions and operational definitions important?

9. In Figure 3.1, financial accounting is shown as part of management accounting. Discuss the logic underlying this concept.

10. Conceptually, how do public accounting, governmental accounting, and management accounting differ?

11. Explain how cost accounting is linked to tax accounting, financial accounting, and managerial accounting.

References

Brimson, J. A. (1991). *Activity Accounting: An Activity-Based Costing Approach.* New York: John Wiley & Sons.

Berliner, C., and J. Brimson. (1988). *Cost Management for Today's Advanced Manufacturing: The CAM-I Conceptual Design.* Boston: Harvard Business School Press.

Garg, A., D. Ghosh, and H. Halper. (2004). "Best Practices in Management Accounting." *Cost Management 18*(2), 21–25.

Johnson, H. T. (1989). "Professors, Customers and Value: Bringing a Global Perspective to Management Accounting Education." *Proceedings of the Third Annual Management Accounting Symposium.* Sarasota, FL: American Accounting Association.

Keller, I. W. (1976, November). "All Accounting Is Management Accounting." *Management Accounting*, 13–15.

Martin, J. (n.d.). *Management Accounting: Concepts, Techniques & Controversial Issues.*

Management and Accounting Web. See the organization website.

National Association of Accountants. (1981, January). "MAP Committee Promulgates Definition of Management Accounting." *Management Accounting,* 58–59. See the organization website.

National Association of Accountants. (1982). "Objectives of Management Accounting." *Management Accounting* (November), 57–59. (MAP Committee Statement No. 1B).

Raun, D. L. (1962, October). "What Is Accounting?" *The Accounting Review,* 769–773.

Spiro, Herbert. (1996). *Finance for the Nonfinancial Manager.* New York: John Wiley & Sons, Inc.

Weston, F., and E. Brigham. (1990). *Introduction to Management Finance,* 9th ed. Orlando, FL: The Dryden Press.

Key Terms

accrual The most commonly used accounting method, which reports income when earned and expenses when incurred. The term *accrual* refers to any individual entry recording revenue or expense in the absence of a cash transaction.

accrued expense An expense that is incurred, but not yet paid for, during a given accounting period.

audit A professional auditor's examination and verification of a company's financial and accounting records and supporting documents.

carrying costs Financial and operational expense associated with operational activity. This can also be thought of as the opportunity cost of unproductive assets, the expense incurred by ownership.

coherence The quality or state of cohering, especially a logical, orderly, and aesthetically consistent relationship of parts.

conformity Action in accordance with some specified standard or authority.

credibility Perception of trustworthiness an individual imparts to other people.

deferred expense Refers to an item that will initially be recorded as an asset but is expected to become an expense over time and/or through the normal operations of the business. Sometimes called prepaid expenses.

depreciation A noncash expense that reduces the value of an asset as a result of wear and tear, age, or obsolescence.

economic ordering quantity The optimum quantity of goods for which, if orders are placed, the aggregate order placing cost and the aggregate inventory carrying cost will be equal and economical.

Generally Accepted Accounting Principles (GAAP) The standard framework of guidelines for financial accounting.

marginalism Changes in the quantity used of a good or of a service, as opposed to some notion of the overall significance of that class of good or service, or of some total quantity thereof.

matching A culmination of accrual accounting and the revenue recognition principle.

materiality A concept or convention within auditing and accounting relating to the importance or significance of an amount, transaction, or discrepancy. All material items should be disclosed in financial statements.

opinion A belief or conclusion held with confidence but not substantiated by positive knowledge or proof.

prepaid expenses Payments made for goods or services that will be received or used in the future.

standards Written definition, limit, or rule, approved and monitored for compliance by an authoritative agency or professional or recognized body as a minimum acceptable benchmark.

CHAPTER 4

Economic Concepts

Objectives

After reading this chapter, the student should be able to:

4.1   Describe an organization and the basic reason for the existence of an organization.
4.2   Describe the role of finance.
4.3   Define financial management and its relationship to operational management.
4.4   Describe the difference between microeconomics and macroeconomics.
4.5   Discuss how supply and demand impact decision making.
4.6   Review the time value of money.

Overview

The purpose of this text is to introduce the concepts of finance to nonfinancial EMS managers. The chapters present valuable information to both new and experienced EMS leaders who may have varying degrees of experience, formal and informal. The goal is to stimulate thinking in order to change the way things are done, to avoid mistakes of the past, and to encourage future growth of EMS as a profession.

Key Terms

annuity	demand theory	fixed costs
cost-benefit analysis	economic efficiency	future value
(CBA)	economics	interest
demand	equilibrium	k

k*	marginal costs	organizations	supply
k_{RF}	microeconomics	payback method	unit
macroeconomics	net present value	present value	
managerial accounting	(NPV)		

WHAT WOULD YOU DO?

Your EMS organization is watching the evolving plans of a proposed residential community being considered within your response area. The community will be built near the interstate and in close proximity to a shopping mall. The community will house 1,500 independent living residences, an assisted living building with 500 apartments, and a skilled nursing facility for 500 patients. The expected call volume increase is 70 calls per month. You realize the plan to build the retirement community will require a substantial investment in resources.

Questions

1. How are operational goals established so that they reflect the financial abilities of the organization?

2. Are the organizational goals based on financial success, or are finances used as a report card to measure the success of an organization goals? Explain.
3. Why should decisions be made based on an objective review of resources?
4. What are the potential resources needed for this proposed community from an EMS response standpoint?
5. Will you need to build another facility closer to this proposed community, or can you handle the increased call volume with current resources? Explain your reasoning.

■ INTRODUCTION

There are many answers to the question, "Why are businesses started?" The most frequent and common answer is "to make money." In a capitalist system, we often equate business with profit. That would seem to make sense because people believe that most business owners work to make as much money as possible. However, the key reason a business begins or continues to exist is to bring about a change or make a difference. The person with the original idea saw a problem and said, "I can do that better!" The belief that people can use their resources to

improve the current situation is an underlying reason for why businesses start. It is the entrepreneurial spirit that moves an idea and turns it into a success.

The secondary result of success is the financial rewards that come with the business. This is true whether the business is for-profit or nonprofit. One could argue that a nonprofit exists to improve a social problem or provide a needed service. For example, Clara Barton founded the American Red Cross to help victims of disasters, not to make money. As of June 2011, records show that the American Red Cross has a little over $1 billion in assets and $732 million in revenue and contributions (American National Red Cross–Chapter Network, 2011). If we look at the number of nonprofits in America, we see the number of organizations has grown by 32.7 percent since 1998. EMS organizations are part of this growth (Table 4.1).

One could argue that only for-profits exist to fulfill a need related to making money.

TABLE 4.1 ■ Nonprofit Organizations in the United States

Number of Nonprofit Organizations in the United States, 1998–2008

	1998		2008		
	Number of Organizations	Percentage of All Organizations	Number of Organizations	Percentage of Organizations	Percent Change
All Nonprofit Organizations	1,158,031	100.0%	1,536,134	100.0%	32.7%
501(c)(3) Public Charities	596,160	51.5%	974,337	63.4%	63.4%
501(c)(3) Private Foundations	70,480	6.1%	115,340	7.5%	63.6%
Other 501(c) Nonprofit Organizations	491,391	42.4%	446,457	29.1%	−9.1%
Small community groups and partnerships, etc.	Unknown	NA	Unknown	NA	NA
501(c)(3) Public Charities	596,160	51.5%	974,337	63.4%	63.4%
501(c)(3) Public Charities Registered with the IRS (including registered congregations)	596,160	51.5%	974,337	63.4%	63.4%
Reporting Public Charities	231,625	20.0%	483,779	31.5%	108.9%
Operating Public Charities	201,175	17.4%	426,033	27.7%	111.8%
Supporting Public Charities	30,450	2.6%	57,746	3.8%	89.6%
Non-Reporting, or with Less Than $25,000 in Gross Receipts	364,535	31.5%	490,558	31.9%	34.6%

(Continued)

TABLE 4.1 ■ (*Continued*)

	1998		2008		
	Number of Organizations	*Percentage of All Organizations*	*Number of Organizations*	*Percentage of Organizations*	*Percent Change*
Congregations (about half are registered with IRS)*	—	0.0%	385,874	25.1%	NA
501(c)(3) Private Foundations	70,480	6.1%	115,340	7.5%	63.6%
Private Grantmaking (Non-Operating) Foundations	67,625	5.8%	110,099	7.2%	62.8%
Private Operating Foundations	2,855	0.2%	5,241	0.3%	83.6%
Other 501(c) Nonprofit Organizations	491,391	42.4%	446,457	29.1%	−9.1%
Civic Leagues, Social Welfare Organizations, etc.	125,504	10.8%	110,924	7.2%	−11.6%
Fraternal Beneficiary Societies	103,065	8.9%	78,109	5.1%	−24.2%
Business Leagues, Chambers of Commerce, etc.	69,734	6.0%	71,887	4.7%	3.1%
Labor, Agricultural, Horticultural Organizations	61,444	5.3%	55,629	3.6%	−9.5%
Social and Recreational Clubs	56,452	4.9%	55,838	3.6%	−1.1%
Post or Organization of War Veterans	34,272	3.0%	32,592	2.1%	−4.9%
All Other Nonprofit Organizations	40,920	3.5%	41,478	2.7%	1.4%

Note: Excludes out-of-scope organizations.

Source: Permission granted by The Urban Institute. http://nccsdataweb.urban.org/PubApps/profile1.php

* = The number of congregations is from the website of American Church Lists (http://list.infousa.com/acl.htm), 2004. These numbers are excluded from the totals for the state since approximately half of the congregations are included under registered public charities.

Most finance books will state the reason for-profits exist is "to improve the position of the stockholders." However, we are talking about the reason why businesses started and why they continue to exist. An example of a business that appears on the surface to be profit-oriented but ended up having an altruistic intent is Ford Motor Company. Henry Ford did not build the Model T to earn as much money as possible or to enrich stockholders. According to Dodes (1965), Ford stated, "A business that makes nothing but money is a poor business" (p. 96). He designed and manufactured the Model T as a result of his desire to "devise ways and means to better transportation." He stated, "I will build a car for the great multitude. It will be large enough for the family, but small enough for the individual to run and care for. It will be so low in price that no man making a good salary will be unable to own one—and enjoy with his family the blessings of hours of pleasure in God's great open spaces" (p. 96). There is no reference to maximizing profit in Ford's philosophy.

EMS **organizations** exist to fulfill a societal need. To accomplish this goal, organizations must develop a philosophical position that identifies an altruistic goal and develops resources to achieve the expected result. EMS organizations did not start as social clubs that just happened to help injured people; they started with people who desired to help people and evolved into a means to socialize. The evolution has taken us from the social club mentality into the realization, due to all of the regulations and requirements, that EMS organizations are a business.

■ ROLE OF FINANCE

Finance engages in two primary functions for management: recording, monitoring, and controlling the financial consequences of past and current operations, and acquiring funds to meet current and future needs. The first set of functions is predominantly internal to the organization. The second set requires interfacing with independent institutions.

> **Side Bar**
>
> William Dinsmoor of the University of Nebraska mentioned that departments of an organization, not the finance department, are responsible for the success of the budget. With this in mind, leadership must hold all departments accountable for the outcomes; finance does not hold managers of the department accountable.

Some of the financial responsibilities of an organization are historical: an accurate portrayal of the financial position of the organization consistent with Generally Accepted Accounting Principles (GAAP). Basically, it provides an answer to the question "What happened?" rather than concerning itself with what should happen. Accuracy, consistency, and reasonableness are key to reporting past events. Issuing accurate statements serves as a basis for providing information on the financial position of the organization to interested board members, the management team, and outsiders such as creditors, governmental agencies, or lenders. Furthermore, it serves to meet the legal requirements imposed by taxing authorities and regulatory bodies.

Managerial accounting is the term used to describe the control aspects of the finance function. It starts with the preparation of financial forecasts, the development and monitoring of performance, budgets, and the determination of costs. Accounting professionals rely on historical data, and the constant input of current activities of operations to make decisions. In larger organizations, these functions could be divided into two separate and distinct jobs: managerial accounting and financial accounting.

Managerial accountants are sometimes called controllers because they deal with the right side of the balance sheet, whereas financial accountants are sometimes referred to as treasurers because they deal with the income statement and activities reflected on the left side of the balance sheet. In smaller organizations, there often is no differentiation between the two functions; however, the person responsible for the finances of an organization must be familiar with and understand the difference between the functions, the tracking of financials, and the debit/credit aspects of running a business.

Managerial accounting almost always relates to the dynamic activities of the liability functions within the organization. An example of these would be the determination of breakeven and revenue gained over expenses (in for-profit organizations, this is considered profit). The treasurer traditionally handles the interactions with other organizations, such as discussing bank loans, determining long-term obligations, meeting regulatory obligations, or the revenue side of the organization.

Financial accounting deals with information reported to people inside and outside the organization. Financial accounting reporting may provide information that is valuable to government agencies or on grant applications that may differ from operational costs. If the manager is unable to read or understand the reports, an unfavorable decision could occur that affects the organization. For example, a supervisor or division chief may request information on the expenses and revenue of a particular station to determine staffing or purchase a new vehicle. Such information would help determine how to staff a station for the best response. However, if the manager attempts to retrieve this information from a report filed with the local government agency, he may misinterpret the information as the financial report and may identify revenues and costs of providing the service. In other words, the government report may contain irrelevant information. Managers promoted from the ranks of providers must be capable of understanding that financial and managerial accounting reports are not interchangeable.

Relevant information affects operational objectives or the choice between two alternatives. The manager must be comfortable determining which information is relevant and which information will not be useful.

Part of the role of the finance manager is to determine what information is viable relative to the alternatives. In determining the relevance, a **cost-benefit analysis (CBA)** may show whether the potential benefit of an expense is worth the estimated cost. In other words, will the financial review improve the manager's decision by saving or earning more for the organization than it costs to fund it?

Accounting's purpose is to provide reliable information to the managers in an organization. This is especially true if there is a separate accounting department in an organization. What happens when the manager is the "accountant"? Basically, the same principles still apply. The manager must be familiar with the purpose of tracking the financial health of an organization. The manager's purpose is to establish an organization's direction and objectives and also coordinate the resources to achieve these objectives. The role of the manager "accountant" is to provide information that helps the organization fulfill its role.

■ FINANCIAL MANAGEMENT ——

Finance is the common language of management. The goals, objectives, and plans of an organization; the allocation of the organization's resources and accomplishments; and the failures of organizational components are increasingly presented and assessed in this language. Effective communication among organizational components requires that managers understand this language and use it in the performance of their assigned responsibilities. The absence of sensitivity to this means of communication may handicap managers in presenting their objectives, plans, and requirements for approval to the board of directors. *Board of directors* is a general term to describe a formal group of decision makers who oversee or offer advice regarding the operations of the EMS organization. The board of directors could be the municipal council that is responsible for public safety, a district board that is directly responsible for EMS, or hospital administrators who oversee all critical units. If there is no board of directors, the manager must have a mechanism in place to justify decisions if the organization is audited by an outside firm or a bank that underwrites a loan. The application of financial concepts and practices to management transcends the legal form adopted by the organization.

An EMS manager must master fundamental financial concepts because external professionals (bankers, suppliers, legislative bodies, benefactors, and trustees) evaluate the performance of the EMS organization on financial terms. Most of the information for assessment is presented in financial terms.

Rarely can the theory and practice of a field of knowledge be compartmentalized neatly into a mutually exclusive package. Finance is no exception. Some issues in finance and management merit discussion in a variety of theoretical and situational contexts. The overlap of finance with operations, operations with human resources, human resources with management, and management with finance should be evident to any decision maker. Financial management concerns itself with many nuances of decision making, but it is not, nor should it be, the sole discipline about which decisions are made. The appreciation of the interrelationships requires exposure to all the disciplines as a whole rather than mastery of one specialized area. Sadly, however, within the relatively short life of the field of EMS, very few decisions makers have been exposed to any of the management specialties, never mind mastering one. Coming from operations as a street medic or EMT does not prepare a person to manage any more than attending a 1-hour class in paramedic school prepares a person to care for a critically ill patient.

One issue that deserves discussion is the role judgment versus analysis plays when making financial decisions. Whenever appropriate and possible, quantitative relationships (objective comparisons between two options) should be explored in order to determine the best course of actions. It is important to keep emotions out of managerial decisions and remain objective. This is not just a legal requirement, though this is extremely important. Managers must be able to explain and defend decisions to board members, municipal authorities, other government agencies, bankers, the public, and the people who work for the organization.

As in any situation, judgment reflects exposure to applicable theory, past experiences, and intuition. The greater exposure to the theory of finance, and the broader a manager's experience, the more appropriate will be the judgment applied to given situations. Finance, like all business disciplines, does not provide a cookbook approach with guaranteed results. Rather it should be viewed as a creative approach to the solution of complex problems facing all organizations. Financial management is an organized way of facing financial uncertainties.

ECONOMIC CONCEPTS

Economics is the social science that studies the production, distribution, and consumption of goods and services. The term *economics* comes from the ancient Greek ο κονομία (*oikonomia,* "management of a household, administration") from ο κος (*oikos,* "house") + νόμος (*nomos,* "custom" or "law"), hence "rules of the house(hold)" (Harper, 2001). Current economic models developed out of the broader field of political economy in the late nineteenth century, owing to a desire to use an empirical approach more akin to the physical sciences (Clark, 1998).

A definition that captures much of modern economics is that of Lionel Robbins (1945) in a 1932 essay: "the science which studies human behavior as a relationship between ends and scarce means which have alternative uses" (p. 16). Scarcity means that available resources are insufficient to satisfy all wants and needs. Absent scarcity and alternative uses of available resources, there is no economic problem. The subject thus defined involves the study of choices as they are affected by incentives and resources.

Economic thought dates from earlier Mesopotamian, Greek, Roman, Indian, Chinese, Persian, and Arab civilizations. Notable writers include Aristotle, Chanakya (also known as Kautilya), Qin Shi Huang, Thomas Aquinas, Ibn Khaldun, and other writers of the fourteenth century. Joseph Schumpeter initially considered the late scholastics of the fourteenth to seventeenth centuries as "coming nearer than any other group to being the 'founders' of scientific economics" as to monetary, interest, and value theory within a natural-law perspective (Stigler, 1954, p. 344).

The concepts of finance are based on economic theory. The tools used to evaluate the financial activities of an organization are a part of economic analysis. Economics deals with the allocation of resources to meet the needs of the end user. The success of the transactions between two individuals, an individual and an organization, or two organizations is analyzed using economic analysis tools. Economics can be divided into two fields: microeconomics and macroeconomics.

MICROECONOMICS

Microeconomics deals with decisions between people, households, firms, or institutions. Microeconomics looks at interactions through different markets, given scarcity and government regulation (Pindyck and Rubinfeld, 1995). A given market might be for a product, such as fresh corn, or services as a factor of production, such as EMS response to a 9-1-1 call. The theory considers aggregates of quantity demanded by buyers and quantity supplied by sellers at each possible price per unit. It weaves these together to describe how the market may reach **equilibrium** as to price and quantity or respond to market changes over time.

MACROECONOMICS

Macroeconomics is concerned with how all of these interactions impact society. In this text, we will focus on discussing the impact of managerial decisions regarding finance on EMS-related topics. However, the reader must understand that any decision made, even in a small organization in the rural foothills of a mountain state, may ultimately affect the financial position of a payer or supplier in the urban setting of a major city. Macroeconomics is the cumulative effect of all microeconomic decisions.

Supply and Demand

Supply and *demand* are terms used to describe the transactions of resources. If there is demand for a product or service, the supply can and will go up or down depending on resources. With the up-and-down movement, prices may also reflect the up-and-down swing. However, as indiscriminately as these terms are used, they do not reflect an accurate representation of the actual activity of trading resources. For example, though there may be an ample supply of ambulances in a particular urban setting, it does not reflect the staff's availability to run the ambulances because the organization may decide not to pay overtime to ensure availability. Economists, therefore, define **supply** in terms of the quantity of a specific commodity offered at a given price.

As the price of the commodity increases, more owners of the commodity are willing to part with the commodity, and thus the quantity increases. Here's an example: As the price of reimbursement for medical services increases, more entrepreneurs will open EMS organizations that under old reimbursements levels were not attractive. Or, as resources (e.g., medical transports) become more scarce, contractual pricing may improve, thus allowing more bidders to compete for the same business. Supply and demand fluctuate around the scarcity of resources and prices attached to the service or product.

There is no immutable law of supply and demand. The amount of **demand** is determined by relationships and equilibrium of conditions during certain situations. The optimal situation is when supply equals demand at a fixed price.

The theory presupposes that the supplier can control the price, and the buyer agrees to pay that price. In EMS, the price paid is normally established by the government or a third-party payer. Often, EMS and economics cross paths when the demand for services exceeds the supply of people to respond. EMS does not follow the normal concept of economics in the same way a grower of corn or a producer of automobiles would. In a normal economic market when the basic relationship between the supply of a product or service is equal to the demand of the product or service, the intersection of these two curves (Figure 4.1)

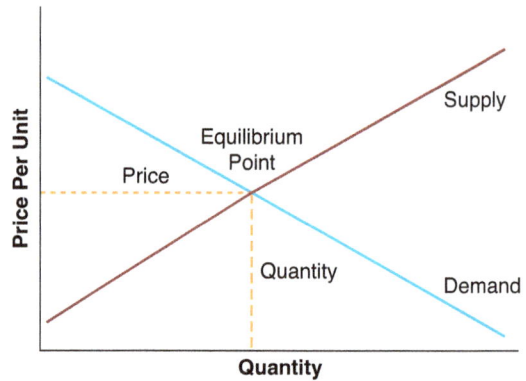

FIGURE 4.1 ■ Basic supply and demand curve.

represents equilibrium. From the perspective of EMS, this means that every time a call for medical assistance is received—be it for an emergency, routine transport, public service, training, standby, or presentation—someone will be available to respond immediately.

In Figure 4.1, we see that, in basic market-driven businesses, there is a specific demand for a product or service. People will seek to enter the business of supplying the answer to the demand. For example, think back to when your EMS organization was founded. There was a reason for the inception of the organization; there was a need to respond to a call for help. The founders realized they had the skill and resources to answer that call, so they organized and gathered money to buy an ambulance, and when that first call came in, a crew responded. One demand, one supply: the equilibrium point. As more and more calls came in, one crew was unable to respond to every call (demand exceeded supply). The decision was made to put another crew in service. So two calls came in, and two crews responded: again, equilibrium point. Price in this example is relevant when considering how much it costs to respond to each call. As the number of EMS calls increases, the cost to respond to each call decreases because the total costs are spread out over the number of calls.

As EMS calls increase, the cost to respond decreases. How does that work? If the ambulance was purchased for $10,000, and the EMS organization had no other expenses, the price for one call is $10,000. If the organization responds to two calls, the price per call is $5,000. Gas, supplies, a building, and other expenses to run an organization are needed. When expenses are added to the equation, the costs per call increase substantially for the organization.

Another way of looking at the price per unit is to consider how much money the organization will receive (reimbursement) for responding to and treating the patient. If the organization receives $300 for responding, then the price per unit is $300. If the crew responds to two calls, and the organization receives reimbursement for only one call, the price per call falls to $150. Subtract any expenses, and the true cost of running each call becomes evident.

Over time changes occur in the cost structure of services. In the case of EMS, the reimbursement (price per unit) and the demand for the service will also change. These changes are referred to as a shift in the supply and demand curves. Any change in the demand of the service is going to affect the supply of the service. In the case of EMS organizations, we will see more shifting on the demand side than on the supply side. Pricing is often set by the payers of the service; therefore, EMS organizations are not as free to alter their fees in the same way a retailer is able to alter prices of merchandise when the demand changes.

The goal is to understand the basic cost structure of the service in order to make incremental, long-lasting changes. If, for example, it is determined that the price per unit is only $2 after all expenses and revenues are calculated in, management may have to make some deci-

sions regarding pricing. If, however, an organization responds to 10,000 calls each year, and additional employee expenses have to be covered, then the organization made $20,000 for the year.

On the other hand, having the same $20,000 at the end of the year with the intent to purchase an additional ambulance at a cost of $35,000 will result in a shortfall. Changes may need to be made in either the expense side or the revenue side. By increasing the revenue per unit through the reduction of expenses, the organization could realize a higher return on activity.

The theory of supply and demand is an organizing principle that explains prices and quantities of goods sold and changes in prices in a market economy. In microeconomic theory, it refers to the determination of price and output in a perfectly competitive market. This has served as a building block for modeling other market structures and for other theoretical approaches. In an EMS organization, this principle may be more apparent if we discuss a program such as community CPR. Given that many organizations can offer CPR classes, the price established is based on what the end user is willing to pay, the number of people who can teach, and the price charged by everyone offering the training.

Here is an economic approach for describing the supply and demand concept. For a given market, demand shows the quantity that all prospective buyers would be prepared to purchase at each unit price of the good. **Demand theory** describes individual consumers as rationally choosing the most preferred quantity of each good, given income, prices, tastes, and so on. A term for this is *constrained utility maximization* (with income as the constraint on demand). Here, *utility* refers to the (hypothesized) preference of individual consumers. Utility and income are then used to model hypothesized properties about the effect of a price change on the quantity demanded.

Let's look at the economic verbiage in easy-to-understand terms. For a given market—that is, for a defined area or population of customers—we see a certain number of customers who need a particular service. For that service, the customer is willing to pay a certain price. The customer will make his choice based on individual criteria. Given that each customer has a choice and that choice is based on variables such as income, price of the service, quality of the service, or apparent need for the service, each will choose the organization that meets their specific criteria. Thus, the organization that offers the service must "guess" at the price in order to meet the customer's expectations.

This only applies to services the customer can choose. In an emergency, 9-1-1 call, the customer cannot choose which service offers the best price (based on the person's ability to pay), the best quality (no way to measure this in an emergency), or the best fit for whatever treatment is necessary (e.g., ALS vs. BLS). Consumers generally have no choice about who is going to respond to their emergency or what kind of quality they will receive. This is different for the CPR training example, where the consumer does have a choice—most of the time.

The law of demand states that, in general, price and quantity demanded in a given market are inversely related. In other words, the higher the price of a product, the less of it people would be able and willing to buy (other things unchanged). As the price of a product or service (commodity) rises, overall purchasing power decreases (the income effect) and consumers move toward relatively less expensive goods (the substitution effect). Other factors can also affect demand; for example, an increase in income will shift the demand curve outward relative to the origin, as in Figure 4.1.

In the example of CPR training, if the local EMS organization is the only group that offers CPR training to the public and busi-

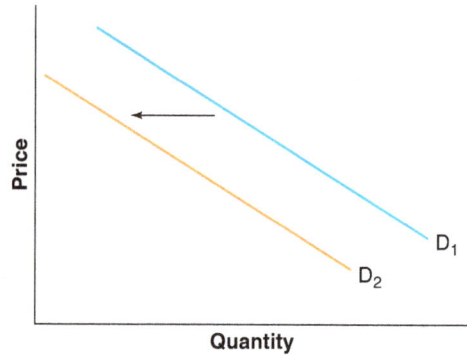

FIGURE 4.2 ■ Illustration of demand curve shifting left.

nesses, then the organization will set a price that not only covers its cost but will generate additional revenue. People and businesses will pay those costs, especially if they are required to have CPR. If another person or organization realizes that money can be made teaching CPR, enters the market, and offers the same training at lesser cost, then the demand for the higher-priced training will decrease (shift to the left) (Figure 4.2).

The original organization will have to make choices: either keep the same pricing and market differently in a way that shows greater value for the cost, or drop the price comparably, or enter into an agreement with the new instructor, or devise a combination of any of these or other options. The point here is that demand can change depending on price and/or supply—in this case, the instructors. The purchaser of the service, in this case CPR, will make a choice based on value, need, expense, or something else.

Supply is the relation between the price of a good and the quantity available for sale from suppliers (such as producers) at that price. Producers are hypothesized to be profit maximizers, meaning that they attempt to produce the amount of goods that will bring them the highest profit. Supply is typically represented as a directly proportional relation between price and quantity supplied (other things being unchanged).

In other words, the higher the price at which the good can be sold, the more of it producers will supply. The higher price makes the product profitable, so producers are apt to increase production. At a price below equilibrium, there is a shortage of quantity supplied compared to quantity demanded. This pulls the price up. At a price above equilibrium, there is a surplus of quantity supplied compared to quantity demanded. This pushes the price down. The model of supply and demand predicts for given supply and demand curves: Price and quantity will stabilize at the price that makes quantity supplied equal to quantity demanded. This is at the intersection of the two curves in the graph, market equilibrium.

In the CPR example, if ten people or organizations can supply training, the price will reflect equilibrium based on what the consumer is willing to pay and the supplier (instructor) is willing to teach *and* make a reasonable profit. If one of the organizations determines that the cost of teaching exceeds the revenue generated, its manager may discontinue offering this service.

For a given quantity of a good or service, the price point on the demand curve indicates the value, or marginal utility, to consumers for that unit of output. It measures what the consumer would be prepared to pay for the corresponding unit of the good. The price point on the supply curve measures marginal cost, which is the increase in total cost to the supplier for the corresponding unit of the good. Supply and demand determine the price in equilibrium. In a perfectly competitive market, supply and demand equate cost and value at equilibrium.

Demand and supply can also be used to model the distribution of income to the factors of production, including labor and capital. In a labor market, for example, the quantity of labor employed and the price of labor (the wage rate) are modeled as set by the demand for labor (from business firms and such for production) and supply of labor (from workers).

Looking at Figure 4.3, we see that the X axis represents quantity, and the Y axis represents the price. The blue line is supply, and the red lines are the demand. As demand moves from D1 to D2, in pure economics, industries

Side Bar

Another example of where supply and demand impact the EMS profession is in determining the amount of resources needed to fulfill the demand for prehospital medical services. If 10 organizations respond to 50,000 calls in a county of 500 square miles (50 square miles per organization or 1,000 calls per square mile) and one organization fails, the distribution of the 1,000 calls to three or four of the remaining organizations may exceed the supply of resources of any one of those organizations. The price to provide the service (revenue per call) will not change as it is a set amount, but the expense to provide the service may change.

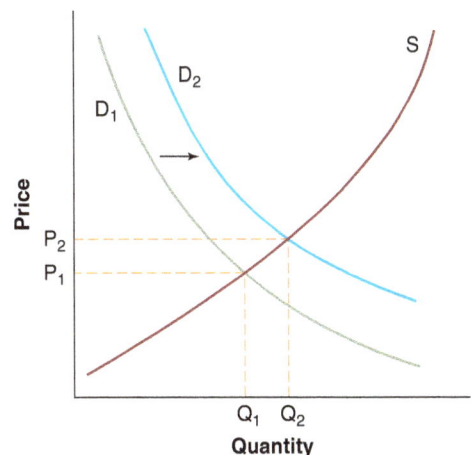

FIGURE 4.3 ■ Movement of demand and price. *S = supply; D = demand; Q = quantity.*

will produce more Q1 to Q2, therefore the supply increases, and the price will increase P1 to P2. If competitors enter the market and provide higher quantities, supply will be great and price will decrease. Thus, equilibrium is obtained based on the new supply available.

EMS organizations do not typically operate under a pure supply and demand structure. Often, when demand exceeds supply due to too many calls and not enough ambulances or staff, alternatives are sought. Some of the options are to place another ambulance in the expanding territory (if the EMS organization is municipally based), a competitor submits a proposal to operate a base in the new territory in exchange for a set fee, or a freestanding nonprofit EMS organization will move into the new territory. Any of these scenarios will satisfy the demand. Each of these answers to the demand will produce benefits (to the consumer who needs EMS services), but it may also produce areas of weaknesses. If the supply of medical personnel is not available to staff the new station, personnel may have to be pulled from other areas; if a contracted arrangement is in place, the expense may be passed on to taxpayers.

Another scenario is based on perceived demand. Many times EMS organizations will create demand for their own organization by positioning a new station at the edge of another EMS organization's territory in order to create more calls for itself at the expense of the other organization. It is this type of business mentality that increases the costs for the entire system, decreases the professionalism of EMS, and opens the door for counteraction. This selfish positioning attempts to alter the delivery of EMS services without improving the balance of supply and demand. Managers who attempt these maneuvers do not have a clear understanding of the financial management of their organizations.

In most service industries, certain fixed costs occur regardless of the volume of output.

Fixed costs are business expenses that are not dependent on the activities of the business. Examples include salaries, rents or mortgages, and utilities.

In the preceding example, the manager who creates demand may not have looked at the increase in fixed costs caused by opening up a new facility. By increasing the total fixed costs and only incrementally increasing output, the manager placed the EMS organization in a weaker financial position. A greater volume of calls will decrease the fixed costs per unit. At the same time as call volume increases and the ability to respond to all of the calls (production capacity) is reached, inefficiencies in the delivery of care will occur. These may be seen in poor documentation, lesser quality of care, overtime, lack of close supervision, waste of supplies, repeated breakdowns in transporting vehicles, or increased sick days. As the inefficiencies increase, the per unit cost goes up. By measuring the average cost per unit (total costs [TC]/quantity of units), management arrives a starting point. The question "How much does it cost per unit?" can then be asked.

We should define what a **unit** is. EMS is different from a manufacturing operation that produces widgets and associates a cost to each one. In EMS, management must determine what a unit is. A unit could be total calls responded to, calls during which a patient was transported, employee paid hours, and so on. To determine maintenance costs, management may look at average costs as units of hours on the engine or miles driven. The point here is that management must decide, as a baseline for determining future needs, how to measure the costs of operating the organization. Part of management's job is determining the additional costs that will be incurred if "production" increases.

This leads to the concept of marginal costs. **Marginal costs** are the costs added to total costs that are required to produce one additional unit at a given output level. As output increases, marginal costs increase due to inefficiencies incurred at the higher level of output. In pure business economics, when marginal costs exceed the selling price that can be realized per unit, production should be curtailed until management can determine a method for adjusting to the additional output.

In EMS, we cannot simply say we are not going to respond because the costs are greater than the reimbursement. The challenge is to minimize the average costs while keeping marginal costs lower than average costs. As soon as the average costs rise above the marginal costs, management should be alerted to the fact that marginal costs are higher than average costs and that output is exceeding the anticipated costs at a given level.

Understandably, a certain amount of output must be maintained to achieve a minimum, average cost. Management must be careful not to make arbitrary decisions because of personal desire, by, for example, entering into a new territory and quickly buying more ambulances and hiring more staff in order to treat and transport potentially more patients. The additional staffing or equipment may result in excess capacity and increased costs for only a small increase in business. Good management practices dictate that when the cost of providing additional services rises above the average cost of services already provided, administrative changes must occur. As difficult as determining average costs, marginal costs, and economies of scale is, performing such an analysis is the cornerstone of quality management.

Economic efficiency describes how well a system generates the maximum desired output with a given set of inputs and available technology. Efficiency improves if more output is generated without changing inputs—in other words, if the amount of friction or waste is reduced. Economists look for Pareto efficiency, which is reached when a change can-not make someone better off without making someone else worse off.

Economic efficiency refers to a number of related concepts. A system can be called economically efficient if no one can be made better off without making someone else worse off, more output cannot be obtained without increasing the amount of inputs, and production ensures the lowest possible per unit cost. These definitions of efficiency are not exactly equivalent. However, they are all encompassed by the idea that nothing more can be achieved related to the resources available.

Cost-Benefit Analysis

Any time a manager examines alternative courses of action, he engages in cost-benefit analysis. In essence, the manager is examining the trade-offs that must be made in exchanging one commodity or policy for another. Managers must look at all costs and benefits of the decision. Often the manager does not look deep enough or ignores the secondary costs or benefits of a decision. Even as managers make decisions, the decision is problematic because of the uncertainty regarding what may or may not happen.

Cost-benefit analysis (CBA) is a relatively simple and widely used technique for deciding whether or not to make a change. As the term suggests, a manager simply adds up the value of the benefits of a course of action and subtracts the costs associated with it.

Costs are either realized once or may be ongoing. Benefits are most often received over time. Management can build this effect of time into the analysis by calculating a payback period. A payback period is the time it takes for the benefits of the change to repay the costs of the change. Many companies look for payback on projects over a specified period of time, such as 3 years.

In its simplest form, cost-benefit analysis is carried out using only financial costs and

Best Practices

The following extract provides an example of how economics and the desire to extract efficiencies from any process, more specifically EMS, are used to make prehospital delivery decisions. EMS managers should understand the impact their organizations have on society and seek to develop sound business practices that minimize organizational as well as societal costs.

> The cost of false emergency responses by ambulance personnel can also be estimated. The percentage of unneeded ambulance service is substantial. A U.S. government study found that for 67% of Medicare reimbursed ambulance trips that did not result in emergency room treatment or hospital or nursing home admission, alternative transportation would not have endangered patient welfare (Inspector General 1998, pp. 5, 10). Thus, nationwide false ambulance calls cost $850 million plus the cost of fatalities, injuries, and property damage. Thus, the total social cost of false alarm responses is about $916 million annually. Solving the false alarm problem for ambulance services could free up the equivalent of 18,300 paramedics. There is already some evidence that competition between public and private providers lowers prices and improves service. For example, in Pinellas County, Florida, a private company (Sunstar) won the contract over a government provider to handle the emergency and non-emergency ambulance services. It has cut emergency response time by 30 seconds and upgraded the equipment, and it is projected to save the County between $13 and $21 million over the decade (Reason 2006). In general, private ambulance firms have more sophisticated equipment than public providers. Seventy percent of private providers have defibrillation devices for heart attacks compared to only 48% of public ambulances. Further, 48% of ambulance companies use automatic vehicle locators compared to 20% of city agencies. Finally, private paramedics earn only 75% of what their public counterparts earn (Johnson 2002). When comparing private to public ambulance service, private companies perform at lower cost and use more sophisticated equipment and technology while some evidence suggests faster response time as well. This finding is consistent with the fact that firms operating in a competitive market are often more efficient than government monopolies.

Blackstone, E. A., A. J. Buck, and S. Hakim. (2006). "The Economics of Emergency Response." *Policy Sciences* 40(4), 313–334. doi:10.1007/s11077-007-9047-6. Accessed September 18, 2012, at http://sbm.temple.edu/ccg/documents/eer2.doc

General Government Division. (1998, April). "Privatization: Questions State and Local Decision Makers Used When Considering Privatization Options." Washington, DC: General Accounting Office, GAO/GGD-98-87. Accessed September 1, 2012, at www.gao.gov/special.pubs/gg98087.pdf

Johnson, R. (2002). "Ambulance Wars." *Michigan Privatization Report*. Midland, MI: The Mackinac Center for Public Policy, *Winter*, 12–13. Accessed September 2, 2012, at www.mackinac.org/archives/2002/mpr2002-01.pdf

benefits. For example, a simple cost-benefit ratio for building a new ambulance building would measure the cost of constructing the building and subtract the economic benefit of improving the time of response to the new area. It would not measure such things as the cost of environmental damage or overtime incurred.

A more sophisticated approach to building a cost-benefit model is to put a monetary value on intangible costs and benefits. This can be a highly subjective determination. For example: Is the proposed building construction planned for land designated as a historic wetland worth $25,000, or is it worth $500,000 because of its environmental importance? What is the value of the new building relative to response time or community feedback? Other cost-benefit questions could include these: Does the call volume support the cost structure of employee wages? Will the increased costs negatively affect other areas of the EMS business or other consumers?

It should be obvious that making financial decisions goes far beyond just saying "I want to do this." Each decision, made by a manager, that spends the organization's financial resources must be objectively analyzed and reviewed with an eye toward improving delivery while not increasing costs to society.

Interest Rates

Administrators have responsibility for the overall success of the organization. In this capacity, the administrator must determine the best use of the resources. These resources include human, financial, governmental, and societal capital. Each resource is precious to the growth and viability of the organization. Administrators have the duty and obligation to look after each of these resources and continuously find the best ways to optimize them. Another requirement for managers is to understand how interest works.

Interest is viewed as the price of money. It arose from the choice between spending today and postponing such consumption until a later date (investing). If an organization can achieve more capital by investing the money in a financial vehicle whose return is greater than the value of spending the same capital—for example, on equipment—management may opt to invest and forgo a purchase. However, if the purchase of equipment can be done during a time when investment interest is low, management may decide to purchase and receive a greater value for the equipment.

In discussing interest rates, the EMS leader must be familiar with the concept of interest. The cost of borrowing is expressed in the interest rate. Interest rates are made up of several measurements: the nominal or stated rate of interest on any given security, k; the real risk-free rate of interest ($k*$) [pronounced *k-star*]; the nominal risk-free rate of interest (k_{RF}); the inflation premium (IP);

the default risk premium (DRP); the liquidity premium (LP); and the maturity risk premium (MRP).EMS managers must stay educated on the economy and the flow of money as the availability of money can affect the financial health of the organization. One may think, "Well, the economy does not affect us because we have money in the bank" or "We always receive funding from grants, municipal contributions, or donations." Historically, this attitude may have helped the organization survive; however, in lean times (as in 2008–2009 and 2011–2012) the availability of money deteriorated and the openness of banks to lend declined.

During lean times, the financial market may require municipalities to watch spending, because as their funding sources from the state or federal government decreases, support of the local EMS organization may slow or even stop. As people lose jobs, donations may cease. With any decrease in financial support, EMS organizations may have to dip into reserves to operate. The point here is that the astute EMS leader/financial manager will constantly be aware of the global financial market and adjust his financial plans accordingly. Without an awareness of and response to current events in financial markets, some EMS managers may suddenly find their organizations are short of cash; they may have committed during positive economic times to pay for capital expenditures but find themselves suddenly unable to do so. By borrowing money, the manager places the organization's financial resources at greater risk due to the potential for incurring higher costs. Understanding the cost of money and how to use interest rates can save the organization money both on short-term and long-term projects.

Interest is the price paid to potential lenders to induce them to postpone the recall of the money lent. Even if monies are available to the administrator from internal sources, interest must be considered in any financial decision. The use of funds entails an opportunity cost for an organization; in other words, the money could be invested elsewhere and earn a return. These possible returns are sacrificed if available funds are earmarked for specific purposes. Consideration also must be given to internal and external environments. Consideration of internal environments might include potential increased costs due to higher employee costs because of poor morale, or due to the value of holding onto an older computer system if it takes twice as long to complete documentation. Consideration of external environments might include how interest rates are rising or falling because of the economy. What is the value of holding onto a computer system versus purchasing a new one? Administrators must consider the current value of money not being invested as well as the value of the investment if purchased.

Interest is stated as a percentage of the original sum on a per annum basis. For example, 8 percent on a $500 loan would obligate the organization to pay $40 to the lender at the end of 1 year, in addition to repaying the original $500 loan. If the loan is renewed for a second year and no interest is paid, the total payment due the lender, at the end of the second year is $540 + ($540 × 8%) = $583.20. This total is comprised of the original principle of $500 and $83.20 of compounded interest.

Interest Rates and Decision Making

By tracking availability, accessibility, and the cost of borrowing and saving of the organization's money, a manager should be able to make properly informed decisions. If interest rates increase, the financial manager must anticipate the consequences of any decisions relative to capital expensing. For example, if an organization wants to build a new building with a 20-year life at a cost of $1 million and decides to borrow the entire amount, how would the manager decide how to analyze his options? Borrowing on short-term debt (say for 1 year) at an interest rate of 8.1%, the cost of borrowing would be $81,000, whereas if long-term debt (20-year financing) is used the interest cost for 1 year would be 8.9% or $89,000. At first glance, it would seem reasonable to use short-term borrowing. However, this could be disastrous, if the loan renews every year because of unforeseen circumstances.

The rate charged on each loan will reflect the current interest rate. If the rate charged jumps to 11%, the organization will now pay $110,000. This would require the manager to either reduce reserves, increase call volume (which there is no control), increase revenue (usually fixed by the payer), decrease expenses (lay off staff or reduce the quality of equipment, forgo any planned improvements, which could affect morale), or try to increase donations, write grants, or approach the local government for help. These options all show that the organization either was not prepared or was unable to plan effectively.

By opting for the long-term financing, the interest costs would remain constant throughout the life of the loan. An increase in interest rates would not negatively affect the organization's financial budget as the expense would be known year after year. Does this mean that organizations should not take advantage of short-term debt? The economy fluctuates, and the unknowns are always a challenge when making financial decisions that will affect the organization every year. The astute EMS manager understands how to look at financial forecasts and build on this knowledge when making financial decisions. Financing decisions would be more profitable if there were an easy method for accurately forecasting future interest rates. Unfortunately, predicting the future with accuracy lies somewhere between difficult and impossible. By looking at the history of interest rates, one could accurately say only that interest rates will fluctuate.

Present and Future Value of Money

Most administrators understand the concept of interest in its simplest form. EMS managers see how interest is applied in the daily operations of the organization and their personal lives. Where administrators need to gain additional understanding is in how interest works to determine the **present value** and **future value** of money for capital budgeting, leasing, and cash management.

When discussing interest and the value of money, it is best to establish some generalized and acceptable expressions that will simplify the calculations. It is easy for managers to review this portion of the discussion and recognize that the calculations can be performed on a calculator. By doing the calculations without a good background on the how's and why's, simply performing the calculation will not generate confidence in understanding the concepts of money management.

The following symbols are essential in defining formulas:

P = the principal, or the present value of a sum

F = the future value of a sum

B = the present value of an annuity

W = the future value of an annuity

R = the annuity

n = the number of periods

i = the rate of interest

Now we can see how the borrowing of $500 at 8% for 2 years can be formulated algebraically. This will be demonstrated step by step.

The initial step requires us to compute the value of the money at the end of the first year. This future value is stated as

$$F_1 = P + Pi$$

where F_1 stands for the future value at the end of year 1. Simplifying the expression, we have

$$F_1 = P(1 + i)$$

If this future value is not repaid after the first year, it becomes the value borrowed for the second year. The future value at the end of the second year becomes

$$F_2 = F_1 + F_1 i$$

Or, simplifying

$$F_2 = F_1(1 + i)$$

As we know, F_1 is equal to $P(1 + i)$, so we can substitute this into the expression and arrive at

$$F_2 = P(1 + i)(1 + i)$$

Or combining like terms:

$$F_2 = P(1 + i)^2$$

Now that we have arrived at a formula, we can substitute the numerical values in the expression:

$$F_2 = \$500(1 + 0.008)^2 \text{ or } F_2 = \$583.20$$

Remember, the formula for 1 year is $F_1 = P(1 + i)^1$ and after 2 years it is $F_2 = P(1 + i)^2$.

The general expression for the future value of a sum of money after compounding for n years at an interest rate of i can be shown as

$$F_n = P(1 + i)^n$$

This general formula is helpful in deriving solutions to many future value problems. Consider the following example. What is the future value of an investment of $1,000 that is held for 3 years at an interest rate of 10% per year?

$$P = \$1,000$$
$$n = 3$$
$$i = 10\%$$

Thus,

$$F_3 = \$1,000(1 + 0.10)^3$$
$$F_3 = \$1,000 \times 1.1 \times 1.1 \times 1.1$$
$$F_3 = \$1,331$$

TABLE 4.2 ■ Future Value of Interest										

Here is a portion of a future values interest table. The entire table is found in Appendix A

n/i	0.01	0.02	0.03	0.04	0.05	0.06	0.07	0.08	0.09	0.10
1	1.010	1.020	1.030	1.040	1.050	1.060	1.070	1.080	1.090	1.100
2	1.020	1.040	1.061	1.082	1.103	1.124	1.145	1.166	1.188	1.210
3	1.030	1.061	1.093	1.125	1.158	1.191	1.225	1.260	1.295	1.331

Calculating this return is cumbersome, especially, when calculating several years. Most EMS managers can do this computation quickly on any calculator; however, it is important to know the fundamental process and the value of the information. Once the concept is understood, the mathematics become easier. Utilizing a calculator makes sense, but it is the hands-on practice that helps the manager gain confidence in how the values are obtained. Tables are available to assist managers with the number of years and interest rate calculations. Each entry in such a table represents the interest factor for the number of periods and rates specified. (See Table 4.2 for an example.)

For this example, go to period 3 (*n*) and follow the interest rate (*i*) to 0.10 or 10%. The corresponding intersecting point is 1.331. By multiplying the amount borrowed with 1.331, the total cost of the use of the money is determined.

Let's consider another view of how calculating the future value of money affects an organization that depends on investments, loans, and/or other nonsustained income. The concept of an annuity will help at this stage. An **annuity** is an equal payment to be paid at set periods of time in the future. Examples of annuities for a nonprofit EMS organization could include payment on a building loan, salaries and wages, payments from bequeaths, or a savings account from which funds will be drawn from in the future (e.g., trust funds).

The formulas used in the financial world provide managers with information necessary to determine the flow of wealth, both present and in the future. For example, the timing of payments either at the beginning or at the end of a period is important to cash flow.

Future Value of an Annuity

Why are annuities important to an EMS manager? In simple terms, annuities allow the manager to anticipate future cash flow, determining whether borrowing over the long term is a better choice than taking money out of a reserve account or planning for a major purchase sometime in the future, in which case saving should begin now.

Assume that payments are conventionally made at the end of the period. The general expression for the future value of an annuity is W. Remember, annuity payments can be viewed as deposits to a savings account. Deposits are made at the end of the year and added to previous deposits, including interest already deposited in the account. The annuity contract is for *n* years.

Example

$1,000 invested in an annuity for 5 years with a 6% interest.

The first deposit made is R. Since it is deposited at the end of the first period, it will remain in the savings account and draw interest for one period, *n*. Let's designate the annuity period as 5 years. The first payment is made at the end of the first year and earns interest for the remaining 4 years. The second deposit will be made at the end of the second year and earns interest for the remaining 3 years. The third deposit earns interest for 2 years, the fourth for 1 year, and the fifth does not earn any interest.

The deposits are laid out in this manner because from a managerial viewpoint if we consider

TABLE 4.3 ■ Future Value of Annuity

n/i	0.01	0.02	0.03	0.04	0.05	0.06	0.07	0.08	0.09	0.10	0.11	0.12
4	4.060	4.122	4.184	4.246	4.310	4.375	4.440	4.506	4.573	4.641	4.710	4.779
5	5.101	5.204	5.309	5.416	5.526	**5.637**	5.751	5.867	5.985	6.105	6.228	6.353
6	6.152	6.308	6.468	6.633	6.802	6.975	7.153	7.336	7.523	7.716	7.913	8.115

a payment on a loan, payments on borrowed funds are made after an elapsed time, not when the money is borrowed. Similarly, returns on investments are earned after the investment decision is made.

The algebraic expression for the above example is

$$W = \$1,000(1 + 0.006)^4 + \$1,000(1 + 0.006)^3 + \$1,000(1 + 0.006)^2 + \$1,000(1 + 0.006)^1 + \$1,000 = \$5,637.10$$

A simplified expression is

$$W = R(1+i)^{n-1} + R(1+i)^{n-2} + \ldots + R(1+i) + R$$

Using standard algebraic techniques, the formula for the future value of an annuity reduces to

$$W = R\frac{(1+i)^{n-1}}{I}$$

The expression in the bracket is also the interest factor T_c (Table 4.3). Interest tables are standardized for time and interest and can be found in many financial books. Thus we have

$$W = RT_c$$

Now if we take the original problem of $1,000 invested in an annuity for 5 years at 6% interest, we can calculate quickly what the value of the account will be in 5 years. Looking at the table we see $T_c = 5.637$. Therefore:

$$W = \$1,000 \times 5.637 = \$5,637$$

Another example
$2,500 is deposited in a savings account each year for 15 years at a 7% annual interest rate. What is the value of the account at the end of year 15 (see Table 4.4)?

$$W = \$2,500 \times 25.129 = \$62,822.50$$

1. For example, let's say that management decides to begin a vehicle replacement program and the organization wants to put one-third of the money down on each vehicle and use grants, loans, or operational revenue to pay off the balance. What monies must be available each time a new vehicle is ordered?

You now have two formulas to assist with determining cash value in the future:

1. $W = RT_c \rightarrow$ future value of an annuity
2. $F_n = P(1 + i)^n \rightarrow$ future value of a sum

The next formula is a combination of these. To determine the present value of an annuity to budget for equal payments over a period of time, a formula is helpful. For example, an organization decides to pay off a building or land and the total payment is $50,000 for 30 years at an interest rate of 9%. What are the payments per year? Let's say $5,000 is received per month through a bequeath of

TABLE 4.4 ■ Present Value of an Annuity

n/i	0.01	0.02	0.03	0.04	0.05	0.06	0.07	0.08	0.09	0.10	0.11	0.12
14	14.947	15.974	17.086	18.292	19.599	21.015	22.551	24.215	26.019	27.975	30.095	32.393
15	16.097	17.293	18.599	20.024	21.579	23.276	**25.129**	27.152	29.361	31.773	34.405	37.280
16	17.258	18.639	20.157	21.825	23.658	25.673	27.888	30.324	33.003	35.950	39.190	42.753

a patient who was transported. The formula (found on a present value of annuity table) would be:

$$B = RT_D$$

where

B (or T_D) = present value of annuity

R = the unknown or the payment

$T = (1+i)^n - 1$

If we set up the problem algebraically, we have

$$\$50,000 = R \times 10.274$$

$$R = \$4,866.65 \text{ per year}$$

The 10.274 is found on a present value of an annuity table, another standardized accounting table. However, the question is, are you taking the future value of a dollar amount and bringing it back to present value?

The organization must have available $4,866.65 each year for 30 years to pay off this loan. The following are the managerial questions that arise from this information:

1. Over time, is 9% a good rate and could we improve this?

or

2. Do we budget for this amount and seek to build up this account by investing the balance for the highest return and pay down the loan faster?

or

3. Do we invest the difference in the $4,866.65 in a high–interest-bearing account and just pay what is due?

Net Present Value

The preceding questions are some of those that managers must ask each budget year or at least during strategic planning sessions. Ultimately the question becomes "Is it worth investing funds today (in buildings, equipment) considering the returns that can be expected in the future from this investment?" What this formula allows a manager to do is compare the present value of future receipts to the present value of cash. To illustrate:

Let

C = the investment

B = the present value of expected returns

As long as B is greater than C, the investment is desirable. When C is larger than B, the future returns are not sufficient to justify the investment. The difference between the present value of expected returns and the initial investment required to generate these returns is the **net present value (NPV)** (see Table 4.5). The decision rule stated above can now be written as

If the NPV is positive, accept the investment proposal.

If the NPV is negative, reject the investment proposal.

TABLE 4.5 ■ Net Present Value

n/i	0.12	0.14	0.16	0.18	0.20	0.22
1	0.893	0.877	0.862	0.847	0.833	0.82
2	1.690	1.647	1.605	1.566	1.528	1.492
3	2.402	2.322	2.246	2.174	2.106	2.042
4	3.037	2.914	2.798	**2.690**	2.589	2.494
5	3.605	3.433	3.274	3.127	2.991	2.864

Of course, an example will help in this situation. Let's assume that the organization has just been given $15,000. Management must decide whether to pay off existing debt, buy new equipment, pay bonuses, or invest the money to pay off long-term debt. To pay off the long-term debt, an annual return of $6,000 for 4 years is needed. To justify the risk of this investment, a minimum return of 18% is needed. Should the investment be made? Using the listed numbers and NPV Table 4.6, we see a difference between Option A and Option B.

Option A

$$NPV = \$6,000 \times 2.69 - \$15,000$$

$$NPV = \$1,140$$

where

$$C = \$15,000$$

$$R = \$6,000$$

$$T_D = 2.69 \text{ (18\% for 4 years)}$$

Since the NPV is positive, this investment should be considered.

Assume that another investment requiring the same $15,000 and returning $6,000 for 4 years is judged to be more risky, requiring a 24% return. Should this investment be made?

Option B

$$NPV = \$6,000 \times 2.404 - \$15,000$$

$$NPV = -\$576$$

where

$$C = \$15,000$$

$$R = \$6,000$$

$$T_D = 2.404 \text{ (24\% for 4 years)}$$

Since the NPV is negative (Table 4.6), this investment should not be made. By comparing the rate of return between the investments, option A should be considered, and option B should be rejected. Amazingly, many EMS managers will choose option B because it appears it will make more money for the organization.

This example is one method managers can use to make a decision on the best use of money. Another method is called the **payback method**. As the name implies, this method identifies the number of periods required to pay back the initial investment. Based on the number of periods estimated, a decision can be made to accept an investment or reject it. Remember, that these decision-making tools are part of a plan of operations established by all members of the organizational team. In other words, the board of directors must establish the plan. So let's say the board decides to invest $32,500 to purchase land to build a new building. The criteria for the investment are that the land must be paid off in 5 years, and the amount of budgeted money for the land is $7,000. The payback method will help determine if this is possible given the current state of the organization.

TABLE 4.6 ■ Net Present Value								
n/i	*0.16*	*0.18*	*0.20*	*0.22*	*0.24*	*0.26*	*0.28*	*0.30*
1	0.862	0.847	0.833	0.82	0.806	0.794	0.781	0.769
2	1.605	1.566	1.528	1.492	1.457	1.424	1.392	1.361
3	2.322	2.246	2.106	2.042	1.981	1.923	1.868	1.816
4	2.914	2.798	2.589	2.494	**2.404**	2.320	2.241	2.166
5	3.433	3.274	2.991	2.864	2.745	2.635	2.532	2.436

Algebraically,

If

C (the investment) = $32,500

R (the annuity) = $7,000

C/R = Number of payback periods

We then have

$32,000/$7,000 = 4.6 (or just less than 5 years)

If the predetermined payback is within a 5-year period, the investment should be accepted. If the numbers exceed the 5-year criteria, the investment should be rejected.

Payback is simple in determining set criteria for investing. However, it does have some weaknesses. It does ignore the time value of money by allocating equal weight to near-term returns and those due later. It is inconsistent with results over time and may mislead managers, especially when returns are uneven over a specific range. It does give a broad idea of investment and forces managers to look at options to making well-qualified decisions.

CHAPTER REVIEW

Summary

Interest is the value of money and must take into account all investment decisions, those requiring outside funding, as well as those that are financed internally. The three basic formulas are the future value of a sum $Fn = P(1 + i)n$, future value of an annuity $W = RTc$, and present value of an annuity $B = RT_D$. Tables, calculators, and computer programs can simplify computations; however, the manager must understand the underlying concepts. It is the decision-making exercises that are important. Too often managers just make decisions with inaccurate information. It is not to say that the outcomes are not good, but managers could do better or at the very least know that their decisions are based on objectivity not just gut reactions.

In subsequent discussions, we will build on these formulas as a way to continue to make decisions.

WHAT WOULD YOU DO? Reflection

You have many things to consider when making a decision to expand services and use organizational and community resources. Understanding short-term and long-term financing, interest rates, and the time value of money can make your decision more objective and less emotional. In this situation, you look at the organization's current resources (staffing), equipment (supplies and vehicles), support services (supervision, human resources, and financial), and community support (agreements with the new residence). You also research the zoning requirements, traffic access, and potential local business support.

In determining if another building is a good investment in the future, you have come to understand the best options for financing the new facility, including interest rates, contract terms, use of current reserve funds, and how to seek community support.

You ask, "Will increases in call volume offset the incremental cost to invest in the new building and staffing as compared to the current costs of running calls without the expansion?" Other items you consider are the drain on current resources if the decision to expand is made without investment in another facility. Each of these decisions will reflect your organizational goals and be firmly rooted in solid financial decision making. Any decision will be based on an

objective review of the pros and cons of the decision and will not reflect an emotional or personal desire to "become the biggest" or be based on arbitrary goals. Each decision will be made based on a time-tested process of evaluation and with an objective view of the long-term goals of the organization.

Review Questions

1. What is an organization?
2. What is the role of management relative to the growth of the organization?
3. How does finance support the role of management in the growth and development of the organization?
4. Why is understanding the role of finance important for an EMS manager?
5. What is the future value of $2,000 at 6% for 3 years?
6. Why does an EMS manager need to evaluate the financial consequences of a project objectively?
7. Why is the knowledge of the value of money so important for the EMS manager?
8. Why is *interest rate* an important concept for understanding how to use financial resources available to the organization?
9. In the grand EMS scheme, how do supply and demand of EMS affect future development of EMS services for communities?
10. How does finance affect the economics of EMS?

References

"Accounting Concepts." BusinessDictionary.com. See the organization website.

Allison, T. (2011). "Guest Op/Ed: Cuts to Reimbursement Will Be Devastating to State's Health Care." *Pacific Coast Business Times.* See the organization website.

American National Red Cross–Chapter Network. (2011, June). "Financial Statements and Schedules for Cleveland Center of Expertise." See the organization website.

American Red Cross. (2007, November). Forbes. com. See the organization website.

Blackstone, E. A., A. J. Buck, and S. Hakim. (2007). "The Economics of Emergency Response." *Policy Sciences 40*(4), 313–334. doi:10.1007/s11077-007-9047-6

Clark, B. (1998). *Political-Economy: A Comparative Approach.* Westport, CT: Praeger Publishing.

Coase, R. (1937). "The Nature of the Firm." *Economica 4*(16).

Department of Business Management and Economics (BME). (2012). "Introduction." Isles Internationale Université. See the organization website.

Dodes, J. W. (1965). *Everyday Life in the Twentieth Century.* London: BT Batsford.

Donchez, R. (n.d.). "Overview of Finance and Financial Markets." See the Leeds School of Business website.

Freeman, R. B. (1987). "Labour Economics." *The New Palgrave Dictionary of Economics*, vol. 3. See the organization website.

General Government Division. (1998, April). "Privatization: Questions State and Local Decision Makers Used when Considering Privatization Options." Washington, DC: General Accounting Office, GAO/GGD-98-87. See the organization website.

Harper, D. (2001–2012). "Economy." Online Etymology Dictionary. See the organization website.

Hons, B. (n.d.). "Economics." See the Shyam Lal College (Evening) University of Delhi website.

Johnson, R. (2002). "Ambulance Wars." *Michigan Privatization Report.* Midland, MI: The Mackinac Center for Public Policy, *Winter,* 12–13. See the organization website.

Khoaanh.net. (2009, January). "Cost/Benefit Analysis: Evaluating Quantitatively Whether to Follow a Course of Action (n.d.). See the organization website.

Nethelper. (n.d.). "Economics." See the organization website.

Pindyck, R., and D. Rubinfeld. (1995). *Microeconomics,* 3rd ed. Englewood Cliffs, NJ: Prentice-Hall.

Robbins, L. (1945). *An Essay on the Nature and Significance of Economic Science.* London: Macmillan and Co., Limited. See the organization website.

Scorecard Dashboard Analytics. (n.d.). "Reporting." See the organization website.

Spiro, H. (1996). *Finance for the Non-financial Manager.* New York: John Wiley & Sons, Inc.

Stigler, G. (1954). "Schumpeter's History of Economic Analysis." *Journal of Political Economy, 62,* p. 344.

Tuon, P. (2009). Economics 101 Book. See the organization website.

Key Terms

annuity An annuity can be defined as a contract that provides an income stream in return for an initial payment. It is also income from a capital investment paid in a series of regular payments, usually payable at specified time intervals. Or it is an amount paid at regular intervals for a set period of time. Mortgage payments are a form of an annuity paid to the lender.

cost-benefit analysis (CBA) An analysis that evaluates the cost-effectiveness of a project or policy.

demand The desire to purchase goods and services.

demand theory Explains the relationship between consumer demand for goods and services and their prices.

economic efficiency How well a system generates the maximum desired output with a given set of inputs and available technology.

economics The branch of social science that deals with the production and distribution and consumption of goods and services and their management.

equilibrium The condition of a system in which competing influences are balanced, resulting in no net change.

fixed costs Fixed costs are business expenses that are not dependent on the activities of the business. They tend to be time-related, such as salaries or rents being paid per month.

future value The value of an asset or cash at a specified date in the future that is equivalent in value to a specified sum today.

interest The percentage or rate charged by a lender to use borrowed money.

k The nominal or stated rate of interest on any given security.

k* The real risk-free rate of interest. It is the rate that would exist in a riskless security if zero inflation were expected.

k_{RF} The nominal risk-free rate of interest. This is the stated interest rate on a security that is free of default risk.

macroeconomics The study of the sum total of economic activity, dealing with the issues of growth, inflation, and unemployment and with national economic policies relating to these issues.

managerial accounting The process of identifying, measuring, analyzing, interpreting, and communicating information for the pursuit of an organization's goals.

marginal costs Additional cost associated with producing one more unit of output.

microeconomics The branch of economics that studies the economy of consumers, households, or individual firms.

net present value (NPV) Today's value of future costs and benefits.

organizations Groups of people who work together; a social arrangement that pursues collective goals.

payback method Method to evaluate an investment project.

present value The current value of an asset or cash.

supply The amount of goods or services a business provides.

unit A unique entity or thing that is a function of a whole and is used to value or compare against something different.

CHAPTER 5

Creating a Fiscally Sound Program

Objectives

After reading this chapter, the student should be able to:

5.1 Describe how the EMS manager should understand the concept of the financial resources that are available and how forecasting will better prepare the decision makers for the future success of the organization.

5.2 List and describe the various methods of forecasting and how each can add to the ability to make an informed decision about the allocation of financial resources.

5.3 Review how the board of directors should function as the last best opportunity to question operational decisions relative to the future financial health of the organization and the allocation of the organization's finances.

5.4 Discuss why an analysis of the organization through a business, community, and financial perspective is essential for short- and long-term planning.

5.5 Introduce analysis tools that can assist the EMS manager in determining risk and the best use of organizational finances.

5.6 Discuss how cash management affects an EMS organization's ability to operate and how the manager should prepare formal plans for the use of cash.

Overview

The purpose of this text is to introduce the concepts of finance to nonfinancial EMS managers. The chapters present valuable information to both new and experienced EMS leaders who may have varying degrees of experience, formal and informal. The goal is to stimulate thinking in order to change the way things are done, to avoid mistakes of the past, and to encourage future growth of EMS as a profession.

Key Terms

allocation	cost of risk	output	uncertainty
assets	deviation	pro forma statement	validity
astute	forecasting	sensitivity testing	variable costs
bias	investments	stewardship	working capital
breakeven analysis	opportunity cost	sustainability	
cash budget	outcomes	toleration	

WHAT WOULD YOU DO?

As a newly hired manager of a medium-size EMS organization, you decide to review the financial position of the organization. You pull together the bank statements, the audited statements from the local accountant, and the investment portfolio. You look over the funding sources, which include money from operations, donations from the annual fund drive, and money from three municipalities in your response area. After a thorough review, you determine that the organization is stable, and you are comfortable with the current financial position. The organization is self-sustainable for the short and foreseeable future. You also foresee the ability to develop additional needed programs that will benefit the community.

You are approached by the board of directors about planning for the next annual fund drive. You also hear that some of the staff are planning to ask for an increase in hourly pay because all the other EMS organizations pay their people more. The other EMS organizations are municipally based and on average run 30 percent more calls. The local auto dealership calls you to confirm the order of a chief's vehicle. Apparently, the previous manager ordered a vehicle to respond to calls if needed; however, he was only trained as a first responder and his role was more of a scene administrator. It was anticipated that he would also use the vehicle for his personal use when not at work.

Questions

1. How will you determine the available financial resources that are allocated to the organization?
2. What method of evaluation would you use to prioritize available financial resources for the pending or anticipated commitments?
3. What process would you implement to ensure that the financial resources are allocated for organizational growth?

■ INTRODUCTION

Financial analysis not only looks at the dollar numbers as they relate to past activities, but the analysis also provides the EMS manager with a method of evaluating what can occur in the future. By developing a systematic method to review how the organization functions, develop trends, and control operational activities, the EMS manager can facilitate the growth of the organization. Financial analysis provides an objective view of the organization relative to meeting the goals, having the ability to fund projects that benefit the community, or improving the work environment. Analysis is not merely the process of generating reports and looking at them once a month at a board meeting. Analysis requires ongoing assessments of the **outcomes** of operations and the effect operations have on the budget, growth, **sustainability**, and consistency in outcomes. Analysis also allows for decision makers to evaluate the EMS organization objectively and determine if management decisions are appropriate and in line with the goals established.

■ BOARD OF DIRECTORS————

EMS organizations have unique reporting structures. The EMS manager may report to a municipal board or supervisory committee. If the organization is a nonprofit, the board of directors may consist of crew members, or community members, or a combination of both. If the EMS organization is affiliated with a hospital, the manager may report to a director or a vice president. If the manager is responsible for day-to-day operations and ultimately reports to another person or an authoritative body, the manager must be capable of presenting objective information that does not show unnecessary **bias**.

A board of directors is comprised of individuals who may or may not be past or present personnel. They may be politicians or community members. The key question to ask is this: Is the board capable of making objective business decisions? If the board is comprised of community members, do the individuals have sufficient knowledge about EMS and the organization to help direct the activities? Can the board make tough business decisions by looking at the merits of a decision objectively?

A board of directors should be comprised of professionals who specialize in business and finance *and* have an interest in putting their talents to work in the field of EMS. The board is the last best opportunity to protect the **assets** of the organization from decisions that could negatively impact future growth or success. Without this high level of oversight, the organization's success could be limited. Too often directors feel they do not have knowledge about EMS and are hesitant to question the EMS manager on operational plans. As a result, projects are moved through the decision-making process without question or challenge. Boards should scrutinize and question plans that require major **investments** and do not demonstrate the value of the investment to the organization.

Another weakness of some EMS boards of directors occurs when the board is comprised of past and present crew members exclusively. A potential bias could exist when all members are emotionally attached to the organization. Objectivity regarding tough business decisions may challenge an all-EMS board. Efforts to build a community board with members who are concerned about the success of the organization, but have a clear concept of their role as the final decision maker, is essential (Figure 5.1).

FIGURE 5.1 ■ A board of directors. *Courtesy of Dennis Mitterer.*

ALLOCATION OF RESOURCES

One of the key functions of financial management is the **allocation** of existing resources with the expectation of reaping benefits in the future Although existing financial resources are known (cash on hand, money in a checking account), expending them is done with purpose, the future benefit is not guaranteed—it is uncertain. When managers direct and approve payments for items purchased, the hope is that the purchased item has or will provide value to the organization. The manager is expecting a return for the outlay of cash. Paying an electrical bill occurs after the organization has used the electricity to power the lights, copier, and appliances. There is an exchange of cash for the electricity, and thus there is value in the purchase.

EMS managers must seek, at a minimum, a one-to-one return in value before allocating the organization's financial resources. In most cases, when investing in a project or service the EMS manager should expect a higher return for the investment. Since financial returns may deviate from those expected for a variety of reasons, in financial terms this **deviation** serves as the definition of **uncertainty** or risk.

Managers should constantly evaluate the assets of the organization and determine, through strategic planning, the growth of the organization and the resources needed to achieve the growth. Growth in this context does not necessarily mean acquisitions or purchase of land. It can mean developing new programs, which may result in the need for additional staff. Planning for growth allows managers the ability to forecast expected results—within certain perimeters.

For example, an EMS organization runs 12,000 calls per year. A developer plans to build a retirement community in the district. Preliminary reports anticipate 7,500 people will live in the center. Based on historical data, your organization can anticipate responding to emergency calls at the new facility at 8 per 1,000 people

per year. Due to the clientele of the facility, the crews will respond to nonemergency transports on an average of 18 times per week.

Base charge for transport = $120

Base charge for emergency call = $350

Based on preliminary information, expected revenues can improve the EMS financial position in excess of $300,000:

Emergency revenue = $3,500 × 56 = $196,000

Transport revenue = $120 × 18 × 52 = $112,320

Total revenue = $308,320 per year

The EMS manager has decisions to make. He could begin to allocate financial resources to purchasing new ambulances, hiring more EMS responders, and purchasing equipment to improve the ability to accommodate this growth. In contrast, he could wait and see how the new facility impacts the call volume and then act on the increase in activity. By purchasing equipment and hiring staff, the manager must commit and allocate financial resources now in anticipation of an unknown future. By waiting, the manager may not be able to accommodate the growth. The operator of the facility may contract all medical services to another, better prepared EMS organization. Either decision is difficult. The take-home points are, first, making this decision without the benefit of a qualified board is difficult. Second, either decision made is going to impact the financial position of the organization. Third, there are no guarantees that one decision is better than the other. However, the EMS manager can determine the risk of the decision by applying financial techniques.

FORECASTING

The operations of most businesses are continually affected by events beyond the control of the management. Some of these events are unanticipated or of such importance that they require specific management consideration to determine the response. Alternatively, during normal operations a tremendous number of events that cannot be controlled or predicted occur. The key to **forecasting** is determining what the future is going to be like financially. It is known only that the future will yield an uncertain number and often a moving target. Trying to determine what an organization's needs are in a future period is difficult; however, even given the uncertainty, educated guesses can be made through forecasting. The manager must prepare for possibilities before committing the organization's financial resources to a project. By knowing the internal and external environment, the manager can research different possibilities. Even if the research provides relevant information, many variables could and will affect any decisions made. By looking at all possible outcomes, the manager can decide the best direction for the organization.

By looking at the example used in the preceding section, "Allocation of Resources," the EMS manager can anticipate a significant increase in revenue. This may look exciting to the manager, and he could begin hiring new staff, purchasing a new ambulance, updating equipment, and anticipating higher call volumes. Those are all exciting projects! But, what if the facility builds a clinic and hires a nurse practitioner to staff the clinic? The retirement community could purchase its own transporting unit and staff it with prehospital providers. In these scenarios, annual revenue would rise and fall based on the uncontrolled variables associated with decisions by the owners of the facility. A variety of scenarios exist with this one possibility. Thus, it is imperative that the EMS manager research as many possibilities as possible before committing any financial resources.

Since deviations from the estimated number of responses are likely, the outcome is uncertain. By looking at an average number of responses, the manager can anticipate a certain level of revenue. This range in revenue is an average of all possibilities that can be expected from very low dollar amounts to very high dollar amounts. In the language of statistics, this is considered expected values. Since the EMS manager cannot predict whether the revenue will be high, low, or somewhere in between, there is uncertainty about how much money the organization will receive. With this uncertainty, the EMS manager cannot plan effectively. Even if the manager's budget anticipates a certain dollar value, he has no idea how much will be received. The greater the uncertainty associated with the expected revenue, the greater the probability is that actual revenue will differ from expected revenue. If the uncertainty is small (revenue is close to budget), the probability is high that actual returns will approach expected returns.

Managers must understand that planning is essential in determining the direction of the organization; however, there will be times when things happen that can deviate from the plans. When managing an EMS organization, holding to a strict fiscal outcome is unrealistic. If the EMS manager develops a budget so rigidly that the dependency on expected revenue provides no leeway when unforeseen events occur, the greater the chance is that the organization will fall on hard times when revenues decrease or expenses increase.

Since uncertainty is unavoidable, it must be treated explicitly in the financial planning process. This can be accomplished by stipulating a range of outcomes, varying the perimeters and observing the changes that occur as assumptions are altered. Thus, in examining a future revenue forecast, management may wish to inspect both a forecast on the high end of the range of possible outcomes and one at the low end.

HIGH-END AND LOW-END FORECASTING

The decision to choose a high-end, middle- or average-range, or low-end forecast is often based on a manager's ability to assess current internal and external conditions. In addition, personal beliefs and **toleration** for risk will influence the manager's decision. Since finance is a more exact science than gut reaction or belief systems, it is important to develop an objective methodology for determining the best outcome. Whether the organization is large and can pay an analyst to determine external conditions or the organization is small and the survivability of the organization depends on management's decision-making ability, the financial success of an organization requires that managers understand their environment by reading, listening, investigating, and evaluating the internal and external environments. Uncertainties facing the organization's management team cannot be controlled, yet the manager must be explicitly aware of uncertainty and include appropriate considerations in the financial planning process.

FORECASTING MODELS

There are different types of forecasting models that a manager can use. Among these are the Box-Jenkins model, exponential smoothing, regression analysis, and trend projection. An overview of each technique is provided in this section. When deciding which forecasting tool to use, the EMS manager should look at what information is needed and what the information will be used for, and he should become familiar with one or two techniques.

Box-Jenkins Model

The Box-Jenkins model represents processes that are stationary or nonstationary. In a stationary process, statistical properties are the same over time. A very straightforward example would be transporting a chemotherapy patient from a nursing home to a radiation facility. A nonstationary process has statistical properties that vary over time. Examples of nonstationary processes are the number of emergency responses during winter; these trends or seasonal behaviors are unpredictable, yet fall around an identified number of occurrences. The Box-Jenkins model is predicated on a time-series analysis of information that tries to find the best correspondence to past information in order to make forecasts about the future.

Exponential Smoothing

When seeking to detect significant changes in data, the EMS manager can use exponential smoothing (also called averaging), which is a statistical technique. The EMS manager should ignore any fluctuations (changes) in the data that are irrelevant. For example, the EMS manager is tracking purchases of IV fluids over the summer months. In the preceding year, a bike race was held during the July 4th weekend. During that time, the weather was uncharacteristically hot and humid. Many bikers were treated for heat exposure with IV fluids. This data are considered irrelevant when looking at the total IV fluid purchases for the summer months. The excess use in this case is an aberration from normal. In exponential smoothing, older data provide progressively less relative weight (importance), whereas newer data maintain progressively greater weight. Exponential smoothing is initiated when making short-term forecasts.

Regression Analysis

A regression analysis is a statistical approach used to forecast changes in a dependent variable (patient revenue) on the basis of change in one or more independent variables (population and income) (Figure 5.2). Regression analysis is also known as curve fitting or line fitting because the process can be used in fitting a curve or line to data points. Relationships depicted in a regression analysis are, however, associative only, and any cause-effect inference is purely subjective. In regres-

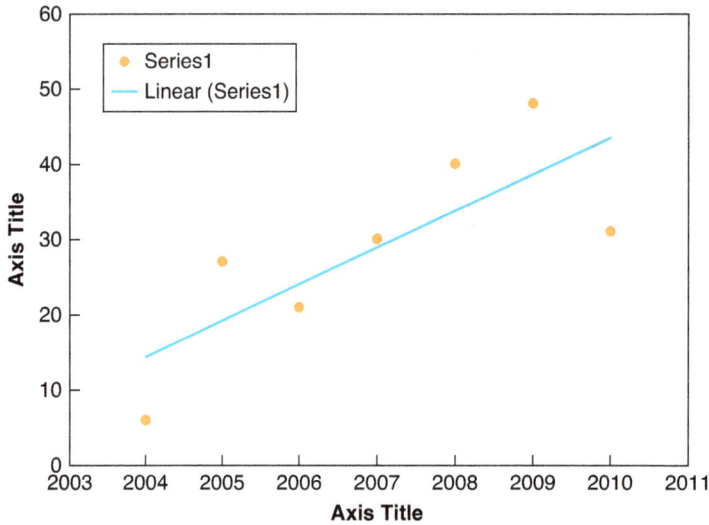

FIGURE 5.2 ■ Example of regression analysis.

sion analysis, the EMS manager would enter data into a chart. The variable used should show some relationship with other variables (e.g., age of patients transported and the reimbursement from Medicare versus other payers). When plotting the data, the manager will see independent data points. Regression analysis applies a line to show how close the relationship is with the central tendency (the line represents the central tendency). The closer the data points to the line, the greater is the predictability that the comparison becomes.

Trend Projection

Trend projection is a forecasting model most frequently used by organizations. Managers use this model to study variables over time. To be effective the manager tracks data over a period of time and graphs the information on a spreadsheet. Trend lines can be added to show the direction of the movement of the data, to indicate how much the data changes, and to provide a visual representation of past and present data. Future decisions or projec-

tions are not reliable because the trend line's plotting for future results can be subjective and open to management bias.

■ FINANCIAL DECISION MAKING—

Decisions, based on financial forecasting, require the evaluation of internal and external factors. Once these factors are identified—through a SWOT analysis, for example (see Box 5.1)—they can help the EMS manager develop priorities. Once the priorities are established, then funding can be allocated to achieve the expected outcomes. Managers should ensure that the factors used in any forecasting application are specific to the organization.

Side Bar

SWOT is an acronym for **S**trength, **W**eakness, **O**pportunity, and **T**hreat. A SWOT analysis is a management tool that looks at the internal and external environment.

Box 5.1

SWOT Analysis

Many different analysis tools are available to an EMS management team. In a SWOT analysis, the manager would look at four areas of the organization.

S = Strength. First, the manager would determine the strengths of the organization. Is it the people, the board of directors, the financial position, the fact that the organization is the only EMS responder in the area, or the reputation of the organization? Any or all of these should be evaluated, plus many more details. The point is that the manager *must* take an unbiased look at why the organization is as good as it is. Not every area in an EMS organization, or any business, is perfect in every area. What are the key strengths that make it what it is?

W = Weakness. After looking at the strengths, the manager would look at the organization's weaknesses. Here the manager dissects where the organization can improve, or what is holding it back. A weakness would not be "We don't cover enough response area" but more on the lines of "We are unable to cover all shifts on the weekend" or "Our pay is not competitive, so we lose well-trained responders to larger units." As for strengths, the manager's view is, or should be, unbiased. For both the strengths and weaknesses, the manager analyzes the internal makeup of the organization. By searching for these answers, the management team can determine what to prioritize and, ultimately, what to fund. This exercise does not have to be completed in a vacuum—in other words, the manager does not need to complete this by himself. Here is an opportunity to solicit community, vendor, staff, and board feedback. What do others perceive to be the organization's strengths and weaknesses?

O = Opportunities. The external evaluation of the organization begins with opportunities. What areas in the external environment or community, given the right resources, move the

organization closer to its goals? What partnerships if developed will jump-start a particular project, such as teaching CPR to high school students, or developing a program that looks after elderly neighbors, or approaching a large church and helping congregants to initiate a medical response team? The question to evaluate is this: What can we do, in the external environment, to better meet our goals? Of course, if the goals are simply to grow the organization, then viewing the external environment may be challenging. Many EMS organizations maintain strictly an internal view of organizational growth and thereby fail to realize that the community is their way to grow and succeed. For example, an external opportunity would be to approach a community college and develop a partnership with its business or computer department. It is often possible to arrange for internships for various students to do work for the EMS organization. Here the student receives valuable work experience and the organization receives input on projects from a fresh perspective or completes work that otherwise would be pushed aside. Whether the intern is paid or not is not the priority; what is most important is that you have identified an opportunity to get the EMS organization involved in other things besides just responding to 9-1-1 calls.

T = Threats. What outside factors can take away or threaten the current activity or direction of the organization? Do the threats come from the payers, the local hospital that opens four more urgent care centers, or the very large long-term-care facility decides to transport its patients, thus reducing your potential income? For municipal-based EMS organizations, the threat could be a reallocation of money away from emergency responders due to unforeseen shortfalls in tax revenue.

The idea behind both opportunities and threats is that the EMS manager must be look outside his organization to evaluate the external environment relative to the EMS organization's existence in that environment.

SWOT Assessment Form

Action Item/Time Line	Estimated Completion Date	Responsible Party	January 1, 20xx Milestone	Results
PHYSICAL PLANT/OPERATIONS				
Discuss areas needing attention: crew room, rooms 1–2, maintenance rooms	12/13/20xx	Team		Committee to develop overall facility plan
Establish priority				
Determine current capital (biggest bang for the dollar)				
PEOPLE				
Complete staffing of front office				
Position 1	9/25/20xx	Manager	In training	
Position 2	12/11/20xx	Manager	Starting orientation	
Position 3	1/1/20xx	Manager	Will start first week of January	
Position 4	12/4/20xx	Manager	Started orienting to office	
Position 5	1/1/20xx	Manager		
Temporary help	12/1/20xx	Manager	Assisting in routine office function	Allowing supervisor time to train new staff
FINANCE				
Maintain budget				
MARKET/GROWTH				
Residential	12/1/20xx	Manager	Residential housing across street	
Opening of new retirement village				
PATIENT SAFETY/EMPLOYEE SAFETY				
Continue to monitor near misses				
Education of new and existing staff				
CUSTOMER SERVICE				
Review intubation success with medical director	12/13/20xx	Manager		Overall acceptable results; unchanged from study done 3 years ago

The manager must carefully watch for any changes in the internal or external environment that could alter the assumptions or that may no longer apply to the organization. If lacking detailed knowledge of the internal and external environments and the relationship between the two, then the manager of the EMS organization is not adequately prepared to make informed, financial decisions about the growth of the organization.

For example, let's illustrate the point about analyzing business decisions based on external factors: The EMS manager at Main Street Ambulance decides to place a unit at a nursing facility solely to protect or enlarge the organization's territory. He heard that Metro Ambulance was staffing a unit at a large outpatient facility located in Main Street's primary running district. Decisions to invest in staffing and vehicles, develop agreements using legal professionals, and spend management time discussing the plan without determining the costs and overall benefit to the organization commenced. These actions were begun based on a perceived threat by a "competing" organization's placement of an ambulance in Main Street Ambulance's district.

Justifications were made to the board of directors that this move was necessary to "protect territory." What Main Street Ambulance did not know was that Metro Ambulance was contracted to do all the transports from the outpatient center. Metro Ambulance was required to be available in the facility and therefore could not respond to other emergency calls. Main Street's management team was threatened and reacted to the external environment without determining if changes were necessary. The money wasted in developing a reactive strategy detracted from the organization's overall purpose. Some may say that this reactive stance was necessary to protect territory. However, the net effect was wasted money, decreased employee morale, questioning of management's decision making, and some

actual loss of employees due to the decision. Main Street Ambulance placed itself in survival mode and reacted to a perceived threat. By only looking at this situation from an internal perspective, the organization's management was blinded by the reality of what was actually happening.

This example provides a two-fold lesson for EMS as a public servant and as a profession. If better communication existed among organizations, then fewer organizational resources, financial or otherwise, would be spent trying to protect "territory." Second, EMS is rooted in public service and should seek to develop processes that benefit the public, not focus on personal or organizational survival. By understanding the implications of "protectionism," EMS could save the community huge amounts of financial resources (macro view) and preserve internal dollars (micro view) for many other worthwhile projects that benefit the community.

TERRITORY AND FINANCE

Management in EMS is not about territory and protecting a set client basis. Unfortunately, that is what it has become in many areas. Short-sighted managers have used the tagline "It's a business decision" to justify actions to protect their organizations, or to undermine or attempt to destroy other organizations while attempting to earn an additional dollar. Many managers develop policies and relationships that protect themselves and their positions rather than working together to deliver better care to the community. The amount of resources wasted on protecting territory is staggering. The profession of emergency services is about protecting the community. In the previous example, Main Street Ambulance spent tens of thousands of dollars to react to a situation that never existed, in essence wasting "community money." The unit placed at the nursing home was in service for 4 months before being pulled out so Main Street Ambulance could revert to its normal business. The short-sighted view was to protect territory to make more money, but the bottom line is not the goal!

Many may say "This doesn't happen to us. We are the only EMS organization in the county" or "We are municipal based" or "We operate out of a fire department." Despite the differences in organizational structure, every EMS organization has similar problems; they are just presented differently. It is the **astute** manager who perceives an opportunity or a threat and investigates what impact it will have on the organization, analyzes objective data, communicates with the people who have a vested interest in the success of the organization and the public, and then makes a decision. Similarly, the astute manager understands his internal environment, recognizes when an opportunity exists, and seeks to capitalize on the opportunity to better the organization. He recognizes weakness and allocates resources to improve the weaknesses before they become anchors. He perceives a threat and seeks clarification before spending financial resources to protect what appeared to be a significant threat and will turn out to be only a minor distraction.

■ SENSITIVITY TESTING

An important part of any planning process is analyzing information and determining its **validity**. Once validity of the information is determined, and management is satisfied with the information, **sensitivity testing** is needed. Sensitivity testing is relevant for financial planning because the results will have far-reaching influence on revenues generated from operations. The main goal of sensitivity testing is to gain insight into which assumptions are critical (i.e., which assumptions affect choice). The process involves various ways of changing input values to see the effect on the **output** values. Frequently, the direction of revenue changes cannot be forecasted. For example, a drop in call volume or a delay in reimbursements may require some additional external financing for short-term projects. Sensitivity testing to identify changes in operations revenue helps to assure management that the organization has the flexibility necessary to cope with any changing financial needs.

Although it may not be feasible to develop support plans for every contingency, the manager can guess what the potential impact may be as the situation unfolds. Obviously, the earlier the EMS manager identifies a problem that could affect revenue and corrects the problem, the better skilled he becomes.

A customary approach to sensitivity testing is to determine high and low forecasts. These forecasts should consider call volume, transport volume, revenue generation, and other programs that contribute to revenue. High/low forecasts are developed with the expectation that they will span events that are most likely to occur. Forecasts cannot cover every contingency. Management cannot anticipate an ambulance crash that renders it useless for calls. Managers cannot foresee a sudden and dramatic jump in call volume due to a pandemic. Although operational contingency plans should be available to ensure that needed services are provided to the community during extraordinary circumstances, it is not realistic to expect an EMS manager to concern himself with financial problems that surface if a disaster strikes. Separate plans are developed and continually updated for these unlikely circumstances.

For each condition, an EMS manager identifies high and low revenue forecasts to determine a "profit" forecast. Profit in this context is not about making money, but rather about revenue over expenses. These forecasts require developing of a **pro forma statement** that reflects the conditions upon which the forecasts are based. For example, the high forecast may require considerable expansion of services (e.g., increase staffing, purchase additional vehicles). If the required additional labor is complex (i.e., training expenses will increase), revenue will need to reflect this level of growth. Profit may equal or even be less than anticipated for the basic revenue forecast. Similarly, special considerations may apply to a lower revenue forecast. It is prudent to anticipate the impact of changes of revenue on profitability in order to develop plans for what could happen, either positive or negative. In other words, preparation trumps reaction.

A useful display of the impact of changing revenue is presented in Figure 5.3. Managers can readily assess the implication of increased revenue or decreases in revenue on cash flow by preparing different forecasts.

Figure 5.3 illustrates a budget forecast (yellow line) showing an increase in revenue over a set period of time. The management team, in this case, believes the budgeted forecast will be positive with some periods showing less of an increase. During periods of decreased revenue, management may decide against spending a large amount of cash for a new vehicle or possibly paying for a long-term expense. The high forecast (brown line) shows a steady increase also, but the management

team may anticipate extra revenue (e.g., due to a long-term note maturing), a higher call volume (e.g., due to an expected merger), or the organization's routine transport business increasing. The low forecast (blue line) depicts a steady revenue stream. An internal analysis may show staff turnover is high because the next closest service is paying $3 more per hour and people are leaving, which increases the cost of recruitment and training, thus reducing overall revenue.

Figure 5.4 represents another view of a financial analysis where the management team uses the baseline as an indicator of budgeted revenue. The high forecast (brown line) is the deviation from expected on the positive side, and the low forecast (brown line) is the deviation from revenue on the low side. This type of analysis is good when tracking cash flow. Both graphs analyze what management anticipates the future is going to look like. It is only after time that management can see how well they did in their forecasting.

Another method of forecasting is to develop a system to view financial information over time. For example, a 5-year forecast with all revenues and expenditures identified, appropriate taxes computed, adjustments made for depreciation, deductions for capital expenditures, and repayment of loans can help

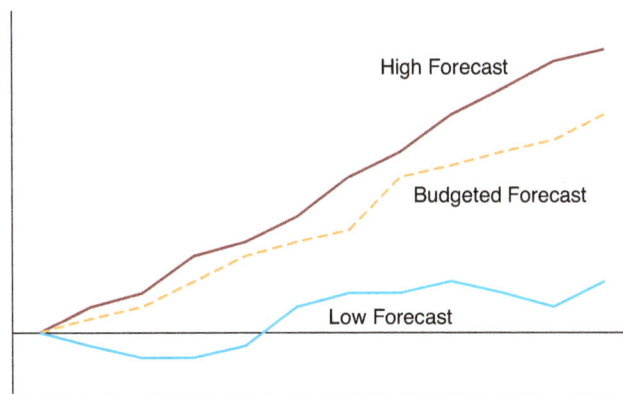

High Forecast

Budgeted Forecast

Low Forecast

FIGURE 5.3 ■ Example of multiple budget forecasts.

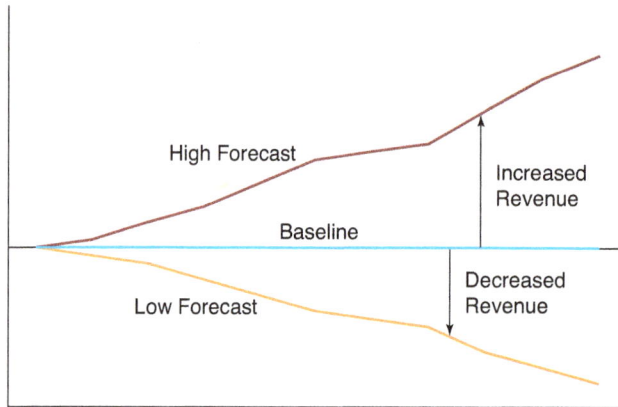

FIGURE 5.4 ■ Baseline comparisons of potential forecasts.

managers identify strengths and weakness in not only their ability to predict operations, but also in how successful they are with managing the operations and reaching established goals. This evaluation is significant information for management when planning for securing funds for future growth.

By entering and tracking financial information in a spreadsheet program, the manager can easily run reports and conduct other types of financial analysis (e.g., internal rate of return where positive and negative cash flows are financed, or regression analysis). Managers who conduct analyses are able to address a significant concern: the early identification of excess funds and shortages that are likely to occur if business conditions change. Excess funds provide revenue or cash flow potential if invested properly to expand services or pay down debt. Shortages require action on minimizing potential negative consequences to operations.

Even more important is the early identification of fund shortages. As long as the financial condition of the organization is healthy and shortages are anticipated, shortages are not necessarily a cause for concern. By estimating cash flow when funds are lower

than anticipated, EMS managers can develop contingency plans for dealing with decreases in revenue. By looking at the organization's financial operations over time, the EMS manager can evaluate the direction the organization is heading—positive or negative.

Table 5.1 shows an example of Main Street EMS's expenses for a given year. The reader can see how entering the data in a spreadsheet allows the manager to track expenses related to individual categories over an accounting period. The manager is further able to make adjustments based on any trends identified. It is relatively easy to break down the actual tracking into manageable concepts. The manager can see what each transported patient costs the organization by looking at the last line in the spreadsheet. By comparing the revenue per patient, the EMS manager can quickly and easily see how successful the organization is over time.

The information presented in Table 5.1 is very complex, and thus it is difficult to determine trends from it. By looking at a spreadsheet, the manager can see the detail that goes into managing financial operations. However, if the manager wants to see how his organization is performing over time, a graph is more

TABLE 5.1 ■ Overview of EMS Financial Activity

Main Street EMS Year 20xx-20xx Expenses	July	August	September	October	November	December	January	February	March	April	May	June
SALARIES												
PTB Accrual	-1036	-338	-2525	3578	-2098	4090	-1365	2106	13153	152	5775	2122
Allied Health								927	0			
Ancillary	2537	2710	2652	2759	2858	3029	2868					
Clerical/Administrative	4193	4593	4193	4393	4661	4325	4776	4153	4569	4361	4776	4361
Bonus												
Total Salaries	5694	6965	4320	10730	5421	11444	6279	7186	17722	4513	10551	95954
BENEFIT EXPENSE												
Non-Physician Payroll Taxes	2433	2768	2386	2715	2869	3234	2966	2488	2708	2653	2760	2770
SUTA	44	49	18	76	55	1247	1394	769	611	378	226	175
Worker's Compensation												
Employee Hospitalization	6832	6879	6359	5446	6328	6346	5784	6423	6701	6409	6409	6742
CME Benefits - Non-Physician												
Total Employer Paid Benefits	9309	9696	8763	8237	9252	10827	10144	9680	10020	9440	9395	20922
Total Employee Expense	15003	16661	13083	18967	14673	22271	16423	16866	27742	13953	19946	116876
MONTHLY EXPENSE												
Utilities	857	941	901	744	729	760	1052	1003	1226	975	768	791
Telephone	1157	939	952	1152	921	944	1037	936	933	1146	933	978
Communication												
Answering Service	361	276	276	877	-520	520	891		106	468	269	277
Cellular	134	50	66	107	100	128	141	87		11	73	91
License and Inspection		285										
Water & Sewer	497			547	221		590		82	294		383
Real Estate Taxes	931	931	931	931	931	931	931	931	931	931	1213	912
Rental Building	9458	9173	7410	7410	7410	7410	7410	7410	7410	7410	7410	7410
Total Monthly Expense	13395	12595	10536	11768	9792	10693	12052	10367	10688	11235	10666	10842
GROUNDS AND MAINTENANCE												
Building Repairs	194	315	75	1134	3673	561	169	250	3654	980	3168	1366
Capital/Minor/Parts/Repairs										99	469	
Janitorial	800	1000	1000	800	800	1000	800	800	1000	800	800	800
HVAC	285						289	1070				359
Medical Equipment Repair		391										
Cleaning/Housekeeping	166	53	304	269	123	153	100	160	231	147	109	53
Total Grounds & Maintenance Expense	1445	1759	1379	2203	4596	1714	1358	2280	4885	2026	4546	2578
PURCHASED SERVICES												
Services	3003	2818	2660	2897	3553	2258	2460	2227	2738	2456	2005	2427
Agency						1604	1829	2515	1365	2155	3021	1758
Equipment Maintenance contract		304		758			304			304		
Purchased Printing	-34	212		92			210		6	123		79

(Continued)

TABLE 5.1 ■ Overview of EMS Financial Activity (Continued)

Hazardous Waste removal	20	20	20	20	93	20	22	99	44	22	22	22
Laundry & linen	212	366	219	443	295	308	384	154	306	219	318	296
Total Purchased Services	3201	3720	2899	4210	3941	4190	5209	4995	4459	5279	5366	4582
SUPPLIES												
Medical Surgical	962	655	882	1451	1028	710	714	842	843	789	910	677
Total Supplies	962	655	882	1451	1028	710	714	842	843	789	910	677
GENERAL OPERATING												
Office Supplies	334	388	1048	950	636	258	927	616	264	388	747	210
Forms	320	−46	256	322	722	226	83	92	335	847	315	196
Postage	300	4	300	904	7	22	7		3		87	328
Journals & Periodicals	166											
Reference Books	304											
Literature												
Membership Dues - professional												
Membership Dues - licenses	420				551	1560	720	1400	2201	−550		551
Meetings & Travel - other	126	203	199	141	231	341	231	327	84	259	729	271
Minor Equipment					485		111		183	137		
Recruiting					111					235		
Rental & Leased Equipment			336	124	−102	144	192		336			
Development - support				102		211	200					
Meals & Entertainment						73					33	200
Other	60		60								15	
collections												
Total General Operating Expense	1970	549	2199	2543	2641	2835	2471	2435	3406	1316	1926	1756
ADMINISTRATION												
Banking	268	239	277	232	293	291	240	320	290	379	253	343
General	239											
Professional Liability	2820	2820	2820	2820	2820	2820	2820	2820	2820	2330	2330	2330
Administrative	4510	5145	4288	5876	5468	4785	5315	4631	5331	6139	5219	5444
PA sales tax												
Total Administrative	7598	8204	7385	8928	8581	7896	8375	7771	8441	8848	7802	8117
Total Marketing	64	744	64	64	64	335	174	−58	57	114	392	57
Total Bad Debt	6906	−2149	2196	264	3164	−937	3560	−532	−1027	4747	1797	−1090
DEPRECIATION												
Major Moveable	343	343	343	343	343	343	307	323	323	323	323	323
Leasehold Improvement	100	100	100	100	100	100	100	100	100	100	100	100
Total Depreciation/Amortization	443	443	443	443	443	443	407	423	423	423	423	423
Total Operating Expense	150875	154880	138539	160995	154908	162840	161061	142922	168675	155543	165177	155053
Number of patients transported	1588	1745	1505	1749	1754	1611	1887	1705	1956	1814	1780	1760
Expense/Patient	$95.01	$88.76	$92.05	$92.05	$88.32	$101.08	$85.35	$83.83	$86.23	$85.75	$92.80	$88.10

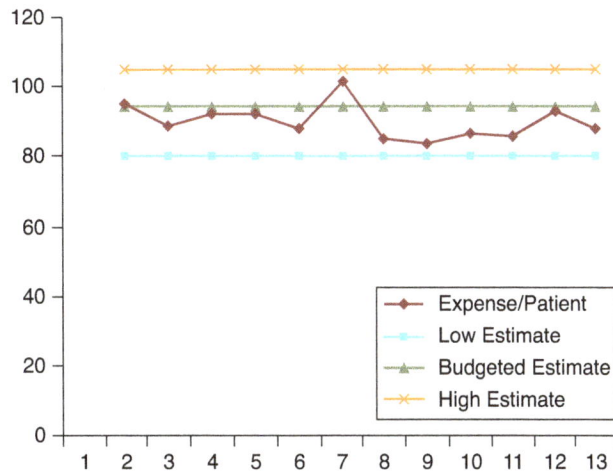

FIGURE 5.5 ■ Overview of EMS finance simplified.

informative. Figure 5.5 illustrates the same information over the same period of time in graph form.

By looking at the Expense/Patient category in Figure 5.5, we can see that the organization chose a moderately conservative expense/patient value (green line) and that the actual figure (brown line) falls consistently under budget, except for one month. This is a good example of how much easier it is to look at information in chart form and find what is pertinent than it is to do so in spreadsheet form.

The manager can also design spreadsheets and graphs to track revenue. Ultimately, the revenue and expense charts can be combined to paint a financial picture of the organization's health.

■ BREAKEVEN ANALYSIS

Breakeven analysis is a technique applied in a wide range of management problems. It is predicated on the observation that some costs vary in direct proportion to output while other costs remain fixed regardless of the level of output. Examples of **variable costs** are direct

labor and direct material expense. Examples of fixed costs are rent or building loans, executive salaries, utilities, and insurances.

The concept of variable costs is identical to that of marginal costs in economic theory. In other words, they are the costs required to produce one additional unit of output. Breakeven analysis assumes that this cost remains unchanged over a wide range of outputs. A similar assumption is implied in the definition of fixed costs. This technical description can be applied to EMS by describing the "normal" or daily functions.

When a group of people meet and decide to form an EMS organization, the only costs for this first meeting are for coffee and donuts. One person may agree to allow the not-yet-purchased ambulance to respond out of a warehouse he owns. Still, no costs are sustained by the organization. When the group purchases its first ambulance, it will begin to incur variable and fixed costs. During the incorporation process, the variable costs will be the legal work (unless the work is done pro bono—which is a good reason to have a lawyer on the board of directors). When this group purchases the ambulance, it could incur

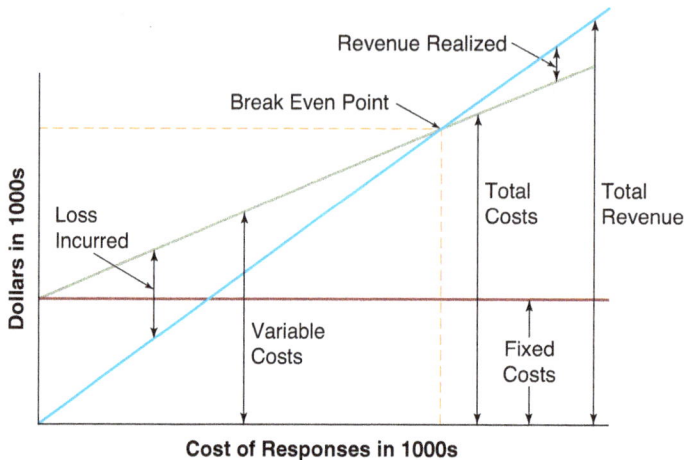

FIGURE 5.6 ■ Example of breakeven analysis.

fixed costs: money that must be repaid over time at specific defined periods. Since the cost must be paid, the ambulance must run a certain number of calls in order to generate revenue that will go to pay for the ambulance. The payback (loan) cost is fixed, yet the more calls that are billed, the more the cash that is available, until this new organization is running so many calls it has to buy another ambulance.

As the organization grows, management may learn that the Good Samaritan who allowed them to use the warehouse is no longer able to provide them a home base. They may also begin running so many calls that staff needs to be paid. Fixed and variable costs will increase and decrease as the business grows. The point here is that managers now need to know when they have enough cash to pay the bills. For every dollar used for an expense, a dollar must be generated in revenue.

Most EMS organizations are past this point; however, the concept applies to mature organizations as well. Managers should know what cash is needed to pay all costs associated with running the organization under various operational scenarios.

A breakeven model can be readily adapted to the problems of cash management. Certain expenses vary little with the volume of responses to calls. Rent, electricity, executive salaries, and insurance are examples. Other expenses such as direct labor and direct materials vary directly with the number of calls run.

Let's look at this graphically in Figure 5.6. You can see that a certain amount of revenue (blue line) is necessary for operations. As the blue line goes from zero (bottom left) upward, it passes through the horizontal fixed costs line. The fixed costs, as discussed, are stable and constant over time. As the revenue increases, a point is reached where the line crosses the cost of response or expenses (green line). Notice how the expense line always starts above zero. (Why does this occur?) When the two lines cross we have the breakeven analysis point for each dollar received that is spent to run the organization. Moving upward, the lines diverge and more revenue is generated than expenses incurred.

Let's look at this concept algebraically:

P = revenue realized per unit

V = variable cost per unit

F = fixed cost

N = number of patients transported

By definition the breakeven analysis is:

$$\text{Total Revenue} = \text{Total Cost}$$

but we see that

$$\text{Total Revenue} = P \times N$$

and

$$\text{Total Cost} = V \times N + F$$

Therefore, at breakeven

$$PN = VN + F$$

Rearranging the letters, we get

$$(N(P - V) = F)$$

or

$$N = F/(P - V)$$

where $P - V$ is the contribution margin.

So, if the EMS organization has the following dollar values we can determine the number of patient transports that are needed to break even.

$P = \$3.00$

$V = \$1.75$

$F = \$50,000$

$N = \$50,000/(\$3 - \$1.75)$

$N = 40,000$ paying patient transports are needed to breakeven

Side Bar
The breakeven point will go up if the amount of fixed expenses goes up or if the gross margin goes down.

Breakeven is good for two types of financial analysis. First, when looking at a new service, managers should determine how much money is needed to sustain the perspective service. If the EMS organization decides to build a new station, determining the breakeven point assists the board of directors in evaluating the potential success of the decision. The breakeven point indicates if the EMS organization is able to make enough money to cover expenses. This financial analysis is used to determine if a project can proceed as conceptualized. The second use for breakeven analysis is for incremental management decisions. There are two sublevels of analysis. The first sublevel is used to determine if the gross margin is so small that proceeding with the project will require too many resources. In this situation, other areas of the organization are affected to the point that no money is made. The second sublevel is used in making decisions about buying new equipment. The breakeven analysis will show if the purchase affects the fixed cost base so much that there is no way the EMS organization can break even.

Do not overuse breakeven analysis. If management becomes so granular that it looks at each service line for a breakeven point and subsequently makes a decision to stop the service, it could be removing needed revenue. Fixed costs remain the same, but more of the costs to cover them is spread over less revenue streams. There is no need to run the breakeven analysis frequently because most fixed expenses do not fluctuate widely unless there are major decisions affecting the financial position of the EMS organization.

CASH MANAGEMENT

In a nonprofit EMS organization, measurement of sound cash management occurs with an increase in the number or quality of services provided by the organization. An organization should develop policies that determine levels of available cash. Too much cash should not be invested, and too little will not provide the needed cushion to weather any unexpected situations that occur. Excess cash not invested is considered lost opportunity cost. **Opportunity cost** is defined as the return that may be realized by the next best alternative. An EMS organization that holds cash in a normal checking or savings account as a result of conservative policies is an example of lost opportunity costing the organization potential cash. Investing in short-term accounts that pay higher interest rates provides the next best alternative. In other words, by investing excess cash in high interest accounts, the organization is letting the money work for the organization. The money is not saved just to spend. Money is saved to improve medical services at a future time.

CAPITAL ACQUISITION

It is useful to compare the stages of organizational growth to the biological life cycle and then to trace the impact of the organization's growth phases on the need for capital, anticipated financing strategies, and managerial practices. To do this, we must differentiate between infancy, adolescence, and maturity. Anything after the maturity cycle evolves into issues of ongoing survival. This analogy is a simple way to describe the growth, development, and potential needs of an organization during these cycles (Figure 5.7).

The life cycle of an organization, like a biological organism, usually follows an S-shaped curve. The curve identifies the stages of growth for the organization. These cycles evolve, are measured, and vary from organization to organization. Some attributes of growth include the addition of physical assets, hiring personnel, increase in call volume, or enlarging response area. All of these can occur simultaneously as an organization moves through the growth stage.

The capital needs of an organization are met in different ways during each cycle. In EMS organizations, these can include public donations, grants, public money in the form of local government subsidies, taxes paid by the citizens, gifts and bequeaths, and investment income. The sources of funding may remain the same over the entire life cycle. The ability to tap any one of these areas at any given time may vary according to the stages and needs of the organization. In most organizations, the early phase of growth requires considerable funding to acquire equipment or facilities. In later phases, heavy demands for funding will cover the costs of personnel.

Many studies show that business risk facing new organizations is extraordinarily high. During the infancy stage, a strong emotional attachment to a nonprofit EMS organization by highly motivated individuals can attract capital through community involvement. Obtaining financing from people who have faith in the principles and objectives of the project is not easy. Usually such faith is only encountered by believers who are willing to provide funding or by friends and relatives of the people involved who may provide initial capital. This is not true of municipally based organizations since the revenue needed to open or expand an EMS organization adds to the tax base as a normal course of business.

The challenge of management in the infancy stage is attracting enough capital to meet the needs of the growing organization, including the purchase of equipment and payroll expenses for staffing the units. If the ven-

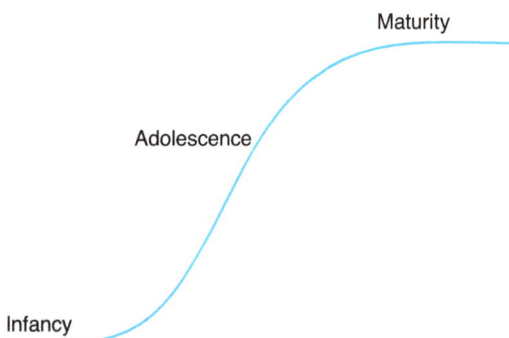

FIGURE 5.7 ■ Life cycle of an organization.

ture survives—and in most cases in EMS the organization will survive because the community identified the need for the service—the adolescent stage will begin. During this stage, accounts receivable will grow, cash balances will be maintained, and new equipment will be purchased. It is a common misconception that as a business grows the pressure for managing finances eases. The contrary is true: The more successful a business, the more pressing the need is for capital and experienced people to manage the activities. During infancy, acquiring capital may be easier due to the developing history with financial institutions, awareness of the organization's existence by the public, and other developing relationships. The adolescence phase of the organization, like that of a human, is hectic and difficult. With proper guidance and skillful management, the difficulties can be overcome.

Although the capital needs of the organization continue to grow through the maturity phase, a profound change takes place. Internal sources of funding begin to supply a large portion of the capital needs. Investments in the facilities and the paying down of loans free needed cash for other services. What occurs in the maturity phase can be simply described as routine. During infancy and adolescence, management activities are creative and innovative. In maturity, the activities become standardized and bureaucratic. This should not be interpreted as implying that the financial problems of mature organizations are necessarily simple and do not require good financial management. On the contrary, the stakes in mature organizations are sufficiently high, so that even very small improvements in operations will show measurable and meaningful results. What has changed? When systems are well thought out and consistent, the crisis management mode during the younger stages is reduced. In young organizations, managers in survival mode focus on short-term problems. Adoption of solutions is not necessarily

sufficient for long-term survival. As the organization moves through the life cycle, managers focus on issues impacting the future as opposed to the present.

Tying this into the preceding discussion, establishing analysis tools provides managers with information needed to allocate financial resources. Without tracking financial inputs and outputs, the EMS manager is not as successful in determining if decisions are meeting the goals of the organization effectively. Knowing where the organization stands financially prepares the manager to move through the stages of growth while being prepared to weather unforeseen circumstances. You must understand that many managers are promoted into their position through a series of steps taking them from street provider to supervisor then to the manager. This occurs without the benefit of formal business or finance training, and subsequently decisions are often made without analysis. Relying on intuition or luck may seem to be the easiest form of running an EMS organization, but it is certainly not the most effective.

WORKING CAPITAL

Working capital is a term almost synonymous with current assets and reflects the short-term disposition of the organization's cash. As business activity increases, the working capital needs of the organization increase. This is caused by increased financing requirements for accounts receivable, increased levels of inventory needed to sustain operations, and higher cash balances required to smooth over the accelerated pace of activities. Managers should monitor the rate of increase. The difference between current assets and current liabilities is referred to as *net working capital*. As the pace of business and revenue increases, sources of funding must be identified to provide necessary additional capital to meet the organization's needs.

To ensure early identification of the need for additional funds, management must monitor the organization's cash position at all times. When performing most financial transactions, the acquisition of cash demands a certain amount of lead time. By identifying deficiencies early (provided the organization is healthy), the appropriate funds can readily be tapped. The same potential sources of capital (e.g., banks) are likely to deny poorly run organizations additional funds under conditions of severe fund shortages. When an organization's cash position becomes weak, it indicates that careless planning and poor management practices are in effect.

Conversely, good financial management implies that all funds available to the organization are effectively used. The accumulation of cash balances in excess of those ordinarily required for the short-term needs of expansion deprive the organization of income that otherwise could be earned in investment vehicles. Management must strive to estimate minimum cash requirements and devise alternative methods for borrowing or investing funds so that the cash balances are neither above nor below the needs of the organization.

Let's take a look at an example. A small EMS organization grows to the point of running two or three emergency calls per day with a few daily transports. Management employs a part-time secretary to answer the phone and schedule transports. The board of directors is made up primarily of older running and non-running members of the organization with one or two local business owners. The organization matures from an all-volunteer unit to a mixed unit of partially paid and partially volunteer. The organization's response area is 20 square miles and is boarded on all sides with other similar ambulance organizations. The total population served is just under 18,000 people.

The operations chief, who also functions as an occasional crew member, approaches the board of directors and presents the case that he needs to have a "company vehicle" so he can be "available to the crew." As the board is primarily running or previously running members, they "feel" what he is saying and agree to buy a $45,000 SUV. They have the vehicle customized and painted with "SUPERVISOR" on the back, and they equip it with radios, lights, and all the same equipment as the transporting ambulance. The total cost of the vehicle is $58,000. If we study this case, we must ask "Where did the money come from to purchase the vehicle?" If it was from a savings account (reserves), how did the organization save enough disposable cash to spend on a vehicle? Could the money have been invested in other community programs, to pay down debt, to provide training, and so on? The organization still requests money annually from the community and the municipality it serves. Is a "personal" vehicle the best use of community and taxpayer money? If the money was available to purchase this vehicle, why would the organization continue to request money from external customers? If grant money from the state was used to purchase the vehicle, an objective question is "Was this the best use of public funds in a broader sense?" If the only reason for the purchase was to satisfy a perceived personal need, one must question the objectivity of the board, the skill of the manager to allocate funding, and the desire of the organization to achieve long-term goals.

Often these tough questions are not raised because many of these decisions are based on desire—desire to keep up with others, desire to look more prestigious, or desire for personal status. In reality, an EMS manager who is in tune with the external environment, the financial position of the organization, and the goals of the organization will ask these questions of himself and of the organization. The EMS manager should always look at the goals, match the strategic plans, and analyze the financial position of the organization before expensing capital resources.

CASH BUDGET

When matching the strategic plans of the organization to making larger purchases, the mechanism for determining the availability of cash is called the **cash budget**. Although the cash budget bears a resemblance to the master budget, it is not used to forecast operational income but, rather, to identify the cash balances that will probably exist in the future. The cash budget traces the flow of funds through the organization, identifying likely sources prior to their occurrence. By discerning levels of cash balances ahead of time, management can plan borrowing or investment strategies appropriately for the needs of the organization. The cash budget becomes the instrument that permits management to plan rather than merely react to emerging situations.

Managers often speak of the need to plan and control cash and operational activities, better. The documents that support better control are sporadically updated and do not reflect ongoing operational changes or developments. If the cash budget serves as a tool to gauge the organization's position, it cannot be handled only "whenever there is time." It must be updated continually and revised as additional information becomes available. At the very least, at the end of a preestablished period an improved forecast should be prepared that will extend over the full span of the cash budget cycle. These procedures will ensure that the cash budget remains an updated and relevant document. Since the cash budget's implications affect the current status of the organization, management cannot rely on forecasts and projections that have become outdated.

Keeping the cash budget current allow managers to identify issues of concern and to develop and execute the appropriate actions to correct negative changes in the organization's finances. Reacting to unanticipated situations is costly. The cash budget is a tool geared to the attainment of organizational goals with a high degree of objectivity.

The cash budget presumes that receipts and payments occur simultaneously each month. In reality, this is generally not the case. It is conceivable that some organizations' payments are due at the beginning of the month, whereas receipts may only materialize toward the end of the month. This could create severe cash deficiencies during the month, even if the budget indicated excess funds.

Three possible suggestions for resolving this issue are presented. First, managers could develop a cash budget on a weekly or even daily basis. This may seem excessive to people who are responsible for an organization that responds to 20 calls per month. However, for those organizations responding to 20 calls in a 12-hour period, developing a daily or weekly cash budget may be necessary. Each manager must evaluate what works for him—as the person who is responsible for the financial, as well as the operational, success of the organization, preparation for any unforeseen situations is essential. A current cash budget frequently will make it possible to pinpoint issues for continued management attention. The second possibility is to move income (receipts) one period out while leaving expenses (disbursements) as originally planned. This will prevent the worst case: all disbursements at the beginning of the period and all receipts toward the end. The third option is to adjust the desired cash balance upward to provide additional slack for slippage in cash receipts.

The cash budget provides essential information to management. Although, over the long run the flow of cash and total revenue can be equal, considerable divergences may occur in the short run. Managers may look at the income statement and see positive results, but it is not a suitable indicator of the short-term financial health of the organization. The cash flow statement is not a sufficient measure of financial health either. Excess cash can readily be attained by disposing of corporate assets—say, by selling two ambulances. Obviously it would appear that the organization is flush with cash; however, this recording of the additional money does not show how financially healthy the organization is, nor does the influx improve business conditions. Management must chart a financial course and take into account all pertinent information, rather than focus exclusively on one indicator. Ignoring cash flow needs in the short run can severely affect the organization in spite of a highly encouraging outlook laid out in a budget.

Earnings are generated through balanced investments, fixed assets, and highly motivated personnel. To acquire any of these requires the disbursement of cash. The larger the cash balances, the greater the opportunity to seek investments that will return more to the organization. For example, the EMS manager determines that the organization has excess cash available. Staff expresses the desires to attend an EMS conference. The excess money could be set aside, in an educational account, and the organization could pay the cost to attend the conference. For these reasons, an astute manager insists on tracing cash flow through an organization.

A simplified example of a cash flow report illustrates how the EMS manager can track the actual cash flow through the organization (Figure 5.8).

Managers should realize that the cash budget provides the means for determining

Cash Flows from EMS Operating Activities	
Case received from customers	$175,000
Cash paid to suppliers	120,000
Cash paid for operating expenses	27,630
Total Cash Flows from EMS Operating Activities	27,370
Cash Flows from Investing Activities	
Proceeds from sale of Ambulance Equipment	43,000
Net Cash Flows for the Period	70,370
Add: Beginning Cash Balance	21,000
Ending Cash Balance	$ 91,370

FIGURE 5.8 ■ Example of cash flow report.

both surpluses and deficiencies. By recognizing when cash shortages occur, the manager can investigate the need for fundraising, including whether borrowing is necessary, what is involved in making a public appeal, or what talking with governmental bodies might achieve. Seeing that cash is readily available, the manager can "give back" by investing in people, programs, or fixed assets in order to grow the organization. As pointed out earlier, managers can also use excess cash to enhance their individual needs (e.g., purchasing an organizational vehicle for personal use). The cash budget allows the manager to plan for investing in people or acquiring additional funds through short-term investments.

Best Practice

First Aid and Safety Patrol in Lebanon, Pennsylvania, uses a concept called sweep checking. As many EMS organizations face cash flow issues, FASP maintains a line of credit. Although the line of credit is established to assist with cash flow challenges, it still must be paid down. With a sweep checking account, money in the checking account can "sweep" nightly to pay down the line of credit. For example, if $30,000 is drawn from the line of credit today to meet payroll and tomorrow the organization receives a deposit of $20,000, the sweep will engage and pay down $20,000 on the line of credit. In addition, if the organization has paid bills and has $10,000 of uncashed checks, that $10,000 is available to pay down the line of credit until the check is cashed. This creates an environment of "holding onto cash for the organization's benefit" for periods of time.

IDLE CASH

Idle cash is money that sits in a noninterest-bearing account, earning no income. Some idle cash is justifiable. If the management team does not properly plan the cash flow of the organization, idle cash may be sufficient to pay bills until formal plans can be enacted. However, poor planning affects spare cash if an unplanned expense suddenly hits the organization. An example of this occurs when an EMS organization experiences a delay in payments for services and receives an unexpected bill. Tracking when idle cash is used to pay for bills will better assist managers in gaining experience as to the frequency of such occurrences so they learn to plan accordingly.

Several options are available to managers when looking to reduce the cost of holding excess cash balances. Remember, every organization is going to incur revenues and expenses. If revenues exceed expenses by a large margin and cash balances are excessive, managers can and should evaluate the best use of the excess cash. The first option is to review long-term projects that, through previous analysis, appeared desirable but could not be financed for lack of long-term funds, though they might now be considered.

Second, short- or long-term debt might be prepaid, helping to reduce the overall interest costs. Taking advantage of trade discounts is also an advantageous method of reducing excessive cash balances. Most growing organizations are not in the position to have excessive cash balances. If they are, management must look at their reason for holding the excess. Are the decisions to provide additional services too conservative? Are funds held just in case something bad happens? There are many reasons for holding excess cash; however, many reasons are neither valid nor good management.

On an annual basis, organizations continue to appeal to local government and community support when it is truly not needed.

EMS managers think, "Make as much money as possible." The arguments for this are "We never know when we will need it," "Make it when you can," "They can take it away," or "They will not give us as much next year if we do not use it this year." The justifications are endless, and managers' philosophical beliefs are understandable, but the "business concept" of nongovernmental EMS organizations should be to work toward becoming self-sustainable and to not rely on outside routine or annual requests for money. Somehow it has become a badge of honor for managers to show how successful they are by reporting a very large investment portfolio, excess money in the checking and savings accounts, and low long-term debt. Yet the organization pleads with the public or the municipal government for "much needed" assistance and funding every year. Not every organization has this luxury, and many do rely on external sources to sustain the business year after year. If this is the case, managers should look at their operations relative to finance and determine whether the current structure allows for growth.

Side Bar

Every business can develop into a self-sustaining organization with the right planning and development.

Unfortunately, in many EMS organizations the key decision makers appeal to outsiders for help in generating operating capital. Tradition guides this in many cases, yet once the money is deposited in the organization's accounts, spent money does not reflect the amount given. The sad part of this system is that many organizations are not transparent and resist any attempt by outsiders to review their accounts. Huge amounts of money build up, and yet the organization seeks funds from others every year. Good financial management will anticipate needs of the organization in the short and long term and will adjust the need for other's assistance accordingly.

When management's primary goal is to build a large reserve, a cash balance, or an investment balance without using the money to develop services, this stretches the concept of public good, or **stewardship** as pointed out earlier. Conversely, if management does not plan sufficiently, cash deficiencies may exist and the organization will have to live from one budget period to the next. In such cases, departments within the organization will be pressured to reduce their activities. Reducing inventories to save costs, or reducing expenses for fixed assets, may have many undesirable effects. First, it may preclude the organization from replacing old equipment with newer, safer equipment. Second, it might restrict the organization from meeting the public's demand for services.

EMS organizations may also generate revenue by pressuring self-pay patients or patients with co-payments to settle their accounts. This has the effect of ruining good public relations with the very people the organization is serving. Neither this nor any of the preceding solutions should be pursued beyond the normal course of operations.

On the payment side of cash deficiencies is the possibility of delaying payment until the last possible moment. This can be costly in two ways. First, it can impair the credit rating of the organization by raising the cost of future funding. Second, delaying payment can lead to the loss of discounts that otherwise would be available. Although a strategy for accelerating receipts and delaying payments may appear favorable in principle, it should only be pursued on a limited basis.

LONG-TERM DEBT FINANCING

Beyond the daily problems of cash management, managers must be concerned with the nature of financing the long-term asset requirements of the organization. Successful

EMS organizations require continuous review of the services provided. Some managers look at their role as always expanding their coverage area. Expansion does not mean increasing competition or challenging operational territories. EMS's role in the community is to provide needed medical care and services. Growing an EMS organization is about developing partnerships with other entities to provide the necessary care. Long-term debt funding (capitalization) requires managers to change their view regarding the needs of the community to how the organization can best meet those needs, rather than focusing on the goals of individuals within the EMS organization.

Improving existing facilities and buying new equipment to facilitate appropriate responses to the demand for services are necessary for growing EMS organizations. In the early years of an organization, any spending of money constitutes a significant addition to the fixed assets of the organization. In a new organization, the acquisition of a new computer system or another ambulance may appear to be a significant increase in the total level of fixed assets. For example, an EMS organization that has $45,000 in fixed assets purchases a $10,000 computer system. This represents more than a 20% increase in assets. As the organization matures, however, any new fixed asset represents a smaller percentage of total fixed assets on hand at any given time. If the EMS organization grows to $3 million, investing $10,000 in a computer system only represents a .003% increase in assets.

The task of management is to obtain the necessary funds from internal and external sources to meet the needs of short- and long-term growth. As pointed out earlier, the cost of short-term funds is usually lower than for long-term funds. The temptation to finance all of the organization's activities with short-term capital should be resisted. This usually does not happen due to strategy but, rather, because managers are inexperienced in planning and cash management.

FINANCING RISK

Financial management allocates existing resources with the expectation of reaping benefits in the future. Returns may not materialize as expected, thus financial investment is risky. The term of any deviation from anticipated results is uncertainty or risk. In other words, spending the organization's financial resources brings a certain amount of risk, and generally a loss of some or all of the investment. Any deviation from the expected outcome will be either positive or negative.

When the deviation is positive, management's decision is good, and the decision was not risky. If the loss were significant, the manager's decision was too risky. Some causes of deviations can include reduced call volume due to changes in the external environment or unexpected loss of a vehicle due to mechanical failure. These are examples that may not be within the direct control of the organization, yet a loss occurs. Decisions specifically made by management affecting long-term capital expenditures, such as buying new equipment or constructing a modern building, can raise the risk exposure if the investment does not materialize as expected. Whether the investment is profitable or not, the organization must be prepared, financially, to pay for the potential loss or essentially be prepared to pay for the risk of making the decision. Money should be set aside to absorb the loss. This is called the **cost of risk**.

Reflect back on the example of the new long-term-care facility that is going to be built. The facility will have mixed uses: assisted living, apartments for fully functional retirees, and an inpatient health care facility. The man-

ager decides to be proactive and purchases land within a mile of the facility, anticipating a substantial increase in call volume. The manager begins construction on the new building. Suddenly the developer decides to relocate the new facility 5 miles from the original site. The investment in the new EMS station is now a moot endeavor, and the EMS organization is stuck with land that has decreased in value. The decision to sell the land is made. The EMS organization is going to take a loss on the deal, either by selling or holding onto the land for the future. The "loss" is the cost of risk that should have been funded at the start of planning.

Borrowing money or taking it from reserves or investments to pay for the land without consideration for funding the potential loss may force management to pull surplus money from operations, which affects daily activities. Preparing for the potential loss keeps daily operations from being affected. Management should seek to minimize surprise outcomes—in other words, management should minimize risk. If a project is somewhat risky, but the investment could propel the organization into a rapid growth stage, then contingency plans should be developed to protect the organization from the risk.

In planning for expenses, anticipated and unanticipated, financial management confronts the need to assess expected returns in accordance with the risk. Managers should understand that looking at financial implications of a program or expenditure is one part of running an organization successfully. When developing an exciting new project, management must focus on the effect any decision has on the overall position of the organization.

CHAPTER REVIEW

Summary

As pointed out, managers must refrain from making the bottom line be the goal of the organization. However, many managers are evaluated on the bottom line because it is easy to measure. Finances should not lead the organization, but more importantly, the mission of the organization should be supported by finance. Finance is the scorecard to good management, not the ends to a day's work.

WHAT WOULD YOU DO? Reflection

After the review, you determined that the organization is currently financially stable. This does not mean the organization has large amounts of disposable income, but it does reflect that the organization is able to pay for current liabilities and to develop ongoing projects. As a new member of the leadership team, a more in-depth review of the finances will buy you some time relative to the concerns raised by the crew members. Since the annual fund drive is approaching, determining how that campaign was conducted in the past may shed some light on the current plans and what resources are needed to move forward. If a committee organized past fund-raising activities, asking for members' assistance may provide you with more time to look into the entire financial picture of the organization.

Looking back through the records (minutes of meetings), signed contracts, or other agreements, you gain some insight into the decision-making process for the purchase of the vehicle. If you determined that the vehicle is not necessary and that there are no contractual obligations for it, cancelling the order will provide additional capital for other projects. If a contract has been signed and there is no way to void the agreement, then taking delivery may be your only recourse; however, the vehicle could be used for other activities and the organization could still recoup the investment.

Review Questions

1. What are a few key duties of an EMS manager?
2. What are the benefits of forecasting?
3. Why is it important that the EMS manager not only learn about forecasting but actively incorporate forecasting in decisions?
4. Describe the concept of low-end and high-end forecasting.
5. How does or should the board of directors' role affect the decisions made by operations?
6. What are the benefits of analyzing the organization with tools such as SWOT?
7. Describe the value of sensitivity testing and what type of information can be gained.
8. How does determining the breakeven point help determine the business needs of an EMS organization?
9. Describe how cash management, capital acquisition, working capital, cash budget, idle cash, and long-term financing affect the success of an organization?
10. How important for an EMS organization is determining the cost of risk and preparing for this cost?

References

Box, G., and G. Jenkins. (1970). *Time Series Analysis: Forecasting and Control.* San Francisco: Holden-Day.

Box, G., G. Jenkins, and D. Bacon. (1967). "Models for Forecasting Seasonal and Nonseasonal Time Series." In *Spectral Analysis of Time Series*, B. Harris, ed., New York: John Wiley & Sons, Inc.

Cacuci, D. G. (2003). *Sensitivity & Uncertainty Analysis,* vol. 1. Boca Raton, FL: Chapman & Hall.

Campolongo, F., J. Kleijnen, and T. Andres. (2000). *Sensitivity Analysis.* K. Chanand and M. Scott, Eds. Chichester, MA: John Wiley & Sons.

Chambers, J., S. Mullick, and D. Smith. (1971, July–August). "How to Choose the Right Forecasting Technique." *Harvard Business Review* pp. 45–74.

Leuthold, R. M., A. MacCormick, A. Schmitz, and D. Watts. (1970, March). "Forecasting Daily Hog Prices and Quantities: A Study of Alternative Forecasting Techniques."

Journal of the American Statistical Association 65(329), 90–107.

Sullivan, A., and S. Sheffrin. (2003). *Economics: Principles in Action.* Upper Saddle River, NJ: Pearson Prentice Hall.

Spiro, H. (1996). *Finance for the Non-financial Manager.* New York: John Wiley & Sons, Inc.

Weston, F., and E. Brigham. (1990). *Introduction to Management Finance,* 9th ed. Orlando, FL: Dryden Press.

Key Terms

allocation The assignment of assets to expense as well as the assignment of liabilities to revenue over a time frame. It is also apportionment or assignment of income or expense for various purposes.

assets In financial accounting, assets are economic resources. Anything tangible or intangible that is capable of being owned or controlled to produce value and that is held to have positive economic value is considered an asset. Simplistically stated, assets represent ownership of value that can be converted into cash (although cash itself is also considered an asset).

astute Having or showing shrewdness and discernment.

bias A particular tendency or inclination, especially one that prevents unprejudiced consideration of a question; prejudice.

breakeven analysis A calculation of the approximate revenue volume required to just cover costs, below which production would be unprofitable and above which it would be profitable. Breakeven analysis focuses on the relationship between fixed costs, variable costs, and profit.

cash budget An estimation of the cash inflows and outflows. Used to assess if an organization has sufficient cash resources to operate and determine if access cash is accumulating in unproductive accounts.

cost of risk Measurement of the total cost related to the risk management function.

deviation The difference between an observed value and the expected value of a variable or function.

forecasting A planning tool that helps management to cope with the uncertainty of the future. It starts with certain assumptions based on management's experience, knowledge, and judgment. These estimates are projected into the coming months or years using one or more techniques such as the Box-Jenkins model, Delphi method, exponential smoothing, moving averages, regression analysis, and trend projection. A forecast (which indicates what "might" happen) should not be confused with a budget (which shows what "ought" to happen).

investments In finance, investments are purchases of financial products or other items of value with an expectation of favorable future returns. In general terms, investment means the use of money in the hope of making more money. In business, investment is the purchase by a producer of a physical good, such as durable equipment or inventory, in the hope of improving future business.

opportunity cost The return that may be realized by the next best alternative.

outcomes A final product or end result, consequence, or issue.

output The act of production or manufacture.

pro forma statement Hypothetical financial statement showing assets and liabilities, or income and expenses that may be recognized in the future. Pro forma statements also can illustrate projected earnings if a company were to merge with another or sell off part of its operations. Business firms often are asked to submit pro forma statements when making a loan application.

sensitivity testing A series of tests of a strategy to find out how its performance changes with changes in the assumptions made. It is also the systematic investigation of the effects on outcomes of changes in assumptions.

stewardship The conducting, supervising, or managing of something, especially the careful and responsible management of something entrusted to one's care.

sustainability For a social entrepreneurial organization, sustainability is the ability to achieve and sustain an impact for as long as there is a need for its intervention. It can also mean the ongoing process of achieving development or redevelopment that does not undermine its physical or social systems of support.

toleration To refrain from intervening, to allow one to participate or function.

uncertainty In finance, uncertainty usually refers to risk or volatility.

validity Describes how well a particular assessment method actually measures the outcome it is intended to measure.

variable costs Expenses that change in proportion to the activity of a business.

working capital A financial metric that is a measure of current assets of a business that exceeds its liabilities and can be applied to its operation.

Budgeting

Objectives

After reading this chapter, the student should be able to:

6.1 Discuss the concept of financial performance including the elements involved.

6.2 Describe four types of budgets and how they are used for different types of costs.

6.3 Outline the main parts of a master budget, including the sequence in which they are developed.

6.4 Discuss the purposes and benefits of the master budget.

6.5 Discuss the limitations and problems associated with the master budget.

6.6 Briefly describe the assumptions underlying the master budget.

6.7 Discuss the sources of the various information needed for the master budget.

Overview

The purpose of this text is to introduce the concepts of finance to nonfinancial EMS managers. The chapters present valuable information to both new and experienced EMS leaders who may have varying degrees of experience, formal and informal. The goal is to stimulate thinking in order to change the way things are done, to avoid mistakes of the past, and to encourage future growth of EMS as a profession.

Key Terms

amortization	cost behavior	effect
budget	cost center	engineered costs
capital budget	department	master budget
cause	depreciation	working capital
committed costs	discretionary costs	

You were recently hired as a new manager for a small EMS unit. The organization is in a transitional period. It was an all-volunteer unit in a small community when a rapid increase in community growth forced the small organization to become busier. After 18 months of trying to run the unit with volunteers, the board of directors (who is made up of previous running volunteers) decided it was time to hire you as the full-time business manager. Within a few weeks of your hire, you notice that the treasurer purchases items (business and medical) simply on request. There is no operational budget and no cash reserves. As you continue to review all the operational and financial functions, you find there are few, if any, formal processes in place.

Questions

1. What would you do to prepare the organization for developing a budget that matches the strategic plan and future growth?
2. How would you introduce the concept of budgeting to the current BOD and staff?
3. How would you achieve "buy in" to formal business practices and demonstrate the value of budgeting for planning and growth?

■ INTRODUCTION

The purpose of this chapter is to introduce the EMS manager to the concept of the master budget or the organization's financial plan. The discussion will include important concepts and techniques that represent the major financial planning activities for an organization as well as the foundation for evaluating the traditional standard budgeting process with contemporary budgeting processes.

Side Bar

Tom Honan of the Hunter group observed that the budget process often is used as a method to create new positions. During the budget process, strategic issues should remain the focus.

■ BUDGETING

Budgeting involves planning for the revenue-producing and cost-generating activities of an EMS organization. The importance of budgeting is emphasized by an old saying from Winston Churchill: "Failing to plan is like planning to fail." Budgeting is planning for the financial performance of the organization (Martin, 2011). Consider the conceptual view of financial performance presented in Figure 6-1. As illustrated, financial performance depends on receiving revenue and allocating cost. Revenue is generated by operational activities, investments, and donations. In addition to producing revenue, EMS organizations generate three types of costs, including discretionary costs, **engineered costs**, and **committed costs**. Various costs fall into one of these three categories based on where they impact the organization (Martin). Although costs can be defined in a variety of ways, categorizing costs in terms of the **cause** and **effect** relationships

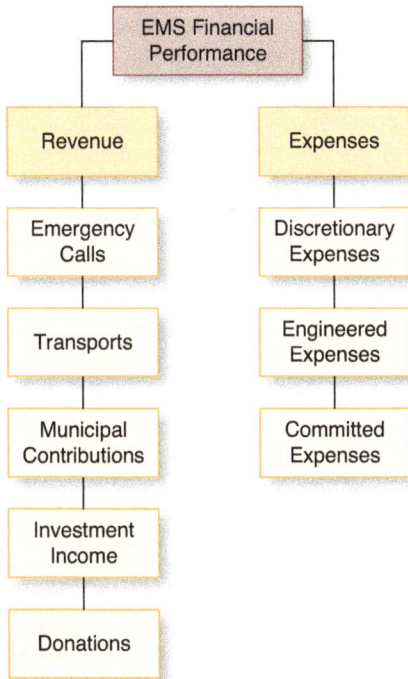

EMS Financial Performance

Revenue — Emergency Calls — Transports — Municipal Contributions — Investment Income — Donations

Expenses — Discretionary Expenses — Engineered Expenses — Committed Expenses

FIGURE 6.1 ■ Conceptual view of financial performance.

is a prerequisite for understanding the different types of budgets introduced in this chapter.

Side Bar

The budget is a control over how the company, as a whole, is operating.

A **budget** is a financial expression of management's plan for the organization. The budget represents the financial intentions of management to all persons interested. It also provides a means for monitoring the implementation of the financial plan.

A budget is a plan that establishes the projected revenues and expenses for certain activities and explains where the required funds are generated. Thus, the operational budget presents a detailed analysis of the required investments in supplies, labor, and capital equipment that is necessary to operate and respond to calls. Each major area or **department** within the EMS organization should develop a sub-budget to track the expenses incurred. The sub-budgets could include training, maintenance, operations, administrative, facilities, and front office or support staff. Generally, budgets should be established on a monthly basis. Managers should develop a budget for each month, and as each month passes the actual figures should be compared to the projected figures. Differences or variances between the projected and actual should be explained and corrected. Projected figures for the rest of the year should be adjusted if the actual values appear to show that the original projections are unrealistic.

■ TRADITIONAL BUDGETING ACTIVITIES

Most organizations develop their budgets by looking at the history of income and expenses. The decision makers arbitrarily establish a percentage increase to expenses and guess what increase or decrease in revenue will occur in the foreseeable future. A paper budget is developed from this activity. Supervisors responsible for specific areas (maintenance, office staff, and training) receive the paper budget. The supervisors may or may not have any say regarding how the numbers are developed for their areas, but they are held responsible for the proposed numbers. Supervisors are responsible for their budgets, and any deviations from the developed budget are reviewed during the supervisor's evaluation and job performance reviews. Each year the process continues with unforeseen fluctuations and unanticipated costs. Simultaneously, EMS decision makers continue to request monies from local governments, expect increased donations from residents and businesses, and hold fund-raisers. Yet very little planning occurs to improve the process of accounting for financial assets. It is this traditional process that continues to find EMS organizations struggling from year to year while spending community money without oversight. Without a systematic process for determining revenue and watching expenses, many organizations will succeed, but they will not maximize or improve their ability to serve or develop more programs that help the community.

Side Bar

Budgets are complex, single transactions that are unlike other transactions that rely on efficiency. Budgets are completed accurately and correctly, not quickly.

Box 6.1

Budgeting Steps

- Establish a direction for the organization.
- Match the mission, goals, and directives to a specific financial plan.
- Allocate necessary and available resources to the goals and objectives that are deemed a priority.
- Communicate the mission, goals, and objectives to all levels of the organization.
- Ensure that all decision makers are aware of the financial position of the organization and how they impact the financial success by their decisions.
- Incorporate the budget into a feedback loop by creating a series of end-of-month reports that are designed to match the responsibility of each employee.
- Establish a realistic financial picture and hold people accountable.
- Practice the art of developing a budget.
- Simplify the budget as much as possible.
- Maintain consistency in how the budget is prepared, evaluated, and implemented.

- Evaluate individual decisions with a broad view that allows for flexibility in the budget where necessary.
- Communicate the financial position of the company to all parties interested in the success of the organization.

FINANCIAL PLANNING AND CONTROL

Financial planning involves revenue projection, asset allocation, growth and marketing strategies, and forecasting of the financial requirements to fund the activities. In the financial planning process, EMS managers should evaluate the long-term plans and identify potential changes in operations that will consistently improve results.

Financial control addresses the process of implementation, monitoring, receiving feedback, and adjusting the processes to either ensure that plans are followed or adjust existing plans in response to changes in the EMS environment. This process begins with agreeing on organizational goals. After determining the organizational goals, managers outline the budgets for the operational areas of the EMS organization's activities. Once the goals are agreed on, the allocation of money is established. The EMS manager develops the system that monitors activities and provides feedback to ensure that the goals and financial resources are aligned.

The projected levels for every operational area are combined during the planning process. The organization's cash flows are then recorded in the operational budget from this new set of data. If the actual revenues increase or decrease, management will make arrangements offsetting the differences. With increases in revenue, management can decide the best use for additional money. In a situation where revenues are less than expected, the manager should establish a plan to make changes to the overall budget and the sub-budgets and should determine how to make up any shortfalls.

Side Bar

Verify the revenue assumptions in areas that can slow down operational efficiency. For example, if the revenue budget calls for an increase in community training dollars, and no money is allocated for publicity about the training classes, the revenue assumptions are incorrect.

After forecasting for all revenues and expenses, the management team develops the income statement and balance sheet. These statements are compared to the actual financial statements. These comparisons can pinpoint reasons for deviations, correct operating problems, and adjust projections for any remaining budget periods. Through the financial planning and control process, management should seek to avoid cash shortfalls and improve the organization's ability to provide services.

Many EMS organizations exist to provide a service without concern for paying investors or stockholders. At best, EMS managers should desire to break even at the end of the year. In other words, revenues and expenses should be equal. The organization should control expenses and maximize revenues in order to build reserves for future use. To determine if the company is breaking even, the EMS manager or the person responsible for the finances should be familiar with breakeven analysis.

Best Practice

During a recent period, The University of Utah Hospitals and Clinics spent, on average, $15.8 million more each year than was budgeted for—representing a 5.8 percent average budget variance. However, a closer look revealed that $7.7 million of the $15.8 million constituted necessary expenses attributed to unforeseen volume growth after the budgets were initially set. The other $8.1 million can, in general terms, be attributed to a failure to control the budget.

Although it can be argued that the extra money needed to be spent, it is hard to conclude that it was necessary to spend an additional $56.7 million (approximately $8.1 million per year over the seven-year time period). Such an amount represents a huge cash outlay, eaten up in operations rather than strategically deployed in capital investments to further the institution's teaching, research, and patient care missions.

To help UUHC achieve optimal financial performance, Richard Fullmer, UUHC's executive director, hired Gordon Crabtree, former managing director of finance for the Salt Lake 2002 Olympic Organizing Committee, as UUHC's CFO and financial coach. He has focused some of his early effort at UUHC on the operating budgeting process, the backbone of all financially healthy institutions.

Among other things, Crabtree is improving UUHC budgeting results by setting budgets based on a strategic point of view to fund future growth and operations. His approach is to first set the volume or revenue side of the budget and then balance it by driving down the cost side and by providing managers with the following year's budgets based on historical performance to hold costs down. Crabtree manages the budget through educating hospital management about budgeting and finance, holding budget variance meetings with managers, and requesting corrective action plans from managers whose budgets are outside targets.

In just two years, Crabtree and his finance team have already helped UUHC achieve improved financial results.

As most managers are aware, the operating budgeting process comprises two parts—budget setting, in which budgets are established prior to the beginning of each fiscal year, and budget management, in which budgets should be monitored and controlled. If either is not properly executed, year-end financial results can be problematic and expectations can be missed.

Best practice budgeting includes, among other steps, setting accurate budgets, establishing accountability, monitoring variances, and managing expenses. The following is a summary of best practice budgeting principles: *Disciplined Growth: Instilling a Culture of Financial Accountability*, and interviews conducted with various healthcare consulting firm executives, hospital CFOs, and hospital budget managers. The principles are categorized into the budget setting and budget managing processes.

Basing the budget on a strategic plan. The budget is based on a five-year strategic plan to understand its capital needs and gain buy-in and managerial support for budget targets. The strategic plan is integrated into a financial plan that calculates cash, debt, capital, and profitability requirements to fund routine and five-year strategic plans and maintain financial integrity.

Collaborating with internal organizations. The budget is based on the mission, strategy, and financial plan of the entire health system.

Presenting and owning the budget. Once the budget and operating margin target are finalized, the CEO and senior management, as a unified team, own the budget and are accountable for meeting it. *The CFO and the finance department do not own it.* The CEO presents the annual budget and operating target to the entire management team to endorse the budget and establish the expectation of obtaining

it. The CEO should also communicate the methodology and need basis for setting the targets to gain buy-in and support from hospital management.

Establishing a culture of accountability. Senior management must have a firm resolve about reaching the budget targets. Budget meetings should involve a department manager and director who meet with a budget team consisting of the appropriate vice president, the CFO, budget director, and controller to instill senior leadership accountability into the process. Job descriptions for managers and higher positions should contain business and budget management requirements and expectations, against which performance can be measured and reviewed. Senior management should explain to managers that they will be evaluated and held accountable in the year-end review.

Managing expenses. Department managers should primarily focus on expenses rather than on gross revenue. A dollar of savings is a dollar to the bottom line, whereas a dollar of revenue is much less. Net revenue and contribution margin should not be reported on department operating statements because they are estimated and inaccurate, and can lead to poor decision making. Individual department budgets should reflect cost savings opportunities from cost-cutting or revenue enhancement initiatives to hold managers accountable for realizing the savings.

Clark, J. J. (2005). "Improving Hospital Budgeting and Accountability: A Best Practice Approach." *Healthcare Financial Management* 59(7), 78–83. Accessed at www.phase2consulting.com/cmsdocuments/HFM_JonClark%280705%29bestpractice.pdf

WORKING CAPITAL

Working capital is a term almost synonymous with current assets and reflects the short-term disposition of the organization's capital. As EMS activity increases (i.e., call volumes, increased community training, and additional transport contracts), working capital needs

increase. This is caused by increased financing requirements for accounts receivable, increased levels of inventory needed to sustain operations, and higher cash balances required to smooth over the accelerated pace of activities. Managers should monitor the rate of increase to offset current assets and current liabilities. The difference is referred to as net working capital. As the pace of business and revenue increases, additional sources of funds must be identified, in advance, to provide necessary additional capital to meet the organization's needs.

Management must monitor the organization's cash position at all times for the early identification of the need for additional funds. As is the case for most transactions, the acquisition of cash demands a certain amount of lead time. If deficiencies are identified early, and as long as the organization is healthy, the appropriate funds can readily be tapped. The same potential sources of capital (banks or governmental agencies) are likely to deny applications for additional funds under conditions of severe cash shortages. An EMS organization will have difficulty asking for money from the usual sources if the sources are struggling. When an organization's cash position becomes weak, often it indicates that negligent planning and poor management practices are in effect. In looking at the tough economic conditions of 2010 and 2011, many organizations and governmental entities struggled to survive for these very reasons.

Conversely, good financial management implies that all funds available to the organization are effectively dispersed. The accumulation of cash balances, in excess of what is required for short-term needs, deprives the organization of income that otherwise could be earned in investment vehicles. Management must strive to estimate minimum cash requirements and devise alternative methods for borrowing or investing funds so that cash balances maintained are neither above nor below the needs of the organization at any given point.

OPERATIONAL REVENUE

An EMS organization is a niche business. Its primary purpose is to deliver emergency medical care to those requesting help. Businesses survival and growth are dependent on having a steady revenue stream. Whether the organization is a nonprofit, for-profit, municipal-based, or hospital-owned entity, an organization requires capital to pay for staff, equipment, and support services.

Depending on the organizational structure, a number of revenue-generating options are available, including the following:

- Third-party pay
- Self-pay
- Transports
- Community training
- Sale of assets
- Contracts for services
- Investment income
- Donations
  - Membership activities
  - Bequeaths
  - Grants
- Taxes
- Bonds

Managers must be explicit about not only what current revenues contribute to the operations of the organization but also what potential opportunities exist for bringing in additional revenue. Additional revenue should provide continued development toward becoming a self-supported organization. By reducing reliance on annual and ongoing community donations or government subsidies as a means of getting by from budget year to budget year, the EMS organization becomes better prepared to control its destiny. Every revenue-generating option has financial and legal implications. The EMS manager should explore all of the requirements for each method of income.

EXPENSES OR COSTS

Expenses or costs are generated from operational activities. It is essential that EMS managers understand where the organization's expenses originate and how to control the disbursement of cash. Some expenses are routinely anticipated, like electricity, payroll taxes, and insurance. Other expenses are controllable; for example, the EMS manager can reduce inventory expenses by developing an inventory ordering system.

Another often overlooked area of expense control is risk management activities. By identifying areas of potential loss, managers can avoid very costly problems. Potential losses might, but do not necessarily, include a sexual harassment charge, theft of equipment by staff or outsiders, poor delivery of care (as seen in monitoring of intubation attempts/successes), driving infractions, and so on. In all of these examples, the potential for financial loss is great, and the EMS manager should become skilled in developing methods not only to monitor the activity but also to abate the possibility of an adverse outcome.

Expenses are necessary in the operation of any business. When attempting to balance the budget, many EMS managers immediately look at cutting expenses. Cutting known, obvious, and unnecessary expenses is the easiest way to manage the bottom line, but that is not always the best way. By searching for areas of improvement, the EMS manager may preserve the necessary expenses *and* reduce those that save revenue. For example, the easiest method for reducing expenses is to look at the highest percentage of expenses paid out. Employee salaries make up 55 percent to 70 percent of most organizational budgets. Managers should look at all expenses. However, most managers just look at obvious expenses, such as reducing staff. EMS managers will often review what positions are needed or expendable, how much of a raise can be afforded for each

person, or what benefit can be eliminated or reduced. The organization can make necessary changes and see direct effects to the bottom line. It is also important to consider what the cost of making changes is to the organization relative to morale and retention.

Side Bar

The more difficult places to look for expenses are the interpersonal areas, such as retention. The cost of replacing a departing employee at that employee's level in the organization can be as much as 50 percent of the departing person's salary. Let's say you have 50 employees with a turnover rate of 25 percent and an average salary of $28,140 per year. This means you will lose 12.5 employees per year at a cost of $337,680 per year. Compare this number with only giving a 2 percent rather than a 4 percent raise. If you provide a 4 percent raise to all employees, using $28,140 as the average salary, the organization will spend an additional $56,280 per year. If you reduce expenses but still provide some increase and give each employee a 2 percent raise, the cost will be $28,140 per year. However, as noted, the turnover rate is 25 percent, and it will cost the organization $337,680 to replace the employees who leave.

Would it not be a better investment to determine why people are leaving? Are people leaving due to a specific person, salary, schedule, working conditions, or lack of care by management? Managers are responsible for using financial resources in the best possible way, even if it means looking at themselves as the reason for higher expenses.

DISCRETIONARY COSTS

Many activities are viewed as beneficial to an organization, even though the benefits obtained, or their value, cannot be defined precisely. The costs of the resources required to perform EMS activities are **discretionary costs**. This means that management must choose the desired level of activity based on intuition or experience because there is no well-defined cause-and-effect relationship between cost and benefits. Discretionary costs are normally generated by service or support activities. Examples include employee training, advertising, promoting the organization to others, legal advice, and preventive maintenance. The value added by each of these activities is difficult to measure. Value added refers to the benefits obtained by either internal or external customers.

ENGINEERED COSTS

Engineered costs result from activities with reasonably well-defined cause-and-effect relationships between inputs and outputs and costs and benefits. Direct material costs provide a good example: Managers can specify precisely how many parts (inputs) are required to generate a single output. Direct labor, for example, would fall into the engineered cost category as well as indirect resources. Direct labor is used for operations such as running emergency calls, transports, or community CPR training. The actual expense may vary depending on how an employee is paid.

The hourly wage for a street provider could be set higher than an employee who conducts community CPR training. Either way, these costs fall under the heading of engineered costs and are considered direct costs because they show immediate value to the organization. The training officer or maintenance supervisor's salary is considered an indirect cost as its value has an indirect effect on the overall operations. A key difference between discretionary costs and engineered costs is that the value added by the activities associated with engineered costs is relatively easy to measure.

COMMITTED COSTS

Committed costs are associated with establishing and maintaining the readiness to conduct business. For example, the costs associated with the purchase of a new parcel of land, dues paid to a certifying organization, and purchase of equipment create long-term obligations that fall into the committed cost category. These costs are typically fixed and expire to become expenses in the form of **amortization** and **depreciation**.

Managers must be sensitive to changes in costs related to the EMS organization's activities. Both an increase in call volume or successful revenue-generating activities could affect an organization's budget. The way a specific cost reacts to changes in activity levels is called **cost behavior**. Cost behavior requires the EMS manager to learn how costs change as the organization's level of activity changes. Costs, such as labor or materials used, vary when the level of activity increases or decreases. Costs unaffected by changes in the level of activity, such as insurance or mortgage payments, are fixed costs. Understanding cost behavior is very important for management's efforts to plan and control total organizational costs. Budgets and variance reports are more effective when they reflect cost behavior patterns. The manager's understanding of cost behavior is also necessary for calculating a company's breakeven point and for any other cost-volume-profit analysis. Unless the cost behavior—variable or fixed—is known, costs cannot be accurately used for forecasting.

■ FOUR TYPES OF BUDGETS———

Four types of budgets are used for planning and controlling the various types of costs. The EMS manager should become familiar with the various types as they provide not only a historical view of budgeting but also a basis

TABLE 6.1 ■ EMS Cost Defined in Terms of Cause and Effect

Type of Cost	Cause and Effect, or Cost-Benefit Relationship	Cost Behavior	Examples
Discretionary	Relationships are difficult or impossible to define.	Fixed, variable, and mixed in the short run	Cost of administrative and support services such as employee training, advertising, organizational promotion, legal advice, and preventive maintenance
Engineered	Relationships are relatively easy to define.	Variable in the short run	Direct resources used in production activities, such as direct materials and direct labor, and many indirect resources, such as electric power
Committed	Relationships can be estimated, but not defined precisely.	Fixed in the short run.	Cost of establishing and maintaining the readiness to conduct business, such as the costs associated with the building and equipment

for developing a higher degree of comfort when constructing an organizational budget (Table 6.1).

Side Bar

Future budget results typically follow historical results unless a significant change occurs in the organization.

APPROPRIATION BUDGETS

The oldest type of budget is referred to as an appropriation budget. Appropriation budgets place a maximum limit on certain discretionary expenditures. Appropriation budgets can fall into one of the following categories: incremental, priority incremental, line item, and zero based.

Incremental Budget

Incremental budgeting starts out with a budget from a prior period. The manager uses this earlier budget as a basis for calculating the new budget. Managers add to or subtract from the previous totals to develop a budget for the upcoming period. For example, last year the EMS organization ran 22,000 calls and received revenue of $1,600,000. This year, the call volume is expected to increase 10 percent. Therefore, the new budget will be $1,760,000 for the year. Budget preparation using previous budgets or actual performance as a basis with incremental amounts added for the new budget period is straightforward. Any allocation of resources is based upon allocations from the previous period.

Advantages of Incremental Budgeting.
Managers may find budgeting in this manner easy as the budget remains stable and change is gradual. Also, managers can operate their departments on a consistent basis. Within a short amount of time, the budgeting system is relatively simple to learn, operate, and understand. A person does not need a lot of business experience to use this form of budgeting.

As EMS managers become comfortable with incremental budgeting, they realize how flexible it is to use. An EMS manager can easily do it from one month to the next. The manager can see changes very quickly when implementing a new policy or when revenue or expenses change. Depending on how large the EMS organization is, conflicts can occur between departments relative to the amount of financial resources that are allocated. With this method of budgeting, it is easier to keep everyone on the same page and avoid conflicts between departments (Financial Web, n.d.).

Disadvantages of Incremental Budgeting.

With incremental budgeting, there are drawbacks for the EMS manager. This type of budgeting assumes EMS activities will continue in the same way. Since it is assumed that the work will never change, there is no incentive for developing new ideas or even reducing costs.

One of the biggest disadvantages is the "Use it or lose it" mentality. Incremental budgeting encourages spending up to the budget limits to ensure a reasonable allocation in the next period. Employees know that next year's budget is going to be incrementally based on this year's. Therefore, if they do not spend everything that is allocated to them, they may not have enough money to work with next year. This creates an environment where waste is encouraged (Financial Web, n.d.).

Over time, the budget may become outdated and no longer relate to the level of activity or type of work carried out. However, the budget continues to increase at some arbitrary rate without an evaluation of why increases are granted or even what the increase is based on. Managers do not reevaluate the business. The priority for resources may have changed since the budgets were set originally. Incremental budgeting is based on the idea that expenses will run pretty much as they did before. However, in business this is rarely the case. There

are always variables. Lastly, budgetary slack may be built into the budget, which is never reviewed. Managers might have overestimated their requirements in the past in order to obtain a budget that is easier to work with and will allow them to achieve favorable results.

Priority Incremental Budget

Priority incremental budgets also involve an increase, but the difference is that it requires EMS managers to prioritize, or rank discretionary activities in terms of their importance to the organization (Martin, 2011). The idea is for the manager to indicate which activities would be changed if the budget were increased or decreased.

Line Item Budget

Budgets in which the individual financial statement items are grouped by **cost center** or department are easily amendable to line item budgeting. This form of budget shows the comparison between the financial data for the past accounting or budgeting periods and estimated figures for the current or a subsequent period.

Line item budgets are typically used by governmental entities in which budgeted elements are grouped by administrative entities. A municipally based EMS organization (whether fire based or freestanding) would become a line item in the local government's financial statements and reports. Line item budgets are used also in private industry for comparison and budgeting for selected departments.

In line item budgeting, the link between financial planning and budget preparation gives the budget document a unique role in governmental organizations. Budgets in the public arena are often considered the official policy document because an adopted budget represents the financial plan used by a government to achieve its goals and objectives. "When a unit of government legally adopts a financial plan, the budget has secured the approval of the majority of the governing board and reflects

- the prioritization of activities in which the unit of government will be involved
- the influence of various participants and interest groups in the budget development process
- the governmental plan for acquiring and using its resources." (National Center for Education Statistics, 2003)

Performance evaluation allows citizens and taxpayers to hold policymakers and administrators accountable for their actions. Because accountability to citizens often is stated explicitly in state laws and state constitutions, it is a cornerstone of budgeting and financial reporting. The General Accounting Standards Board (GASB) recognizes the importance of accountability with the following objectives:

- Financial reporting should provide information to determine whether current-year revenues were sufficient to pay for current-year services.
- Financial reporting should demonstrate whether resources were obtained and used in accordance with the entity's legally adopted budget. It should also demonstrate compliance with other finance-related legal or contractual requirements.
- Financial reporting should provide information to assist users in assessing the service efforts, costs, and accomplishments of the governmental entity. (Executive Office of the President, 1993)

Line item budgeting is still the most widely used approach in many municipally based EMS organizations because of its simplicity and its control orientation. It is referred to as the "historical" approach because administrators and chief executives often base their expenditure requests on historical expenditure and revenue data. One essential aspect of line item budgeting is that it offers flexibility in the amount of control established over the use of resources.

Advantages and Disadvantages. The line item budget approach has several advantages that account for its wide use. It offers simplicity and ease of preparation. It is a familiar approach to those involved in the budget development process (National Center for Education Statistics, 2003). This method budgets by organizational unit (training, maintenance, support staff) and is consistent with the lines of authority and responsibility. As a result, this approach enhances organizational control and allows the accumulation of expense data at each level. Finally, line item budgeting allows the accumulation of expense data for use in trend or historical analysis.

Although this approach offers considerable advantages, critics have identified several shortcomings that may make it inappropriate for certain EMS organizations. The most severe criticism is that it presents little useful information to EMS managers on the functions and activities of the organization. Since this budget presents proposed expenditure amounts only by category, the justifications for such expenditures are not explicit and are often unintuitive.

In addition, it may invite micromanagement by EMS managers and governing boards as they attempt to manage operations with little or no performance information. However, to overcome its limitations, the line item budget can be augmented with supplemental program and performance information.

Zero-Based Budgeting

Zero-based Budgeting (ZBB) is an alternative approach to resource planning, decision making, and financial management. Rather than starting with estimates for the current financial year, as with incremental budgeting, the starting point for ZBB is zero. For each product or service, the total estimated costs should be fully offset by projected income. For an EMS organization, this means that estimated expenditures for each program or operational area must be balanced by income from revenues, grants, subsidies, and other sources.

The basic concept of ZBB is that program activities and services must be justified annually during the budget development process (National Center for Education Statistics, 2003). The budget preparation starts by dividing all EMS operations into units where decisions are made at relatively low levels of the organization. Every unit evaluates its specific needs for the next budget period. All departments submit their revenue and expense projections. In nonprofit EMS organizations, each department could also submit an explanation on the value that the department will bring to the organization or the customer. Each submission is aggregated into a program package based on activities, program goals, organizational units, and so forth. Each program receives a dollar amount based on the level of revenue or service provided to produce defined outputs or outcomes. Departments are then ranked by their importance in reaching organizational goals and objectives. Therefore, when the proposed budget is presented, it contains a series of budget decisions that are tied to the attainment of the entity's goals and objectives.

The central thrust of ZBB is the elimination of outdated efforts and expenditures and the concentration of resources where they are most effective. This is achieved through an annual review of all program activities and expenditures, which results in improved information for allocation decisions. However, proper development requires significant staff time, planning, and paperwork. Experience with the implementation of this approach indicates that a comprehensive review of ZBB decisions for some program activities may be necessary only periodically. The review of program activities makes ZBB particularly useful when overall spending must be reduced. With ZBB, all spending requests must be justified in detail. Requests are assessed against requests from other departments before a decision is made. To gain the most positive affect in using a ZBB approach, the EMS manager can follow the three steps outlined here:

Step 1 *Developing a Program Package.* A program package is a document that explains a proposed activity, its goals and objectives, what benefits are expected, how performance will be measured, and all costs that will be incurred. In addition, a program package should outline what alternative courses of action have been considered and why these were rejected.

Step 2 *Ranking the Program Packages in Order of Priority.* After each department submits its program package, the packages are ranked in order of priority. They are then ranked in terms of the priorities of the institution as a whole. The revenue allocation in each program package is also reviewed to ensure that it is not excessive or unrealistic.

Step 3 *Allocating Funds.* Where activities do not generate their own revenue and require a contribution from organizational funds (for support staff or maintenance), then whatever resources are available are allocated to the various activities on the basis of their ranking. From a control perspective, individual budgets are limited in the amount of expenses that can be incurred. Since each department effectively starts at zero dollars and has reviewed its specific needs for the preceding accounting period, each department should conceivably determine an adequate dollar amount needed for operating. In this way the EMS manager can review the individual department needs against the strategic plan and prioritize where funding is needed. Each year the level of need may change within the departments. The manager should be capable of looking at the operations to determine if any decreases or increase in submitted budgets is reasonable.

FLEXIBLE BUDGETS

Flexible budgets are based on a cost function such as $Y = a + bX$, where Y represents the budgeted cost, or dependent variable. The constant *a* represents a static amount for fixed costs and the constant b represents the rate of change in Y expected for a unit change in the independent variable X. The expression bX is the flexible part of the budget cost function. The flexible budget technique is used for planning and monitoring all types of costs. The constant amount *a* includes both discretionary and committed costs, while the flexible bX includes various types of engineered costs. The characteristic of this technique enables the flexible budget to play a crucial role in both financial planning and performance evaluation.

EMS managers can look at their organizations' expenses and allocate them into specific categories. Once the expenses are allocated, the managers can apply the flexible budget formula to determine the specific budget that is necessary. For example,

a = $10,000

b = a range of expected calls for a given period (1,500 to 2,200 calls per month)

X = cost per call

The EMS manager can determine the total revenue by plugging in the known figures to calculate a budget that encompasses a range of possibilities. By determining the range of budget possibilities, the manager is not tied to a rigid or fixed budget. The manager can adjust allocations to programs based on actual revenue activity.

CAPITAL BUDGETS

Capital refers to fixed assets accrued in the process of doing business. A budget is a plan that details projected outflows and inflows during a defined future period, and a **capital budget** outlines the process of analyzing projects and deciding which to include as considerations for financing. The process is fundamentally important to the success or failure of the organization because capital budget decisions determine the future of the organization. Capital budgeting procedures recognize this by focusing on cash flows as the relevant indicator of returns realized in each period. For these reasons, an astute manager insists on tracing cash flow through an organization.

While leading an EMS organization, management's job is to continually allocate available resources for planned projects that return a benefit. In EMS, the benefit's focus is on improving the health of the community. The activity of allocating resources to achieve the goal is the essence of EMS management planning. The long-run survival of the organization demands continuing and meticulous attention by management on the goals and the resources needed to fulfill it. EMS managers must be concerned that current organizational resource allocation maximizes services delivered (Figure 6.2).

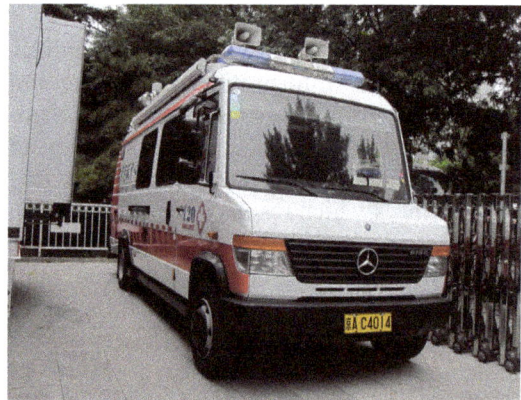

FIGURE 6.2 ■ Ambulance. *Courtesy of Dennis Mitterer.*

For the most part, from management's perspective capital budgeting is straightforward. Management simply estimates the cost of a project, and its expected future impact or returns to the organization. By determining the present value of the project and calculating the return on investing, management can decide whether investing in the project will bring more value to the organization.

A number of factors must be considered when making capital budget decisions. First, results of capital budget decisions continue over an extended period of time. Decision makers must know in what direction the organization is heading. If the organization invests in purchasing an asset with an economic life of 10 years, the organization must determine how the asset fits into the organization's strategic plan. Furthermore, since the purchase is spread out over 10 years, managers must also determine the expected income from the asset over the asset's life.

EMS managers should be able to assess the organization's needs based on its resources and long-range goals. For instance, smaller EMS organizations may feel that they cannot afford to invest in overhauling an antiquated computer system to document patient encounters or track personnel hours. However, when that antiquated system results in a loss of productivity due to lost patient care reports written on paper or inaccurate paychecks, the small EMS organization cannot afford not to invest in more updated technology. The capital budgeting process requires a realistic assessment of the value of equipment, facilities, and people.

Generally, the decision to invest in a capital item originates from a nonfinancial person. A supervisor may identify a need, or the training officer may determine the necessity of additional equipment. To receive authorization for the needed equipment, it behooves the requester to present his information in a way that facilitates management's review process. Most EMS personnel are uncertain

how to do this, and one could argue most EMS administrators are also. As the health care dollar becomes more and more scarce, entities that provide EMS with revenue may begin to demand greater scrutiny of the money. From a practical standpoint, it is management's job to ensure that the organization uses resources in the best manner. It is important that all of the EMS organization's personnel understand the correct process for determining the value of a capital item or project, requesting money for it, and evaluating its value to the organization and/or community.

The degree of confidence that EMS managers have about determining if a project is funded depends on the complexity of the project. Some parts of the project may be difficult to estimate for costs and returns. One-of-a-kind projects may also be difficult to estimate for costs due to the data needed to make an informed decision. Precise estimates for risky projects may also be difficult to track down. Such projects require greater scrutiny. The difficulty in encouraging managers to think this way is apparent: Managers tend to make decisions based on emotion or personal preference for the project without evaluating the effect on the organization. In other words, they use the organization's resources (the money given by others) as if it was their own to fund their pet projects. However, the need to evaluate the effectiveness of the investment against the needs of the community or return to the community is paramount.

All costs that go into the capital project must be considered to be investment costs in this context. Managers should understand that any expense incurred as a result of a capital project affects cash outflows. Cash is needed for the project to generate the expected returns.

Similar considerations apply to the determination of revenue resulting from the project. As mentioned earlier, the analysis must focus on the cash flow resulting from the project, not the "profit" associated with it. An EMS manager should track the returns on the investment of cash and document the returns within each of the time frames under consideration. One must avoid thinking that cash flow and "profit" are one and the same—they are not.

When determining the efficacy of a project and looking at the annual cash flow—all cash outflows must be subtracted from anticipated cash inflows associated with the project. Outflows include increased labor, additional materials, and applicable taxes. In standard financial analysis, reviewers focus on revenues and costs. Reviewers are concerned with marginal revenues and marginal costs. Allocating all overhead expenses to a project is only appropriate if the extra expenses result from the particular project and do not impact other operational activities. The normal cost accounting procedures of spreading the cost of a capital project over all existing activities, regardless of the impact, must be avoided, since doing so can distort the true cost of the new project.

Thus, careful attention to accurate data estimation is a fundamental requirement when preparing a capital budget. Costs and benefits should be estimated in terms of cash inflows and outflows directly associated with the project under consideration. Any overhead that is not directly associated with the project should be excluded.

In other words, to determine the true cost of the project and avoid forcing the numbers to make the project work, managers must look at revenue received and outgoing expenses for a specific project individually, irrespective of the overlap in other operational areas. For example, if the capital project entails buying new training equipment and storing that equipment will involve allocating 10 times more footage of storage space, the cost of the space should be considered as part of the project cost.

The life expectancy of any project is a judgment call. For example, if management upgrades its antiquated computer system, the equipment's life expectancy may be very short because technology is likely to change very soon. In comparison, management can invest in equipment with a life expectancy that is likely to be very long; investing in training mannequins is an excellent example of long life expectancy.

Another issue that management needs to evaluate is the interest rate being applied. Two approaches can aid in this assessment. First, managers should determine the different levels of success and calculate the present value of each assumed return. Large variances will indicate high-risk projects, and slight variances will indicate low-risk projects. An alternative approach is to judge the risk based on a similar project.

EMS managers must determine the cost of capital to the organization. A low-risk investment can only be justified if the returns equal at least the cost of acquiring additional capital. Riskier investments must generate returns commensurate with the increased risk exposure. For example, if the cost of capital to the organization is 10 percent, a moderately risky investment should be expected to generate from a 15 to 25 percent annual return to merit serious consideration.

Another method to determine the desirability of a capital investment is the internal rate of return. This method consists of equating the initial investment with the present value of returns and solving for the interest rate. The resulting interest rate is then viewed in the context of the riskiness of the project. If the returns are equal or in excess of those projects with similar risk, then the project is accepted. If the project's expected returns are less, then it is rejected. An example will help illustrate this:

Investment required = $80,000

Annual cash flow expected = $28,000

Number of years = 5

T_D = (Refer to the interest rates found in Table D in the Appendix.)

Therefore:

$$\$80,000 = \$28,000 \times T_D$$

$$T_D = 2.857$$

Looking at a present value of an annuity table for 5 years, the interest rate for a T_D of 2.857 is around 22 percent. If the organization set a 20 percent limit for interest, this exceeds the established limit and the project should be rejected. However, if the data change and the interest rate falls within the acceptable perimeters established, then the project should be considered.

The relevance and importance of capital budgeting techniques to skillful management cannot be overemphasized. They deal with the core issue of management: allocation of available resources to secure organizational success.

Every manager is faced with capital budget decisions. Although, in many instances, it may be exceedingly difficult to estimate all necessary inputs to the net present value (NPV) or internal rate of return (IRR) models, this exercise is of great value to the manager. By determining ranges of reasonable estimates, success of the project may be evaluated. In people-oriented programs such as training, it is often impossible to arrive at a reasonable estimate of cash flow. In such cases, the problem may be stated in another way: What benefit does a certain investment have on the organization?

It is recognized that certain capital investments are essentials and are not subject to debate. Among these are employee health and safety and programs regulated by governmental agencies. Yet even in such cases an analysis can be conducted to develop an appreciation for the magnitude of the commitment by the organization. With computers and accounting software, there is no reason not to engage in proper analysis of capital projects. Good management is concerned with revenues, costs, and timing of projects. By using these exer-

cises, capital budgeting decisions can be readily ascertained.

Capital Budgeting Process

The capital budgeting process may vary among EMS organizations, but the goal remains constant: to assess current operating procedures, equipment, personnel, and capabilities. The process also helps determine if more cost-effective means to increase productivity and profitability exist. It is also useful in devising investment proposals that make a good case for improving or expanding facilities (Christianet, 2012). EMS managers will want to conduct research on all aspects of the organization to prove to municipal authorities, boards of directors, and other decision makers that an investment in new facilities and equipment will translate into increased goal achievement and revenues. EMS capital budgets will also include proposed expenditures for equipment upgrades, along with a comparison of the benefits and costs associated with an alternative.

The capital budget process is a systematic review of the current assets and organizational state of position. Managers determine, based on information available from the various departments and matched with the outcomes of the strategic planning process, what investments are needed or should be made to grow the organization. Capital budgets are not to be confused with operational budgets or the budget process.

An EMS manager should look at the end result and attempt to forecast the effect any capital purchase will have on the organization. A forecast that is not well thought out can have a disastrous effect. If the organization invests too heavily in the asset, it will incur unnecessary expenses. On the other hand, if the organization does not invest enough, two problems may arise. First, the current or existing asset may not remain sufficiently useful for the expected life, and second, once purchased it may be underutilized relative to the expected use.

The most important part of analyzing a capital project is estimating the cash flow. This is simply the cost of investment and the annual return on investment in revenue that went into the project or purchase. Two general rules which help in this financial analysis. First, capital budget decisions are based on cash flows, not accounting income, and second, only incremental cash flows are relevant to the decision-making process.

Annual cash flows, not accounting profits, are used in the capital budgeting process. Cash flows and accounting profits are very different. If an organization anticipates building and equipping a new building, the loans, grants, or reserves used to fund the project would not be documented as net revenue produced. Only the revenues generated by the call volume would be considered cash flow for this project. Let's use an example of building a new building in a new response area.

The first step in the example analysis is to summarize the investment requirements for the project. Investment requirements include buying more equipment, hiring staff, and so on, which are not considered capital investment but are necessary to make the capital investment successful. The capital outlays consist of the purchase price of the building and land, the price of needed equipment, and the required investment to run calls out of the building. Having estimated the capital requirements, we must now estimate the cash flows once calls start in the new building. The call volume will be estimated using historical run data, population data, economic data, and other information that would assist decision makers in determining revenue and expenses. Often, EMS organizations determine capital projects based on gut reaction without working through the formal process of objectively looking into the financial implications.

Decision makers must see when the investment will be balanced by the net cash flow of operations. An estimated book value of the building, the replacement/salvage value of the equipment, depreciation, and other costs must be calculated to determine the project's value. The organization should also determine the expected payback period for the project. One does not just decide to build and equip a building just because it is the right thing to do. As a steward of the community's resource, management of the EMS organization should seek to justify any large projects and be prepared to explain it to the community whom they represent.

The EMS capital budgeting process should also take into account the downtime required to replace older equipment with newer models. Managers will have to compute lost staff hours and productivity due to the facility or equipment expansion or replacement. Incurring additional costs for training on the new equipment should be factored into the budget.

Effective capital budgeting improves the timing of the asset purchase and the quality of the asset purchased. An organization that forecasts its needs for a capital asset and can adequately plan for the payment of the asset will be better prepared to acquire and utilize the asset.

In any organization, competing projects may require evaluation. For example, EMS organizations routinely determine when the purchase of new vehicles or enlarging a building needs to occur. A systematic approach to determining the priorities should be built into the process of the asset purchase. As previously noted, emotional decisions should not be used as the criteria for pet project investments.

To avoid the uncertainty of investing in unnecessary equipment, managers should objectively evaluate their capital assets and the associated life expectancies. For example, if the organization owns and maintains five emergency response units and each unit has accumulated 30,000 miles in 1 year, a life expectancy of 5 years would anticipate each vehicle having accumulated 150,000 miles at the end of its useful life. Replacing all five vehicles at the same time would require a huge financial investment by the organization and might cause unnecessary strain on the organization's resources. Putting the replacement of the ambulances on a 2-year cycle after a set number of miles would spread out the capital investment necessary for the organization. In this manner, the organization can build into the budget a fixed cost of vehicle replacement without having to scramble for large sums of money at one time.

Similarly, if management is aware of a population increase in a certain area and the citizens would better be served with another building, management can plan on proactively setting aside monies for investment and purchase of the grounds and building costs. Generally speaking, the organization should have a process for determining the correct budgeting decision.

1. The decisions must consider all cash flows throughout the entire life of the project or purchase.
2. The decisions must consider the time value of money—that is, they must reflect the money that comes in early in the project as being more valuable than the money received in the future.
3. The decisions must determine that each project is mutually exclusive, and each project must maximize the goals of the organization.

The entire budget is comprised of operational budgets and the capital budget. The capital budget is the investment made, by the management team, in the organization's future. The following is a mathematical formula for objectively determining if a project's financing should be part of the capital budget:

P = Principle or present value of a sum

F = Future value of a sum

B = Present value of an annuity

W = Future value of an annuity

R = Annuity

n = Number of periods

i = Rate of interest

$$W = RT_C$$
$$B = RT_D$$
$$F = PT_A$$

Two decision rules were previously discussed; the NPV and the IRR. As discussed, most investment decisions can be made if the NPV is positive and the project is, therefore, accepted.

To illustrate, assume management is considering replacing its computer system. The estimated cost is $110,000. This seems high for a new system, but the IT manager is pushing for it. You know the manager's brother-in-law is the salesman, so you are not sure how much of this is nepotism. You have seen the software program, and it contains a lot of impressive content, such as communication interfaces and download capabilities for mobile computers. However, the organization's accountant is not convinced it is a good investment.

You ask the team to look at the decision objectively. There is some dissent about this approach, but your will prevails. Estimates indicate that this system will improve documentation, improve billing, and reduce the time needed to document patient interactions, for a savings of $32,000 per year for the next 4 years. Should the investment be made?

To answer this question, an appropriate interest rate must be selected. In other words, the interest rate should reflect how much interest is paid on borrowed money or how much money is lost if you use reserve capital. Numerous factors enter into this determination: the cost of capital to the organization, returns that could be realized on other investments (opportunity costs), the criticality of the need, the reason for contemplating the acquisition, crew training, and the cost of the learning curve, to name a few things. Assume that

20 percent is an appropriate interest rate for this project.

Therefore:

$$NPV = \$32,000 \times T_D - \$111,000$$

T_D for 4 years and 20% is 2.589. Therefore:

$$NPV = \$32,000 \times 2.589 - \$110,000$$

$$NPV = -\$27,152$$

Despite the IT manager's disappointment and arguments, the project should be rejected as a negative return on the investment occurs. Objectively, rejecting the project is the correct decision. It is possible, however, to seek concessions that may make the project affordable. Using superior negotiating skills, you discuss the situation with the computer salesman. He submits a second proposal. The new estimates indicate that your returns might be realized in 5 years instead of 4 years, the interest rate is lowered to 14 percent, and the salesman can reduce the cost of the system to $108,000. T_D now is equal to 3.433.

Therefore:

$$NPV = \$32,000 \times 3.433 - \$108,000$$

$$NPV = \$1,856$$

The project now appears desirable. Note how sensitive the results are when the factors are laid out objectively. Through negotiation and working with vendors, you could make this project decision easier. Just because the NPV is positive, does not, in this case, make this project a definite go. The idea here is to show managers how to make the best use of the resources available and decide how to make decisions objectively. Too often managers make decisions based on nonobjective information and either never realize their mistakes or falsely believe they do not matter. The point here is that the organization could continue to function, but what is the opportunity cost to the organization?

Foremost among these decisions is the need for impartiality and an objective review of the data. This imparts a large amount of trust to those supplying the data. For these reasons, and more, any proposal must be developed, researched, and presented. The advocates for any project will tend to estimate costs at the low end and returns at the high end of the range. The task for the EMS manager is to be that impartial voice and assess the value of the project. This is especially difficult when the project is the brainchild of the manager.

Since estimates are crucial to decisions, managers must explore the source and nature of the data. Good documentation of the estimation process improves the credibility of the data. Managers should be provided the opportunity to review all significant assumptions made in the preparation of the estimates. This assumes that someone else is providing the estimates. Managers must be as diligent if they are providing the data to the administrative team or the board of directors.

PROJECT CASH FLOWS AND RISK

Risk analysis is important in all financial decisions, especially those relating to capital projects. Three separate types of project risk can be identified: (1) the project stands alone on its own risk, (2) the project is contained within the organization's risk, and (3) the community assumes the risk.

Project risk is the set of external circumstances or events that cannot occur for the project to be successful. Any capital project is but one part of the organization. EMS management must determine the risk of project failure by incorporating the assumption that it will be the only project undertaken by the organization. Specifically, what is the viability of the project's return relative to the investment? Will the investment ultimately provide enough cash flow, in a reasonably short period of time, to pay for the project? Having an understanding of NPV and future expected values is necessary to make these critical assessments. If the NPV of the project is less than the future return, the project would most likely be a worthwhile investment. However, if the current value of the financial resources is greater now than the future value, the money should be used for projects that have a current higher net value for the organization.

Computer programs can determine the sensitivity of a project and conduct scenario analysis to determine the best and worst-case scenarios for an investment. These tests are very important in helping the EMS manager determine whether a project is worthwhile. Often, the EMS manager may need to consult with an accountant or other professional to run these computer tests. Obviously, if the EMS organization is large enough and has a staff accountant to assist in these exercises, the decision can be effectively evaluated. The concept of capital project risk management is to introduce objectivity into the assessment process, again to better utilize the community's resources.

The first step in determining the risk of a single project is to look objectively at that particular project as if it is the only one. It is then easier to determine how one project stacks up against other projects that the organization is considering. Within the organization, the risk of one capital project is determined by the project's viability relative to other projects that are being considered by the organization. It is measured by the effect the project has on the organization's revenue or value to the community. For example, Main Street Ambulance believes it can open an EMS training institute for its county and possibly draw in people from other counties. Before beginning such an aggressive project, Main Street Ambulance's management should evaluate the risk of its investment (money, time, and personnel) relative to other operational requirements.

The community risk is defined as the effect on the community and the loss of the financial resources contributed by outside sources. What is the community able to absorb

if the project fails? For example, the management of Broad Street Ambulance decides to erect a new building to house two new ambulances at a location that is 3 miles from its current building. The decision makers believe calls will be covered faster on the other side of town, so they invest all of their reserves in purchasing the land, erecting the building, and buying new ambulances and equipment. Within 6 months, the call volume, which has now split, does not generate enough money to support either building. Broad Street Ambulance files for bankruptcy. The community is now at risk of EMS service being unavailable to respond to 9-1-1 calls.

MASTER BUDGETS

The **master budget** is the primary financial planning mechanism for an EMS organization. It provides the foundation for traditional financial control systems. More specifically, it is a comprehensive, integrated financial plan developed for a specific period of time, such as for a month, a quarter, or a year. This is a much broader concept than for stand-alone appropriation, flexible, and capital budgets. The master budget includes various appropriation budgets (typically in the administrative and service areas) as well as flexible budgets, a capital budget, and much more.

The basic document is called the master budget. This document represents the expectations of the financial position of the organization in the future. The information is based on history, current realities, and management's insight on business activity. The master budget identifies financial activities for various segments of the organization and traces the activities to various measurement tools and reports.

There are pros and cons to developing a master budget. Though management should be aware of historical trends, the master budget is a look into the future. Determining the outcomes in future periods is impossible;

therefore, the master budget may not reflect actual events as time passes. The master budget becomes static, and the people who are responsible for the various cost centers within the budget and are held to a rigorous outcome may become frustrated. These measurements can become a source of contention if management adheres to the financial projections that are laid out 9 months earlier, especially if significant changes in operations have occurred.

The advantage for developing a master budget is that the document provides the opportunity to evaluate operations and think through expectations of the organization's activities. It also should identify areas of opportunities and point out areas of weaknesses.

One begins developing a master budget by looking at expected revenues. If the EMS organization is municipally based (fire company or freestanding), revenue will come from the money allocated from government officials. The revenue allocation is based on historical needs and future expectations, tax revenue, and the municipality's current financial status. If the organization is a freestanding nonprofit, revenue can come from services rendered and payments by third-party payers, fund drives, fund-raisers, and donations.

Once revenue determination is complete, the management team allocates revenue to specific cost centers. Input from the people responsible for the cost centers is encouraged. Giving staff members responsibility for a cost center budget, and holding them accountable for the outcome without allowing any input, will discourage buy-in to the overall financial plan.

The master budget contains two major parts: the operating budget and the financial budget (Figure 6.3). The operating budget begins with the revenue budget and ends with

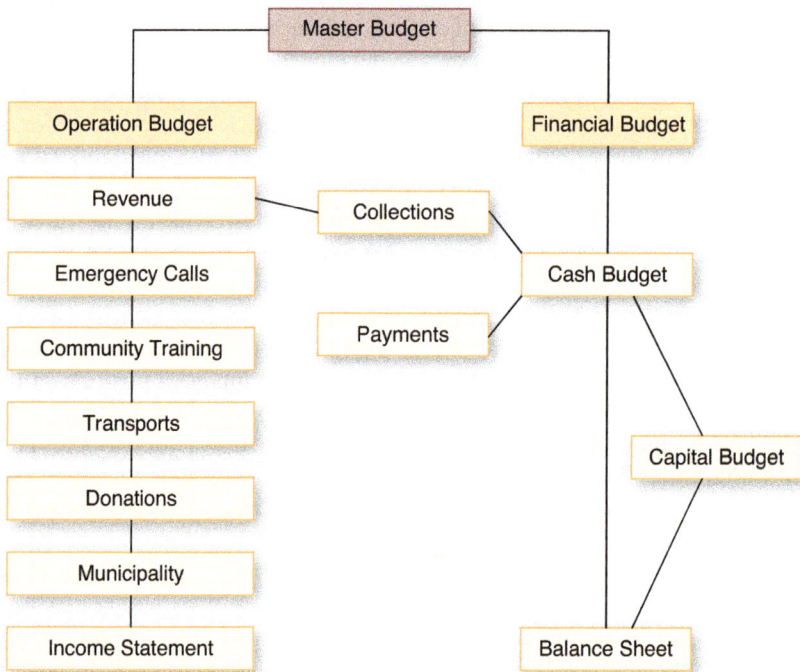

FIGURE 6.3 ■ Diagram of master budget for EMS.

the budgeted income statement. The financial budget includes the capital budget as well as a cash budget and a budgeted balance sheet.

Purposes and Benefits of the Master Budget

A variety of purposes and benefits are obtained from master budgeting. Consider the following:

Integrates and Coordinates.

The master budget is the principal planning device for an organization. It is used to integrate and coordinate the activities of the various functional and operational areas within the organization. For example, a comprehensive plan helps ensure that all the needed inputs (equipment, materials, labor, supplies, etc.) will be at the right place at the right time. It also helps ensure that EMS operations staff reviews the potential call volumes, transport volumes, training, and or hours needed for staffing. The integrative nature of the budget provides a way to implement concepts and constraints that emphasizes performance of the total system (organization) rather than the various subsystems or functional areas (cost centers).

Communicates and Motivates.

Another benefit of the master budget is that it provides communication through which the organization's personnel can see how their efforts contribute to the overall goals of the organization. This communication tends to be good for morale and enhance job satisfaction. People need to know how their efforts add value to the organization. The behavioral aspect of budgeting is extremely important.

Promotes Continuous Improvement.

The planning process encourages managers to consider alternatives that might improve customer value and reduce costs. The planning cycle supports specific improvements in the operational processes. The master budget and subsequent financial performance measurements reflect the financial expectations and consequences of those efforts.

Guides Performance.

The EMS master budget also provides a guide for accomplishing the objectives included in the financial plan. After approval, the budget becomes the basis for acquisition and utilization of necessary resources. Anticipating resource needs and reviewing the strengths and weaknesses of the budget can significantly reduce the amount of uncertainty and variability in EMS operations.

Limitations of Master Budgets

Management should consider several limitations and problems associated with the master budget. These problems involve uncertainty, behavioral bias, and costs.

Uncertainty.

Budgeting includes a considerable amount of forecasting, and this activity involves a degree of uncertainty. Uncertainty affects both revenues and expenses, but uncertainty on the revenue side presents a more serious limitation for planning. Revenue is frequently based on a forecast supported by a variety of assumptions about call volumes, transport volumes, donations, and other sources of EMS income. This uncertainty forces management to constantly monitor and analyze changes in the community and the reimbursement environment. From the planning perspective, the inability to accurately forecast the future reduces the usefulness of original budget estimates for staffing, inventory, and planning for other resource needs.

Uncertainty on the expense side tends to be less of a problem because management has more influence over the quantities of resources consumed than over the services needed by the community. From an evaluation and control perspective, uncertainty on both sides of financial performance is not as much of a problem because flexible budgets are used to fine-tune the original budget to reflect expectations at the current level of activity.

Behavioral Bias. Behavioral conflicts are created when the budget is used as a control device. To be effective, the budget must be used by the managers it is designed to help. Thus, it must be acceptable to all levels of staffing impacted by the budget. Literature on budgeting supports the view that budgets should reflect what is most likely to occur during normal operations. A budget is an effective planning and monitoring device, and it should encourage a high level of performance and efficiency throughout the organization. It should also be fair and attainable. If the budget is viewed by staff responsible for the budget as unfair (too optimistic), it may intimidate rather than motivate.

One way to gain acceptance is to implement what is referred to as participative (rather than imposed) budgeting. The idea is to include all levels of management in the budgeting process. The EMS manager should coordinate this process to ensure attainment of a fair budget that will help achieve the goals of the entire organization.

Costs. A third problem or limitation is that budgeting requires a considerable amount of time and effort. Many EMS organizations maintain a 12-month budget that is repeated year after year. While this does not create a substantial expenditure for large or medium-size EMS organizations, smaller organizations may find it difficult to justify the costs involved. Many small EMS organizations do not plan effectively and eventually struggle as a result. Cash flow problems or not having a bank line of credit are common reasons an organization cannot pay for medical supplies or meet the payroll. Many of these problems can be avoided by preparing a budget on a regular basis.

Assumptions of the Master Budget

Typically, the following simplifying assumptions are made when preparing a master budget:

1. Call volumes are constant during the budget period.
2. Variable costs per unit of output are constant during the budget period.
3. Fixed costs are constant.
4. Revenue mix is constant when the company offers more programs or has access to different revenue streams.

These assumptions facilitate the planning process by removing many of the economic variables.

At all levels, the management team should attempt to develop the master budget as realistically as possible. Optimism may lead to higher expectations. For example, if the management team expects higher revenue due to an increase in call volume, the training department may plan for more training equipment. The training officer may develop an aggressive schedule for recertifications, purchasing videos, or training programs and begin to schedule staff a few months ahead. If a shortfall occurs, then the nonproductive work to undo everything increases costs and adds to overall employee frustration.

Conversely, if the master budget is too conservative, then the staff responsible for the cost centers may not do any planning. For example, if management anticipates a flat or decreasing call volume and the volume increases, then the staff trainer may need to hurriedly conduct new employee orientation or increase available training that was otherwise unanticipated, again leading to increased employee frustration and possible overtime expense.

The master budget should have a level of variability built into it. As stated, EMS managers cannot predict the future: The budget is an educated guess on what the future may look like financially. Having a financial plan that allows for changes is optimal. Once the budget is established, many managers adhere to the final product with a sense of duty. In an ideal world, the revenues will come in at or higher than expected and expenses will occur at or below what was planned. In reality, events in the EMS world and the financial world are not so predictable. Therefore, managers should develop a few variations of an acceptable budget and measure success based on the ability of all persons to use organizational resources to better the organization with an eye to stewardship of a scarce resource.

Preparing a Master Budget

The EMS management team should receive input from all departments and decision makers who are affected by the budget. Pulling all parties together to generate a realistic and workable budget for the future is essential to optimize the success of the organization. Multiple, separate budgets must be developed, and each person who is impacted by one or more should provide insight into the development of the master budget.

Operating Budget.   Preparing an operating budget is a sequential process of developing sub-budgets. Except for one or two exceptions, the sub-budgets must be prepared in the following order: revenues, response volumes, inventory, direct labor, overhead, ending inventory, cost of services, administrative, and income statement. Every organization determines if sub-budgets are necessary or more are needed. For example, a municipally based EMS system may not be concerned about call volumes because the revenue received is determined by the local government.

Revenue Budget.   Developing a revenue budget involves the following calculations:

Budgeted Revenue \$ = (Budgeted Response Volume)(Budgeted Reimbursement Prices)

This is done for all levels of responses.

Current Period Cash Collections = Current Period Cash Receipts + Contracted Collected in Current Period + Prior Period Contracted Collected in Current Period

These calculations are relatively simple, but where does the EMS manager obtain this information? EMS forecasting is often based on statistically tracking the historical call volumes and determining the number of calls per 1,000 population. Other revenue estimates are generated by looking at contracted transport volumes and increasing contracts, or by determining community training programs by discussing future needs with customers (businesses or community organizations).

Statistical forecasting techniques also can be used to make estimates of expected future responses or training programs, based on the company's previous volumes, various assumptions about the future economic climate, the actions of the government related to reimbursements and government revenues, and activities of other neighboring EMS units and consumers.

Pricing for training is a marketing function, but various prices are based on costs plus a markup (the supply function) and consideration of what consumers are willing and able to pay for the product (the demand function). Thus, the budgeted sales price is usually determined after the budgeted unit cost has been calculated.

Direct Materials Budget.   The direct materials budget is based on the volumes of specific equipment or supplies used. This is a historical view; however, the EMS management team should determine a common denominator when trying to anticipate inventory needs. For example, how frequently are

IV starts attempted and completed for each call per 1,000 population?

Cost of Material Used = (Quantity Needed for Responses) × (Budgeted Material Prices)

The cost of materials used is needed to determine the money needed to buy inventory.

Cash Payments for Direct Material Purchases = Current Period Purchases Paid in Current Period + Prior Period Purchases Paid in Current Period

The information needed to determine budgeted cash payments is usually based on past experience. Normally the budget should reflect a situation in which the company pays promptly to take advantage of all cash discounts allowed.

Direct Labor Budget. Labor hours are slightly easier to budget for because they cannot be stored in the inventory for future use. Time can be wasted, but not postponed.

Direct Labor Hours Needed for Coverage = (Hours to Be Covered) × (Direct Labor Hours Budgeted per Unit)

The amount of direct labor time needed per unit is determined by the number of ambulances that are staffed for a specific number of hours per day.

Budgeted Direct Labor Cost = (Direct Labor Hours Needed for Coverage) × (Budgeted Rates per Hour)

The budgeted rates per hour for direct labor are provided by the human resources department or by tracking hours worked. Many different types of labor may be required, with different levels of expertise and experience. Thus, to be as accurate as possible, labor rates should be calculated based on the variable rates. Obviously, the EMS manager should not look at each person's rate and attempt to calculate the direct labor costs. If one basic hourly rate applies to running emergency calls as compared to running transports or conducting training, then the EMS manager can group rates for an estimate of each function.

CHAPTER REVIEW

Summary

An assumption of budgeting is that the EMS organization has established separate centers that are controlled in a top-down manner. However, this separation inevitably fails to consider many of the interdependencies within the organization. Ignoring the interdependencies among cost centers often prevents teamwork and creates the need for such buffers as additional inventory, workers, supervisors, and capacity. Remember, the EMS manager develops a budget for everyone, and each cost center is going to strive to obtain its share of the money.

A system that prevents teamwork and creates excess competition is inconsistent with using community financial resources in the best manner. For this reason, critics of traditional accounting control systems advocate managing the system as a whole to eliminate the need for buffers and excess. They also argue that EMS organizations need to develop process-oriented learning support systems, not financial results or fear-oriented control systems. Investment is necessary in information systems that reveal the organization's problems and constraints in order to empower users to identify and correct problems, remove constraints, and improve the process.

Given the importance of compliance with the approved budget, the financial reporting system must control the use of financial resources and ensure that budgetary appropriations and allocations are not exceeded. To demonstrate compliance, accounting systems are normally operated on the same basis of accounting used to prepare the approved budget. The actual financial information captured by the accounting system is in a form comparable to the approved budget. Through budgetary integration, the financial accounting system becomes the primary tool to prove financial accountability.

Finally, the budget is evaluated for its effectiveness in attaining the organization's stated goals and objectives. Evaluation typically involves an examination of how funds were spent, the outcomes that resulted, and the degree to which these outcomes achieved the stated objectives. This phase is fundamental in developing the subsequent year's budget. In effect, budget preparation is not only an annual exercise to determine the allocation of funds. It is also part of a continuous cycle of planning and evaluation to achieve the stated goals and objectives of the EMS organization.

WHAT WOULD YOU DO? Reflection

You meet with the board of directors and begin to introduce the concept of budgeting and the importance of tracking revenues and expenses. While describing how important the process of budgeting is to achieving organizational goals, you also point out that tracking revenues and expenses reduces the chance of organizational assets. While discussing the budgeting process, you begin developing a formal budgeting process and prepare reports that show how the organization is achieving expected results and the positive affect the results are having on operational activities.

While discussing the importance of budgeting with the board of directors, you introduce the need to identify the major goals and objectives, both short term and long term. You know you must follow up to determine levels of responsibility and accountability. Once these two steps are complete, to the satisfaction of both you and the board, you know you will actively communicate these goals to the rest of the management team. Once everyone knows what the organization is working toward, you can begin looking at the financial requirements, establishing measurements, and delineating responsibilities, including establishing a tracking process for purchasing requests and actual purchases. The treasury can continue to be responsible for the actual purchases, but you insist that all purchases be worked through the process until the system is operational.

Once the process is established for purchasing, you plan to meet with all of the people responsible for the sub-departments so you can explain how the budget process works and answer questions. As your middle-level decision makers become comfortable with the budgeting process and after reviewing the history of purchases, you will be better positioned to initiate a formal process of reviewing revenues and expenses, allocating expenses to specific cost centers, and holding people accountable for their financial contributions to the organization.

Eventually you will sit with the board of directors and show how important matching the financial activities are to the strategic plan. That is when you will begin to develop short- and long-term goals.

Review Questions

1. Define three types of expenses in terms of (a) the relationship between the inputs and outputs involved, (b) the behavior of the cost (i.e., fixed, variable, or mixed), (c) whether the cost are viewed as short run or long run, and (d) how the cost are evaluated.
2. Define four types of budgets.
3. Discuss four types of appropriation budgets.
4. Discuss the purposes of budgeting or financial planning.
5. Discuss the limitations of budgeting.
6. What are the two main parts of the master budget?
7. What type of costs are associated with risk management?
8. What is the connection between the income statement and the balance sheet?
9. What are four assumptions underlying the master budget? Explain each.
10. Discuss how an EMS manager can look for reduction of nonobvious expenses.

References

Bett, A. (2010). "Capital Budgeting in the Healthcare Industry." Ezine Articles. See the Ezine website.

Bobinski, D. (2006). *Strategic Screening and Hiring: Six Steps to Finding the Best Applicants for your Organizations.* Boise, ID: Development Press. See the organization website.

Branch, S. (1998, November 9). "You Hired 'Em, But Can You Keep 'Em?" CNNMoney. See the organization website.

Christianet. (2012). "Capital Budgeting Process." See the organization website.

Clark, J. J. (2005). "Improving Hospital Budgeting and Accountability: A Best Practice Approach." *Healthcare Financial Management* 59(7), 78–83. See the organization website.

Dayananda, D., R. Irons, S. Harrison, J. Herboun, and P. Rowland. (2002). *Capital Budgeting.* Cambridge, UK: Cambridge University Press.

Dube, A., E. Freeman, and M. Reich. (2010). "Employee Replacement Costs." Berkeley: University of California–Berkeley, Institute for Research on Labor and Employment. See the organization website.

Executive Office of the President, Office of Management and Budget. (1993,

September 2). "Objectives of Federal Financial Reporting. Statement of Federal Financial Accounting Concepts," Chapter 3: Accountability and Users' Information Needs the Foundation of Governmental Financial Reporting. See the organization website.

Financial Web. (n.d.). "Pros and Cons of Incremental Budgeting." The Independent Financial Portal. See the organization website.

Graham, J., and C. Harvey. (2002, March 2). *How Do CFOs Make Capital Budget Decisions?* Social Science Research Network. Durham, NC: Duke University.

Kendrick, T. (2003). *Identifying and Managing Project Risk.* New York: AMACOM.

Martin, J. (n.d.). "The Master Budget or Financial Plan." In *Management Accounting: Concepts, Techniques, and Controversial Issues.* Management Accounting Web. See the organization website.

National Center for Education Statistics. (2003). "Chapter 3: Budgeting." IES: Institute of Education Sciences, U.S. Department of Education. See the organization website.

Reh, F. J. (2012). *"What Good People Really Cost: It's Not Really Blackmail, Is It?"* About.com: Management. See the organization website.

Siegel, G., and J. Sorensen. (1994, September). "What Corporate America Wants in Entry-Level Accountants." *Management Accounting*, pp. 26–31.

Key Terms

amortization The gradual elimination of liability, such as a mortgage, in regular payments over a specified period of time. The writing off of an intangible asset over the projected life of the asset.

budget Generally refers to a list of all planned expenses and revenues. It is a sum of money allocated for a particular purpose.

capital budget The planning process used to determine whether an organization's long-term investments are worth pursuing.

cause A reason for an action or response.

committed costs Money that is already spent on such things as long-term investments, mortgages, and equipment.

cost behavior Examination of specific variable costs to determine their response to changes in business activity (production) or business volume.

cost center A unit for which costs are accumulated. It can be a designated department that incurs costs in an effort to carry out the purposes of the organization.

department A specialized division of a large organization.

depreciation A decrease in value of an asset due to obsolescence or use.

discretionary costs A cost that management uses and can be easily changed such as advertising, repairs, and training.

effect Consequence that follows an action. The change in an outcome that results from an intervention.

engineered costs Have a direct and clear relationship with output.

master budget The comprehensive budget plan encompassing all the individual budgets related to the operations of an organization.

working capital Reflects the short-term disposition of the organization's capital.

CHAPTER 7

Purchasing

Objectives

After reading this chapter, the student should be able to:

7.1 Define and discuss the purpose of purchasing and procurement.

7.2 Describe the value of developing a mission statement, objectives, and goals for the purchasing process.

7.3 Outline the main objectives of purchasing and the implication of good purchasing processes.

7.4 Discuss the benefits of green purchasing decisions to the overall success of the organization.

7.5 Explain the benefits of cooperative purchasing arrangements and limitations.

7.6 Briefly describe the proactive purchasing arrangements.

7.7 Discuss the sources of contracts and the various considerations necessary when entering into a formal agreement.

Overview

The purpose of this text is to introduce the concepts of finance to nonfinancial EMS managers. The chapters present valuable information to both new and experienced EMS leaders who may have varying degrees of experience, formal and informal. The goal is to stimulate thinking in order to change the way things are done, to avoid mistakes of the past, and to encourage future growth of EMS as a profession.

Key Terms

bilateral contract	competitive edge	material breach
bonds	congruency	monitor
breach	efficiency	overhead
competitive	inventory control	preferred

proactive	resource dependency	systematic	waiver
procurement	theory	time breach	
purchasing	sustainability	unilateral contract	

WHAT WOULD YOU DO?

Your EMS organization is projected to grow 15 percent to 20 percent every year for the next 7 years. At this rate, you calculate that you will enlarge your staff by 25 percent, construct two more buildings, purchase at least four new vehicles and replace a few in the current fleet, increase equipment and supply purchases, and look at replacing the computer system and office equipment. With all of this activity, you believe you can handle the purchasing requirements with your current management team. The organization does not have a formal process for evaluating areas for improvement and determining short- and long-term purchasing needs, and only proactively matches purchases with expenses to determine future purchasing needs. Board members have also indicated that during this growth stage they would like to move toward a greater emphasis on environmental friendliness.

Questions

1. How would you prepare the organization for this explosive growth?
2. What will you need to do to develop and implement processes for evaluating purchasing objectives, needs assessments for ongoing purchases, and tracking mechanisms for determining how and what to purchase?
3. How can you assess your current purchasing processes and organize them to gain financial efficiencies?
4. How does risk management factor into decision making about purchasing?
5. What are the operational differences between proactive purchasing and reactive purchasing?
6. How will you evaluate and implement the board of directors' goal of going green?

■ INTRODUCTION

All EMS organizations must buy equipment and supplies. Depending on the size of the organization, the EMS manager may perform this function, or he may delegate it to another person. In either situation, the manager is responsible for the outcomes of purchasing decisions. Most managers or their delegates have little experience in developing purchasing programs, grading equipment or supplies, negotiating pricing, and analyzing supplier activities. The idea that the organization needs amount X of supplies per year and that supplier Y can deliver what is needed is usually the basis for how most EMS organizations function. Larger EMS organizations may have varying degrees of experience with a formal program, and municipally or hospital-based EMS organizations may have very stringent requirements for purchasing needed supplies. The point here is that purchasing has become such a specialized science that a person can earn a college degree in procurement and supply management.

EMS managers should understand the possibilities of operational **efficiency** gained

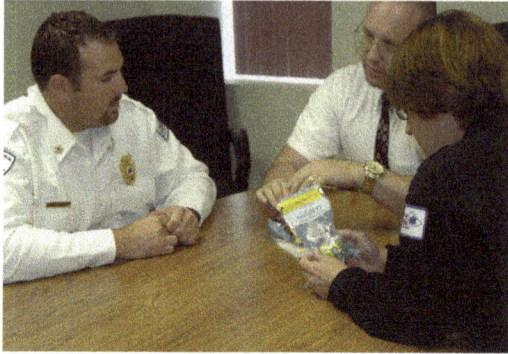

FIGURE 7.1 ■ EMS responders are involved in purchasing decisions. *Courtesy of Dennis Mitterer.*

by developing a **systematic** process of evaluating the purchasing activities of the organization. Buying equipment and supplies is an ongoing activity and is certainly needed to fulfill the function of the organization. The purchasing function does not have to be left up to chance. Nor does the purchasing function have to rest on which vendor has the best price, brings in the best incentives, or takes the boss out for lunch and a round of golf. Clearly, good operational decisions can lead to increased productivity. The basis for better decisions is better information for input. Too often, EMS managers are either not provided with the relevant and timely information they need to make decisions, or they are not sure what information is valuable (Figure 7.1).

Having a systematic process for determining what supplies and equipment are needed, evaluating the quality of supplies, determining the right quantity to buy, determining the right price, and evaluating the purchase for correctness can save hundreds, thousands, or even tens of thousands of dollars. This additional money can easily be returned to the operational budget for program development or other patient care investments.

■ DEFINITION AND PURPOSE

According to the *Business Dictionary*, **purchasing** is management's ability to control all significant purchases and **monitor** for the right authorization of the right item, at the right price, quality, and quantity, from the right supplier at the right terms, and at the right time.

The following are the major objectives of purchasing:

* Maintain the quality and value the firm's products or services
* Minimize cash tied up in inventory
* Maintain the flow of inputs to maintain the flow of outputs
* Strengthen the firm's **competitive** position

Purchasing may also involve the following:

* Receiving and processing requisitions
* Advertising for bids
* Evaluating bids
* Awarding contracts
* Inspecting the materials received
* Coordinating appropriate storage and release

In many traditional texts, a reader may find additional content about achieving the best pricing of equipment in order to improve the stock price of the business, increase the return on investment, and even improve competitive bidding in order to undercut organizations that perform similar functions. In the case of EMS purchasing, this text has maintained a consistent position of noncompetitiveness. The tenets of purchasing apply regardless of whether the EMS organization is municipally based, hospital based, freestanding, nonprofit, or for profit. In fact, depending on the EMS organization, the manager's knowledge of the purchasing process is very specific and detailed.

MISSION OR GOAL STATEMENT

The initial step in establishing the direction of purchasing activities is developing a mission, goals, and an objectives statement for the purchasing department. The organization should establish the expectations for the people who are spending organizational money. Should the purchasing activities focus on buying "green" products? Will only one vendor be utilized? Will the organization sign contracts, and what type of contract will be used? Will the goal be the lowest cost or the best quality?

The mission of purchasing must align with the mission of the organization. If the EMS organization commits to community health and improvement, then the purchasing mission statement should follow the same basic tenets. Having a purchasing mission statement that follows fiscal responsibility as its primary purpose will conflict with a community-focused mission statement. This occurs when a request for special equipment is made for a community project that brings little financial value but high public relations value to the organization. The purchase of particular equipment may go against the premise of spending money on financially sound projects. Evaluate the following purchasing mission statement, compare it to the stated organizational mission statement, and determine the **congruency**.

The goal of Main Street Ambulance Association is to provide out-of-hospital medical services to all who request evaluation, care, treatment, and transportation in every capacity by qualified and competent emergency medical responders. Our associates are dedicated to preserving and improving the health of all human beings under our care. We will maintain the highest degree of integrity, respect, and medical knowledge in preparation for caring for any individual who requests our services.

The goal of Main Street Ambulance Association is to reduce the adverse environmental impact of our purchasing decisions by buying goods and services from vendors who share our commitment to protect human health and the environment. By incorporating environmental considerations into purchasing decisions, our organization will remain fiscally responsible while promoting practices that improve public health and safety by reducing pollution, conserving natural resources, and supporting manufacturers and vendors that reduce the adverse environmental impact of their products.

The organization's goal statement is the umbrella philosophy, and the purchasing goals statement aligns and supports the organizational philosophy. Decisions are easier, there is less debate about the value of requests for materials or the purchasing of equipment, and the organization should see financial gains from consistent decision making.

Once a mission statement is formulated, the EMS manager or management staff should develop a process for requesting and purchasing needed equipment, supplies, and services. When developing this process, managers should determine the level of sophistication required for the purchasing function. For example, is there a need for a purchasing checklist, or are the organization's purchases so infrequent that a person buys based strictly on a need?

PURCHASING FUNDAMENTALS—

As with any management concept, certain basic knowledge is needed in order to lead an organization to success. The person responsible for buying or managing the inventory must want this responsibility, have requisite knowledge about the effects of purchasing on the financial success of the EMS organization, and understand the purchasing process.

Box 7.1

Purchasing Processes

- Develop a systematic approach to purchasing and inventory control.
- Assign a person to be responsible for purchasing and a separate person to be responsible for inventory control.
- Conduct audits on a frequent basis on both the purchasing and inventory.
- Review all journal entries on the accounts that encompass purchasing and accounts payable.
- Avoid obsolete inventory.
- Minimize the number of people who have access to the inventory and computer programs that track inventory.

PURCHASING PROCESS CHECKLIST

The EMS manager who personally performs the purchasing function or who oversees the people who are responsible should develop a process that establishes consistency and evaluates the effectiveness of the performance. Without a standardized process, purchasing supplies and equipment may result in increased costs, decreased quality, and unnecessary problems with vendors. The following checklist for EMS managers can serve as a template in developing an organizational process for purchasing.

In some of the listed steps, additional administrative processes must be developed to support the listed requirement. For example, step 9 states, "If [the purchase price is] over $5,000, what is the account code to be

utilized?" Thus, the organization must have a process for assigning an accounting code to purchased items.

Step 1 Identify the needed product or service.
- Develop a needs assessment if the request is for a new item.
- If currently purchased, determine if any change (increase or decrease in quantity) is necessary.
- Justify the needed change.
- Does the item need to be compatible with other items?
- Are there maintenance issues to be considered?

Step 2 What type of funds will be utilized to pay for the required goods or services?
- Reserve funds
- Grant funds
- Operational funds
- Request for additional funds (community, municipality, administration)

Step 3 Is the required product or service an appropriate use of funds?

Step 4 Is the required product or service available from an internal source?
- Facilities Operations
- IT
- Other

Step 5 Is the request an emergency, urgent, or of normal urgency?
- If emergent or urgent, complete a Purchasing Request and Emergency Questionnaire.

Note: An emergency questionnaire should address the urgent needs of the request by highlighting the costs to purchase, the benefits to the organization, and all reasons for the immediacy of the purchase. The emergency request's purpose is to shorten the approval process and accelerate the acquisition of the needed materials. This process should be used rarely. Most situations that require an emergency request are caused by extenuating circumstances that fall outside normal operations and are not planned in normal operating budgets or capital allocations.

Step 6 Is the item or service available from a **preferred** use or optional use contract?

Note: An optional use contract is a secondary source used to fulfill the needs of the organization. Many organizations establish preferred vendors. In some situations, the preferred vendor is not able to fulfill the organization's needs. A secondary or optional use contract may exist for rare occasions.

- If so, purchase the item or service from the contract vendor regardless of the dollar amount.

Step 7 If the item is not from a preferred or optional contract or not available to meet your needs, then determine the estimated cost of the transaction.

Step 8 If under $5,000, departments are free to purchase from the vendor of their choice.

Step 9 If over $5,000, what is the account code to be utilized?

- Refer to account code information.

Step 10 What purchasing procedure is assigned to the applicable account code?

Step 11 If competitive bids are required for the designated account code, is there an applicable prior authorization exemption among Main Street Ambulance's purchasing procedures?

- If so, please complete a Purchasing Request and Questionnaire.

Step 12 Submit a Purchasing Request to Purchasing Services.

DECISION TREE

Another purchasing method EMS managers can use is a formal system: the decision tree. A decision tree, which is much like other medical guidelines (e.g., Advanced Cardiovascular Life Support [ACLS] guidelines), provides a consistent framework for making the best decision. Ultimately, the person making the final decision feels secure that the requester has evaluated the need for the product, service, or equipment sufficiently to justify the purchase (Figure 7.2).

Best Practice

Rod Shirken, Vice-president of Pillsbury Canada Ltd. pointed out the importance of purchasing to operational success of an organization. He stated that managers are often unaware of the amount of revenue spent on purchasing materials or the space used to store the materials. Indirect costs of insurance, employee benefits, and transportation adds expense to process of purchasing. He contends that management attitude is often the biggest hurdle to reaping the benefits realized in looking at the purchasing process.

Shirken feels management must be involved in the purchasing process, by having purchasing professionals involved in upper level management decision making, like strategic planning. Other areas he believes are essential include:

- *Hiring the right people for the responsibility.* People in the position to purchase should understand the entire operational process. They should have a keen sense of detail, be inquisitive, and seek objective information. Additionally the employees responsible for purchasing should not be rigid in their thinking, but open minded and looking for better ideas and products. They should have a firm grasp of the financial position and when dealing with internal customers and outside vendors, should seek win-win solutions.

- *Set measurable goals.* By setting goals and measuring outcomes, the executives and the purchasing professional can gauge how effective the process is and what value is added back to the organization. By developing best practices, the organizational targets are known and the process supports activities to meet objectives.

- *Seek to improve, constantly.* Each year many organizations establish slightly varied goals and objectives. Shirken believes that purchasing should seek to find better ways of doing things and look for unexplored opportunities that translate into more effective outcomes.

Sherkin, R. (2000). "Five Principles for a Healthier Bottom Line: Stressing Better Purchasing Practices Makes Dollars and Sense." *Canadian Plant* 59 (9), 20.

PROCUREMENT

Current business language and practice have introduced an umbrella concept, procurement, to the process of purchasing. Procurement is relatively the same as purchasing; however, the procurement process encompasses greater responsibility. Purchasing is the act or process of acquiring needed equipment, supplies or services, whereas the **procurement** process or procurement management process is a method by which the process of assessing the need for products or services, the evaluation of purchases for appropriateness, and the ongoing tracking of all products purchased occurs. "The procurement management process involves managing the ordering, receipt, review and approval of items from suppliers. A procurement process also specifies how to manage supplier relationships and ensure that a high level of service is received. This is a critical task in Procurement Management. In essence, the procurement process helps you 'get what you have paid for'" (Method123, n.d.).

Initiation of the procurement process occurs any time an item is purchased from an external supplier. By using a preestablished procurement management process, the EMS manager can ensure that purchased items

meet the organization's needs. It also helps the EMS leadership team manage supplier relationships, ensuring that any issues are resolved quickly. By implementing a procurement process, the EMS manager can ensure that the organization receives the maximum value from the supplier relationship.

PROCUREMENT MANAGEMENT CONCEPTS

In a procurement management process, the first activity for the EMS organization's purchasing professional is the *planning of purchases and acquisitions*. This is the process of determining the items to purchase for the organization or specific projects and when they are needed.

The second activity is *evaluating the need for a contract*. This process creates requirements for all products and services the requesting department or the project team needs. Purchasing should also start identifying potential companies that can supply the products and services (TechRepublic, 2012).

After determining the organization's needs, the purchasing or procurement specialist can look at *developing a request for seller responses*. Identifying a list of vendors to consider is important. Requesting information on

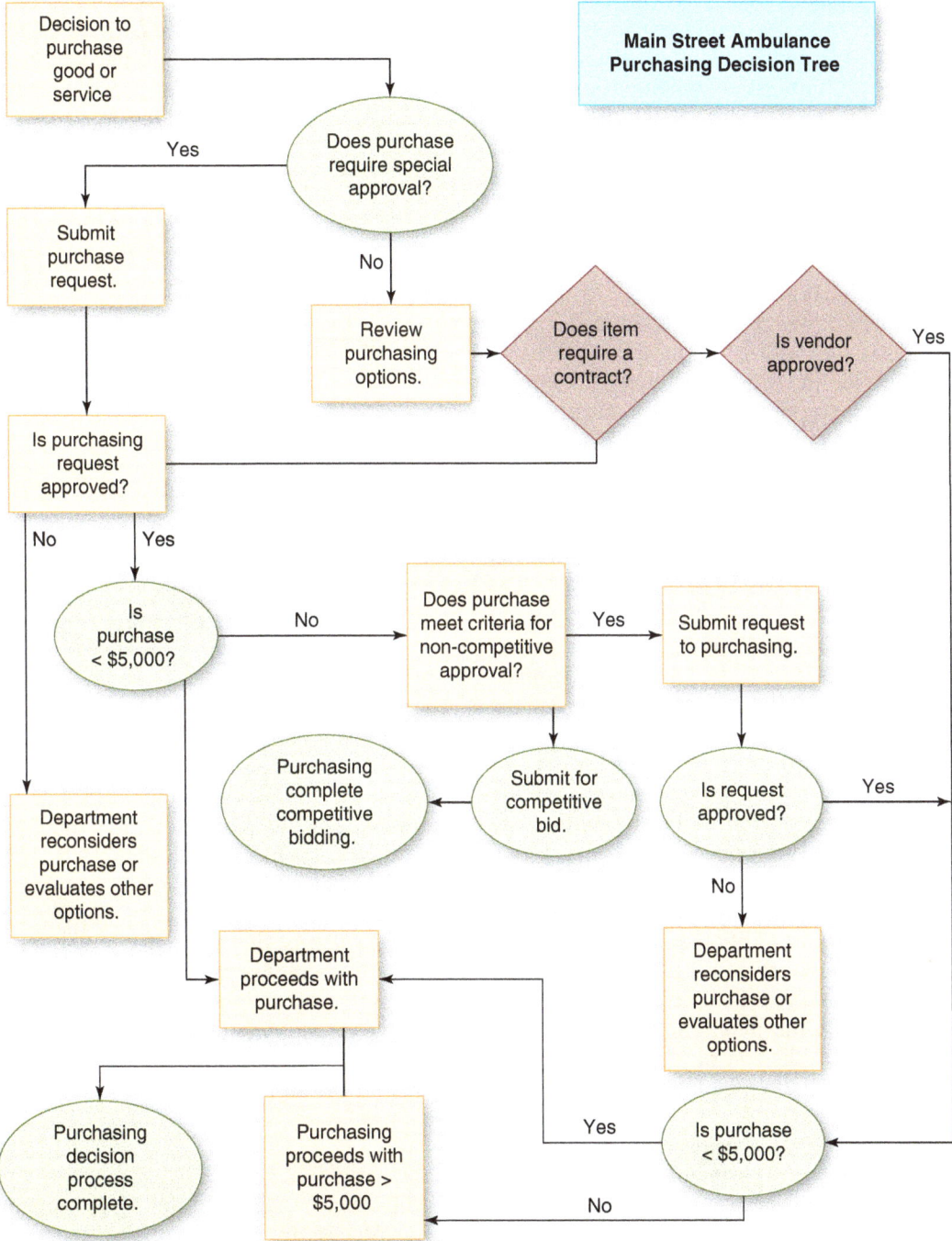

FIGURE 7.2 ■ EMS purchasing decision tree.

their capabilities and prices through vendor proposals and price quotes provides an opportunity to narrow the list of potential companies to a short list of qualified companies. In order to request quotes, the procurement specialist generates a procurement document. **Procurement documents** are used to solicit proposals from prospective sellers. The procurement document then becomes the basis for the seller's proposal.

The fourth step in the process is *selecting the sellers or vendors*. Selecting is the process associated with choosing the vendor that will provide the product or service. Depending on the size of the EMS organization, the supervisor may make the final selection, but only with the guidance of the manager or purchasing department. The manager or purchasing department signs the final contracts. Most organizations do not want supervisors or project managers to enter into legal, contractual relationships.

Once the contract is signed, the purchasing department engages in *contract administration,* which is the process of managing the relationship with the vendor's company.

When the project is completed or the need for a service or product has ended, the purchasing department will facilitate the *contract closure*. This occurs if the contractual relationship existed only for the life of the project. For instance, if the contract was in place to build an addition to an existing structure, then the contract will probably end after the project is over. The project team will be involved with the purchasing department to ensure that all the contracted work was completed and to gather feedback about the vendor relationship.

In most EMS organizations, the bottom line is that the department head or project manager should understand the basics of procurement management, but that is frequently a responsibility shared with the procurement department. The project manager should provide requirements to the procurement specialist to ensure that the correct vendor is chosen, and the procurement specialist in turn provides guidance to the project manager on managing the vendor relationship successfully.

PROACTIVE PURCHASING MANAGEMENT

In the book *Purchasing and Materials Management*, the authors Leenders and Fearon (1993) discuss five major categories of purchasing strategies. EMS managers can benefit from understanding how **proactive** purchasing is more advantageous than reactive or routine purchasing. The following are some concepts of proactive purchasing:

1. Assurance of supply
2. Cost reduction
3. Supply support
4. Environmental change
5. Competitive edge
6. Backward vertical integration
7. Supplier quality assurance programs

Assurance of Supply
The supplier should be capable of delivering the supplies needed to the EMS organization relatively quickly. If the EMS manager/ purchasing agent places an order and must wait days to weeks for the supplies to arrive, this increases the chance of running out of supplies. Often in such a scenario, the EMS manager learns that he must order greater numbers of supplies to avoid delays in receiving shipments. As stated, ordering greater number of supplies ultimately increases the cost of doing business for the EMS organization, and the supplier does not lose anything by the delay.

Cost Reduction
Savings can be achieved during the procurement process by implementing some of the following ideas. Suppliers or vendors can also contribute to suggesting cost reduction

ideas. The procurement department can have a prime role in contributing to saving unnecessary and often hidden expenses for the EMS organization. Some of the ideas can be expanded to include other EMS organizations in an effort to reduce overall purchasing costs for everyone.

Bulk buying. The companies that have greater geographical presence or have multiple locations can obtain better prices by buying in volume rather than for individual units. Central buying policies are recommended over single unit purchases. Bulk buying is commonly arranged with an annual contract in effect for 6 to 12 months, with prices remaining fixed for the entire period (Figure 7.3).

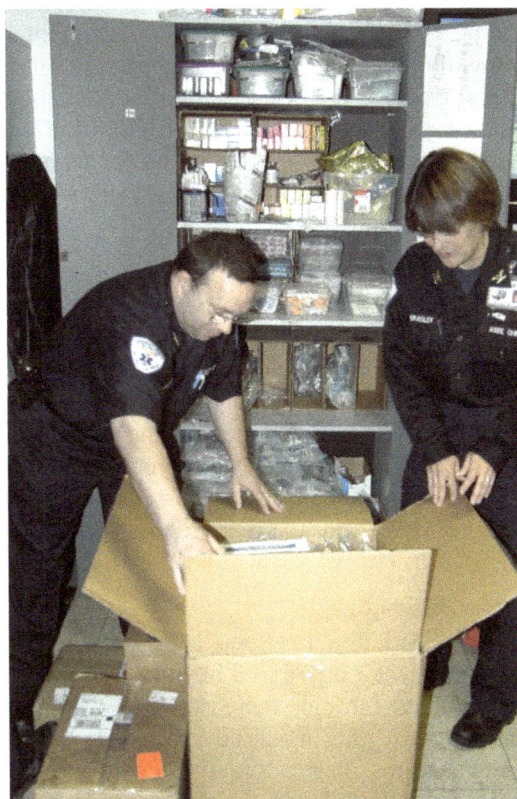

FIGURE 7.3 ■ Bulk purchasing. *Courtesy of Dennis Mitterer.*

Opportunity buying. Many items exhibit a seasonal cycle as prices peak and fall in intervals or are sold off due to overproduction or to reduce manufacturing inventory. Hence the astute purchaser can maximize scarce financial resources by developing relationships with vendors and asking them to look for special or opportunity purchases.

Local vendors. EMS organizations should choose vendors located nearby so that they can keep inventories and freight costs low.

Partnerships with major vendors. Partnerships with vendors that include equity or technical collaboration are highly recommended in order to reduce unnecessary expenses. Vendors are assured of business and should willingly offer savings in exchange for the relationship (Figure 7.4).

E procurement. Purchasing via the Internet may save time and money since the EMS manager or purchasing specialist will not need to meet with vendors or sales representatives. This is most beneficial for regular and bulk purchases of supplies.

Alternate material. Where quality will not be sacrificed, replace items made of high-cost ma-

FIGURE 7.4 ■ Vendor partnerships can be seen in bulk purchasing. *Courtesy of Dennis Mitterer.*

terials with those made of low-cost materials (e.g., replace steel with plastic or aluminum products). Knowing what your purchasing needs are and understanding the technology for manufacturing items with less expensive resources may save the organization money. The other benefits can include supporting green purchasing and recycling. The key is not to sacrifice quality when purchasing alternative and often nontraditional materials.

Vendor-managed inventory (VMI). With the appropriate incentives, suppliers can assume responsibility for replenishing the inventory. Suppliers' control of their inventory and production schedule can almost always be managed to efficiently meet the EMS organization's demand.

Vendor stocking program (VSP). Used primarily for maintenance inventories but applicable to all types of inventory, VSPs requires a supplier to commit to an extremely high service level for delivery of a specific product within a fixed time at a predefined markup. VSPs can reduce or eliminate inventories for slow-moving products. The key to managing inventory successfully is to continuously measure performance and look for new ways to improve.

Supply Support

Many businesses—whether commercial, nonprofit, or governmental—have been under pressure to reduce costs, improve customer service, and focus on core competencies. EMS organizations share the same challenges of operating under many budgetary challenges. Constraints have led top commercial firms to reexamine the purchasing structure. Many of these businesses recognize that an organizational structure built from traditional specialization makes purchasing difficult to coordinate.

Accordingly, they have reorganized to consolidate the various material management functions—purchasing, inventory management, and distribution—to provide a more

integrated systems approach (Shumaonline. com, n.d.-a). Under a systems approach, the objective is to optimize the performance of the system, rather than to optimize the performance of individual operating units. A systems approach also promotes a closed-loop feedback mechanism, whereby the organization can respond more readily to any changes in its core businesses.

Putting these concepts into practice has led firms to create new methods, implement strategic policies, and develop strategic relationships with suppliers. The key for EMS organizations is to recognize the need to change the task-oriented idea of purchasing and develop methods that will improve the use of scarce financial resources.

To successfully transition from a traditional purchasing concept into a streamlined procurement structure, the organization must develop the processes to support the change and ongoing activity. Developing a centralized system, as opposed to having each department or supervisor decide what to buy, supports a streamlined procurement structure.

Environmental Changes

Environmental changes encompass the new and expanding requirements for organizations to consider buying environmentally friendly materials and developing processes that consider the impact on the environment. The "Green Purchasing" section later in this chapter covers this in greater detail.

Competitive Edge

Many EMS organizations have grown and expanded their operations beyond their initial capabilities through increased call volumes. To minimize the increased level of expense, organizations have creatively developed methods to increase the level of revenue. Naturally, a certain degree of competition may develop between EMS organizations that are located near each other. An increase in competition between stations within the same municipally supported EMS organization can also occur. Even though EMS organizations should not compete with other public service organizations for funds, competition does occur. When describing **competitive edge** involving purchasing, the purpose is to show how good purchasing processes and system development can improve the financial position of an organization in order to reduce the competition for funding among organizations.

For example, the EMS organization receives funding from the public through fund drives or even municipal support and has historically needed $100,000 of assistance. The municipality also supports the fire department, and its needs are $100,000 for operations. Due to economic conditions, the municipality can only provide $150,000 to both. The municipal decision makers agree that splitting the money evenly is the fairest method. By developing a systems approach to purchasing, the EMS organization reduces operating expenses to a level that requires only $80,000 of outside support. The fire department continues to need the full $100,000. Since each organization is only going to receive $75,000, the EMS is in a better position to continue to provide the needed services because it needs to make up only $5,000 compared to the $25,000 the fire company will need to make up to balance its operational needs. In this way, the EMS organization has gained a competitive edge related to organizational functionality.

A number of other specific strategic purchasing concepts are considered proactive. Examples include backward vertical integration, establishing supplier quality assurance programs, and risk sharing with the supplier.

Backward Vertical Integration
An EMS organization assumes ownership or increased control of its supply systems in a backward vertical integration purchasing system. The process serves to streamline the process of purchasing, for better cost controls, and to reduce the effects of increased costs added to a product by local vendors. In many small to medium-size EMS organizations, contacting the manufacturer directly for high-ticket items (e.g., defibrillators and patient handling equipment) may save money. For regular purchases on soft supplies (e.g., oxygen and pharmaceuticals), organizations routinely rely on vendors. Buying directly may occur if large organizations spend significant dollar amounts on supplies. Organizations that are municipally or hospital based may take advantage of volume buying and purchase all their supplies directly from the manufacturer.

Many EMS organizations have formed cooperatives for purchasing. In a sluggish economy, where every dollar is essential, multiple EMS organizations can partner and agree on what standardized equipment to use. Using the purchasing power of higher numbers to request lower prices on regular supplies is an example of collective backward vertical integration.

Supplier Quality Assurance Programs
In a supplier quality assurance program, the purchaser requires each supplier to meet certain predetermined quality objectives. As stated earlier, small to medium-size EMS organizations may be at a disadvantage when requiring suppliers to meet stringent quality programs. The size of an EMS organization should not discourage the EMS manager from setting high quality standards for products purchased. This is another argument in support of EMS organizations developing a purchasing cooperative.

In a supplier quality assurance program, the purchaser develops expectations that all suppliers must meet in order to do business.

The following are examples of quality expectations:

* High-quality systems
* High-quality products with few DPM (defects per million)
* On-time delivery
* Few rejections
* Corrective actions issued where appropriate
* Formal requests issued for deviations
* A signed partnership agreement

By developing high expectations from suppliers, the EMS manager can control purchasing and the money spent on supplies, equipment, and services. EMS managers can implement any of these at various degrees of complexity in order to meet the purchasing objectives. Implementing proactive purchasing activities strengthens the financial position of the organization.

INVENTORY CONTROL

Controlling inventory is as important as buying the proper materials for the EMS organization. Each organization has an idea about how much inventory it uses in a week, month, or year, depending on the business of the organization. EMS units that respond to 20 calls per month require less inventory than organizations that run 20 calls per day. Both organizations require an inventory control program that not only tracks the use of inventory but also accounts for the cost of inventory through the organization's accounting system.

WHAT IS INVENTORY CONTROL?

Inventory control is a means of supervising the organizational supplies, storage of inventory, and accessibility of clinical items in order to ensure that an adequate supply is available for responders. The primary aim is to reduce the **overhead** costs associated with keeping an adequate supply available. Many organizations attempt to keep a surplus of supplies available—just in case—which requires the use of financial resources that could be better used in other areas of the organization.

Inventory applies to every item that the EMS crew, office staff, or maintenance person uses to keep the organization running. When an EMS unit responds to a call and uses monitor pads, 4×4s, oxygen, and so on, these items must be replaced out of the organization's inventory. *Inventory control* covers every aspect of controlling available stock, from purchasing and delivery to using and reordering.

INVENTORY CONTROL SYSTEM

Since the purchase of inventory requires an outlay of money, the accounting of inventory is the key to the control system. Each purchase of inventory has an associated monetary value. These values can be high, medium, or low. A high-value item may be an ambulance or new monitor. A medium-value item may be a radio or a new training mannequin. A low-value item may be paper supplies for the office.

The inventory can also have a value that is not directly measured by the cost to purchase. A case of paper is low cost relative to the cost of the ambulance, but most businesses cannot survive without an adequate supply of paper. What happens to the operations when someone forgets to order paper? Thus, paper can be a high-value item because of usage. Placing a value on miscellaneous items will help determine, from an accounting standpoint, what inventory items are essential for the continued operations of the organization, especially in lean times. The EMS manager must decide where to concentrate the organization's financial resources to bring about the greatest value.

Efficient inventory control allows the organization to have the right amount of hard and soft supplies in the right place at the right time. It also ensures that needed financial capital is not tied up unnecessarily. The EMS manager should establish control mechanisms that account for the movement of inventory and then assign a person to be responsible for controlling the inventory. In large organizations, the use of office supplies may constitute a large portion of the cost of running an office with the use of paper, ink cartridges and toner, and other needed items. In the maintenance department, oil and lubricants, equipment for repairs, tires, and belts may make up the cost of inventory. The crew inventory consists of the supplies used on calls and during training. All of these areas require good inventory control systems.

When deciding to establish an inventory control system, the EMS manager must determine that the system's purpose is to control costs. Often people who work in the organization will "borrow" a pen or some paper, but what about the employees who "borrow" a ream of paper for their home computer or a quart of oil for their car? The EMS manager must understand that this does occur. The inventory control system is not intended to catch people but to ensure that inventory is accounted for correctly. The size of the organization does not impact the need for an inventory control system. Even if the organization is relatively small, EMS managers must purchase inventory in order to be prepared to respond to calls. Not having a system of tracking the inventory can ultimately lead to wasted financial resources.

ASSIGNING RESPONSIBILITY

Having control of the inventory is an essential part of the smooth operations of the EMS organization. Every organization benefits from having one person responsible for the organization's inventory. Part of the job function is to maintain complete accuracy of the inventory. Many organizations assign the responsibility for the "shop inventory" to the maintenance person because that is who is most familiar with the equipment. But what if this person is also responsible for the purchase of that inventory? The conflict that could develop is obvious. This is about accountability, not trust. Assigning an impartial person to the inventory control team that is kept separate from the area that is evaluated allows for objectivity. Since all purchases affect the financial success of the organization, having an accurate count of inventory on hand is essential to determining if excessive financial resources are sitting on a shelf. The person who is assigned the responsibility for controlling inventory must exhibit a high degree of accuracy and attention to detail.

Side Bar

Control of the cost of inventory is often tied just to being neat and orderly.

INVENTORY TRACKING PROCEDURES

Having an excess amount of obsolete inventory contributes to losses recorded on the balance sheet in the form of write-offs. To avoid this, stock should be rotated based on the purchase date, and all removals should be tracked on a computer to ensure that the oldest inventory is used first. If the inventory usage is tracked on a computer, access to the computer system should be limited to just a few people.

The EMS manager should review all journal entries made in the general ledger that has a component of inventory in the account. For example, accounts payable or purchases for large amounts of stock should be checked against budget.

The EMS manager should also review overhead costs frequently. Overhead costs should not vary greatly from month to month, so any large deviation should prompt an immediate investigation.

EMS managers should record all inventory as an asset, although it can be looked at as a liability because it costs money to order, store, handle, and account for it. It also can cost money if the inventory is not tracked systematically on a regular basis.

> **Side Bar**
>
> The best control of inventory is to keep it as low as possible.

THE ROLE OF RISK MANAGEMENT

Risk management is the avoidance or prevention of losses and can cover financial, human, and property losses. Risk management looks at a situation and helps determine what decision is best for the organization. According to Sitkin and Pablo (1992), high-risk decisions are defined to the extent that (1) their expected outcomes are more uncertain, (2) decision goals are more difficult to achieve, or (3) the potential outcomes include some extreme consequences. To better appreciate risk in the context of purchasing, the EMS manager should understand the perspective involved in the purchasing process. Purchasing occurs as a routine process. Many tasks associated with purchasing are viewed as clerical (Sitkin and Pablo, 1992).

Let's assume that one of the organization's support departments (maintenance) instructs the staff member responsible for purchasing to buy needed materials. Purchasing, acting in a reactive manner, prepares requests for quotes and selects a supplier. A purchase order is issued, materials are received, and the invoice is paid. Purchasing is responsible for relatively routine procedures, but several risks and potential consequences still exist that can damage the firm's ability to satisfy the maintenance department. The major risks for the purchasing function are clerical errors and poor judgment in supplier selection. Poor judgment in supplier selection can lead to late deliveries and missed shipments. In that case, the maintenance department bears responsibility for quality, timing, and specifications. The clerical person who completed the purchase does not have significant responsibility for strategic decisions that affect the material purchased.

Now consider a situation in which purchasing is an integral member of the management team. Purchasing is responsible for material availability and cost, so the person in charge of purchasing works closely with potential suppliers during the early stage of the relationship. Subsequently, purchasing works with a selected supplier to develop a long-term alliance in which material procurement risk will be shared. Purchasing is responsible for both the analysis and management of the purchasing effort. During this process, changes are made as products are used or revised. Purchasing is then responsible for nonroutine activity and thus incurs higher risk than when it had less strategic involvement. The consequences of poor judgment, poor timing, and poor quality can be laid squarely on the person responsible for purchasing. However, for the organization as a whole, risk is now shared with the supplier.

The transaction cost and resource dependency theories will help explain why frequent purchasing functions are not proactive.

TRANSACTION COST THEORY

This theory views negotiating, monitoring, and enforcing contracts as transactions, all of which have associated costs. By reducing the number of transactions, management reduces the associated costs of the transactions.

In addition to transaction costs, each transaction also incurs an associated risk of opportunism. Opportunism is the practice of adjusting one's decisions to take advantage of another regardless of the potential sacrifice to one's moral or ethical principles. This includes, but is not limited to, lying, stealing, and cheating. More commonly, opportunism is the incomplete or distorted disclosure of information in a transaction, especially in a calculated effort to mislead, distort, disguise, obfuscate, or otherwise confuse. All transactions carry the risk of supplier opportunism. Again, by reducing the number of transactions, the risk of opportunism can be reduced.

The definition of risk also encompasses the concept that the riskier the decision is, the more difficult goal achievement will become. When the complexities of transactions are minimized or made routine, goals are easier to achieve. When purchasing decisions are complex, or the potential for risk is high, there is an incentive for purchasing to remain under the control of administrative activities. In this case, the person responsible for purchasing would be accountable to the administrative team, but he may not be a member of that team.

RESOURCE DEPENDENCY THEORY

This theory helps managers understand why delegating the purchasing responsibility to another is avoided. **Resource dependency theory** attempts to explain how managers and organizations adapt to their environment. In the most simplistic form, it states that for a manager or organization to survive, it must not become dependent on others. Managers' dependency on others is risky because it potentially leads to uncertain outcomes. This implies that the more critical the resources are to the organization, the more the manager wishes to control them.

Some proactive purchasing management practices are considered contrary to resource dependency theory because they create greater risk. For example, when an organization reduces its supplier base, it relies on fewer suppliers for critical materials, possibly increasing the risk of a supply interruption. Also, when major activities are outsourced to suppliers, dependency on those suppliers increases. This creates higher risk for the manager and the organization. In summary, dependency creates risks, making goals more difficult to achieve, and increases the potential for serious consequences.

Proactive purchasing management is the management of risk—it actually mitigates risk and, at the same time, provides a higher return. An analogy to reducing risk and increasing return on purchasing can be made with increasing quality while at the same time increasing profits. Forward-thinking EMS organizations are learning that risk reduction for the entire organization, through proactive purchasing, can increase profitability.

Proactive purchasing management includes activities that are beyond the traditional administrative purchasing cycle. Such activities include reducing the supplier base, developing long-term alliances, achieving early supplier involvement, and outsourcing.

RISK SHARING

Risk sharing is a process in which the EMS organization (the buyer) and the supplier (seller) agree to share the risk of purchasing services or inventory. In a normal economic relationship, both the buyer and seller want to maximize their advantage over the other. The buyer attempts to squeeze the lowest price out of the supplier by controlling volumes purchased in order to drive down costs and use inventory as a buffer against business fluctuations. The supplier tries to maintain the highest profit margin. This is not always the best approach. Buyers may have limited information about suppliers' behaviors, technology, and costs. Suppliers may take advantage of this lack of knowledge by inflating the cost of buying supplies.

Small negotiations may provide success for either party, but the traditional goal is to improve the economic position of one party at the expense of the other.

Under risk sharing, buyers are concerned with short-term reductions of the cost of their supplies, but also with building and maintaining long-term relationships with trusted suppliers (Dawid and Kopel, 2003). Risk sharing provides an opportunity to develop a long-term relationship between the buyer and seller by agreeing to minimize potential financial losses by either party. Providing support to suppliers and sharing business and technology information with them helps establish lasting relationships, which eventually improves the overall business performance (Dyer, 2000).

For example, one risk-sharing method is having a buy-back agreement in which the seller agrees to buy back any unused or outdated inventory. Another risk-sharing option is called a quantity-flexibility agreement, in which the EMS organization agrees to purchase a set quantity of a product, regardless of demand, and as a result price discounting is agreed upon by the supplier. Within this framework, EMS organizations should consider absorbing part of the risk of the unpredictable cost of supplies they purchase. If EMS organizations do not provide suppliers with some incentives against cost fluctuations, the performance of the supplier and their commitment to the EMS organization will **waiver** and, eventually, will negatively affect the EMS organization's bottom line. A common interest between buyers and suppliers exists in pursuing agreements that consider the profitability and potential risk to each partner. The goal is to ensure that one partner does not improve at the expense of the other (Simchi-Levi, Kaminsky, and Simchi-Levi, 2004). What does all this mean?

Essentially the EMS manager should seek to develop relationships with suppliers who are willing to reduce costs (absorb some of the business risk) for a guarantee of continued business. In areas where there is only one supplier, this becomes a little tricky, but if there is any inclination on the part of the EMS manager that he is not getting the best deal from the supplier, the relationship is one sided. Discussing the concerns may lead to a risk-sharing relationship.

Proactive purchasing does not start with the buyer and the supplier. It begins in the administrative makeup of the organization. Often in EMS organizations, the person who purchases supplies and equipment is considered support staff and the job is simply a normal, clerical function. Only when the purchase of high-ticket items occurs does management become involved, and then a piece of equipment undergoes at least a partial review and assessment.

The purchasing function should be considered in any strategic planning process, both short term and long term. Heinritz, Farrell, Giunipero, and Kolchin (1991) identify several risks that occur when purchasing is not included in the strategic planning process. These risks include threats to ensuring the availability of supplies, decreased selection of supplies, problems with environmental hazards, and increased EMS liability. When these perspectives are taken into consideration, proactive purchasing becomes a viable option for EMS managers.

Other authors also provide additional insight about the term *proactive*. They believe purchasing is moving from a transaction activity to a supply management orientation. As this transition occurs, two shifts in focus are occurring:

- From internal processes to value-adding benefits
- From tactical management to strategic management

Burt and Pinkerton (1996) recognize that procurement of material and services is a process that involves all portions of the organization, and implementation of an integrated procurement system results in proactive procurement, as distinguished from reactive purchasing. They also define proactive procurement management as the process of adding value during the following four stages required for effective procurement:

1. Determining what to buy
2. Identifying and developing the appropriate relationship with the supplier
3. Obtaining the lowest total cost associated with purchasing and converting the required material or service
4. Ensuring that the required material or service is received in a timely manner and that future supply will be available (Burt and Pinkerton, 1996, p. 4)

Reactive Purchasing

To understand proactive purchasing management, EMS managers should be familiar with the opposite belief: reactive purchasing management. Reactive purchasing management treats the purchasing function as a response to the needs of the requester. This is a traditional approach to the purchasing function. The person responsible for purchasing receives a request from an area of the organization and proceeds to place an order with the vendor. The purchasing department may track the purchase through the process but, in many cases, once the order is placed may not hear about it unless there is a problem. If goods are delayed, a crisis may develop to which purchasing must react. In this situation, the purchasing department is largely a transaction-oriented, secretarial function. The people performing the purchasing service often perform other functions within the EMS organization. More time is spent expediting than planning.

The reactive purchasing function is typically evaluated on two criteria: administrative costs and savings on the price of materials or supplies. EMS organizations can track the purchasing activity by determining the number of requisitions filled per employee, cost per requisition, or total number of employees per dollar spent. However, these are often just measurements of employee activity and do not provide information on whether the organization is effective in the purchasing process. The focus for purchasing is on controlling administration costs and on negotiation skills that result in reduced contract costs. Adversarial relationships with suppliers may be encouraged.

STRATEGIC PARTNERSHIP AND VENDORS

The individual who is responsible for purchasing should also be capable of establishing relationships with a select group of vendors. The ability to communicate and develop trust with vendors is essential to negotiating not only the best price, but also service after the sale. Often EMS managers or purchasing professionals discuss their needs with multiple vendors in order to force competition. Often this competition is based on price. At any given time, a vendor may be capable of taking price concessions on products on the short term to gain business. Over the life of any product, however, the low-ball price is not sustainable and the price increases. By developing a relationship, both the purchaser and the seller understand each others' needs and cooperatively work together in seeking the best outcome.

When preparing to purchase supplies, services, or equipment, the EMS manager or person responsible for purchasing should evaluate and determine the need for goods and services. The manager should extend an invitation for this evaluation to associates who are affected by the purchased goods. The associates and management should conduct a thorough evaluation of the potential vendors who sell the required equipment or supplies. Remember: The goal to reducing expenses on equipment, supplies, and services is to develop a relationship with vendors because goods and services are potentially used throughout the life of the relationship with the vendor.

Vendors should be chosen for their ability to provide the best mix of quality, service, and price. Accordingly, if a strategic partnership agreement exists for goods and services, then the preference for the strategic partner will carry over to most transactions involving those supplies or equipment.

In *The Deming Management Method* (Walton, 1986), the author discusses Dr. Deming's fourth point: End the practice of awarding business on the price tag alone. She quotes Dr. Deming as having stated, "Price has no meaning without a measure of quality being purchased" (p. 62). To serve the organization best, the EMS manager should develop a relationship based on trust with a single vendor who will work with the organization to succeed. Deming also points out that "defects beget defects" and low price begets low quality (p. 63). That inferior quality can be seen after the sale or in poor service or poor-quality workmanship. Many managers like to have multiple vendors compete for the business. As stated, this may drive down the price, but ultimately it tends to alienate good vendors and exceptional service.

Deming further states, "Purchasing should be a team effort and one of the most important people on the team should be the chosen supplier. He should be chosen for his record of improvement and his effort to learn and help your organization" (Walton, 1986, p. 63). A gentleman's agreement works well for building trust. It is a powerful route to developing a long-term business relationship. Of course, long-term relationships are all relative, but a contract entered into by the EMS manager and the supplier can be changed by a skilled lawyer. If a contract is necessary, the EMS manager should understand the basics of bidding and contracts.

COMPETITIVE BIDDING

EMS managers have many options when planning to purchase equipment and supplies. For small items (soft supplies) the EMS manager does not need to request bids unless, of course, the purchase is over a certain dollar amount, or the organization is required to ask for bids by its governing body. If the manager determines that a bid process is necessary, a few different bid structures may be utilized (Shumaonline.com, n.d.-a).

Box 7.2

Types of Bids

- *Request for Quotation (RFQ)*. Generally used when the supplies, materials, equipment, goods, property, or services are to be acquired on a one-time basis.
- *Invitation for Bids (IFB)*. Typically used when the supplies, materials, equipment, goods, property, and services, to be acquired will be provided via contract on a recurring basis over a specified period of time.
- *Request for Proposal (RFP)*. Generally used when multiple factors exist that make it difficult or impossible to define a product or scope of work that allows an evaluation to determine the best bid from a responsible bidder. Evaluations are based on the factors set forth in the RFP in order to determine which proposal(s) best meet(s) the needs of the organization.
- *Direct Competitive Negotiation (DCN)*. This bid method is used after an unsuccessful RFQ, IFB, or RFP process if the EMS manager determines that time does not permit resolicitation.
- *Competitive Reverse Auction (CRA)*. An option for very large commodity purchases wherein vendors bid against each other to provide the item(s) at the lowest price.

Very little trust is built in during the bidding process. Someone always wins, and someone always loses. EMS managers convince themselves that this is the fairest method to secure the best price. It may very well be one way, but if the EMS manager seeks to grow the organization for the long term, developing a relationship with a vendor or two so that when working together everyone wins is the best way to purchase supplies and equipment.

CONTRACTS

In today's business world, EMS managers often have come to believe that once an agreement becomes a contract it formally binds each party to the terms of the agreement. A contract allows for legal recourse if one of the parties does not honor the terms of the agreement. "Binding" a person connotes a notion of mandatory compliance. If a relationship is strong and trusting, an argument can be made that a formal contract is unnecessary—both buyer and seller are agreeing to work toward the mutual success of both parties. Until EMS and vendors can work toward this level of trust, however, the contract is available to formalize the agreement. The two ways in which a contract can originate are unilaterally and bilaterally.

A **unilateral contract** is a common form for a contract. It is a relatively simple document, such as a purchase order. A purchase order is used when routine, fixed cost items are needed. A purchase order is legally binding and should be specific. In a **bilateral contract**, each party is both promisor and promisee.

Contract types are grouped into three broad categories: cost-reimbursement contracts, fixed-price contracts, and unit-price contracts.

COST-REIMBURSEMENT CONTRACTS

Cost-reimbursement contracts are suitable when known uncertainties exist that could impact the ability to complete the contract performance, or costs cannot be estimated with sufficient accuracy. (An example of a cost-reimbursement contract is a cost-plus-fixed-fee contract, as described below.)

FIXED-PRICE CONTRACTS

A price that is not subject to any adjustments is established for a particular purchase. This type of contract places minimum risk and full responsibility for all costs and resulting profit on the contractor. It provides maximum incentive for the contractor to control costs and perform effectively.

Firm-Fixed-Price Contracts.

This is the preferred method of contracting from the government's perspective. It is used when a sealed bid process is involved and for acquiring supplies, services, and/or commercial items. One variation of fixed-price contracts allows for an economic price adjustment. It also allows for a revision of prices for specific contingencies. Adjustments are based on increases or decreases from an agreed-upon level in either published or established market prices for specific items. Adjustments are based on actual increases or decreases in the price of specific items or labor that the contractor incurs. Adjustments are also based on increases or decreases in the specific labor or material cost standards or indexes, such as the U.S. Bureau of Labor Statistics indices. An example of a fixed-price contract is a fixed-price-plus-incentive-fee (FPI) contract (see below).

UNIT-PRICE CONTRACTS

Unit prices can take the form of a simple purchase order or a fixed price per unit for goods or service. In unit pricing, the purchasing agent evaluates the cost of buying a product based on the unit cost. For example, a plumber who is hired to fix a sink is paid by the hour, or the EMS organization may purchase normal saline by the case. In either example, the purchase order (P.O.) will reflect the cost per unit.

■ RISK-AVERSION CONTRACTS——

The EMS manager should be familiar with different types of contracts because each one presents a certain level of financial risk to the organization. To reiterate, many of these contract types are generated when the EMS organization is working on a large project and huge financial resources are at risk. The everyday or customary purchases may not fall into this level of risk. The following contracts are listed in order of increased risk to the seller and decreased risk to the buyer.

Cost-Plus-Percentage-of-Cost Contracts
The seller is reimbursed for allowable costs of performing cost-plus-percentage-of-cost (CPCC) contract and receives as profit an agreed-upon percentage of the costs. There is no limit on the seller's profit. If the seller's cost increases, so does the profit. This contract is the most undesirable contract from the buyer's standpoint. The CPPC is prohibited for federal government use, but it is used in private industry, particularly construction projects.

The CPPC contract is susceptible to abuse. There is no motivation for the seller to decrease costs, and the buyer bears 100 percent of the risk. The buyer's project manager must pay attention to the control of labor and material costs so that the seller does not purposely increase these costs. The bottom line is that there is no limit on the seller's profit.

CPPC

Estimated Cost of Project	$1,000 K
Percentage Markup	10%
Estimated Total price	$1,100 K
Estimated Cost + 10% × Estimated Cost	

If the cost increases to $1,500 K due to overruns, the total price would increase relative to the increase in actual cost. Now the buyer would pay $1,100 K + $500 = $1,650 K.

Cost-Plus-Fixed-Fee Contracts
In the cost-plus-fixed-fee (CPFF) contract, the seller is reimbursed for allowable costs of performing the contract and receives as profit a fixed-fee payment based on the percentage of the estimated costs. The fixed fee does not vary with actual costs unless the scope of work changes. This contract is open to abuse because there is an upper limit on profit but no motivation to decrease costs.

This contract is primarily used in research projects where the work required to achieve success is uncertain at the time of signing the contract. The bottom line is that there is a limit on profit but no incentive to control costs.

CPFF

Estimated Cost	$1,000 K
Percentage Markup	10%
Estimated Total Price	$1,000 K
Estimated Cost + 10% × Estimated Cost	

If the cost increases to $1,100 K, the total price would be $1,100 K plus 10% of the original estimated cost = $1,200 K.

Cost-Plus-Incentive-Fee Contracts
For a cost-plus-incentive-fee (CPIF) contract, the buyer pays the seller a fee for performing the work, a predetermined fee, and an incentive bonus. If the final costs are less than expected, both the buyer and seller benefit by the savings based on a prenegotiated sharing formula. The sharing formula reflects the degree of uncertainty faced by each party.

This contract is commonly used when contracts involve a long performance period with a substantial amount of hardware development and test requirements. The risk is shared by both buyer and seller. The bottom line is that the CPIF contract provides an incentive to the seller to reduce costs by increasing profit potential.

CPIF

Estimated Cost	$1,000
Predetermined Fee	$100 K
Sharing Formula	85/15

The buyer absorbs 85% of the uncertainty, and the seller absorbs 15% of the risk.

Actual Cost	$800 K
Savings	$200 K
Seller Receives	$800 K + $100 K + $30 K = $930 K
	Actual Cost + Fee + (15% × savings)
Buyer Saves	$170 K

Fixed Price-Plus-Incentive-Fee Contracts

The fixed-price-plus-incentive-fee (FPI) contract is the most complex type. It consists of target cost, target profit, target price, ceiling price, and share ratio. The seller and buyer share any savings, based on the share ratio, for every dollar the seller can reduce costs below the target cost. The share ratio is a negotiated formula that reflects the degree of uncertainty faced by each party. If the costs exceed the ceiling price, the seller receives no profit. Regardless of the actual costs, the buyer pays no more than the ceiling price.

The risk is shared by both buyer and seller, but the risk is usually higher for the seller. This type of contract is used when a substantial sum of money is involved and a long production time is anticipated. The bottom line is that this contract provides an incentive to decrease costs, which in turn increases profits. If costs exceed a ceiling, then the contractor is penalized.

FPI

Target Cost	$1,000 K
Target Profit	$1,000 K (seller's fee)
Target Price	$1,100 K
Ceiling Price	$1,200 K (maximum the buyer will pay)
Share Ratio	70/30

Example:

Actual cost	$800 K
Savings	$200 K
	Target cost − actual cost
Seller Receives	$800 K + $100 K + $60 K = $960 K
	Actual Cost + Fee + (30% × savings)
Buyer Saves	$140 K

Firm-Fixed-Price Contracts

With a firm-fixed-price (FFP) contract, the seller agrees to perform a service or furnish supplies at the established contract price. This predetermined price is also called the lump sum. The seller bears the greatest degree of risk, so the seller is motivated to decrease costs by producing efficiently. When developing an FFP, the buyer determines the best specifications that are available and the buyer also has relative certainty of the costs. This is the most common type of contract.

FFP (Lump Sum)

Price	$1,000 K
Actual Cost	$700 K
Seller's Profit	$300 K
	Price − Actual Cost

SPECIAL CONSIDERATIONS FOR CONTRACT EXECUTION

Each contract agreement is entered with the expectation that the contract will or could have nuances requiring special language. The EMS manager should look at the entire project and determine beforehand if any variables or exceptional circumstances are evident. If so, he should make sure those items are included in the contract.

Changes

The change control system should be defined and included in the changes clause of the project. The system should cover who initiates a change request, how it is processed and funded, and who has final approval. The change process is used for major projects, and a control committee should be established to oversee any changes. The change proposal must be explicit in terms of the impact of the change in the contract work statement, specifications, drawings, and costs. From a legal standpoint, there must be mutual agreement to modify a contract, and that agreement must be supported by consideration (the change clause is very important), or the change may also be accomplished by unilateral action if pursuant to the exercise of options contained in the terms of the original contract.

Specifications

Contract specifications can be either standard in nature, as in a specific design that has been accepted throughout the industry, or tailored and unique to the situation at hand. A behavioral component is associated with the development of specifications and includes the following:

- *Drive for competency.* The EMS manager or seller keeps changing the design, which results in increasing complexity and cost. (The buyer and seller cannot come to closure.)
- *Safety margin coefficient.* This is related to design parameters in terms of how much is enough. At some point, costs increase exponentially, but safety gains do not.
- *Indifference methodology.* This is related to an attitude that promotes a contingency approach to specifications even when not warranted. (The design is too flexible; the engineer or architect is "indifferent" to the final structure of the product.)
- *Monument syndrome.* This syndrome is based on the desire to build a product that will last forever regardless of the cost (e.g., Great Wall of China).
- *Budget expansion.* The designer develops the specifications with an eye to the available funds. The more money available, the more complex and costly the design.

- *Sole-source shelter.* Specifications are developed so that equipment, materials, and supplies are tailored to require the products of a specific manufacturer or supplier.

When a major project is undertaken, the EMS manager must carefully review the contract and documents during the drafting stage. Correcting problems after signing the contract may rarely be done without costly negotiation or litigation.

QUALITY CONTROL

Once an item is bought and the organization receives it in inventory, the end user (the person on the street) determines if the product works sufficiently. Let's say the EMS manager desires to improve the bottom line and either purchases the lowest-cost product available or asks someone else to perform this task. All stock items are bought with costs as the only criteria. The EMS organization projects saving $10,000 dollars each year, thus justifying it as a way to improve salaries or buy essential equipment. With the new plan in place, the organization purchases cheap IV catheters and while inserting a 20-gauge in the hand of a construction worker, the tip of the needle breaks in the patient's hand. How much is this avoidable event going to cost the organization?

Quality cannot be overemphasized when it comes to patient care. There may be some situations when buying the most expensive items will not add to or improve patient outcomes and purchasing a cheaper, no-name item may suffice. However, even when it comes to materials used by staff, quality can make a huge difference in comfort while performing activities.

The following are a few facts about quality:

- Quality cannot be inspected into the product—it must be built into it.
- The attitude of quality must be present when the product is designed.

- Controls must be established to ensure that quality is kept in mind as work progresses.
- Periodic checks for specification conformance are a must.
- Defects can be costly and damaging to the reputation of the company, the project manager, and the project team.

When evaluating materials for purchase, the EMS manager should insist on high quality when absolutely necessary. He should determine when a lower-cost product will suffice. From IV catheters to toilet paper, spending additional money may mean the difference between a good day and a rotten one, but that may not always be sufficient reason to do so. For example, while spending top dollar for automotive towels to clean the outside of ambulances may make the maintenance man (and your best friend) happy, the additional cost does not justify the increase in quality.

In any contract or verbal agreement, quality should be included in the terms. In case the product does not meet the highest reasonable standards expected, the agreement should contain a mechanism for exchanging the product or receiving a refund. Another concept that supports the idea of quality is the ability to return the product or have recourse if the product or equipment does not live up to expectations. This is the warranty.

WARRANTIES

A warranty is based on one party's assurance to the other that the goods will meet certain standards of quality, including condition, reliability, description, function, or performance.

Express Warranty

An express warranty applies when a service or product does not meet the level of quality specified in the contract (Cornell University Law School, n.d.).

Implied Warranty

"Implied warranty . . . is measured by *merchantability* or *fitness for a particular use. . . .* The implied *warranty of merchantability* arises in every sale of goods made by a merchant who deals in goods of the kind sold. It means the goods must be reasonably fit for the ordinary purposes for which such goods are used (applies to goods which can be resold)" (IBM Education and Training, 2000). Generally, this is not a concern for EMS organizations because reselling is not a usual part of the business.

The implied warranty applies to both merchants and non-merchants. The warranty is implied if the seller knows the purpose of the products the EMS manager is purchasing the item for, and the seller also knows the manager is relying on the seller's judgment in selecting the best products. The implied warranty is *not* relevant in the following cases:

- The purchaser is knowledgeable about the product, has inspected it, and has made his own independent judgment without relying on the seller's skill.
- The product meets the specifications and plans furnished by the client project manager.

Analogy: If you buy a lawn mower, you would expect it to cut grass. If you use it on the carpet, the warranty does not apply.

WAIVERS

The EMS manager or purchasing agent must continually be aware of the waiver pitfall. "Under the doctrine of a waiver, a party may relinquish rights he otherwise has under the contract" (IBM Education and Training, 2000). If the EMS manager or purchasing agent knowingly accepts incomplete inventory, defective products, or late performance, and accepts these without objection, the person has waived his right to strict performance.

BONDS

Bonds contain penalties sufficient to ensure payment and performance. When appropriate, bonds are drafted into the contract. A performance bond secures the performance and fulfillment of the contract, including all the terms, conditions, and undertakings contained therein. Penalties for failure to perform could be as much as the total contract price (IBM Education and Training, 2000). A payment bond secures the payment of subcontractors, laborers, and others by the prime contractor. In addition, the EMS manager may include a clause that requires the contractor to secure a bond from any subcontractor on the project.

BREACHES

A **breach** of the contract is the failure to perform a contractual obligation. The measure of damages for a breach is the amount of loss the injured party has sustained. A **material breach** of contract states that the non-faulted party is discharged from further obligations under the contract. The breach is so serious that it also deprives the non-faulting party the expected benefits of the bargain. A **time breach** states that no time for performance are stated or implied in the contract but the performance was not completed within a reasonable amount of time. However, if time is critical, the contract should explicitly state that "time is of the essence." When time is of the essence, and it is explicitly stated within the contract, failure to perform within the allotted time will constitute a material breach of contract and the buyer will not be required to accept late performance.

■ NEGOTIATION

Miller and Kelle (1998) point out that in a traditional purchasing environment the purchaser and supplier may have an adversarial relationship. The authors contend that each party tries to enhance its own position, which increases the costs for the other party. For purchasing to be effective, the two parties should have a cooperative relationship. They should work together to enhance both positions. Rubin and Carter (1990) showed that "compromises by the buyer, as well as by the seller, can serve to improve profitability for both" (p. 22).

STAGES OF NEGOTIATION

There are several stages in negotiation. The first stage is protocol. Introductions are made, and the negotiators get to know each other. The atmosphere for the rest of the negotiations is determined at this stage (IBM Education and Training, 2000). The second stage is probing. Negotiators begin the search process. Each party identifies issues of concern. Strengths and weaknesses are identified as well as possible areas of interest (IBM Education and Training).

At the third stage, the negotiators conduct scratch bargaining. During this stage, bargaining occurs and concessions are made. Points of concession are also identified.

- *Closure.* The two positions are summed up and final concessions are reached. The agreements are summarized and documented.
- *Agreement.* The main difficulty in this stage is ensuring that both parties have an identical understanding of the agreements. This stage should establish the plans for recording the agreements in a written contract. (IBM Education and Training, 2000).

NEGOTIATION TACTICS

The EMS manager should be aware that negotiation is not only an art but also a science. The following negotiation tactics are commonly used to gain an advantage over a person who is not as skilled (IBM Education and Training, 2000):

- **Imposing a deadline for reaching an agreement.** A powerful tactic because it implies a possible loss to both parties. The purchasing party does not have to accept deadline, but often does.
- **Surprise.** One party springs information such as a price change on the other party.
- **Stalling.** One party may claim that he cannot finalize an agreement because he has limited authority and cannot commit the company's resources. A party may claim that the person with final authority is absent. The "missing man" technique—when the party does not have the information asked for by the other party—may also be used.
- **Fair and reasonable**. The negotiator may claim the price for a piece of equipment (like a computer or copier) is equitable because that is what another company is paying.
- **Delays.** Useful when tempers are beginning to flare, a team member is going astray, or diversion from a particular subject is desired.

Examples of delays: arrival of refreshments, request for recess, etc.

- **Reasoning together.** Used to confuse the other party. Deliberately distorting issues and figures. (If this is done, someone should speak up before agreeing to anything.)
- **Withdrawal.** Sometimes done to divert attention from an area of weakness. One party may make an attack on an issue, then retreat. Or they may make the other party appear unreasonable by pointing out all the concessions made by the party.
- **Arbitration.** A third party may be brought in when agreement cannot be reached.
- **Fait accompli.** A party may claim that what is being asked for has already been accomplished and cannot be changed.

PREPARATION FOR NEGOTIATION

When negotiating; be clear about exactly what you are after. Conduct research to prepare to discuss every aspect and respond to every question and comment. Be persistent. Do not expect to "win." Your first goal is to start the other person thinking. When looking to enter into a relationship, both parties must understand each other's position. Negotiation is not about winning at all costs, but to seek a win-win for both parties (Business Coach, n.d.). If the EMS manager attempts to pressure for the lowest cost, the vendor may become protective of their position and seek higher dollars in other areas.

Develop a relationship with the person with whom you are bargaining. Put your needs in terms of his by expressing the advantages and the benefits. Discuss how the relationship is beneficial for both parties.

Keep your sense of humor. Sure it is about business. Depending on the purchasing levels, there are many financial implications. In the end, if the relationship that is developing between the buyer and seller is about getting the best deal out of the other person, then the interactions will be stressful at best and suspicious at the worst.

Separate the relationship with people from the substance of the deal. Be hard on the deal but soft on the people. You are protecting the assets of the organization and the community, whether volunteer, municipally based, or hospital based. View the deal from everybody's perspective. Make the proposal consistent with their values.

Focus on shared values and interests, but not on the positions that each side takes. Values define the agreement. Each side has diverse interests, so be explicit about yours and discover theirs.

When stuck on a point, brainstorm for options that have mutual benefits. Be creative, and think outside the box. Identify shared interests. Use objective criteria for decision making. A deal is based on principles, not pressure. Agree on fair standards and procedures. Frame issues as a collaborative quest (Shumaonline.org, n.d.-b).

Set the tone early, and offset any false rumors. Be candid and open about feelings and motives because this builds trust. Avoid discussing too many issues at one time, and emphasize the most relevant ones. Unless there is a critical reason to set deadlines, avoid them. In addition, summarize frequently because doing so provides an opportunity for understanding and a chance to clarify. Do not personalize any arguments. When discussing differences, ensure that your arguments are logical; personal opinions in arguments will slow negotiations. Also avoid ultimatums and other forms of nonnegotiable demands, and admit when the other party has a valid argument (Business Coach, n.d.).

GREEN PURCHASING

A purchasing concept that is relatively new and gaining a lot of attention is green purchasing. What is environmentally preferable (green) purchasing?

BACKGROUND AND PURPOSE

With growing frequency and urgency, organizations are realizing the need to consider environmental stewardship. Increasing costs of waste management, worker safety and public health concerns, and the emergence of severe and chronic environmental problems are a few of the issues spurring businesses to improve the environmental characteristics of their operations (Native Green, n.d.). Though EMS organizations typically do not consider "green purchasing," the local, regional, and global demand for all organizations to adopt an overall "greener" approach is increasing rapidly.

In response, a growing number of local governments are now intent on avoiding the costs of environmental degradation and are committed to instituting more sustainable practices. If

a municipally based EMS organization is contracted to provide services or is supported in some way by municipal or state government, the organization may be requested to develop an environmentally friendly approach to operations.

Green or environmentally preferable purchasing (EPP) not only helps improve environmental conditions, but it also results in significant (but not always immediate) savings in budgets (Native Green, n.d.). EPP can also influence the behavior of other sectors by setting an example. The purchasing decisions of an EMS organization can influence other emergency service organizations to look at their purchasing habits. When organizational purchasing policies favor ecologically sensible products and services, these goods become more readily accessible to other organizations. It makes sense, economically as well as environmentally, for EMS organizations to establish and implement EPP programs.

EPP consists of the selection and purchase of products and services that most effectively minimize environmental impacts over the product life cycle. Environmentally preferable characteristics that maximize conservation of energy and water and minimize the generation of waste and release of pollutants are beginning to receive a lot of attention. Products made from recycled materials that are reusable or recyclable; retrieving energy from renewable resources such as bio-based fuels; solar and wind power; alternate fuel vehicles; and products using alternatives to hazardous or toxic chemicals, radioactive materials, and biohazardous agents are being implemented in many organizations (I.S.O. International, n.d.).

Growing interest and involvement in EPP have resulted in the increasing number of environmentally preferable alternative products. This growing availability is making the transition to sustainable purchasing easier.

When developing a green environment, it should start at the top with the EMS board of directors or the management team establishing a company-wide environmental program with the goal of reducing solid waste, increasing recycling, and purchasing environmentally friendly products. Examples of such wastes include packaging materials, metal scrap, food waste, yard waste, and organic waste. Among these, packaging materials account for 30.3 percent of the municipal waste stream, which is the largest single component (Min and Galle, 1997, p. 12).

Side Bar

When developing a green environment, it should start at the top with the EMS board of directors.

EMS professionals are becoming aware of green efforts, especially those in municipal systems or hospital-based organizations. There is increased attention to environmental regulations, and organizations have begun to perform environmental compliance audits to review applicable environmental regulations, identify new restrictions, and evaluate how environmental initiatives help their organizations conform to evolving regulatory guidelines.

Every EMS manager can evaluate his organization for environmentally friendly activities. Each manager can view the front end by developing purchasing guidelines that spell out how to assess for environmental hazards. On the backside, EMS managers can establish source-reduction strategies.

Effective source-reduction strategies should reduce the amount or change the waste generated at the beginning of the supply chain through recycling, reuse, and source changes and control. Purchasing can enhance the effectiveness of a source reduction strategy in a number of ways, such as the following:

- Reducing the purchased volume of items that are difficult to dispose of or are harmful to the ecosystem
- Reducing the use of hazardous virgin materials by purchasing a higher percentage of recycled or reused content
- Requiring that suppliers minimize unnecessary packaging and use more biodegradable or returnable packaging

AUDITS

Perhaps the best method for evaluating an organization's environmental footprint is to develop more aggressive, proactive, environmental audit programs. As a guideline, the following audit process is suggested:

1. Identify applicable environmental statutes.
2. Develop standard checklists for environmental compliances.
3. Organize an audit team comprised of both internal management and outside third-party inspectors (e.g., private contracting consultants).
4. Maintain records related to handling, storage, use, and disposal of waste.
5. Assess the nature and degree of potential violations and liabilities.
6. Develop a corrective action plan and monitor its progress.

PRICE AND PERFORMANCE OF GREEN INITIATIVES

Price and performance are important factors to consider for individuals who are responsible for purchasing. Adhering to quality and performance standards need not be sacrificed. All these vital considerations could be expressed as follows:

Environment + Price + Performance = EPP

An initial strategy in EPP consists of buying products with recycled content that are themselves recyclable. There is growth potential for the purchase of recycled content products.

Simply by instituting a "Buy Recycled" program, any EMS organization can start an EPP initiative (Native Green, n.d.).

Why does an EMS unit want to buy green? Consider the following ways that buying green helps an organization:

- Improves safety and health of patients, associates, and the public
- Reduces pollution
- Conserves natural resources and energy
- Develops new, more environmentally friendly products
- Stimulates new markets for recycled materials and thereby creates jobs
- Improves awareness of environmental stewardship
- Protects the research mission
- Provides potential cost savings
- Reduces liabilities
- Complies with environmental laws and regulations

There are many areas where an EMS organization can save money as a result of going green. Consider the following examples of where cost savings can occur.

Energy

By evaluating its air conditioning, roofs, appliances, lighting, office equipment, and building insulation, EMS organizations can begin to replace, upgrade, or repair equipment or structures and save money over the long term.

Heating, Ventilation, and Air Conditioning (HVAC). In many areas under the HVAC umbrella, an evaluation has the potential to save money and reduce the drain on the environment. If the EMS manager uses maintenance contracts that check system conditions periodically, then ensuring that filters are changed regularly will save money through increased efficiency. A reduction in maintenance can translate to additional

money for the operational budget. Other methods for reducing costs on HVAC include the following:

- Ensuring proper operation of energy-saving features such as economizer mode, which makes best use of cooler air during spring and fall, and can be used to reduce the hours of costly compressor use.
- Using the cooler air at night to cool the building. As soon as the outside temperature drops lower than inside, open the windows and turn on a window fan to exhaust the hot air and bring in cooler air from other windows. As soon as the temperature rises outside in the morning, close all windows to retain the coolness.
- Closing window shades, drapes, and blinds to block any incoming sunlight.
- Using portable or ceiling fans instead of operating the air conditioner. Even mild air movement of 1 mile per hour can reduce the temperature three or four degrees.
- Programming an Energy Star thermostat to automatically raise the air conditioning setting at night.
- Turning the thermostat below what is comfortable (train yourself to enjoy 75°F, 80°F, or even higher temperatures).
- Moving lamps or TVs away from the air conditioning thermostat. The heat from these appliances will cause the air conditioner to run longer.
- Adding insulation in the floor of the attic, and walls if possible. The thicker, the better to keep the building at a comfortable temperature.
- Installing white window shades, drapes, or blinds to reflect heat away from the building.
- Applying sun-control or other reflective films on south-facing windows.
- Checking the air conditioner's efficiency. Use a household thermometer to measure the temperature of the cool air coming out and the temperature of the return air at the return-air grill. (Keep the thermometer in place for 5 minutes to get a steady temperature.) The

difference should be between 14 and 20 degrees. Less than 14 degrees could mean low refrigerant or leaks. A unit cooling more than 20 degrees could have a severe blockage.

- Purchasing the right heating and cooling equipment for the space, and ensuring that it is installed correctly. Remember: Bigger doesn't always mean better. If the air conditioner is too large, not only will energy costs increase, but the staff will be less comfortable.

Cooling that leaks outside the building wastes valuable financial resources. EMS managers can conduct an inspection of the building to determine where basic improvements can be made to improve cost savings. By looking closely at structural defects and repairing them, the EMS manager is returning money to the organization. Consider the following when inspecting a building:

- Caulking and weather stripping will keep cool air inside during the summer.
- If there are holes or separated joints in your ducts, repair them.
- Add insulation around air conditioning ducts when they are located in unconditioned spaces such as attics, crawl spaces, and garages; do the same for fans where they open to the exterior or to the attic. Use duct insulation material rated at least R-6.

By determining where the generation of excess heat occurs, the EMS manager can reduce the cost of cooling. By looking at the following, not only will the EMS manager save money, but he will also create a more comfortable environment:

- Replace all incandescent bulbs with compact fluorescents.
- Plug electronics, such as TVs, VCRs, computers, printers, cell phone chargers, and so on into power strips and *always* turn power strips *off* when equipment is not in use. (Any AC adapter that is plugged in is always drawing power, creating heat, and costing money. In the

average business, 40 percent of all electricity used to power electronics is consumed while the products are plugged in and turned off.)

- Turn off computers and monitors when not in use.
- Lower the thermostat on hot water heaters; 115° is comfortable for most uses.
- Air-dry dishes instead of using the dishwasher's drying heat cycle (if you have such an appliance on the premises).
- Don't use the oven (if one is present). Use a stovetop burner or grill outside.
- If dishes or clothes are washed on the premises, wash only full loads.

Landscaping. Many EMS organizations are situated on property with parking lots, lawns, and large driveways while other organizations are surrounded by other buildings. By looking at the exterior of the building, EMS managers should evaluate the area immediately around the building and determine any potential for cost savings. Examples of some improvements to the grounds include the following:

- Plant trees or shrubs to shade air conditioning units without blocking the airflow. An AC unit operating in the shade uses less electricity.
- Avoid landscaping with lots of unshaded rock, cement, or asphalt on the south or west sides because it increases the temperature around the building and radiates heat to the building after the sun has set.
- Deciduous trees planted on the south and west sides will keep the building cool in the summer. Just three trees, properly placed around the building, can save between $100 and $250 annually in cooling and heating costs. Daytime air temperatures can be 3 degrees to 6 degrees cooler in tree-shaded areas.

Lighting. In the absence of expensive air conditioning costs, lighting becomes a substantial portion of energy costs. Affordable technologies are available that can improve the efficiency of lights and lower utility bills.

Compact fluorescent lamps (CFLs) are an efficient alternative to traditional A-type light bulbs (Santa Monica Office of Sustainability and the Environment, n.d.). The same light level is produced for one-fourth the energy when using CFLs. Improvements in fluorescent light technology have made the light almost indistinguishable from incandescent light in terms of color.

The relatively high price of a CFL may cause the EMS manager to avoid this product. The typical incandescent light bulb may cost only 50 cents, but it will cost approximately $12 in electricity costs for 1,000 hours of use (the life of the bulb). A CFL, with the equivalent light output and ten times the lifespan, can be purchased for approximately $5, but will only cost $3 a year in energy (Santa Monica Office of Sustainability and the Environment, n.d.). The savings for a CFL are $9 every year—and it will last for 10 years. Money is recovered in the first year, and ongoing savings occur every year after that.

Lighting controls provide another area for going green. Occupancy sensors, twist timers, or energy management controls can also be used to reduce the hours a fixture is on. Warehouse lighting can be changed to bi-level controls and day-lighting control systems that reduce lighting during low-use periods or when skylights provide sufficient light levels in storage areas *(Santa Monica Office of Sustainability and the Environment, n.d.)*.

Efficient Office Equipment. An increasing proportion of an EMS business's energy use is due to the greater reliance of operations on technology such as computers, printers, copiers, servers, fax machines, and other communications equipment. EMS organizations use refrigerators, microwaves, toaster ovens, and water coolers.

When purchasing products labeled with the Energy Star designation of the U.S.

Environmental Protection Agency (EPA) and Department of Energy (DOE), and FEMP-designated products, managers should understand that although the Energy Star label makes it easier to choose energy-efficient equipment, opportunities to save money are often ignored or deemphasized when it comes to technology. For example, desktop and notebook computers routinely include energy-saving features, such as sleep modes for the monitor and central processing unit (CPU). The simple practice of turning off computers at the end of the day is often overlooked, partly because there is no impact on the employee failing to do so because he is not responsible for paying the electric bill (Santa Monica Office of Sustainability and the Environment, n.d.).

Using screen savers on computers can increase electricity consumption. The complex graphics of screen savers often require more CPU energy than if the computer were allowed to operate in sleep mode after a preset period. Although nearly every computer has this savings capability built into its software, it is seldom used to its benefit. An office policy that requires monitor sleep mode, and where possible also CPU sleep modes, is recommended for energy efficiency (Santa Monica Office of Sustainability and the Environment, n.d.).

Oil and Oil Filter Recycling

Recycling motor oil used in vehicles or other gasoline-powered equipment conserves energy and natural resources. Oil can be re-refined for use as motor oil or as fuel for ships. Oil filters, which are up to 80 percent steel, are recyclable into useful products. EMS organizations can ensure that used oil and oil filters are collected and taken to a recycling facility.

LOOKING AT SUCCESS

When evaluating the need for purchasing energy-efficient products or equipment. The EMS manager, or other purchasing staff, should consider choosing products with the following features:

- Low-standby power energy-efficient products
- Energy-efficient items, including Energy Star products
- FEMP-designated products
- Water-efficient products, including those meeting EPA's Water Sense standards
- Products designated in EPA's Comprehensive Procurement Guidelines as containing material from renewable sources or recycled content
- Biobased products designated by the U.S. Department of Agriculture in the BioPreferred program
- Environmentally preferable products and services, including EPEAT-registered electronic products
- Alternative fuel vehicles and alternative fuels required by the National Environmental Policy Act
- Products with low or no toxic or hazardous constituents
- Non-ozone depleting substances, as identified in EPA's Significant New Alternatives Program

When comparing costs, EMS managers should focus on calculating and comparing total costs over the life of the item, not just on the price of the product. The total costs include the initial cost, maintenance and upkeep, operating costs, insurance premiums, disposal at the end of use, replacement, safety and health, training, and hazardous waste compliance.

CHAPTER REVIEW

Summary

Purchasing is a potentially important area for review and improvement. The size of the EMS organization is unimportant when assessing how an organization buys products or services. The size of the EMS organization is irrelevant to becoming more environmentally friendly. What is important is for the EMS manager to recognize that there are many opportunities to improve the purchasing process, and money can be saved in both the short and long term. It is the EMS leadership team's proactive review of successful business practices in other industries, commitment to looking at current purchasing processes, and appropriate adaptation for the organization that will continue to refine a sound financial approach to EMS **sustainability**.

WHAT WOULD YOU DO? Reflection

You look at the size of your staff and each staff member's ability to do his current job and to take on additional responsibilities under the new plan. You choose to have faith in the current staff, but you are realistic about whether or not they will be capable of fulfilling these new responsibilities. You develop a plan to reorganize and, if necessary, to expand the decision-making role of members of the leadership team. Since there is the potential for many purchasing or procurement services, you know you may need to reorganize the purchasing area. With this amount of new activities and new board direction, you will consider adding an experienced purchasing professional to the staff. In order to accomplish all of the planned growth and the desire to become environmentally responsible, you instruct your purchasing department to adapt and successfully accomplish all of the new mandates.

Review Questions

1. Describe the four main objectives of purchasing.
2. Often the main task of purchasing is to place orders from various departments within the EMS organization. Describe other functions an expanded purchasing department can play in operations.
3. Discuss why the mission statement of the purchasing department must align with the overall mission and goals of the EMS organization.
4. Discuss the main tenets of procurement management processes.
5. Discuss the main concepts and ideas of proactive purchasing management.
6. What are the main points related to how risk-management knowledge and techniques can improve the purchasing process?
7. When discussing transactional costs, why is it important for the EMS manager to understand this theory?
8. What is the benefit of having a proactive purchasing program as compared to a reactive purchasing program?
9. Describe the stages of negotiation.
10. Discuss the purpose of green purchasing.

References

Ammer, D. S. (1989). "Top Management's View of the Purchasing Function." *Journal of Purchasing and Materials Management 25*(3), 16–21.

Auguston, K. A., N. Staples, and J. Weston. (1990, June). "Packaging in the 90s: The Environmental Impact." *Modern Materials Handling*, 54.

Biggs, J., E. Long, and K. Fraedrich. (n.d.) *The Integration of Accounting and Planning and Control Will Enable U.S. Manufacturing to Operate More Productively*. Unpublished working paper.

Burt, D. N., and R. L. Pinkerton. (1996). *A Purchasing Manager's Guide to Strategic Proactive Procurement*. New York: AMACOM.

Business Coach. (n.d.). "The Art of Negotiating." See the organization website.

Cornell University Law School. (n.d.). Uniform Commercial Code, Section 2-313(1)(a). See the organization website.

Dawid, H., and M. Kopel. (2003). "A Comparison of Exit and Voice Relationships Under Common Uncertainty." *Journal of Economics & Management Strategy 12*, 531–555.

Dobler, D. W., D. N. Burt, and L. LaMar. (1995). *Purchasing and Supply Management*, 6th ed. New York: McGraw Hill.

Dyer, J. H. (2000). *Collaborative Advantage: Winning Through Extended Enterprise Supplier Networks*. New York: Oxford University Press.

Eisenhart, T. (1990, November). "There's Gold in that Garbage!" *Business Marketing*, 20–24.

Freeman, V. T., and J. L. Cavinato. (1990). "Fitting Purchasing to the Strategic Firm: Frameworks, Processes, and Values." *Journal of Purchasing and Materials Management 26*(1), 15–20.

Heinritz, S., P. Farrell, L. Giunipero, and M. Kolchin. (1991). *Purchasing: Principles and Applications*, 8th ed. Englewood Cliffs, NJ: Prentice-Hall.

Hill, C. (1990). "Cooperation, Opportunism and the Invisible Hand: Implications for Transaction Cost Theory." *Academy of Management Review 15*(3), 500–513.

IBM Education and Training. (2000). "PMP Project Procurement Management: Study Notes in Preparation for PMP Exam." See the organization website.

I.S.O. International. (n.d.). "Green Purchasing." See the organization website.

Keough, M. (1994, April). "Buying Your Way to the Top." *Director,* 72–75.

Leenders, M., and H. Fearon. (1993). *Purchasing and Materials Management.* Irwin, CA: Burr Ridge.

Litvan, L. (1995, February). "Going 'Green' in the "90s." *Nation's Business,* 30–32.

Method123. (n.d.). "Procurement Management Process." See the organization website.

Miller, P., and P. Kelle. (1998). "Quantitative Support for Buyer-Supplier Negotiation in Just-in-Time Purchasing." *International Journal of Purchasing and Materials 34*(2), 25–30.

Min, H., and W. Galle. (1997). "Green Purchasing Strategies: Trends and Implications." *International Journal of Purchasing and Materials 33,* 10–17.

Native Green. (n.d.). "Executive Summary: Environmentally Preferable Green Strategy." *Green Purchasing: A Proposed Guide for EPP Procurement Management.* See the organization website.

Pfeffer, J., and G. Salancik. (1978). *The External Control of Organizations: A Resource Dependency Perspective.* New York: Harper & Row.

Rubin, P., and J. Carter. (1990). "Joint Optimality in Buyer-Supplier Negotiations." *Journal of Purchasing and Materials Management 26*(2), 20–26.

Santa Monica Office of Sustainability and the Environment. (n.d.). "Efficient Lighting." See the organization website.

Shumaonline.com. (n.d.-a). "Manufacturing: Cost Reduction Strategies for Manufacturing Industry." See the organization website.

Shumaonline.org. (n.d.-b). "Negotiation Strategy." See the organization website.

Simchi-Levi, D., P. Kaminsky, and E. Simchi-Levi. (2004). *Managing the Supply Chain: The Definitive Guide for the Business Professional.* New York: McGraw-Hill.

Sitkin, S., and A. L. Pablo. (1992). "Reconceptualizing the Determinants of Risk Behavior." *Academy of Management Review 17*(1), 9–38.

Stock, J. L. (1992). *Reverse Logistics.* Oak Brook, IL: Council of Logistics Management.

TechRepublic. (2012). "Understand the PM's Role in Procurement Management." See the organization website.

Walton, M. (1986). *The Deming Management Method.* New York: Perigee, 62–65.

Williamson, O. E. (1998). *The Economic Institutions of Capitalism.* New York: Free Press.

Winsemius, P., and U. Guntram. (1992). "Responding to the Environmental Challenge." *Business Horizon,* 12–20.

Key Terms

bilateral contract A contract in which each party is both promisor and promisee.

bonds A debt investment in which an investor loans money to an entity that borrows the funds for a defined period of time at a fixed interest rate. Bonds are used by companies; municipalities; and state, U.S., and foreign governments to finance a variety of projects and activities. Bonds are commonly referred to as fixed-income securities and are one of the three main asset classes, along with stocks and cash equivalents.

breach The failure to perform a contractual obligation.

competitive Comparative concept of the ability and performance of a firm, subsector, or country to sell and supply goods and/or services in a given market.

competitive edge The ability of an organization to utilize its resources and services more effectively than others do, thereby outperforming them. This means they must stay ahead in four areas: being responsive to customers, innovation, quality, and efficiency.

congruency The quality of agreeing; being suitable and appropriate; the state of being congruent. The quality or state of corresponding, agreeing, or being congruent.

efficiency Competency in performance.

inventory control A means of supervising the organizational supplies, storage of inventory, and accessibility of clinical items in order to ensure that an adequate supply is available for responders.

material breach Occurs when the non-faulted party is discharged from further obligations under the contract.

monitor The act of observing something (and sometimes keeping a record of it).

operating expenses Rent, gas/electricity, wages, and so on.

overhead Refers to the ongoing expense of operating a business.

preferred Preference refers to the set of assumptions relating to a real or imagined "choice" between alternatives and the possibility of rank-ordering these alternatives, based on the degree of happiness, satisfaction, gratification, enjoyment, or utility.

proactive Acting in advance to deal with an expected change or difficulty. Being proactive is about being anticipatory and taking charge of situations.

procurement A method by which the process of assessing the need for products or services, the evaluation of purchases for appropriateness, and the ongoing tracking of all products purchased occurs.

purchasing To obtain in exchange for money or its equivalent; buy.

resource dependency theory For a manager or organization to survive, it must not become dependent on others.

(continued)

sustainability The ability to sustain something; a means of configuring civilization and human activity so that society, its members, and its economies are able to meet their needs and express their greatest potential in the present, while preserving biodiversity and natural ecosystems.

systematic Of or pertaining to a system; consisting in a system; methodical; formed with regular connection and adaptation or subordination of parts to each other, and to the design of the whole.

time breach No time for performance is stated or implied in the contract but the performance was not completed within a reasonable amount of time.

unilateral contract A relatively simple form for a contract, such as a purchase order.

waiver The act of intentionally relinquishing or abandoning a known right, claim, or privilege; also, the legal instrument evidencing such an act.

CHAPTER **8**

Analysis of Activity

Objectives

After reading this chapter, the student should be able to:

8.1 Describe why analyzing the EMS organization is essential for continued growth.

8.2 Identify specific areas that an EMS manager can or should analyze.

8.3 Discuss why the EMS manager should choose appropriate areas to analyze.

8.4 Discuss the various types of analysis tools and methodologies that can be used.

8.5 Describe how statistical process control is used to generate information.

8.6 Describe how to implement an analysis process.

8.7 Discuss why analyzing the EMS organization serves as a loss prevention technique.

8.8 Review the key analysis ratios and determine how they fit into painting the overall picture of the activities of an EMS organization.

Overview

The purpose of this text is to introduce the concepts of finance to nonfinancial EMS managers. The chapters present valuable information to both new and experienced EMS leaders who may have varying degrees of experience, formal and informal. The goal is to stimulate thinking in order to change the way things are done, to avoid mistakes of the past, and to encourage future growth of EMS as a profession.

Key Terms

analysis	deductive	ratios	theory
Balanced Scorecard	hypothesis	spreadsheets	trends
control chart	inductive	statistical process	
data points	observations	control (SPC)	

WHAT WOULD YOU DO?

After much debate about the membership of the board of directors, it was decided to reduce the number of crew members and increase the number of community members with knowledge of business growth and strong community relationships. After identifying and recruiting well-respected community leaders, the new board members are seated. During one of the meetings, a director requests an analysis of the financial position of the organization that encompasses the last 5 years. He further requests a breakdown of ratios that demonstrate how operations control the business. The director instructs you to gather information and prepare a report for the next meeting. He is looking to see if the EMS organization is meeting established goals and how the organization's financial activities are analyzed.

Questions

1. How do you feel about the director's requests for information, particularly since his concerns were never an issue in the past?
2. Which mechanism will you use to determine the information needed for the analysis of the financial position, and how will you report on the information requested?
3. What analysis techniques would provide sufficient information to show the financial position of the EMS organization?
4. How will incorporating an analysis of EMS operations provide better information for present and future decisions?
5. How does incorporating strategic business tools, like the Balanced Scorecard, assist EMS decision makers with planning?
6. What operational decisions benefit from data collection, analysis, and interpretation for the continuous improvement of the EMS organization?

■ INTRODUCTION

EMS managers have many responsibilities. Tracking operational activities, ensuring appropriate clinical procedures, managing human resources, ensuring financial success, and preparing for the unknown or unexpected are among the variety of functions that encompass an EMS manager's thoughts and concerns on a daily basis.

The EMS manager is responsible for all of these, and many more, activities. In addition, he is accountable for the activities even if the actual function is delegated to others.

So how does one individual maintain adequate control of all of the activities and use information provided by others to build an EMS organization? Managers should develop tracking mechanisms and analysis tools in order to provide valuable information on the financial function of the organization. As stated in previous chapters, many businesses equate the success of an organization with the bottom line. The thinking is that the greater the bottom-line number is at the end of the year, the greater the success of the business, and the more valuable the manager will be. This philosophical belief is confirmed if compared to other business models.

In a very simplified view of the bottom-line philosophy, leading organizations are judged by other businesses and stockholders. At the beginning of each year, Wall Street expects organizations to submit their business plans to show how successfully they will perform over the next 12 months. Businesses performance is then evaluated throughout the year. The company's stock price is adjusted according to how well the projected success goals are met. The number of events that must come together to meet the demands of Wall Street and company stockholders is overwhelming. If the company does not forecast accurately, the company receives less-than-satisfactory reviews and the stock price falls. The company leadership is questioned about the ability to deliver as promised. To meet financial expectations, people lose their jobs. Some say this is how business works. The straightforward question is this: How can anyone accurately predict the future to the extent that promises are fulfilled successfully without negatively affecting the people doing the job or sacrificing the organization's purpose for existence?

The point here is that most EMS organizations are not listed on the stock exchange nor do they have to answer to Wall Street. However, the underlying philosophy in many EMS organizations is that the bottom line is the ultimate judge of its success. One could easily argue that an EMS organization can end the financial year with a zero bottom line and be completely successful. Obviously, an EMS organization that operates at a loss will not survive, so the bottom line should not be the sole determinant of organizational success. However, EMS should report, or at least look, at its finances on a quarterly basis so as not to let anything important slip away unnoticed.

How does an EMS organization measure how successfully it is functioning? There are many ways. Measuring different functions provides a good overview of how the organization is meeting the established goals. A cautionary note: Even though all activities are measurable, it is not necessary to track them all. As the person who is responsible for guiding the organization closer to its goals, the EMS manager can decide what vital processes require measuring. The basis for deciding what is going to be tracked is dependent on the value of the information gained through whatever is measured.

ANALYSIS

Many methods can be used to analyze a business. Managers look at their organization based on their experiences and the education they have. Some EMS managers look at clinical tracking of skills as an analysis of how well their staff is performing. Others may just look at the bottom line on the financial statement as an indication of how well they are doing to make a profit. **Analysis** is more than that; it means separating the organization into its distinct parts in order to better understand what value each part adds to the organization. Once the parts are analyzed, the manager can join all the parts together and look at the organization's ability to function.

Analysis is multifaceted. The analyst interprets data in order to provide objective insight into the functions of the organization. Analysis is used to acquire information, evaluate **trends**, identify performance gaps, and, most important, evaluate opportunities.

Side Bar

An analysis compares the changes in the amount already paid with the expected amount budgeted.

Analysis is a process that combines science and art. It depends on raw data—and not just any data, but data collected appropriately and without bias. The assessment must also be conducted accurately and objectively. Not all data are of equal quality, so the manager must be certain that the data collected provide the needed information.

SUCCESSFULLY ANALYZED DATA

The Society of Competitive Intelligence Professionals (SCIP) suggests the following strategies for considering the process of analyzing data:

- Recognize the interaction of the collection and analysis stages.
- Employ both deductive and inductive reasoning.
- Understand the basic analytical models.
- Know when and why to use various analysis tools.
- Recognize the existence of gaps and blind spots.
- Know when to cease analyzing to avoid "analysis paralysis."

DEDUCTIVE AND INDUCTIVE REASONING

Deductive reasoning starts with the general and leads to the more specific. This is informally called a top-down approach. Begin by thinking about a **theory**—for example, how the budget will look or how well responders provide medical care. Then narrow that down

into a more specific **hypothesis** that we can test. For example, the budget will be better than expected or the providers deliver great care. More specific data are then collected in the form of **observations**. This ultimately leads to testing the hypotheses with specific data—a confirmation (or not) of the original theories.

Inductive reasoning works in the opposite way, moving from specific observations to broader generalizations and theories. Informally, this a bottom-up approach. In inductive reasoning, observations and measures are acquired, and patterns are detected for regularity. A tentative hypothesis is formulated, and then general conclusions or theories are developed.

These two methods of reasoning yield very different results when conducting research. Inductive reasoning, by its nature, is more open ended and exploratory, especially at the beginning. Deductive reasoning is more narrow in nature and is concerned with testing or confirming hypotheses.

ANALYSIS OF AN EMS ORGANIZATION

Every organization has a purpose for its existence. EMS managers are employed to move an EMS organization toward stated goals. In order to move an EMS organization through economic challenges and social changes, managers must make decisions. In many cases, decisions are formulated with incomplete information, are based on personal views, and have no historical reasoning. Thus, there is often no way to measure the effect of the decision, either prospectively or retrospectively. Many of management's decisions have significant financial impact on the organization, yet there is often no method for determining if the decision was the best one for the organization.

Managers should look at how the organization's activities fit into the community and then make the best use of the organization's resources in order to meet the community's needs. Meeting those needs means working within the organization's resources. The allocation of resources should not be decided on personal desire or ego but on what is necessary to function within the framework of the goals.

Therefore, analyzing the activities, resource utilization, delivery of services, and financial impact of decisions provides EMS managers with the pertinent information they need to guide the organization. The output of an analysis can point to actionable steps that are future oriented. Analysis can help EMS decision makers develop better strategies for fulfilling the purpose of EMS at the organizational level and as a profession. Ultimately, analysis is done to produce better results.

Without adequate knowledge, managerial decisions are less effective due to missing key elements that contribute to making a proper decision. Knowledge allows managers to act because they have the information necessary to evaluate the pros and cons of the decision. Having business insight comes from knowledge gained by evaluating EMS activities, applying formal education, and understanding the results of the evaluation. Once a manager has gained the necessary insight by analyzing the organization, he can turn the insight into action.

Analysis is not just about looking at ratios or spreadsheets. An analysis determines what processes are working, how well they are working, and what is not working as well as planned. If managers become comfortable with analyzing the organization, they can gain a better perspective and make better decisions for the organization.

When making decisions based on an analysis of a process, managers should understand that the information provides a look back at how the organization performed. This is very different from conducting a strategic analysis of where the business is currently or is going in the future.

Side Bar
Using various analysis tools helps determine why actual results vary from a standard that is currently established.

There is a significant difference between financial analysis and strategic analysis. In strategic analysis, the manager should look at where the organization is situated relative to other similar providers, how others view the organization, how the organization plans to meet its goals and objectives, and how the organization is prepared to use all its resources to grow.

Financial analysis looks at the past and determines if operations are functioning up to their potential or if changes are needed. The EMS manager can use many analysis tools, and each one provides a different view of the organization. For example, if the EMS manager looks at just the balance sheet, the results may provide inaccurate information about how well the organization and the EMS manager are growing the business. Similarly, if one looks at financial ratios and relies on the results to make decisions, the manager may fail to understand that a ratio only shows a comparison between two **data points**. A ratio does not explain why the variability exists.

■ METHODS OF TRACKING

Tracking information can take many forms. Tracking can occur through **spreadsheets**, written reports, financial statements, or a

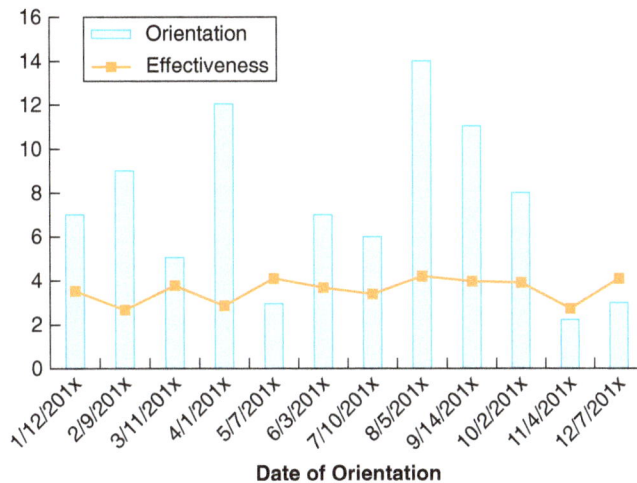

Date of Orientation

FIGURE 8.1 ■ Orientation example.

number of other forms. Information can be exchanged through written reports, verbal conversations, and spreadsheets. The flow of information should be concise, accurate, and readily understandable. Reading a two-page narrative, submitted by the human resources director, of how many people completed orientation is less effective than looking at a graph that shows the number of people who completed the orientation. With the graph, a compilation of the results of a survey describing how the new hires felt about the orientation may provide more, usable information (Figure 8.1).

The graph is a simple depiction of how information is viewed. By looking at the information, EMS managers are able to see trends and can then ask pertinent questions. Such a simple tracking tool does not provide enough information for making decisions; however, it does provide the opportunity to visually evaluate how well a process is accomplishing its goals. In Figure 8.1, the data indicate that the average effectiveness of orientation is approximately 3.5 (using a Likert scale of 1–5). If the rating is consistent over a longer

time, the EMS manager might consider what improvements are necessary to raise the rating. A follow-up survey may provide the additional information.

The design of the tracking method should provide the required information and the trends expected. It also should not be so overwhelming as to confuse to the reader.

■ FINANCIAL TRACKING

Many organizations develop extensive and detailed reports that show the financial position of the organization. Such detail is often important when looking at the overall condition of an organization, but the amount of information also can be too much for people to understand.

In Table 8.1, Main Street EMS has recently expanded and opened a new station and management has tracked the first few months of calls, revenues, and expenses. It is easy to see by looking at the gain/loss line that the new station is losing money. The question is this: Do these few months

TABLE 8.1 ■ Cost Spreadsheet for Main Street EMS

	7/11/xx	8/11/xx	9/11/xx	10/11/xx	11/11/xx	12/11/xx	1/11/x1	2/11/x1	3/11/x1	4/11/x1	5/11/x1	6/11/x1	7/11/x1	8/11/x1
Number of emergency calls	1623	1882	1694	1739	1819	1790	1849	1837	2040	1778	1856	1721	1593	1814
Revenue/patient visit	$60.97	$59.42	$62.65	$65.40	$58.96	$61.72	$58.97	$ 64.84	$59.72	$67.26	$65.76	$64.69	$70.16	$61.56
Expense/patient visit	$73.49	$66.12	$72.66	$72.07	$69.63	$69.64	$71.75	$ 68.32	$63.50	$74.93	$75.84	$76.73	$72.36	$67.24
Gain or Loss	$(12.5)	$(6.70)	$(10.01)	$(6.67)	$(10.6)	$(7.92)	$(12.78)	$(3.48)	$(3.78)	$(7.67)	$(10.08)	$(12.04)	$(2.20)	$(5.68)
Hours worked by EMTs		920	852	911	902	1339	982.3	931	938	848	938	1318	1109	1037
% by patient		2.05	1.99	1.91	2.02	1.34	1.88	1.97	2.17	2.10	1.98	1.31	1.44	1.75
Hours worked by paramedics		951	904	907	938	1340	836	921	944	907	963.4	1277	795	772
% by patient		1.98	1.87	1.92	1.94	1.34	2.21	1.99	2.16	1.96	1.93	1.35	2.00	2.35
Hours worked by support		383	394	278	378	546	359	377	398	391	482	670	271.4	312.9
% by patient		4.91	4.30	6.26	4.81	3.28	5.15	4.87	5.13	4.55	3.85	2.57	5.87	5.80
Hours worked by Administration		890	894	932	912	1338	825	992	893	901	976	1117	709	744
% by patient		2.11	1.89	1.87	1.99	1.34	2.24	1.85	2.28	1.97	1.90	1.54	2.25	2.44

of financial loss indicate how the new station will operate or how successful it will be? That is hard to tell at this stage, but answering the question becomes even more difficult if we add another 12 months of information. Information must be easily read if it is to be analyzed. Looking at rows and rows, and column after column, of numbers can confuse experienced managers. It is likely that a community board making a decision on the information will be more challenged. Who is capable of looking at spreadsheets and making an informed decision?

Let's look again at the information in Table 8.1, but in a different format (Figure 8.2). If we look at the lines for revenue/patient, expense/patient, and gain/loss in a graph format, we can predict the overall outlook of the new station over time. By watching these three categories and their upward and downward movement, the EMS manager can see how the new station is contributing to the finances of the EMS organization.

When analyzing the information in Figure 8.2 over a longer period, a manager can develop a clearer picture of trends in the station's financial position. This graph by itself should not set in motion shutting the station down because it is consistently losing money. The data provide very little information and are, unfortunately, typical of what EMS managers use to make decisions. The crucial point is that analyzing a single set of criteria is often shortsighted. What management should look at is how this information fits into the overall strategic plan. It is easy to decide to close the station strictly from a financial perspective if management is only concerned about the bottom line. However, if we look at this graph to evaluate success, we can see that multiple pieces of information are missing, such as the number of calls to which the crews responded. Every business has a breakeven point. It could be that the new station has not yet hit that point.

The preceding illustrations are examples of information tracking. Information entered into a spreadsheet is time consuming but ultimately relevant, and looking at numerical information on a spreadsheet can cause frustration. Managers can turn the information into a readable format such as a bar graph or pie chart. Even if the new format is easier to look at and provides a clearer picture, the information still may not provide information sufficiently important or valuable enough for making a decision.

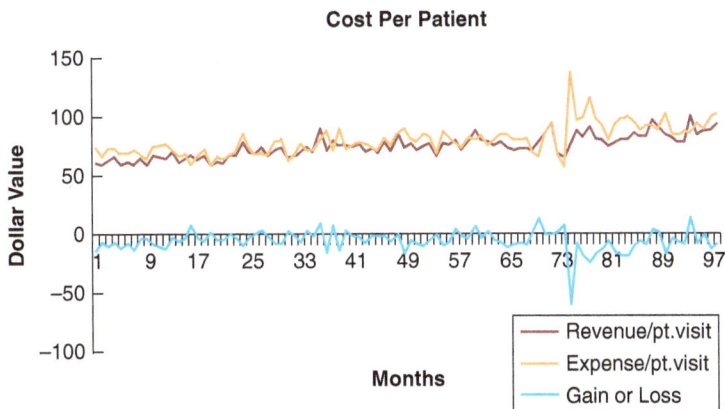

FIGURE 8.2 ■ Example of graph format for looking at data.

Best Practice

Physician offices make it possible to see patients, bill for services, and become successful when revenues exceed expenses. Most physicians understand the basics of business management, but tracking and evaluating business activity interfere with seeing patients. EMS organizations are often designed on this model; the emphasis is placed on having ambulances available for emergencies and/or transports.

A small physician office in South Central Pennsylvania was not unlike many small health care businesses. The physicians in the office worked hard and saw many patients, but from a business perspective, they were losing money. A business manager was hired, and he immediately began to evaluate and analyze every aspect of the business—from answering the phone to medical records tracking to physician schedules. The manager developed spreadsheets to track all activities and established parameters of performance acceptability. While including key people in the decision making, many processes were reengineered, and many activities were reworked. As new information was acquired on the results of the changes, it was added to the spreadsheets. Within 18 months of initiating the process, the health care practice demonstrated significant improvement. Within 24 months, the practice went from losing $18,000+ per month to covering expenses and making money. During this time, the physicians had made significant schedule changes that decreased their work hours, but increased patient throughput, improved patient accessibility by jettisoning the traditional mode of scheduling, and improved revenue. By analyzing the process and tracking the results of decisions, this physician office avoided closure and added value to the staff and the community.

■ SPECIFIC ANALYSIS TOOLS

A manager can use many analysis tools to look at information generated by operations. The EMS manager should become familiar with the various types of tools and find a few that provide the needed information that fulfills the purpose. Tools are used on a long- and short-term basis. However, when choosing and using tools the manager should remain consistent with the information provided. If the tool changes, the manager must communicate the change to all other decision makers who use the information.

Side Bar

Management cannot take action on one or two examples of variance analyses—they must drill down further.

STATISTICAL PROCESS CONTROL

Statistical process control (SPC) was originally developed by Walter Shewhart in the early 1920s, and was further adopted and refined by the Japanese after World War II through the efforts of Dr. Edward Deming. SPC uses techniques to measure and analyze variations in a process. The intent of SPC is to monitor quality and consistency and to maintain a process to a predetermined endpoint. SPC does not improve a poorly designed process. It is used to show how consistently the process is operating. The benefits of SPC are its ability to provide surveillance and feedback for keeping a process in control, signal when a problem has occurred, detect variation, reduce the need for ongoing inspection, and provide a mechanism to make process changes and track the effects of the change.

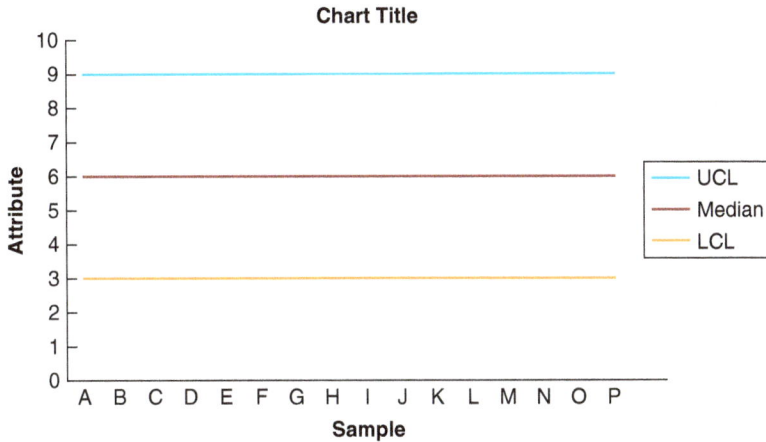

FIGURE 8.3 ■ Basic control chart setup.

Control Charts

Control charts are central to SPC (Figure 8.3). The control chart has a few key factors: the upper control limit (UCL), the lower control limit (LCL), the sample, and the attribute.

The median is the expected value to which information is compared. This value could be the budget, a historical call average, or a set number of hours worked.

The upper control limit is the maximum acceptable limit for the measured value. Likewise, the lower control limit is the lowest number management will accept. The difference between the UCL and the median and the LCL and the median should be enough to provide variability in the process but not so great that the process is completely out of control. The usual difference is 3 percent on either side of the median. A word of caution: If starting out with this process, and the EMS manager is unfamiliar with the process that is chosen, it may be best to expand the percentage between the median and the UCL and LCL until the process has enough information to guide any adjustments. Let's look at a few examples (Figure 8.4).

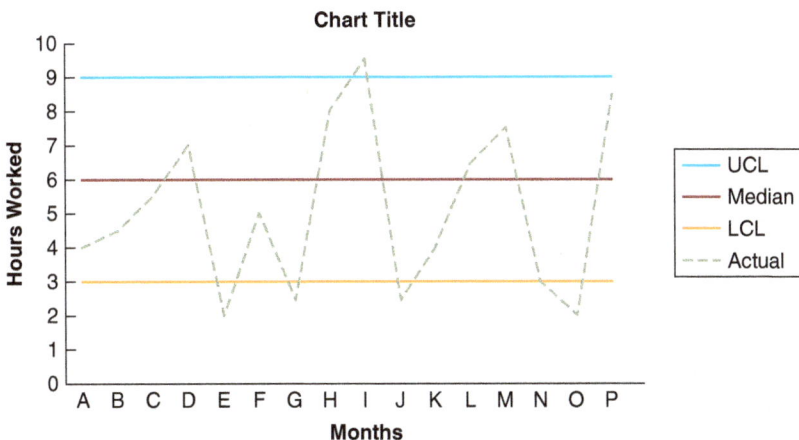

FIGURE 8.4 ■ Control chart with data.

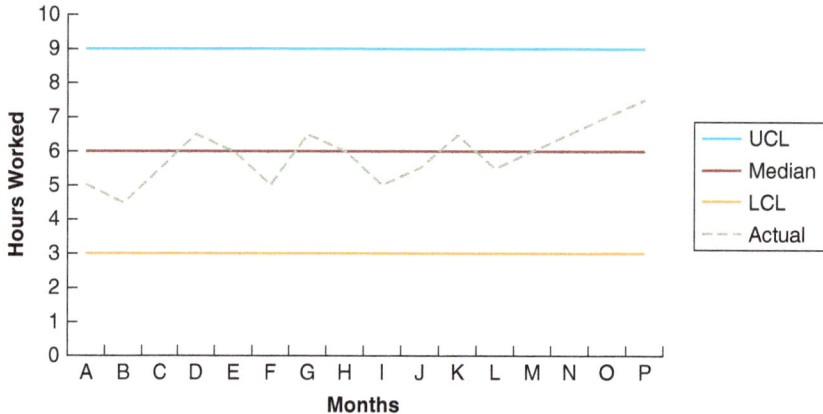

FIGURE 8.5 ■ Control chart with upward trend.

The graph in Figure 8.4 demonstrates the addition of actual data. A specific attribute label (hours worked) and sample label (months) were added. On evaluation, the data fall within the UCL and the LCL most of the time. The question to ask is this: Is this process out of control? Sure it is, because there is no way to predict what will happen next. The goal of a control chart is to provide enough information to determine subsequent data points with some degree of certainty and confidence. The actual data fluctuate wildly, and on 5 separate occasions the actual falls either above or below the control limits. The EMS manager or leadership team should notice that there are no trends to assess and no ability to plan for the next few months. By attaching a dollar figure to this graph, one can quickly see the difficulty in determining labor costs that will be absorbed by the organization.

The first question is, "Is this process in control?" There is another way of looking at this information. Can management better predict the next series of events with more confidence? In looking at this additional information, the data align closer to the median. It is easy to determine that this process is in control. A manager cannot predict the actual data point, but the data points M, N, O, and P indicate the start of a trend. Many authors define a trend as a specified number of data points in the same direction, usually 5 to 7. In this case, four data points are trending upward (Figure 8.5).

Does Figure 8.5 tell the nature of the process? An EMS manager does not know if the graph represents higher hours worked due to an increased call volume, staff members who stayed beyond their shifts, a person who accepted new responsibilities, or any other cause. What we do know is that there is a steady increase in hours worked over a defined period of time.

The value of looking at information over time provides the EMS manager with the opportunity to evaluate how changes in the control chart impact the direction of a process or activity. In Figure 8.6, we see a large amount of information represented by the standard line diagram.

The graph in Figure 8.6 represents time spanning 120+ pay periods or approximately 6 years of data. When analyzing this graphical information (imagine looking at a spreadsheet with all of this information and attempting to make an informed decision) the reader can immediately see that

Total Paramedic Hours

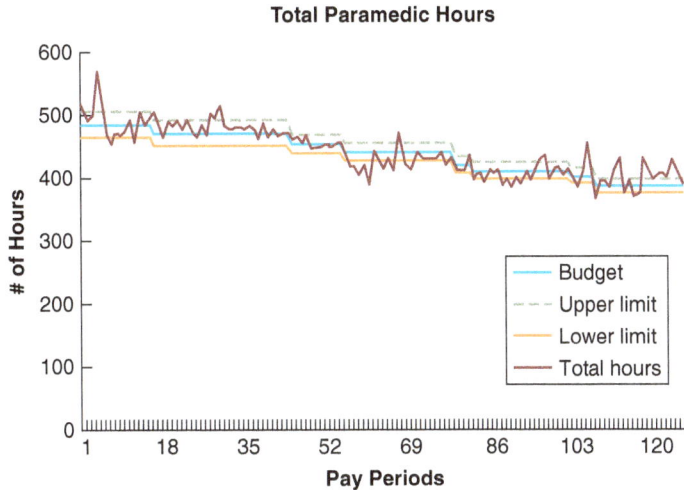

FIGURE 8.6 ■ Graph of paramedic hours.

the budget, UCL, and LCL are decreasing over time. The budgeted hours were reduced by 100 hours, and the actual hours, though fluctuating, were reduced significantly. This reduction occurred for many reasons, such as eliminating inefficiencies, reducing staff duplication, or consolidating jobs and then not replacing the position with another staff member. If the reduction of overall hours was positive, this graph represents a highly engaged management team. Looking at this from a financial perspective, if each person is paid $20 per hour, the organization saved over $52,000 per year in unnecessary direct payroll costs and probably twice that in indirect costs associated with labor.

On the flip side, if the graph in Figure 8.6 represents a negative movement, the analysis could highlight a management team that is dictatorial or disconnected. These numbers may reflect the number of people who ended their employment and the organization's inability to hire qualified replacements. It could represent a reduction in call volume, in a defined area of the run district. Developing a tracking

mechanism such as a **control chart** does not provide the decision, but it does provide an easier way of looking at the information and correcting deficiencies or questioning excessive variabilities.

IMPLEMENTING THE PROCESS

To implement SPC, the EMS manager must look at a few key concepts. First, define the process. Determine what process needs tracking and why. SPC can only be effective if the right process is identified. As stated earlier, any business process is traceable. The EMS manager must decide what information is needed to make decisions and what effect the information has on the organization. Finances, human resource, department expenses, call volumes, and so on are all examples of areas appropriate for tracking. Tracking for the sake of doing so provides useless information and wastes valuable time. The EMS manager should determine what information is necessary, what will be gained by tracking information, and what will be achieved by tracking this process. How will it help make better decisions? By using this information, how can management reach the established goals? How does this information fit into the rest of the business activities? How can a manager best analyze the results of the information? Processes that help establish meaningful information on specific goals are best suited for SPC.

Second, choose the appropriate measurements. "Measurements that provide insight into the performance of a process or activity are adequate, especially if the measurements are related to the process or activity goal" (Quanterion Solutions Incorporated, 2012). Measuring the monthly revenues over expenses, for example, is directly related to the financial health of the organization. Looking at overtime as it relates to late call volume is another example. Tracking information over an extended time has a direct relationship on budget determination, labor hour allocation, or determining when another person should be hired.

Next, design the measurement tool that focuses on process trends. Control charts should be constructed to detect trends, not individuals or nonconforming events. If the measured process exceeds the established limits, the manager should not ask who but why. Even if the limit is exceeded once, this does not indicate a trend. Focusing on trends allows the EMS manager to evaluate the process, not people.

Calculate the control limits correctly. Design the control limits so they are realistic and reflect what is happening. Do not make the upper and lower control limits so tight that the data exceed the limits or so loose that limits are never challenged or, worse, that the variation of results encompasses the whole chart. When establishing the UL and LL, look at history and use the goals established by the strategic or financial planning strategies.

Next, investigate the collected data and act. SPC only signals the existence of a possible problem. Without a thorough investigation, as in an audit of the process, the problem will only continue. Once the EMS manager determines if a problem exists, adjustment and implementation of corrective action are required.

Whatever method of data tracking is used, providing training to other decision makers on the results and any changes is essential. All levels of the organization should understand what is being measured and why. Engage people so the variances that are identified can be corrected at the closest level to the problem.

THE BALANCED SCORECARD

Dr. Robert Kaplan and David Norton developed the Balanced Scorecard as a performance measurement framework (Figure 8.7). The **Balanced Scorecard** adds a nonfinancial performance measure to traditional financial metrics to give managers a more balanced view or organizational performance (Balanced Scorecard Institute, 2012). It aligns the business activities with the vision and strategy of the organization, improves internal and external communication, and monitors organizational performance against strategic goals. The Balanced Scorecard approach provides clear direction as to what organizations should measure in order to balance the financial perspective. It provides feedback from both the internal business processes and external outcomes in order to continuously improve all areas of performance (Balanced Scorecard Institute).

The Balanced Scorecard covers four perspectives on business activity: the Learning and Growth Perspective, the Operational Activity Perspective, the Patient Perspective, and the Fiscal Responsibility Perspective. When developing each perspective, management develops metrics to collect and analyze data with the goal of implementing necessary changes.

The Balanced Scorecard

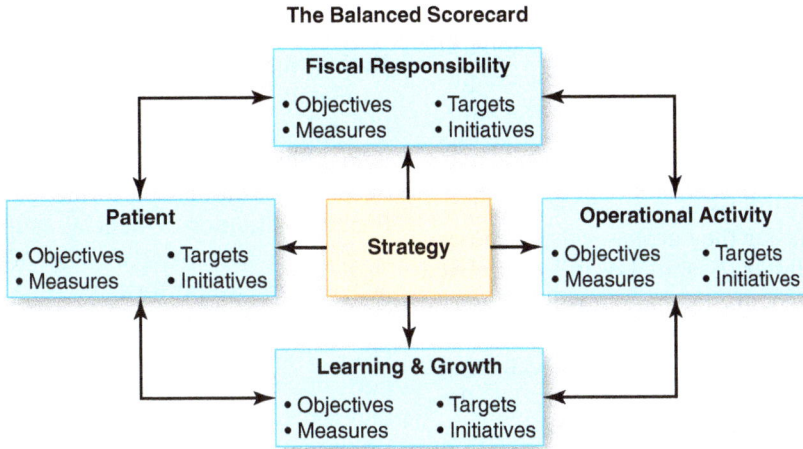

FIGURE 8.7 ■ The Balanced Scorecard.

The Learning and Growth Perspective

This perspective includes personnel training and organizational beliefs about improvement. In today's business climate, organizations need to steer toward the knowledge-worker concept in which people are repositories of information. Developing an organization that emphasizes a model of continuous learning supports the concept of self-improvement, which benefits the organization. Metrics can be developed to help managers allocate financial resources for the learning process. Learning is not the same as training. Learning encompasses, mentoring, communication, problem solving, and personal growth.

The Operational Activity Perspective

This perspective refers to processes occurring inside the business. Developing metrics allows managers to know how well the business is functioning and whether the services conform to professional and customer expectations. Designing analysis tools that measure conformity to medical protocols, driving standards, or patient handling best practices are examples of specific clinical, operational metrics.

The Patient Perspective

Many studies have shown a positive, monetary value in developing a customer-focused organization and measuring customer satisfaction. The premise for many organizations is that the customer will not return if dissatisfied. Organizations that build their business on repeat customers strive to provide exceptional service. Customers who are in a position to make a choice between two alternatives will choose the organization that exceeds their expectations. Unlike a hotel chain or airline, where reservations are made in advance, the EMS customer will only use prehospital medical services in emergent situations. EMS interacts with the customer, most times, when the customer is most vulnerable. EMS customers cannot choose the responding EMS unit, nor can they choose who provides the medical care. However, the EMS manager can measure customer service, often retrospectively, and make decisions based on data accumulated from past calls or actions. With the data in hand, the EMS manager can proactively address any problems to avoid a future bigger problem. In other words, the data can help the manager protect the customer from poor service.

The Customer Perspective is a somewhat different orientation, especially if we look at traditional EMS belief systems. For example, many EMS providers will argue that a satisfied customer orientation would allow the provider to respond lights and sirens (L&S) to all calls regardless of a medical condition, because the faster they arrive at the scene or hospital, the faster the initial or follow-up ER treatment, the better the patient will feel.

The EMS manager may agree with the thought of responding L&S to all calls and support the argument. The support for the rapid response from a management perspective could also include that the unit will become available quicker, and thus will be able to "service" other customers. Showing a higher response activity may be the basis for garnering greater financial support from the local municipalities. On the surface, this may look appealing. The EMS manager may write a policy that allows for an L&S response on all 9-1-1 calls.

This myopic view may cost the organization tens of thousands or millions of dollars when its ambulance is involved in an accident. For example, when responding L&S while transporting a patient with a broken ankle to the hospital, the driver runs a red light and kills a child in the car the ambulance broadsided; the family, driver, organization, and community suffer. Customer service takes on a different meaning in EMS, and the manager must determine which customer perspective is the priority.

The Fiscal Responsibility Perspective

Timely and accurate funding data are essential to the success of any organization. The point with the Balanced Scorecard is that finance is not the priority, and any emphasis on just the finance makes the organization unbalanced. Including areas of risk and cost-benefit provide an additional perspective for managers when making decisions.

RATIOS

Ratios make a comparison between two unrelated items. Ratios can also disclose the relationship between two independent items. Financial ratios are useful indicators of an organization's performance and overall financial situation. Financial ratios are used to analyze and compare the organization's activities to past performance or a peer group. Many financial ratios are available to managers. Before arbitrarily beginning to measure performance of the organization, it is important for the EMS manager to understand the meaning behind ratios, the types of ratios, what the ratios measure, and how the ratios will help with decision making. Table 8.2 provides a list of business ratios that EMS organizations could implement. These ratios provide a means of assessing a firm's strengths and weaknesses. Ratios are divided into operating, liquidity, financial, inventory, and performance ratios.

Financial ratios have their limitations. First, in nonprofit or municipally based EMS organizations, the goal is not necessarily to make a profit. (Profit is measured as revenue over expenses.) Second, a reference point is needed. To be meaningful, most ratios must be compared to previous values, the organization's future forecasts, or a peer group (Everett Community College Tutoring Center, n.d.). Third, ratios by themselves are not highly meaningful. They should be viewed as indicators, which, when combined with other tracking tools, paint a picture of the organization's situation. Fourth, year-end values may not represent a 100 percent accurate picture of the organization. Average values should be used when available. In addition, ratios are subject to any limitations of accounting methods used to generate the data. Different accounting choices may result in significantly different ratio values (Everett Community College Tutoring Center).

TABLE 8.2 **Business Ratios**				
Operating Ratios	*Financial Ratios*	*Inventory Ratios*	*Performance Ratios*	*Liquidity Ratios*
Capital	Fixed Assets	Average Collection	Delinquency	Solvency
Expense/Income	Long-term Assets	Inventory Turnover	Charge-offs	Quick
Profit Margin	Short-term Cash			Acid Test
Net Capital	Gross Income			
Salary and Benefits	Cost of Funds			
Operating	Net Income			
	Current			
	Cash			
	Debt			
	Interest Coverage			
	Return on Assets			
	Accounts Receivable			
	Accounts Payable			

Ratios Explained

Ratios used by EMS can show how well an organization is performing as compared to past practices and other EMS organizations of similar structure. Not all the ratios listed are applicable in every EMS situation. Three of the more common business ratios are explained here.

Current Ratio.   The first ratio discussed is the current ratio. The current ratio is obtained by dividing current assets by current liabilities. It represents the organization's ability to cover short-term liabilities with assets that are easily converted to cash. Current assets include cash, accounts receivable, and inventories. Current liabilities consist of accounts payable, short-term notes payable and current long-term debt due, accrued taxes, or other accrued expenses.

The current ratio measures whether or not a firm has enough resources to pay its debts over the next 12 months. It calculates how many dollars are likely to be converted to cash within 1 year in order to pay debts that come due within 1 year.

$$\text{Current ratio} = \frac{\text{Current assets}}{\text{Current liabilities}} \frac{\$14,000}{\$11,000}$$
$$= 1.2$$

The current ratio measures the EMS organization's liquidity and ability to meet creditors' demands. Acceptable, current ratios vary from industry to industry. If an EMS organization's current assets are in an acceptable range, then it is considered to have significant short-term financial strength. If current liabilities exceed current assets (the current ratio is below 1), then the organization may have problems meeting any short-term obligations. If the current ratio is too high, then the company may not be efficiently using its current assets. For most industries, 1.5 is an acceptable, current ratio.

Once this number is calculated, the results are compared to EMS peers to determine how well the organization is performing. Assume the industrial average is 1.7. The preceding example indicates that liquidity is lower than the industry average; thus the organization would have higher difficulty paying off existing debt.

Unfortunately, most EMS organizations do not report these measurements to any professional organization. Determining how the EMS profession performs in any analysis is difficult. In many EMS organizations, managers can acquire data that are reported to state or national organizations and compare their results with other EMS organizations. By benchmarking their results with others, the manager is able to adjust EMS activities appropriately. Financial performance is difficult to benchmark. The best an EMS organization can do is review similar industries and build a historical perspective of its own to measure against.

It is also important to note that industrial averages are not magic numbers. Some well-run EMS organizations or other nonprofits may have averages that are way above the norm and others that are below. EMS decision makers should determine if their numbers are very different from like organizations, if the analysis differs from year to year, or why the variance occurs.

A current ratio that is 3 or 4 in an EMS organization signifies that management has so much cash on hand it might be doing a poor job of using it to meet goals.

Quick Ratio. The quick ratio is the measurement of the EMS organization's short-term liquidity. This ratio measures the ability of the EMS organization to meet short-term obligations with its most liquid assets. The higher the ratio, the better the EMS organization can use assets in an emergency. Having liquidity allows managers to use funds to pay for unforeseen expenses. The following is the formula to determine this:

$$\text{Quick Ratio} = \frac{\text{Current Assets} - \text{Inventories}}{\text{Current Liabilities}}$$

The EMS manager should determine if this ratio is a better indicator for the organization's use of funds. This ratio is more conservative than the current ratio because it excludes inventory. EMS organizations may have difficulty selling inventory over the short term to raise cash. In the event that short-term obligations need to be paid immediately, this ratio does not include inventory to determine what assets could be sold.

Acid Test. The acid test indicates whether the EMS organization has enough short-term assets to cover immediate liabilities without selling inventory. In most EMS organizations, selling inventory is highly unlikely because there is a limited market for IV fluids and C-collars. This ratio allows for the inclusion of inventory assets. The formula is calculated thus:

$$\text{Acid Ratio} = \frac{\text{Cash} + \text{Accounts Receivable} + \text{Short-term investments}}{\text{Current liabilities}}$$

Organizations with a ratio less than 1 are unable to pay for their current liabilities, and managers should be wary of increasing liabilities (buying more equipment or adding jobs).

Regression Analysis and Forecasting

Regression analysis is widely used for prediction and forecasting (see Figure 8.8). It is also used to understand which variables (independent) are related to other variables (dependent) and to explore the relationship of these variables. In other words, the EMS manager may want to determine what

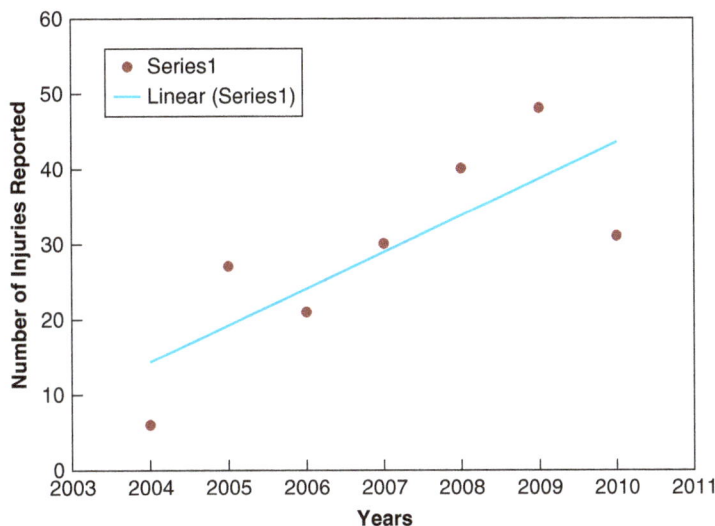

Figure 8.8 Regression analysis.

relationship the number of 9-1-1 calls has on income and then further evaluate the relationship of income between self-pay, third-party payers, and noncollectable write-offs. Another analysis would be used to determine the possibility of future losses relative to workers' compensation or insurance claims related to ambulance accidents.

An example may help. Let's say Main Street Ambulance has experienced an increased number of work-related injuries. The manager decides to analyze the number of events and determine how to prevent subsequent injuries. Using regression analysis, the manager can determine potential future activity. The results may assist with developing a program that minimizes losses. Looking at the raw numbers listed, 6 injuries were reported in 2004, 27 in 2005, 21 in 2006, and so on. Management cannot determine by looking at these numbers the severity, dollar value, number of days off, or any other important information related to the circumstances surrounding the injuries. What is known is that a

certain number were reported. How can the EMS manager determine, with a high degree of confidence, the 2011 injury rate?

2004	6
2005	27
2006	21
2007	30
2008	40
2009	48
2010	31

With regression analysis, in 2011 the organization will have approximately 48 reported incidents of employee injuries.

Side Bar

Analyzing variances only shows what happened in the past. They are calculated at the end of a specific period. The long-term health of the organization looks at multiple periods.

CHAPTER REVIEW

Summary

Conducting an analysis provides the EMS manager with a snapshot and ongoing view of how the organization is functioning and how it is progressing toward established goals. Analysis is a formal process of measuring and then using those measurements to change any negative variations, learn from positive trends, and seek to understand what effect decisions have on the organization. One of the goals of analysis is to find areas of organizational activity that are being performed with the greatest value for the organization. The difficulty for analysis is not locating the problem but developing an organizational structure and process to change the identified issue.

Analysis is the result of looking at the effectiveness of operations. No decisions about operations are possible without relevant information being available to decision makers. Analyzing business activities can yield a report on how well the EMS organization is functioning. In other words, it is a report card upon which decisions can be based. Because an analysis is designed to objectively look at all operations, it provides a clear picture of how management is doing. Are financial goals aligned with strategic goals? Are community service goals aligned with allocating community resources? Analysis is the tool used to better understand the business in order to help make better decisions. Box 8.1 provides a summary of how to use this tool.

Box 8.1

Process for Analysis

1. Develop acceptable standards with which to compare your results.
2. Use more than one tool to analyze the financial activities of the EMS organization.
3. Determine a process to evaluate the results of the analysis, and actions to correct any variance from the standard, and then adjust activities, maintain control, and reevaluate.
4. Communicate to the management team the results of the analysis and the decisions made on adjustments.

WHAT WOULD YOU DO? Reflection

In many EMS organizations, the board of directors is comprised of past and present members of the EMS unit. It is commonly believed that only members of the organization know how to run it. Assigning a unit member to a seat on the board of directors is also a way to reward him for many years of service. In many such situations, past or existing unit members have no formal education or experience in analyzing any business, let alone doing so for a complex organization such as an EMS organization. It is this reluctance to give up this "earned" board position that keeps EMS organizations stagnant, with growth resulting from external forces rather than from controlled actions. When community leaders become involved, they bring their expertise to the organization. The manager and crew members should embrace the alternative views, and they should also be prepared for doing things differently.

So, you learn what analysis is, identify what tools can provide the best information, and decide on a format that provides the requested information in a clear and concise manner. You create a spreadsheet of the raw data. You know that submitting a verbal or written report only provides an opinion, and possibly a biased opinion, on the activities of the organization, whereas the board of directors typically seeks an overall analysis of the organization's financial position: How well is it doing relative to the goals? How are the community's resources being used? How affective are the processes of the operations?

Although many managers may feel that this is an intrusion into their ability to manage, or they perceive these requests as a threat to their job, you do not. By proactively looking at the value of analyzing the operations from clinical, operational, and financial positions, you astutely prepare to show how effectively you actually are running the EMS organization.

Review Questions

1. Describe how EMS measures business success when compared to other businesses?
2. Define the general concept of analysis.
3. Discuss the six key points that the EMS manager would follow to look at the process of analyzing data.
4. Explain the difference between deductive and inductive arguments.
5. Discuss why it is essential that the proactive EMS manager analyze organizational activity.
6. Review why looking at spreadsheets can become overwhelming and provide an inaccurate view of the organization.
7. What is the benefit of looking at information on graphs or charts?
8. Describe the various methods of analyzing the EMS organization.
9. Discuss the various types of ratios that are used to determine the success of the organization.
10. Discuss why choosing one type of analysis is detrimental to growing the EMS organization.

References

Balanced Scorecard Institute. (2012). "Balanced Scorecard Basics." See the organization website.

Bensoussan, B., and C. Fleisherm. (2008). *Analysis Without Paralysis: 10 Tools to Make Better Strategic Decisions.* Upper Saddle River, NJ: Pearson Education.

Best, M., and D. Neuhauser. (2006, April). "Walter A. Shewhart, 1924, and the Hawthorne Factory." *Quality and Safety in Health Care* **15**(2), 142–143.

Cavender, N., and H. Kahane. (2010). *Logic and Contemporary Rhetoric.* Belmont, CA: Wadsworth.

Everett Community College Tutoring Center. (n.d.). "Financial Ratios." See the organization website.

Helfert, E. (2001). *Financial Analysis Tools and Techniques.* New York: McGraw-Hill.

Ishikawa, K. (1982). *Guide to Quality Control.* New York: Quality Resources"

Quanterion Solutions Incorporated. (2012). Software Acquisition Gold Practice: Statistical Process Control. See the organization website.

Value Based Management. (2012). "Regression Analysis Method of Statistical Forecasting." See the organization website.

Key Terms

analysis An investigation of the component parts of a whole and their relations in making up the whole.

Balanced Scorecard A metric that gives managers a more balanced view or organizational performance.

control chart A graph with limit lines that is used to detect changes in a process from the graphed data that are collected.

data points Items of factual information derived from measurement or research.

deductive A form of reasoning in which conclusions are formulated about particulars from general or universal premises.

hypothesis A proposal intended to explain certain facts or observations.

inductive Of reasoning; proceeding from particular facts to a general conclusion.

observations What is seen or viewed.

ratios Proportion; the relationship between things (or parts of things) with respect to their comparative quantity, magnitude, or degree.

spreadsheet A program used for managing, analyzing, and presenting information. Spreadsheets allow information to be sorted or displayed in a chart or graph for calculations to be performed on data.

statistical process control (SPC) The use of statistical techniques and tools to measure an ongoing process for change or stability.

theory An unproven conjecture; an expectation of what should happen, barring unforeseen circumstances. A coherent statement or set of statements that attempts to explain observed phenomena.

trends Tendencies: general direction(s) in which something tends to move. Gradual change(s) in a condition, output, or process moving in a certain direction over time.

Billing for Services

9 CHAPTER

Objectives

After reading this chapter, the student should be able to:

9.1 Describe the payment trilogy and how the EMS manager determines the importance of each factor for the operations of the organization.
9.2 Define GNP and discuss how health care (and more specifically EMS) contributes to the GNP.
9.3 Discuss the partners involved in the payment process for EMS billing.
9.4 Describe how the government determines payment for EMS health care services to defined populations.
9.5 Describe the federal legislation involved in the creation of DRGs and RVUs and discuss how these coding processes affect how EMS is paid.
9.6 Describe how fraudulent behavior can affect the EMS organization and its leadership team.
9.7 Review the ten steps of developing a good collections process.
9.8 Describe the importance of medical documentation in receiving correct payment.

Overview

The purpose of this text is to introduce the concepts of finance to nonfinancial EMS managers. The chapters present valuable information to both new and experienced EMS leaders who may have varying degrees of experience, formal and informal. The goal is to stimulate thinking in order to change the way things are done, to avoid mistakes of the past, and to encourage future growth of EMS as a profession.

Key Terms

account balances	customary charges	fraud	self-pay
beneficiary	deductible	qualified	standardization
claims	diagnosis-related	reform	supplemental
clean claim	groups (DRGs)	reimbursement	uninsured
co-insurance	entitlement	relative value units	
co-pay	expenditures	(RVUs)	

WHAT WOULD YOU DO?

You are the manager of a medium-size community-based EMS organization. You have recently returned from a state EMS conference during which you attended some very good presentations on leadership, a review of medical and trauma topics, and the keynote speaker's talk. The participants in a few breakout sessions discussed the need for billing and understanding the finances of an EMS organization, and you decided not to attend these in lieu of going sightseeing.

When you return to work, you are sitting at your desk catching up on email and other documents when you open a letter from one of your suppliers requesting information on why the organization has not paid its invoice for 120 days. This alarms you because you thought all bills were paid within 30 days, taking advantage of any discounts. When you ask questions, you learn that your accounts payable are all behind and your accounts receivable balance is very high. You sit down with the billing professionals to ask for their input. They indicate that the EMS crews are not getting the information necessary to submit **claims** and are spending more time chasing information that could easily be gathered at the time of the call.

Questions

1. What steps would you initiate to align the goals of patient-centered care with acquiring information for business and financial purposes?
2. How would you educate the EMS responders on the importance of acquiring the necessary information for billing and the effect on the business when the information is not gathered at the time of the response?
3. What resources must be in place to ensure a timely and proper response to any inquiry regarding your billing for services?
4. What steps should you take to avoid any questioning of your billing practices?

■ INTRODUCTION

Historically, EMS organizations are viewed as providing urgent care to the sick and injured. There is a rapidly growing trend to use emergency services for what is considered routine medical care. Responding lights and sirens with a fire truck and an ambulance for shoulder pain, at three o'clock in the morning, does not meet emergency criteria. It is also counterproductive to send an ambulance to the home of a patient who calls 9-1-1 three times in one day for transportation to three different hospitals for the primary purpose of social interaction.

Of the 114 million visits to U.S. emergency departments (EDs) in 2003, an estimated 16 million arrived by ambulance (14 percent). Given that basic ambulance transport average charges equal $550 to $660 per trip, EMS transports to the ED cost the nation almost $10 billion annually (Larkin, Claassen, Pelletie, and Camargo, 2006).

One area that poses many challenges for EMS managers is receiving payment for services rendered. In the complex world of determining who will pay, under what circumstances, how much will be paid, the correct **reimbursement**, and whether the difference can be billed, managers can become confused. In addition, some EMS organizations solicit the public for membership fees or receive monies from a supporting municipality. Each situation has a significant effect on the organization and the leadership team. Reimbursement policies are continually changing, and keeping up with the complex contracts and submission rules will always challenge the best EMS departments.

Understanding the basics of reimbursement will provide a footing on the changing landscape. It is imperative, however, if the EMS organization bills for services, that someone in the organization becomes knowledgeable about the reimbursement process in order to maximize revenue while simultaneously reducing the amount of work that goes into each submission. This person must also keep current with the changes that occur with each payer group and understand how any changes affect the EMS organization.

■ THE PAYMENT TRILOGY ————

The payment trilogy consists of (1) the provider, (2) the payer, and (3) the patient. The provider is anyone who provides medical care and treatment. The payers are those entities that have contracted to pay for the care and treatment received by the provider. The payer can be an employer, the government, or a third-party firm that pays benefits on behalf of another entity. There are two types of patients: self-pay and uninsured. The **self-pay** patient is someone who has insurance benefits. When the patient uses prehospital services, a claim for benefit payment is sent to the insurance company. After the claim is processed, the provider may pay a portion of the bill. The payer will convert the balance of the account from insurance responsibility to patient responsibility. After claims processing, the patient may be responsible for payment of **account balances** due to (1) the difference between the insurance company payment and the provider's usual and **customary charges**, (2) an unpaid **co-pay**, (3) the **deductible**, or (4) **co-insurance**. **Uninsured** patients have no health insurance benefits. The uninsured patient is usually responsible for full payment of the provider's usual and customary charges.

■ CURRENT ECONOMIC STATE————

For many years, spending on health care in the United States has grown faster than the economy has, representing a challenge not only for the government's two major health insurance programs—Medicare and Medicaid—but also for the private sector. As health care spending consumes a greater and greater share of the nation's economic output, Americans face increasingly difficult choices between health care and other priorities (Congressional Budget Office, 2007a).

Health care costs have increased for several years. **Expenditures** on health care surpassed $2.3 trillion in 2008, more than three times the $714 billion spent in 1990, and more than eight times the $253 billion spent in 1980 (Figure 9.1). Stemming this growth has become

National Health Expenditures

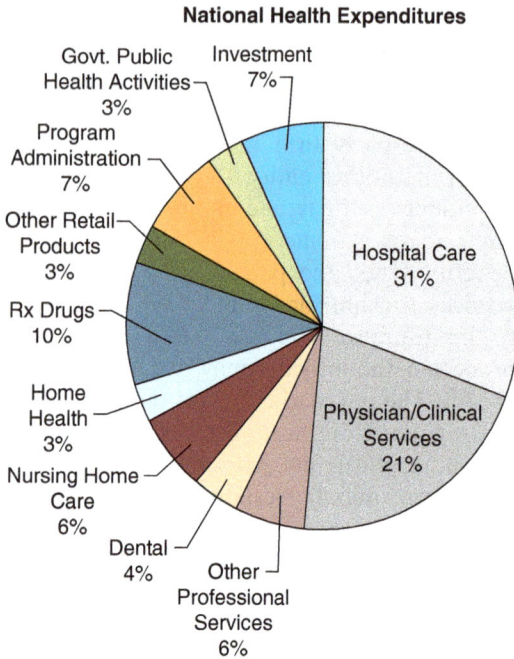

FIGURE 9.1 ■ National health care expenditures. *Centers for Medicare and Medicaid Services, Office of the Actuary, National Health Statistics Group.*

a major policy priority, as the government, employers, and consumers increasingly struggle to keep up with health care costs (Centers for Medicare and Medicaid Services, 2010).

In 2008, U.S. health care spending was about $7,681 per resident and accounted for 16.2 percent of the nation's gross domestic product (GDP); this is among the highest of all industrialized countries (Centers for Medicare and Medicaid Services, 2010). Total health care expenditures grew at an annual rate of 4.4 percent in 2008, a slower rate than recent years, yet still outpacing inflation and the growth in national income. Absent **reform**, there is general agreement that health costs are likely to continue to rise for the foreseeable future (Centers for Medicare and Medicaid Services).

As shown in Table 9.1, hospital care and physician/clinical services combined account for half (51 percent) of the nation's health expenditures.

When looking at the activity of EMS and the costs of responding to emergency and

TABLE 9.1 ■ Hospital Visits, 2007

Patient age	Number of visits in thousands	Total	Walk-in	Ambulance	Public service	Unknown
All visits	116,802	100.0	75.2 (1.0)	15.5 (0.6)	2.3 (0.6)	7.0 (0.8)
Age						
Under 15 years	22,308	100.0	87.6 (1.0)	4.2 (0.5)	1.4 (0.4)	6.8 (0.8)
Under 1 year	3,766	100.0	87.2 (1.4)	4.1 (0.9)	−	7.1 (1.0)
1–4 years	8,340	100.0	88.1 (1.4)	3.6 (0.6)	1.0 (0.4)	7.3 (1.1)
5–14 years	10,202	100.0	87.4 (1.0)	4.6 (0.5)	1.7 (0.5)	6.3 (0.9)
15–24 years	18,983	100.0	80.3 (1.3)	10.3 (0.7)	2.5 (0.9)	6.9 (0.9)
25–44 years	33,485	100.0	78.3 (1.1)	11.7 (0.6)	2.8 (0.7)	7.1 (0.9)
45–64 years	24,491	100.0	70.9 (1.1)	19.1 (0.7)	2.6 (0.6)	7.3 (0.9)
65 years and over	17,535	100.0	53.7 (1.5)	37.6 (1.4)	1.8 (0.4)	6.9 (0.9)
65–74 years	6,908	100.0	63.9 (1.5)	26.5 (1.3)	1.6 (0.4)	8.0 (1.2)
75 years and over	10,627	100.0	47.1 (1.8)	44.9 (1.8)	1.9 (0.5)	6.2 (0.9)

Source: Centers for Medicare and Medicaid, Office of the Actuary, National Health Statistics Group.

nonemergency calls, the activity is tracked by the number of admissions to hospital emergency rooms. In 2007, patients arrived by ambulance at EDs for about 18 million (15.5 percent) visits. About 44.9 percent of patients 75 years of age or over arrived by ambulance at EDs (Institute of Medicine of the National Academies, 2006).

According to the Institute of Medicine, emergency room visits in the United States grew by 26 percent between 1993 and 2003, while in the same period, the number of emergency departments declined by a total of 425. As a result, ambulances are diverted from overcrowded emergency departments to other hospitals. In 2003, ambulances were diverted 501,000 times (Institute of Medicine of the National Academies, 2006).

Obviously, EMS services play a large part in the medical economy of the United States. EMS does not utilize a high percentage of the economic dollars; however, the services contribute to the economic health of the United States. In this context, EMS managers must understand why operating an efficient and financially sound organization will not only provide superior services to the public and assist in preparing for evolving changes in the reimbursement environment, but also will prepare the organization for future survival.

◼ OBTAINING REIMBURSEMENT ——

The EMS organization can receive reimbursement for its services in many ways. An all-volunteer organization that responds to very few calls may operate on community memberships, subscriptions, or donations as a sole means of revenue. A larger department may receive assistance from the local municipality in addition to donations. An EMS organization that is supported by the municipality and funded by tax dollars for all operational expenses may not concern itself with billing

for services. A hospital-based system will bill for services, but the EMS manager may not have much control over the actual billing process. However, a nonprofit, freestanding EMS organization may hire either a team of professionals or an independent firm to handle the billing and collections. Likewise, a for-profit EMS organization will have internal professionals manage the submission of claims and the collection of reimbursements.

Whatever method the EMS organization incorporates into its business model, the EMS manager must understand a few essential concepts. The first is that each outside organization which receives a claim for payment has its own set of rules and requirements. Second, each organization will expect accuracy, timeliness of submission, and assurances that the services provided are appropriate. Third, the rules and requirements will change, and the EMS manager must know how to adjust his organization's specific practices to accommodate the changes. Let's look at the players.

GOVERNMENT PROGRAMS

The GDP is the primary measure of total economic activity, and it defines the market value of all products and services in 1 year. Since providing medical care and EMS activities are considered under the umbrella of the service industry, EMS is measured in the GDP. Studies show that the United States spends more money, per person, on health care than does any other nation in the world. The graphs in Figures 9.2 and 9.3 depict the projected expenditures for health care for the U.S. government.

Figure 9.4 shows a steady increase in government spending and the anticipated amount of spending through the year 2021. Projections of total spending on health care will rise from 16 percent of GDP in 2007 to 25 percent in 2025, 37 percent in 2050, and 49 percent in 2082 (without changes in the current process).

Health Care
Government Spending in United States - FY 2011

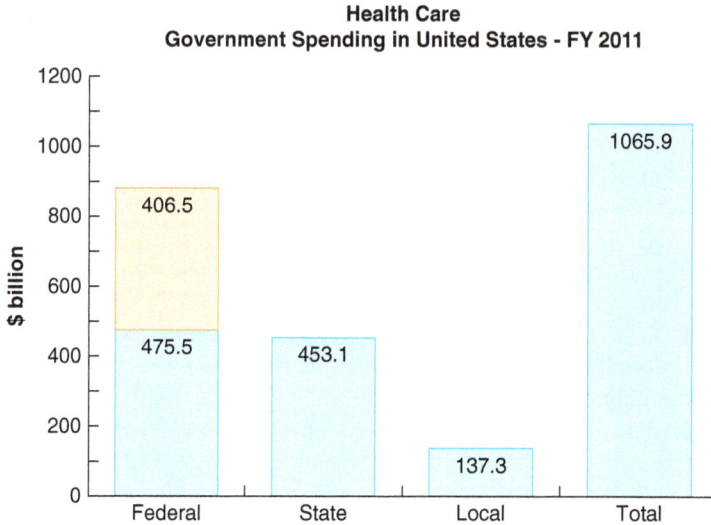

FIGURE 9.2 ■ Total dollars expected to be spent for health care by federal, state, and local governments. *Centers for Medicare and Medicaid Services, Office of the Actuary, National Health Statistics Group.*

The U.S. government spends an inordinate amount of money for health care, and the best projections indicate more money will be spent in the future. As a result, legislators are searching for ways to reduce the financial burden on Americans, and through cost containment strategies the overall percentage of the GDP spent on health care should decrease. The effect on EMS is going to change not only the way EMS organizations are paid but also increase the requirements to receive the maximum reimbursement allowed.

Health Care
Government Spending in United States - FY 2011

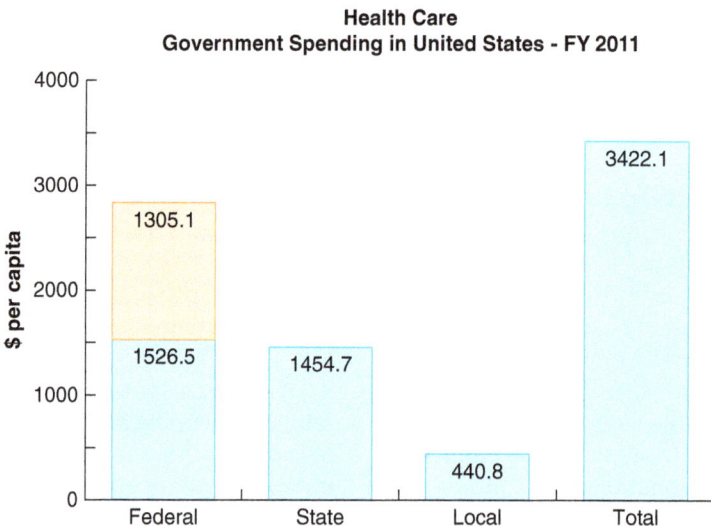

FIGURE 9.3 ■ Per capita government spending on health care, the highest of any nation. *Centers for Medicare and Medicaid Services, Office of the Actuary, National Health Statistics Group.*

Health Care Spending in the US from FY 2001 to FY 2021

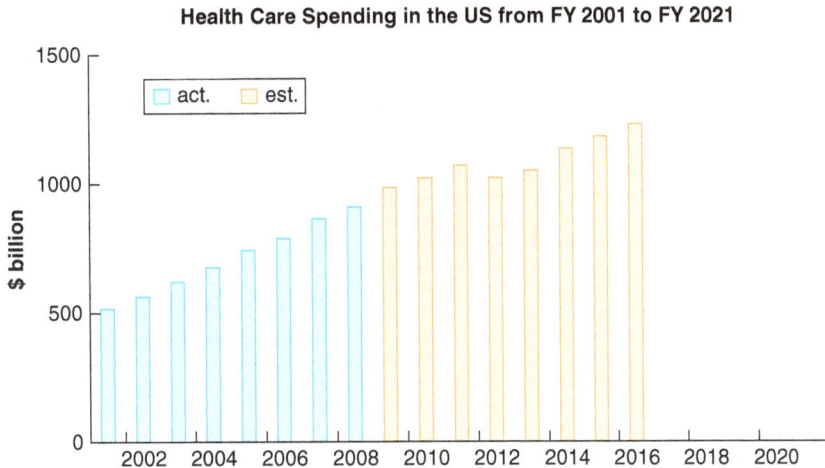

FIGURE 9.4 ■ Health care spending over time. *Centers for Medicare and Medicaid Services, Office of the Actuary, National Health Statistics Group.*

Medicare

Medicare and Medicaid are the nation's public health insurance programs. After Social Security, Medicare and Medicaid are the largest federal **entitlement** programs. Together, they provide federally funded health insurance coverage to millions of low-income, disabled, or elderly beneficiaries (Congressional Budget Office, 2007b).

The Medicare program was enacted in 1965 to provide health insurance coverage to Americans age 65 and over. Eligibility for the program was expanded in 1972 to include individuals under age 65 who qualify for Social Security disability benefits. When Medicare was enacted, only about half of the elderly had any private health insurance, which covers inpatient hospital costs, and that coverage was often quite limited (World Health Organization, 2009). Much of the health care spending incurred by the elderly was paid out of pocket by the individual or family members.

People pay into Medicare throughout their working lives, and are currently eligible for Medicare at age 65. Medicare covers most health care services but does not cover long-term services such as nursing home care. Although Medicare enjoys broad support among seniors and the general public, it faces a number of policy challenges, including addressing the affordability of health and long-term care for beneficiaries, financing the program over the long-term, and addressing the role of government versus the private sector in Medicare.

In 2006, Medicare spending totaled an estimated $381.9 billion, of which $374.9 billion (or 98 percent) covered benefits for enrollees (Congressional Budget Office, 2007b). About 26 percent was paid for services provided by physicians and other professionals as well as outpatient ancillary services. EMS falls into this area (Congressional Budget Office).

Most Medicare beneficiaries receive their benefits in the traditional fee-for-service program, which pays providers for each covered service they provide. Each **beneficiary** must pay a portion of the incurred costs of care through deductibles and coinsurance. Unlike many private insurance plans, Medicare does not include an annual cap on beneficiaries' cost sharing. Nearly 90 percent of beneficiaries who receive care in the fee-for-service program, however, have **supplemental** insurance that covers many or all of Medicare's cost-sharing requirements. The most common sources of supplemental coverage are plans for retirees offered by former employers (held by 37 percent of beneficiaries in the fee-for-service program), individually purchased Medigap policies (34 percent), and Medicaid (16 percent) (Institute of Medicine of the National Academies, 2006).

Medicaid

Medicaid is the nation's major public health insurance program for low-income Americans, financing health and long-term care services (Henry J. Kaiser Family Foundation, n.d.) for more than 52 million people, including children and many of the sickest and poorest in the United States. The program was created in 1965 by the same legislation that created Medicare, replacing an earlier program of federal grants to states to provide medical care to people with low income (Congressional Budget Office, 2007b). Since its enactment in 1965, Medicaid has improved access to health care for low-income individuals, financed innovations in health care delivery, and functioned as the nation's primary source of long-term care financing.

In 2006, federal spending for the program was an estimated $180.6 billion, of which $160.9 billion covered benefits for enrollees (Congressional Budget Office, 2007b). The federal government's share of Medicaid spending for benefits varies among the states but currently averages 57 percent. States administer their Medicaid programs under federal guidelines that specify a minimum set of services that must be provided to certain indigent individuals. Mandatory benefits include inpatient and outpatient hospital services, services by physicians and laboratories, and nursing home and home health care (Congressional Budget Office).

Medicaid is now one of the centerpieces of expanding coverage in national health reform bills. By 2019, the program is expected to cover nearly one in five Americans (Henry J. Kaiser Family Foundation, n.d.). Changes to the Medicaid program have enormous implications for federal and state governments, which are safety-net providers in the health care delivery system, nursing homes across the country, and millions of low-income families.

EMS Billing Rules and Regulations

As legislators tackle the increasing federal deficit, all health care organizations will need to transform not only their operations and responses but, most importantly, their philosophy regarding how they do business. EMS is a business: a business of providing medical services to the community. When someone else is paying the bill, payers need assurances that what they are paying for is a quality service. EMS managers must understand how to position their organizations to respond to the ever-changing billing rules. EMS managers must adjust current EMS operations when prehospital activities are often controlled by the people paying the bill.

Many large hospital systems closed down in the 1990s because they failed to recognize or refused to adjust to the changing financial climate of health care. The introduction of **diagnosis-related groups (DRGs)** and **relative value units (RVUs)** have changed how providers receive reimbursement for the work completed or performed. Ask any family practitioner how RVUs have changed the way he sees patients and how the documentation of the work affects how much he is paid. Similarly, EMS leaders must adjust their thinking and anticipate an increasing use of quality measures and payment structures in order to receive payment under the fee schedule for participants in Medicare and Medicaid.

Section 4531 (b) (2) of the Balanced Budget Act (BBA) of 1997 added a new section, 1834 (1), to the Social Security Act, which mandates implementation of a national fee schedule for ambulance services furnished as a benefit under Medicare Part B. The fee schedule applies to all ambulance services, including volunteer, municipal, private, independent, and institutional providers (e.g., hospitals and critical access hospitals, except when it is the only ambulance service within 35 miles), and skilled nursing facilities (California Department of Industrial Relations, 2011).

When an EMS organization agrees to receive payment from Medicare, it agrees to be paid based on the lower of the Medicare rate or the ambulance fee schedule. The fee schedule was fully implemented as of January 1, 2006. EMS leaders should maintain a high degree of awareness regarding the many nuances within this act. Any ethical breaches can have disastrous effects for the EMS organization. Related to billing, such breaches as accidental or known fraudulent billing can result in enormous fines and potential jail time. Given the complexity of operating an EMS organization, the manager must delegate the responsibility for billing practices and prepare the organization to financially support the billing process. If the manager believes he can run the organization and perform the billing function, the EMS manager places the organization and the people in the organization at risk for prosecution.

An example of details related to billing is seen in the reimbursement for mileage as stated in a provision of the Medicare Prescription Drug, Improvement and Modernization Act (MMA).

> The MMA directs the Secretary to provide an increase in the base payment rate for ground ambulance trips that originate in a rural area with a population density in the lowest quartile of all rural county populations, through 2009. The bonus amount to be applied for the designated rural areas is a multiplier determined by Centers for Medicare & Medicaid Services (CMS). Medicare contractors apply the "super-rural" bonus amount as a multiplier to the base rate where the point of pickup (POP) is in one of a group of designated rural ZIP codes. (California Department of Industrial Relations, 2011)

The EMS billing professional would need to know (1) that this provision existed, (2) whether the ambulance organization is located in a defined rural area, (3) who the Medicare contractor is, (4) what the multiplier is, and (5) if the point of pickup is in a designated rural zip code so he can bill correctly for services—none of which is an easy task.

Defining Rural. Trying to define what "rural" is, for such a diverse geography, can be difficult. People concerned with rural health care and human services must be precise in the definition. Federal and state policy makers, as well as service providers and researchers, need a clearly stated definition that is current in its interpretation.

Three government agencies have definitions of rural in wide use: U.S. Census Bureau, Office of Management and Budget, and Economic Research Service of the U.S. Department of Agriculture (USDA).

The U.S. Census Bureau defines specific urban entities. An urbanized area (UA) has an urban nucleus of 50,000 or more people. Individual cities with a population of 50,000 may or may not be contained in these UAs. UAs have a core (one or more contiguous census block groups [BGs]) with a total land area less than 2 square miles and a population density of 1,000 persons per square mile (Mills and Bhandari, 2003; Congressional Budget Office, 2003).

The Office of Management and Budget (OMB) defines a metropolitan statistical area—metro area—as a central county with one or more urbanized areas, and outlying counties that are economically tied to the central county. Outlying counties are included if 25 percent of workers living in the county commute to the central counties, or if 25 percent of employment in the county consists of workers coming out from the central counties (Mills and Bhandari, 2003; Congressional Budget Office, 2003).

Nonmetro counties are outside the boundaries of metro areas and are further subdivided into two types. A micropolitan statistical areas—micro area—is any nonmetro county with an urban cluster of at least 10,000 persons or more. It is further defined as the central county of a micro area. The second type of nonmetro county is the noncore county. ERS researchers and others who discuss conditions in "rural" America often refer to nonmetropolitan areas that include both micropolitan and noncore counties as rural areas (USDA Economic Research Service, 2012).

The Economic Research Service of the USDA; the Department of Health and Human Services, Health Resources and Service Administrations Office of Rural Health Policy; and the WWAMI Rural Health Research Center, University of Washington, collaborated to develop the Rural-Urban Commuting Area system (RUCAs) (Rural Assistance Center, 2012). This is a census-based classification that utilizes the U.S. Census Bureau's definitions in combination with commuting information to characterize rural and urban status of census tracts.

The Goldsmith Modification is a method used to identify small towns and rural areas within large metropolitan counties that are isolated from central areas by distance or other features. This variation expanded the eligibility for Rural Health Grant programs to assist isolated rural populations in large metropolitan counties (Rural Assistance Center, 2012).

The number of rural counties fluctuates over time, and disparities with conventional designations continually exist. The need for a clearer definition to meet the needs of new programs and new policies has encouraged other agencies to create more detailed definitions, such as those found in the collaboration between the WWAMI Rural Health Research Center and the Economic Research Service (Rural Assistance Center, 2012).

HCPCS. Another area that managers must understand is the Healthcare Common Procedure Coding System (HCPCS). Each year in the United States, health care insurers process more than 5 billion claims. **Standardization** exists to ensure that processing claims occurs in a consistent manner, thus the need for standardized coding. There are two levels of HCPCS. Level I codes derive from Current Procedural Terminology (CPT), which is a numeric coding system maintained by the American Medical Association (AMA). These CPT codes identify services and procedures that are billed to health insurance programs.

Level II is a standardized coding system used to identify products and services not included in the CPT codes. This area covers ambulances and durable medical equipment supplies. Level II codes consist of a single alphabetic letter followed by four numeric digits. Billing for services under HCPCS requires knowledge of the codes and continuous updating of any changes. A full range of HCPCS services is available under the Medicare Ambulance Fee Schedule.

RVUs. EMS managers and finance professionals who are responsible for the billing of medical services must understand the changing world of reimbursement. Since the passage in March 2010 of the Patient Protection and Affordable Care Act (PPACA), there has been much debate on how this act will survive, what form it will take after negotiating all of the challenges, and what effect it will have on professionals providing health care services. Despite all of the political activity surrounding this act, certain provisions in the bill do affect EMS services.

For example, sections 3105 and 10311 affect ambulance payments. The point here is to show how legislative actions impact EMS services. Someone within the organization must take responsibility for ensuring that completed billing processes are accurate. Accuracy is determined by applying standard codes to procedures or services performed. When submitting services to an insurer, the relative value unit (RVU) is used to determine the level of payment.

An RVU is a numeric value for ambulance services relative to the value of a base-level ambulance service. Because there are significant differences in resources necessary when responding to emergency calls, different levels of payment are appropriate for various levels of service. The different payment amounts are based on the level of service. An RVU expresses the constant multiplier for a service (including, where appropriate, an emergency response) (California Department of Industrial Relations, 2011). An RVU of 1.00 is assigned to the basic life support (BLS) level of ground service (e.g., BLS has an RVU of 1; higher RVU values are assigned to the other types of ground ambulance services, which require a higher level of service than BLS) (California Department of Industrial Relations).

The standard RVUs are as follows:

> BLS 1.00
>
> BLS–Emergency 1.60
>
> ALS1 1.20
>
> ALS1–Emergency 1.90
>
> ALS2 2.75
>
> SCT 3.25
>
> PI 1.75

The following definitions apply to both land and water ambulance services and to air ambulance services unless otherwise specified:

> *Basic life support* (BLS) means transportation by ground ambulance vehicle and medically necessary supplies and services, plus the provision of BLS ambulance services. The ambulance must be staffed by an individual who is **qualified** in accordance with State and local laws as an emergency medical technician-basic (EMT-Basic).
>
> *Advanced life support* (ALS) assessment is an assessment performed by an ALS crew as part of an emergency response that was necessary because the patient's reported condition at the time of dispatch was such that only an ALS crew was qualified to perform the assessment. An ALS assessment does not necessarily result in a determination that the patient requires an ALS level of service.
>
> *Advanced life support* (ALS) intervention means a procedure performed that is beyond the scope of authority of an emergency medical technician-basic (EMT-Basic).
>
> *Advanced life support, level 1* (ALS1) means transportation by ground ambulance vehicle, the use of medically necessary supplies and services and either an ALS assessment by ALS personnel or the provision of at least one ALS intervention.
>
> *Advanced life support, level 2* (ALS2) means either transportation by ground ambulance vehicle, medically necessary supplies and services, and the administration of at least three medications by intravenous push/bolus or by continuous infusion excluding crystalloid, hypotonic, isotonic, and hypertonic solutions (dextrose, normal saline, lactated Ringer's solution); or transportation, medically necessary supplies and services, and the provision of at least one of the following ALS procedures:
>
> 1. Manual defibrillation/cardioversion
> 2. Endotracheal intubation
> 3. Central venous line
> 4. Cardiac pacing
> 5. Chest decompression
> 6. Surgical airway
> 7. Intraosseous line
>
> *(ALS) personnel* means an individual trained to the level of the emergency medical technician-intermediate (EMT-Intermediate) or paramedic. The EMT-Intermediate is defined as an individual who is qualified, in accordance with State and local laws, as an EMT-Basic and who is also qualified in accordance with State and local laws to perform essential advanced techniques and to administer a limited number of medications. The EMT-Paramedic is defined as possessing the qualifications of the EMT-Intermediate and also, in accordance with State and local laws, as having enhanced skills that include being able to administer additional interventions and medications.
>
> *Emergency response* means responding immediately at the BLS or ALS1 level of service to a 9-1-1

call or the equivalent in areas without a 9-1-1 call system. An immediate response is one in which the ambulance supplier begins as quickly as possible to take the steps necessary to respond to the call.

Paramedic ALS intercept services means a paramedic ALS intercept unit responds in an area that is designated as a rural area (as determined under the most recent Goldsmith Modification) and be under contract with one or more volunteer ambulance services that meet the following conditions:

(i) Are certified to provide ambulance services as required under § 410.41.
(ii) Provide services only at the BLS level.
(iii) Be prohibited by State law from billing for any service. (State of Connecticut, 2012)

From a financial standpoint, ensuring that the crew makeup is in accordance with the rules and regulations *and* that they are performing the skills within their scope of practice *and* documenting the assessment accurately is essential to submitting claims correctly.

A general rule to remember: Medicare covers ambulance services only if services are provided to a beneficiary (patient) whose medical condition warrants an ambulance and for whom other means of transportation are contraindicated. The beneficiary's condition must require both the ambulance transportation itself and the level of service provided for the billed service to be considered medically necessary (Center for Medicare Advocacy, 2008).

Nonemergency transportation by an ambulance is appropriate if either the beneficiary is confined to bed and it is documented that the beneficiary's condition is such that other methods of transportation are contraindicated, or if his medical condition, regardless of bed confinement, is such that transportation by ambulance is medically required. Thus, bed confinement is not the sole criterion used in determining the medical necessity of ambulance transportation. It is one factor that is considered in medical necessity determinations (Center for Medicare Advocacy, 2008).

Payment. Payment under the fee schedule for ambulance services includes a base rate payment plus a separate payment for mileage. The payment covers both the transport of the patient to the nearest appropriate facility and all items and services associated with such transport. In addition, it does not include a separate payment for items and services furnished under the ambulance benefit (Centers for Medicare and Medicaid Services, 2001).

Payment for items and services is included in the fee schedule payment. Such items and services include but are not limited to oxygen, drugs, extra attendants, and EKG testing (e.g., ancillary services), but only when such items and services are both medically necessary and covered by Medicare under the ambulance benefit (Centers for Medicare and Medicaid Services, 2001).

False Claims Act

EMS is a business. When operating the business, EMS managers maintain responsibility for the success of the organization. This point cannot be overstressed. The success is multifaceted and requires the manager to balance the needs, wants, and desires of the community, personnel, and resources. As managers attempt to balance competing interests and priorities, one thing is certain: The EMS manager must operate the organization ethically. There are costs to taking shortcuts, and the importance of honest and ethical behavior in the billing arena must be stressed emphatically.

When an EMS organization submits a medical claim for payment, the submission must be accurate and timely. Any deviation from accuracy can present an opportunity to question not only the claim submitted but also prior claims. People within the organization, an outside auditor, or any other person familiar with the organization's practices can raise questions.

The False Claims Act (FCA; also called the Lincoln Law) is a federal law that allows people who are not affiliated with the government to file actions against federal contractors they believe have committed **fraud** against the government. The act of filing such actions is informally called whistle-blowing. Persons filing under the act stand to receive a portion (usually about 15–25 percent) of any recovered damages. The law provides a legal tool to counteract fraudulent billings turned in to the federal government. Claims under the law have been filed by persons with insider knowledge of false claims that have typically involved health care, military, or other government spending programs.

On May 20, 2009, the Fraud Enforcement and Recovery Act (FERA) was signed into law. It includes the most significant amendments to the FCA since the 1986 amendments. The FCA now prohibits knowingly submitting for payment or reimbursement a claim known to be false or fraudulent. The FCA does not require the government to prove "intent," just a "reckless disregard" or "intentional ignorance." Ignorance and/or lack of "intent" are not a justifiable defense.

Durable medical equipment (DME) companies and EMS organizations are two of the most frequently excluded organizations on the OIG's Excluded list (Office of Inspector General, 2012). Any organization on the Excluded list cannot participate in Medicare or Medicaid billing. The reason is always fraudulent or "erroneous" billing.

"Medically necessary" means that "the services provided are absolutely necessary to protect and enhance the health status of a patient, and could adversely affect the patient's condition if omitted, in accordance with accepted standards of medical practice" (McGraw-Hill, 2002). For ambulance transports, this means that transportation could not reasonably be done in another way. This is important since Medicare and other insurance coverage are often based on medical necessity. For most insurance companies, emergencies that have occurred suddenly and appear to need prompt medical treatment in order to avoid serious medical consequences are not usually questioned. Nonemergencies, to be medically necessary, ordinarily require the patient either to be bed confined and unable to be moved by any means other than a stretcher or to have a condition that would cause transportation by other means to be a danger to the patient's health or safety. *A doctor's order, without supporting documentation, rarely justifies medical necessity.*

Office of Inspector General

The mission of the OIG, as mandated by Public Law 95-452, is to protect the integrity of the Department of Health and Human Services (HHS) programs, as well as the health and welfare of the beneficiaries of those programs. The EMS manager should understand the consequences of errors in billing and the relationship of that error to the consequences if the error is discovered. The OIG is responsible for investigating and recommending penalties for any occurrence of fraud in billing. The consequences of an investigation and findings of improper billing can bring about monetary penalties, loss of inclusion in Medicare, and jail. From a risk standpoint, the incremental gains in a positive bottom line are negligible as compared with the personal, professional, and organizational consequences brought about from the desire to submit inaccurate medical claims to the government.

The OIG may seek civil monetary penalties (CMPs) for a wide variety of conduct. For example, the OIG may seek CMPs against any person who presents claims to a federal health care program for a service that the person either knows or should know was not provided or is false or fraudulent, or presents a claim that the person knows or should know is for a service for which payment may not be made. The OIG is authorized to seek different amounts of penalties based on the violation. For example, in a case of false or fraudulent claims, the OIG may seek a penalty of up to $10,000 for each item or service improperly claimed, and an assessment of up to three times the amount improperly claimed (Office of Inspector General, n.d.).

OTHER PAYERS AND PAYMENTS

The American health care system is comprised of a patchwork of health insurance programs. In contrast to most other nations where the government finances health care for the majority of its residents, private employer-sponsored insurance is one of the primary sources of insurance in the United States, covering more than 60 percent of Americans. This system is costly and complex, resulting in a complicated array of players, including insurance companies, employers, and regulators. Insurance coverage also affects a patient's interactions with the health care delivery system, particularly in terms of the providers they can see and the out-of-pocket costs they incur. Furthermore, currently 50 million Americans do not have any health insurance. Although national health care reform will extend coverage to many uninsured individuals by 2014, many will remain uninsured until that time.

Health insurance and other third-party payment programs pay for a substantial majority of health care services. As noted in 2002, national health expenditures were approximately $1.6 trillion. Private health insurance paid for $549.6 billion (35 percent), other private funds paid for $77.5 billion (5 percent), and public funds paid for $713.4 billion (46 percent). Consumer out-of-pocket expenses accounted for an additional $212.5 billion in private expenditures (14 percent) (Heffler, Smith, Keehan, Clemens, Zezza, and Truffer, 2004).

Participants in insurance pay a premium to a third party directly or, in most cases, through an employer via payroll deductions.

A third party is any corporation; insurance company; or public, private, or governmental entity that is or may be liable, by law, to pay all or part of a participant's medical cost of injury, disease, or disability. Regarding order of payment, third-party insurance carriers and private health insurance carriers must process the claim before Medicare or Medicaid does so. Each insurer will have unique procedures for submitting claims for payment. The EMS manager must ensure that any claims submitted are accurate because the payers can, and will, reject any claims with errors or missing information.

Claims for medical payment can occur as a result of many different circumstances. Vehicle accidents, receiving an injury at work, sustaining a medical illness, receiving injuries as a result of assault or other violence, and traumatic injuries as a result of falls or unexpected illnesses during the normal activities of life. All of these can result in claims to a number of different payers. Submitting claims to an auto insurer, a workers' compensation administrator, a health insurer, an insurance company that handles liability payments, or a patient's homeowner's insurer can be challenging for an EMS manager. It is the knowledge of how to submit a claim, what information is necessary, how to determine the correct payer, handling rejections, and preparing resubmissions that increase the organization's ability to receive reimbursement for services. The difficulty in understanding insurance payments include the insurance industry's ever-changing rules and regulations, the requirements of the submitting health care provider, the diversity of insurance products and coverage, and contracts written by the legal professionals within the insurance companies. Add to this complexity the need to understand the concept of self-funded employers, third-party administrators, supplemental insurance, and stopgap insurance, and we can see how the billing process requires a very knowledgeable professional.

Par vs. Non-Par

There are a few angles to consider when looking at par (contracted) or non-par (no contract) claims. The first consideration is this: Does the patient participate in an insurance plan? If yes, then the EMS manager must determine how to submit a claim and how the payment will be made. If the EMS organization responds to a call for assistance, 9-1-1 or otherwise, the EMS organization can generate a claim for payment. In such instances, having the patient sign the insurance form at the time of the call is extremely helpful. The signature acknowledges that EMS providers assisted; however, the form and signature do not mean that the patient agrees that the treatment billed occurred. This is where complete and accurate documentation is essential. Complete documentation requires that all necessary information is included in the PCR, the information documented is accurate and describes the events of the situation, a precise assessment is performed, the findings are recorded, and subsequent treatment and patient response are truthful. Once the call is completed, and the necessary paperwork is finished, a request for reimbursement is submitted.

If the patient participates with a certain medical insurance plan, the administrator of the plan will review the charges and determine the amount of reimbursement. Once the reimbursement is received, the EMS accounts receivable professionals should match the money with the claim and determine if the amount is correct relative to the insurance plan's reimbursement schedule. Most EMS organizations will not have every insurance company's contracted reimbursement schedule, so diligence is necessary in determining the terms of the contract. The key point to remember is this: In a situation in which the EMS did not contract with the patient's insurance company and the patient contracted with the insurance company through the employer, auto policy, or other entity, then the EMS organization has provided the service and may expect to be paid the reasonable and allowable rate.

Side Bar
EMS does not contract with the patient's insurance company; the patient contracts with the insurance company through the employer, auto policy, and so on.

As a nonparticipating provider, there is no requirement (but check individual state statutes for clarification or consult the EMS organization's legal professional for guidance) to submit a claim to the insurance company. Generally, the EMS organization can submit a claim to the patient. However, the risk of not being paid may increase for two reasons. First, the patient may not submit for payment. Second, if the patient does submit for payment and the payment is returned, the patient may not reimburse the EMS organization. The EMS organization must have a very strong collections policy in place and the fortitude to enact it in order to collect money that is due. EMS managers must understand the effect on cash flow and the financial success of the organization of having large accounts receivable. In addition, the EMS manager must believe that the money is legally owed to the organization and should actively and reasonably pursue collections.

As stated, if the EMS organization has not contracted with the insurer, the cost of services reverts back to the patient. However, if the EMS organization does participate, the EMS organization must follow the contracted service agreements. All of the rules apply to this scenario, such as timely filing, completed information, accurate documentation, and so on.

To improve the timeliness of satisfying the accounts receivable, EMS organizations should apply for and receive a National Provider Identification (NPI) number to facilitate submission and payment of claims.

Indemnity Carriers

Indemnity health insurance plans are also known as fee-for-service plans. Such plans existed before the rise of health maintenance organizations (HMOs), individual practice associations (IPAs), and preferred provider organizations (PPOs). With indemnity plans, the patient pays a predetermined percentage of the cost of health care services, and the insurance company (or self-funded employer) pays the balance. For example, an individual might pay 15 percent for services and the insurance company pays 85 percent. The fees for services are defined by the providers of the health care service. In most situations, the EMS service will bill a rate that is consistent with other payers and the insurance plan will pay an amount similar to what Medicare pays for the service(s).

An indemnity plan is a medical plan that reimburses the patient and/or provider as expenses are incurred. A few different plans fall under the category of indemnity plan. The conventional indemnity plan allows the participant to choose any provider without effect on reimbursement. Obviously, in emergency services the person calling 9-1-1 will not pick and choose which ambulance responds. However, when being transported in a routine fashion, a person may have a choice. Such situations can occur when the patient is a resident of a long-term-care facility and requires nonemergent transportation to a hospital or other treatment facility.

Another form of an indemnity plan is a PPO. With this indemnity plan, coverage is provided to participants through a network of selected health care providers (such as specific hospitals and physicians). Enrollees may choose a non-network provider but are likely to incur higher costs in the form of higher deductibles, higher coinsurance rates, or non-discounted charges from the providers. Insurers do not assign a specific EMS service to handle their enrollee's emergencies, and EMS organizations do not respond just to emergencies. For many organizations that handle both emergency and nonemergent responses, a PPO may contract with a specific EMS organization for nonemergent transportation of the participants enrolled in its plan.

An exclusive provider organization (EPO) plan is a more restrictive type of PPO that requires employees to use providers from the specified network of physicians and hospitals to receive coverage; there is no coverage for care received from a non-network provider except in an emergency situation.

An HMO is a nontraditional indemnity plan and assumes both the financial risks associated with providing comprehensive medical services (insurance and service risk) and the responsibility for health care delivery in a particular geographic area to HMO members, usually in return for a fixed, prepaid fee. Financial risk may be shared with the providers participating in the HMO.

A point-of-service (POS) plan is an HMO/PPO hybrid, sometimes referred to as an open-ended HMO when offered by an HMO. POS plans resemble HMOs for in-network services. Services received outside of the network are customarily reimbursed in a manner similar to conventional indemnity plans (e.g., provider reimbursement based on a fee schedule or usual, customary, and reasonable charges).

A self-insured plan (or, technically, a self-funded plan) is offered by employers who directly assume the major cost of health insurance for their employees. Some self-insured plans bear the entire risk. Self-insured employers protect against large claims by purchasing stop-loss coverage. Some self-insured employers contract with insurance carriers or third-party administrators for claims processing and other administrative services; other self-insured plans are self-administered. The EMS organization may see this coverage from a large employer who retains the cost of their workers' compensation.

All of the plan types previously discussed (conventional indemnity, PPO, EPO, HMO, and POS) can be financed on a self-insured basis. Employers may offer both self-insured and fully insured plans to their employees.

An individual or firm hired by an employer to handle claims processing, pay providers, and manage other functions related to the operation of health insurance is considered a third-party administrator (TPA). The TPA is not the policyholder or the insurer.

Self-Pay and the Uninsured

There are no social or economic boundaries for the uninsured. Some are young and healthy, and some are not. Many uninsured are below the poverty line, and others are reasonably wealthy. Those most likely to lack health insurance are young adults (18 to 24 years old), people with less education, and Hispanics. In 2002, 23.5 percent of the uninsured were in households with annual incomes of less than $25,000; 8.2 percent were in households with annual incomes of $75,000 or more (Mills and Bhandari, 2003; Congressional Budget Office, 2003). The uninsured population is large, but fluid. A substantial majority of those currently uninsured will not be uninsured a year from now. A Congressional Budget Office study found that 45 percent of the uninsured were without coverage for 4 months or less and only 16 percent (or approximately 6.9 million Americans) remained uninsured for more than 2 years (Black Ink Systems, 2010). A second study suggests that approximately 12 percent of the uninsured remain so for more than 4 years (Short and Graefe, 2003). In many instances, the uninsured cannot pay for the care they receive.

Research reveals that of the patients transported by EMS an average of 36 percent are self-pay patients. Historically, there are two distinctive types of patients. The first are those who have the means to pay at least a portion of the charges. The second group consists of the indigent patients who have no means to pay. Unfortunately, both types of self-pay accounts are combined in one large collections category. Typically, after internal attempts fail to collect money owed, EMS organizations turn over the unpaid accounts to a collection company as bad debt. Collection companies excel in tracking down and setting payments for those self-pay patients who have the means to pay. However, collection attempts on the indigent self-pay population will continue to be unsuccessful (Black Ink Systems, 2010).

How this affects EMS services is important, because as more and more people use an ambulance for their access to the health care system, the greater the cost to EMS locally and nationally. As costs increase and services go unpaid, EMS organizations will continue to struggle to remain financially viable. In a study conducted at the A. I. duPont Hospital for Children and Thomas Jefferson University, researchers found that 121 (41 percent) patients covered by private or commercial insurance, 126 (43 percent) patients were insured by Medicaid and 45 (15 percent) were listed as self-pay (Kost and Arruda, 1999). During the same period, 61 percent of the total ED patient population was covered by private or commercial insurance, 29 percent were covered by Medicaid, and 10 percent were self-pay. A total of 294 patients transported by ambulance were determined to have used ambulance transportation unnecessarily. Of these 82 patients, 49 (60 percent) were insured by Medicaid and 12 (15 percent) were listed as self-pay. Patients insured by Medicaid were significantly more likely to have used ambulance transportation unnecessarily (Kost and Arruda, 1999).

In another study, conducted at numerous hospitals, 30,455 patients arrived by ambulance and 162,091 arrived by walk-in/self-transport. Overall, patients with Medicare insurance were more likely to rely on ambulance transport (34 percent) than the privately insured (11 percent). Among the critically ill, privately insured patients were less likely to rely on ambulance transport (47 percent) than those with Medicare insurance (61 percent), the publicly insured (60 percent), or the uninsured (57 percent). Among the critically ill, patients aged 15 to 24 years and those older than 74 years were most likely to rely on ambulance transport (63 percent and 67 percent, respectively). Of the critically ill, 57 percent used EMS versus 15 percent of noncritical patients (Squire, Tamayo, and Tamayo-Sarver, 2010). At first glance, patients with Medicare insurance or public insurance, the uninsured, the elderly, and the critically ill disproportionately rely on ambulance transport to the ED.

For more and more families across the United States, paying for health care is increasingly difficult. Fewer workers receive health coverage through their jobs. Those who do have employer-based coverage must pay increasing amounts out of pocket.

Sometimes the uninsured, and sometimes the underinsured, are charged full price for their medical services—a price that is significantly higher than what insured patients are charged (Scribd, 2007). In the current health care system, insurance companies negotiate for lower prices. These insurance companies can obtain discounts that are, in some cases, 40 to 60 percent off the maximum price (Scribd). EMS organizations, which have large multiple-county response territories, may experience insurers offering discounts for 9-1-1 services or nonemergent transports. Uninsured and underinsured patients, who do not have the same negotiating power, typically must pay full price for emergency, prehospital care (Scribd).

Not surprisingly, more and more families must go into debt to pay for the health care services they need. Many state legislators and advocates have recognized this trend and have started to take action to ensure that low-income, uninsured, and underinsured Americans are charged fair prices for their care and are protected from aggressive debt-collection practices (Scribd, 2007).

Medical debt is recognized as involuntary debt and not subject to the same kind of punitive debt collection tactics used when someone intentionally buys a car or high-definition television and does not pay the bill. Most people do not plan to call for an ambulance, nor do they anticipate the need for transportation if they reside in a long-term-care facility. Legislators want to reduce what medical providers charge low-income patients who are uninsured or underinsured or who can demonstrate an inability to pay the EMS organization's full charge. EMS organizations may also choose to reduce or discount their collection of co-payments or deductibles from insured patients who can demonstrate an inability to pay (Scribd, 2007). Taking into account that many of the people transported by EMS cannot pay, EMS organizations may need to implement a sliding scale payment system for patients with incomes near or below the federal poverty level.

As the ranks of the uninsured continue to grow, EMS managers can employ certain strategies for dealing with self-pay patients. As the U.S. economy continues to fluctuate, employers will continue to look at all aspects of their expenses and make adjustments. EMS organizations may also face difficulties in dealing with insured patients. As deductibles rise and co-pays represent an increasingly high percentage of the overall cost of receiving care, EMS managers will see more self-pay or out-of-pocket payments, even among the insured. In keeping with the concept of service to the community, EMS organizations should learn to be a lot more creative and flexible when working with patients and their families to help them pay what they owe.

Payment Schedules and Discounts. Nearly every EMS organization must deal with self-pay patients who pay late or not at all. Patients expect prompt and professional medical care, but they do not always adhere to the same standard when it comes to paying their EMS bills. Bills not paid in a timely manner can severely affect the EMS organization's cash flow. Yet EMS professionals are often so sensitive to patients' problems that EMS managers may hesitate to emphatically request the money they are owed. Establishing a clearly defined and carefully communicated payment policy can help prevent difficult collections.

One technique for accommodating the self-paying population is offering a flexible payment plan that incorporates either a prompt-payment discount or extended payment schedules (Vasko, 2010). The EMS manager may expect that these patients will have insurance again one day. Knowing the local health care environment, knowing the patients, and offering prompt-payment discounts offer a promising approach for EMS organizations looking to reduce the accounts payable bucket. EMS managers should examine a discount policy within the parameters of their pricing schedule as well as any other contracts they have signed (Vasko).

It is permissible to provide a discount to an uninsured patient. The OIG published these guidelines several years ago. The OIG did not say it is permissible to provide a discount to a patient with insurance who has a contracted out of pocket payment.

The creativity needed to adjust to current and future medical cost containment activities, increasing numbers of people becoming uninsured or watching their out-of-pocket contributions increase will challenge most successful EMS organizations. There are steps the EMS manger can take to improve the collection of unsettled funds.

In addition, even if the patient is never transported again, he could remember the organization's kindness at a later date and make a future contribution or bequeath death benefits to the EMS organization.

Best Practice

In mid-2010, Wake County EMS learned that its ePCR vendor, HealthWare Solutions, was going out of business and that the ePCR system would not be supported going forward. There was no money budgeted or in a pipeline to do a major technology project. At the same time, the transport billing contract was up for renewal. The organization also had a variety of unmet technology needs, including a scheduling program, an inventory program, and an incident reporting program. At that time, Wake County EMS was paying 7 percent to its billing contractor.

To address all of this, Wake County EMS developed an RFP that bundled billing services and required prospective billing vendors to assemble a technology suite that met Wake County EMS's specifications. Several qualified bidders responded, and when all was said and done, Wake County EMS got billing services (interestingly from the same vendor as before, HealthWare Solutions) and a first-class technology suite, all for the same amount it had originally paid just for billing.

10 Steps. Traditional business models champion an organization's need for success as a priority, and managers will do what it takes to get everything that is owed to the organization. Yet, the manager requests leniency from others when the organization struggles. This one-sided approach leads the manager and the organization down a path of expecting from others what they abhor when others ask the same thing of them. From the perspective of contemporary management theory, everyone is viewed as a customer and treated with respect. This is not to say that EMS managers allow others to take advantage of the relationship. When people know the expectations, they routinely follow through with their commitments. For those who do not follow up, a mechanism should be in place to work with them—in this case to pay their bills.

It is not advantageous to business success to believe that there are only two views on accounts receivable: pay it all or go to collections. After all, EMS is about service to others. The following are ten straightforward steps that when implemented can improve collection results:

1. *Have a defined credit policy.* Let patients know when the payment is expected. When sending a bill, mail the payment policy with the first invoice.
2. *Invoice promptly and send statements regularly.* Establish a systematic invoicing and billing process. Just as early medical treatment can forestall a potentially serious illness, prompt billing can prevent an account from becoming a collections problem.
3. *Use "Address Service Requested."* It is difficult to collect from a patient who has moved without providing a forwarding address. Deal with this possibility by using the U.S. Postal Service's "Address Service Requested" procedure. Print these words, or have the words printed, on the envelope of any statement or correspondence, just below the organization's return address. If the addressee has moved, the Postal Service will search for a change of address and, for 50 cents, will send you a form containing the correct address. This also keeps the organization's address file up to date.
4. *Contact patients with overdue accounts more frequently.* The adage "The squeaky wheel gets the grease" has merit when it comes to collecting past-due accounts. Contact late payers every 10 to 14 days.
5. *Use your aging sheet, not feelings.* Many EMS organizations have allowed an account to age beyond the point of possible collection due to feeling that the patient would eventually pay. Although this may happen occasionally, it is the exception rather than the rule. Stick to a systematic follow-up plan. It will become evident who intends to pay and who does not.
6. *Train staff.* Even experienced collection associates can grow jaded from dealing with indebted patients who make false promises of payment. Train staff to treat such patients courteously, yet firmly. Collection employees may benefit from customer service training because, in effect, they must sell patients on the idea that payment is expected.
7. *Admit and correct mistakes.* Sometimes patients do not pay because they believe the organization made a billing error. If so, quickly admit it and correct it. Patients know that mistakes can happen. Denying an error only heightens a patient's resentment.
8. *Follow state collection laws.* Many states enforce collection activities using the same laws that govern collection agencies. Collection practices, such as calling patients at odd hours or disclosing to a third party that someone owes money, can result in serious repercussions to the EMS agency. If uncertain about the law, contact the state's department of finance.
9. *Consider using a third party.* If the organization has systematically pursued a past-due

account for 60 to 90 days from the due date and it is not paid, the patient is sending a does-not-intend-to-pay message. The time and financial resources budgeted for internal collection efforts should focus on the first 90 days when the bulk of accounts can and should be collected. From that point on, consider using a third party to motivate a customer to pay. Use a contingency collection agency (which takes a percentage of the patient's bill), go to small-claims court or an attorney, or use a flat-fee collection service.

10. *Remember that nobody collects every account.* Even with a carefully designed and administered collection plan, a few accounts will be uncollectible. Identify such accounts early to save the organization time and money. The EMS organization will benefit from improved cash flow since the vast majority of patients will pay.

Side Bar

Figure out what you want to do, figure out what you are actually doing, try some new ways of doing things, choose some combination of improvements as your new standard practice, then track performance to make sure it has gotten better and is staying that way. Your terminology—define, measure, analyze, improve, and control—are not trendy, but they will help your organization have a healthy future.

Depending on the size of the community the EMS organization serves and the relationships that are built, some EMS managers may feel badly about asking for payment from their neighbors. Money issues can damage healthy relationships, but just as a person cannot go into a grocery store and purchase items without paying for them, people who use community medical services should pay the cost of that service. If the patient values the service and the relationship, he or she will not expect the bill to be forgiven and will pay for the service.

Dunning Letter.   The term *dunning* stems originated from the seventeenth-century verb *dun*, meaning "to demand payment of a debt." It is the process of communicating with patients to ensure the collection of accounts receivable. Communication progresses from gentle reminders to increasingly stronger letters as accounts become significantly past due. Laws in many states regulate the form that dunning can take. It is unlawful to harass or threaten the patient. EMS managers can issue firm reminders and pursue all allowable collection options.

The EMS organization should develop a series of letters, with each subsequent letter using increasingly strong wording. As the account ages, the letters should be sent systematically to the patient. Always be receptive when a patient responds to a letter and requests options for payment. When providing options, establish expectations and advise the patient that failure to pay will result in formal collection actions.

■ DOCUMENTATION AND BILLING—

When receiving payments from payers—whether directly from an insurer (governmental or employer), a third-party administrator, or the patient or family—the process does not begin in the office of the EMS organization. It is not the billing professional's responsibility to look at the patient care documentation and determine the level of service and then bill the appropriate amount. Some EMS responders believe that all they need to do is respond to the call, complete the patient care report (PCR), and hand in the report for money to be collected.

However, the billing process starts at the time of the call.

Best Practice

In 2000 Virtua Home Care was losing revenue due to a decrease in volume as a result of deficiencies and poor quality outcomes. The executive team had two choices; close or change the way they operated. Leadership decided the latter and developed a plan to analyze the causes and develop an action plan to correct the current processes. A team of employees were asked to look at operations. They concluded that poor documentation led to unclean bills sent to payers, frequent denials, and higher costs. The documentation also was found to represent the quality of care delivered with an analysis that showed poor referral and coordination of care failures resulting in reduced revenues. The Director of Performance Improvement stated that Virtua needed to rework its processes by standardizing the billing, improving documentation to indicate the care provided, and streamlining the referral services. As a result of tracking performance, revenues increased, expenses decreased, and the quality of the care delivered to patients significantly improved.

Source: Elberfeld, A., S. Benni, J. Ritzius, and D. Yhlen. 2007. "The Innovative Use of Six Sigma in Home Care." *Home Healthcare Nurse* 25(1), 25–33.

PROPER DOCUMENTATION

EMS personnel must realize that the connection to the patient starts when the call is taken by the dispatch center and the ambulance is dispatched. To close the loop, the EMS responder must document the entire response process, starting with the time and location of the call. Many EMS providers mistakenly believe that writing the PCR is simply an exercise to protect them against legal action. The true purpose of writing the PCR is to communicate the events of the medical interaction to all people who will eventually become involved in care, treatment, and payment for the patient. The PCR is the only written "form" that links the patient to the EMS organization, the medical professionals in the hospital, and the financial entities that pay for the treatment. Without proper documentation, which can only be completed by the professionals who responded to the call, treatment and payment will fall below the expectation of a professional.

In addition, insufficient documentation will increase the probability of financial loss due to the inability to support the care provided. Good documentation not only paints a picture of what occurred to prompt the 9-1-1 call or request for nonurgent transport, but it also provides an objective and subjective step-by-step view of what occurred during the interaction. The PCR communicates these medical and other findings to all team members who interact with the patient. This prehospital information is important not only to the emergency department staff but also to the medical professionals who care for the patient, the social service professionals who will assist the patient during the discharge process, and the professionals who will use the information to report to state agencies the effectiveness of the entire care process.

The documentation also provides medical information that billers can use to submit a claim for payment. Good documentation supports the highest level of service that is legally billable. Without appropriate documentation, any reimbursement may be less than the cost of the actual service provided. It is communication that the PCR provides and why proper documentation is essential.

Point of Pickup

The EMS responder can improve the billing process by understanding what is needed in order to submit a claim. Many details and items are often missing in documentation. For example, point of pickup (POP) is the location of the patient at the time he or she is placed in the ambulance. The zip code of the POP must be reported on each claim so the correct geographic adjustment factor (GAF) and rural adjustment factor (RAF) may be applied.

> If providers knowingly and willfully report a wrongful ZIP Code because they do not know the proper ZIP Code, they may be engaging in abusive and/or potentially fraudulent billing. Furthermore, a provider that specifies a surrogate rural ZIP Code on a claim when not appropriate to do so for the purpose of receiving a higher payment than would have been paid otherwise, may be committing abuse and/or potential fraud. (Centers for Medicare and Medicaid Services, 2011)

Legible Signature

The EMS provider's signature is undergoing more scrutiny than ever. The Contractor Error Rate Testing (CERT) Review Contractor (CRC) has announced that it may assess penalties when medical record documentation does not include a legible signature. To avoid penalties, Medicare advises providers to make certain that their signature is legible and that they include a signature sample when responding to a CERT Documentation Contractor (CDC) request for medical records (EMS Billing Services, 2009).

Medical Necessity

An EMS responder does not have any control of when a person calls 9-1-1 for assistance or to request a nonemergent transport. After arriving, the EMS professional must quickly evaluate the situation, determine the medical situation, and formulate a treatment plan, but unconsciously he determines if his services are necessary. *Medical necessity* is a legal concept, related to activities that are considered reasonable, necessary, and/or appropriate, based on evidence-based standards of care. The term *clinical medical necessity* is also used. The question asked is this: Are the response, eventual treatment, and transportation medically necessary? After the fact, the billing question is this: Can we justify the service as medically necessary in order to be reimbursed for the cost?

Medicare Medical Necessity.   Medicare pays for medical items and services that are "reasonable and necessary" (Congressional Budget Office, 2007b). Medicare may only pay for items and services that are "reasonable and necessary for the diagnosis or treatment of illness or injury or to improve the functioning of a malformed body member" (Congressional Budget Office). Medicare has a number of policies that describe coverage criteria. Even if a service is determined to be "reasonable and necessary," coverage may be limited if the service is provided more frequently than allowed under Medicare coverage policies (Congressional Budget Office).

Health Insurance Medical Necessity. Health insurance companies provide coverage only for health-related services that they define or determine to be medically necessary (Bihari, 2010). They often follow the Medicare definition of medically necessary as "Services or supplies that are needed for the diagnosis or treatment of a medical condition and meets accepted standards of medical practice" (Medicare.gov, 2012). The EMS manager should begin to see how quality of care plays a greater role in treating the patient and receiving payment for services provided. Medical necessity refers to a decision by the patient's health plan that the EMS response, treatment, and transportation were necessary for the patient. This determination only occurs after the claim was submitted. Most health plans will not pay for health care services that they deem to be not medically necessary (Bihari, 2010). Again, complete and accurate documentation should demonstrate medical necessity. It cannot be emphasized enough that the importance of accurate documentation also includes avoiding embellishing the report, in order to receive payment, by stating that the patient's condition was worse than it was. Any perception by a reviewer that the EMS professional who completed the documentation was making the patient's condition appear more serious is potentially committing fraud.

CMS View of Medical Necessity. The governmental organization responsible for the oversight of Medicare payments is the Centers for Medicare and Medicaid Services (CMS). The CMS recommends that providers document any preexisting medical problems or extenuating circumstances supporting the medical necessity of response, treatment, and transportation. Factors that may result in an inconvenience to a beneficiary or family do not, by themselves, justify treatment or transportation.

When looking at transportation decisions, EMS professionals could ask themselves if emergency care or inpatient services would be required to improve the patient's medical condition, safety, or health. Would seeking care and treatment with services other than the emergency room significantly threaten the patient's health if care was provided in a less intensive setting? These are some concepts that should be used to guide documentation. For example, the EMS provider could simply document that the patient is nervous and breathing fast. Treatment: IV, oxygen, transport.

However, complete documentation that supports the services would include a fuller history: Increasing dyspnea for 2 days. Tachypnea and dyspnea with exertion. Increase in temperature. Increase in productive cough

for brown secretions. Decrease in oral intake and oliguria. Fatigue and vomiting. Treatment: IV, oxygen, and aerosolized medication. The difference is which picture is incomplete and which one would hold up to the scrutiny of medical necessity for the level of treatment provided. Items that should be documented include the severity of the signs and symptoms exhibited by the patient, the possibility of something adverse happening to the patient if not transported, and the need for ongoing treatment at a higher level of medical care.

Another area that is becoming less common is the legibility of the documentation due to the increasing use of computer-generated PCRs. By investing in a computer program that eliminates the need to hand write the PCR, EMS organizations can improve the return on submitted claims. Illegible documentation has a direct effect on the Recovery Audit Contractor (RAC) reviewer's ability to support that the billed services were medically necessary and provided in an appropriate setting. When using a computer-generated PCR, providers are encouraged by the CMS to ensure that all fields (such as assessments, flow sheets, checklists, etc.) are completed. CMS recommends that providers use an entry such as "N/A" to show that the questions were reviewed and answered. Fields left blank often lead the reviewer to make an inaccurate determination.

CMS also recommends that providers document any changes in the patient's condition or care. This is one area that is routinely missed on the prehospital PCR. The standard of care for EMS professionals is to assess and document the effects of treatment or at the very least an update on vital signs and status before moving the patient into an emergency room. Lastly, providers are reminded to check that any information that affects the billed services and is acquired after the completed documentation must be added to the documentation in accordance with standards for amending medical record documentation.

Timeliness

When an EMS provider completes the PCR and submits it to the billing professionals, it is reviewed for completeness. If the billing professional believes the claim is complete and submits it for payment, the hope is that the EMS organization will receive proper payment. If the claim is rejected due to lack of medical documentation, the billing professional must attempt to gather the additional documentation and resubmit the claim.

The EMS manager must see the inefficiencies of this process. Each time the bill is rejected and more information must be submitted for payment, the actual cash received for use in operations is reduced: On the surface, the organization may receive the entire expected amount of money, but to get payment the organization spent twice the amount of staff hours in order to receive the money, thus reducing the actual amount received. This inefficiency is avoidable if the EMS responder completes the PCR completely the first time. Submitting a clean claim is the goal each and every time. A **clean claim** can be processed without obtaining additional information from the provider or a third party.

A clean claim does not contain any errors requiring the Medicare contractor to investigate before making payment. Claims that do not meet the definition of a clean claim are classified as "other-than-clean" claims (Centers for Medicare and Medicaid Services, 2012). These claims require manual intervention on the part of the contractor. The Social Security Act (Section 1869(a)(2) mandates that the CMS process all "other-than-clean" claims and notify the individual filing such claims of the determination within 45 days of receiving such claims (Novitas Solutions, 2007).

The Change Request (CR) 5355 instructs the Medicare contractor (carrier/MAC) to process all "other-than-clean" claims and notify the provider and beneficiary of the determination within 45 calendar days of receipt (Centers for Medicare and Medicaid Services, 2012). Until the determination is complete, the Medicare contractor processes the claim by asking the provider or beneficiary for additional information (Centers for Medicare and Medicaid Services). The contractor will (1) cease counting the 45 calendar days on the day that the contractor sends the development letter requesting the additional information and (2) resume counting the 45 calendar days upon receiving the materials requested in the development letter from the provider/supplier and/or beneficiary.

What does this mean for the EMS manager? If a claim and supporting documentation are incomplete, delays in a payment will occur until the information can substantiate the payment. Often insurers follow similar policies, thus payments will be delayed for any claim that includes incomplete documentation. If the internal or contracted billing professionals are unable to retrieve information from the EMS provider, greater delays occur. Financially, the organization's cash flow is affected. If the organization was relying on the infusion of cash to initiate a project or pay off debt, any delay will push these goals further behind.

Authorization

In numerous emergency situations, it is difficult for the EMS professional to acquire the necessary information. Often the information is only accessible after the patient is transported to the hospital, where the family provides the necessary information to the registration or admission professionals. For EMS responders, waiting around for information is rarely an option, but the EMS organization requires complete demographics, insurance information, and the medical condition of the patient in order to submit a claim. Without the information, EMS cannot bill for its services.

To facilitate the acquisition of the information, EMS professionals must attempt to complete as much of the documentation as possible at the time of the response. If the EMS responder cannot document the necessary information during the 9-1-1 call, he should make every attempt to have the patient or responsible family member sign a release-of-information form. With the signature, the billing professional can request the needed information from the receiving hospital. Without the signature, the billing professional will have to contact the patient or family to obtain the information.

Contacting the family during a time of stress to ask for insurance information and other pertinent details adds to the difficulties the family is they are experiencing. Asking questions may come across as being insensitive or rude. Even though family members may understand why they are being asked

for information, it may damage relations with the family later. The take-home message is this: Have the patient or family complete the authorization form during the response in order to save resources. The more work the EMS billing professionals need to do to submit a claim, the less money the EMS organization will receive in reimbursement.

Similarly, when completing a nonemergent transfer or a routine transfer, the EMS professional should also have the release-of-information form signed by the patient, the patient's authorized family member, or an individual with the power of attorney (POA). At some long-term-care facilities, it may be possible to obtain a copy of an authorization on record that allows for release of medical and billing information.

CHAPTER REVIEW

Summary

Billing for services is essential for many EMS organizations that rely on more than community contributions and municipal or hospital support. With all of the requirements enacted to reduce medical fraud, the government, insurers, and third-party administrators are becoming more diligent about identifying abuses. EMS leaders must be intimately familiar with the ins and outs of billing. They also must understand the effects of delayed submissions and reimbursements on the organization's cash flow and goal achievement.

Developing a comprehensive billing system, investing in the appropriate technology,

and education for billing professionals (if the billing function is maintained in-house) are necessary for ongoing billing activities. If the services are outsourced, developing a robust checks and balances system will increase cash flow for the EMS organization. Continuously communicating with EMS responders about the importance of gathering the necessary information and holding them accountable are essential functions of the EMS manager. Without the constant infusion of cash, the EMS organization will see the accounts receivable grow, the accounts payable increase, purchases delayed, and goal achievement put on hold.

WHAT WOULD YOU DO? Reflection

First, you know you have a fiduciary responsibility to use organizational money correctly. It is imperative that the organization

commit resources to send you to a conference so you can attend the sessions that are going to benefit the organization the most.

Since you are the business manager, looking for valuable management and leadership sessions is an appropriate use of organizational funds. Learning as much as possible about the newest ideas, trends, and requirements in EMS management and financing will benefit your organization. Although attending sessions might not seem interesting, attendance does provide managers with valuable financial information that can be applied easily. Skipping sessions to do personal sightseeing, even if it is sponsored by the conference organizers, is unethical—and you know it.

As the EMS manager, you are responsible for understanding and tracking the AR and AP accounts. If you are unaware of the delinquencies on either account, then reorienting yourself is a priority. Delegating the activity does not absolve you of the responsibility for knowing what is going on in the organization.

Once you determine where the backlog is, you address the reason why the bills are not being submitted in a timely manner. When you find that the EMS responders are falling short on their duties, you hold an education session to motivate the responders to be more thorough. You also implement a checks-and-balances system which will ensure that providers who are not documenting the correct information (medical or financial) will be held accountable. You know that more education may be necessary. In most cases, EMS providers do not understand the importance of gathering the information, have never been shown what information to gather, or, if they have been told, are reluctant because "It is not a part of my job—it's billing's responsibility."

To address discrepancies in the medical documentation, you schedule a documentation class that will review all aspects of documentation and emphasize the true reasons why medical documentation is performed and is necessary.

Review Questions

1. What is the economic effect of EMS to the cost of medical care in the United States?
2. What is meant by the patient trilogy?
3. Explain the current economic state of health care spending in the United Stated related to the GDP.
4. Describe who the payers are in EMS medical reimbursement.
5. Describe Medicare and Medicaid.
6. How does the Balanced Budget Act affect EMS services?
7. How is *rural* defined?
8. What is the difference between self-pay and uninsured?
9. Why is it important for the EMS organization to develop payment plans for patients transported by their organization?
10. Define *medical necessity*.

References

Bihari, M. (2010). "Medical Necessity." About. com: Health Insurance. See the organization website.

Black Ink Systems. (2010, July). "Case Study: What Is The Largest Problem Facing Ambulance Companies Today?" See the organization website.

California Department of Industrial Relations. (2011). "CY 2011: Ambulance Fee Schedule Public Use Files." See the organization website.

Center for Medicare Advocacy, Inc. (2008, February). "Medicare's Coverage of Ambulance Services: Coverage Criteria." See the organization website.

Centers for Medicare and Medicaid Services. (2001). "Program Memorandum. SUBJECT: Implementation of the Ambulance Fee Schedule." See the organization website.

Centers for Medicare and Medicaid Services. (2010). "National Health Care Expenditures." See the organization website.

Centers for Medicare and Medicaid Services. (2011). "Medicare Claims Processing Manual: Chapter 15–Ambulance." See the organization website.

Centers for Medicare and Medicaid Services. (2012). "Timeliness Standards for Processing Other-Than-Clean Claims." See the organization website.

Congressional Budget Office. (2003, May). "How Many People Lack Health Insurance and for How Long?" See the organization website.

Congressional Budget Office. (2007a, November). "The Long-Term Outlook for Health Care Spending." See the organization website.

Congressional Budget Office. (2007b, November). "Appendix A: Medicare and Medicaid–An Overview. See the organization website.

Elberfeld, A., S. Benni, J. Ritzius, and D. Yhlen. 2007. "The Innovative Use of Six Sigma in Home Care." *Home Healthcare Nurse* 25(1), 25–33.

EMS Billing Services. (2009). "Articles." See the organization website.

Government Printing Office. (2002, February). *Federal Register* 9099–9135. See the organization website.

Heffler, S., S. Smith, S. Keehan, M. K. Clemens, M. Zezza, and C. Truffer. (2004). "Health Spending Projections Through 2013." *Health Affairs,* doi: 10.1377/hlthaff.w4.79. See the organization website.

Henry J. Kaiser Family Foundation. (n.d.). "Medicaid/SCHIP." See the organization website.

Institute of Medicine of the National Academies. (2006). "Fact Sheet—The Future of Emergency Care: Key Findings and Recommendations." See the organization website.

Kost, S., and J. Arruda. (1999). "Appropriateness of Ambulance Transportation to a Suburban Pediatric Emergency Department." *Pre-Hospital Emergency Care 3*, 187–190.

Larkin, G., C. Claassen, A. Pelletie, and C. Camargo. (2006). "National Study of Ambulance Transports to United States Emergency Departments: The Importance of Mental Health Problems." *Prehospital Disaster Medicine 21*(2), 82–90.

McGraw-Hill. (2002). *McGraw-Hill Concise Dictionary of Modern Medicine.* New York: The McGraw-Hill Companies, Inc.

Medicare.gov. (2012). "Glossary." See the organization website.

Mills, R., and S. Bhandari. (2003, September). "Health Insurance Coverage in the United States." Rockville, MD: U.S. Census Bureau. See the organization website.

Novitas Solutions. (2007). "Medicare Part B: News & Sites Updates (2007)." See the organization website.

Office of Inspector General, U.S. Department of Health and Human Services. (n.d.). "Civil Monetary Penalties and Affirmative Exclusions." See the organization website.

Office of Inspector General, U.S. Department of Health and Human Services. (2012). "LEIE Downloadable Databases." See the organization website.

Rural Assistance Center. (2012). "What is Rural? Frequently Asked Questions." See the organization website.

Scribd. (2007, March). "A Pound of Flesh: Hospital Billing, Debt Collection, and Patients' Rights." See the organization website.

Short, P., and D. Graefe. (2003). "Battery-Powered Health Insurance? Stability in Coverage of the Uninsured." *Health Affairs 244*, 247–248.

Squire, B., A. Tamayo, and J. Tamayo-Sarver. (2010, March). "At-Risk Populations and the Critically Ill Rely Disproportionately on Ambulance Transport to Emergency Departments." *Annals of Emergency Medicine 56*(4), 341–347.

State of Connecticut, Department of Public Health. (2012, May). "Re: Short-Form Rate Application Package for Requesting 2012 Rates." See the organization website.

The Henry J. Kaiser Family Foundation and Hewitt Associates. (2006). "Retiree Health Benefits Examined: Findings from the Kaiser/Hewitt 2006 Survey on Retiree Health Benefits." See the organization website.

USDA Economic Research Service. (2012). "Rural Classifications." See the organization website.

Vasko, C. (2010). "Strategies for Accommodating Self-Pay Patients." Medical Management Professionals, Inc. See the organization website.

World Health Organization. (2009, May). "World Health Statistics 2009." See the organization website.

Key Terms

account balances The amount of money in an account equal to the net of credits and debits at that point in time for that account; the equality of debit and credit totals in an account.

beneficiary In insurance, the person or (more rarely) organization that receives money from the insurance company when the insured event occurs.

claims A legal action to obtain money in accordance with an insurance policy.

clean claim A PCR that is complete and free of errors.

co-insurance A form of medical cost sharing in a health insurance plan that requires an insured person to pay a stated percentage of medical expenses after the deductible amount, if any, was paid.

co-payment A form of medical cost sharing in a health insurance plan that requires an insured person to pay a fixed dollar amount when a medical service is received.

customary charges Amounts a provider normally charges the majority of patients for particular medical services.

deductible A fixed dollar amount during the benefit period, usually a year, that an insured person pays before the insurer starts to make payments for covered medical services.

diagnosis-related groups (DRGs) A system of classifications for identification of services that medical provider offers.

entitlement The right granted by law or contract (especially a right to benefits).

expenditures Money paid out; an amount spent.

fraud A false representation of a matter of fact that deceives and is intended to deceive another so that the individual will act on it.

qualified To specify as a condition or requirement in a contract or agreement; in other words, meeting requirements.

reform Make changes for improvement in order to remove abuse and injustices.

reimbursement Pay back for some expense incurred.

relative value units (RVUs) Used to calculate compensation for medical providers using a set formula that is tied to various services.

self-pay A patient or guarantor responsible for the balance owed; a self-pay account.

standardization The condition in which a standard has been successfully established.

supplemental insurance A private health insurance coverage that may be purchased to supplement or fill gaps in health plan coverage.

uninsured Not covered by insurance.

Risk Financing

10 **CHAPTER**

Objectives

After reading this chapter, the student should be able to:

10.1 Describe how the EMS manager should understand the concept of risk and how identifying losses will better prepare the organization for future success.

10.2 Describe how losses affect the organization directly and indirectly.

10.3 Understand the importance of establishing a process for funding losses, and determine the impact of financing risk on the overall budget of the organization.

10.4 Explain what is meant by risk management, risk control, loss control, and loss management.

10.5 Explain the benefits of purchasing insurance.

10.6 Understand why financing safety and training is an inexpensive method of risk management.

Overview

The purpose of this text is to introduce the concepts of finance to nonfinancial EMS managers. The chapters present valuable information to both new and experienced EMS leaders who may have varying degrees of experience, formal and informal. The goal is to stimulate thinking in order to change the way things are done, to avoid mistakes of the past, and to encourage future growth of EMS as a profession.

Key Terms

allocate	frequency	mitigate
catastrophic	insurance	probability
deductibles	liability	risk
economics	loss	severity

You decided to take a day off from work. You are getting ready to start needed repairs to your house when you receive a phone call from your EMS organization. The voice on the other end is extremely upset. You are told that one of the ambulances was involved in a vehicle accident. You immediately stop what you're doing, change clothes, and head to the EMS building. While driving, you review in your mind who was on the crew and remember that the driver is a longtime member of the organization. You have had some difficulty with him related to his excessive speed, but you thought he had improved. When you arrive at the building, you are updated on the extent of the accident.

You find out that your driver ran a red light while responding to a person struck by a car. He had his lights and sirens on. He was reported to have been traveling approximately 35 miles per hour through the intersection. The driver he hit is in critical condition with a closed head injury. The crew chief was ejected from the ambulance, because he was not wearing a seat belt, and is in critical condition with a spinal injury resulting in quadriplegia. The driver is in fair condition. Despite the seriousness of the situation, you have to look at the overall impact of this accident on operations.

Questions

1. How will you manage the immediate and long-term consequences of this situation?
2. What financial impact will this situation have on the crew, current and future contracts, organizational recovery, and the ability of the organization to continue to function?
3. What operational matters that might have led to this incident do you need to review?
4. What preventive measure could have been implemented prior to this situation, with the goal of avoidance?
5. What processes must change to provide a culture that looks at the risks of potential losses so that everyone making decisions reduces the potential for loss?
6. How do you prioritize the financial investment in risk avoidance with the ongoing needs of everyday operations?

■ INTRODUCTION

In all businesses, the emphasis for management focuses on delivering a product or service. This emphasis is no different for EMS. While performing management activities, EMS managers determine ways to fund operations in order to continue the delivery of emergency medical care. With performance of each activity, there is a risk for a loss. That loss can take any form from direct loss of money or equipment to a key person, supplier, or donor. It is essential for EMS managers to understand the concept of a loss and the impact a loss has on an EMS organization.

■ LOSS ECONOMICS

Every business produces something that adds value to another person or entity. That something is a product or service. In exchange for producing the product or providing a service, the business expects something in return. In EMS, the service provided is made possible by the knowledge of and skill with people and equipment. A business certainly would not last long if the management team gave away the product or service without some level of an exchange.

The idea of exchange is central to **economics**. Everyone who needs something—let's call it X—must be willing to give up something else—let's call that Y. In order to acquire anything, a person who desires X must be willing to give up Y to receive it. The more value a person places on X, the more of Y the person is willing to give up.

Not everyone can make X's, nor does everyone have an overabundance of Y's. People find different ways to improve their number of Y's in order to get more X's. This is true with any business. For example, when a 9-1-1 call is received, or the nursing home calls for a transport, the request is for the services of the local, available EMS service. To receive the service (X), the patient is willing to give up dollars (Y) to pay for it. In most cases, the person does not write the check to the EMS responders in the same way that people pay for groceries, but the EMS organization still expects to be reimbursed for the service. Often, the payment comes through a third party, such as the government or an insurance plan. In both situations, the patient receives the service (X), and the EMS organization receives the payment (Y).

In this example, a few things are occurring simultaneously. Let's assume, before the person becomes a patient, that he is currently working or has previously worked (now retired). While the person is or was working, the employer's benefit plan provides some or all medical coverage in the form of insurance; the employee may give up a portion of his salary (X) to purchase insurance (Y). A retired person may have insurance coverage provided by the employer or the government. What is insurance?

Insurance is simply the transfer of financial risk. Using the preceding example, since the employee is unable to calculate when or if an emergency will occur, and is unable to anticipate the level of **severity**, the purchase of insurance offsets the economic impact of an event that does occur. Many people erroneously believe that purchasing insurance

transfers to an insurance company the risk of an event occurring. The insurance company cannot control whether or not a person will fall and sustain an intracranial bleed any more than can the person can control whether he falls and sustains an intracranial bleed.

Whether or not the now head-injured patient is severely impacted by the cost of care is dependent on who pays the bill. If the employee purchased the insurance offered by the employer, the insurance company would pay the cost of care (under the terms of the contract).

To recap, employees give up salary (X) to receive insurance coverage (Y). When an emergency occurs, the employee requests EMS services (X) and agrees to pay (Y) through his health care insurance for the transport.

Obviously, it is essential for the employee to have a steady stream of income in order to pay for the cost of having insurance, which, in the event of an emergency, pays for all or some of the costs of the emergency. Similarly, EMS organizations must make money in order to offer their services to others and cover the costs of potential losses. Just as the head-injured employee may be unable to work for a period of weeks or months, so too might the EMS organization that is ill-prepared to cover the cost of a loss be unable to deliver the services that are expected. Obtaining money is crucial to fulfilling the goals and objectives of the organization. In striving to reach those goals, the EMS manager must understand that there is always a potential for loss. The impetus for managers is to understand what types of loss can occur and prepare for the financial impact of the loss. In order to continue to provide the services expected, the EMS organization must be capable of recovering from a loss and returning to everyday activities.

There are many ways to build assets in an organization. By receiving cash for services, the organization can purchase assets (e.g., buildings, ambulances, equipment). These assets provide a mechanism to generate more cash. Organizations can invest excess cash for future use (e.g., certificates of deposit, bonds). The selling of assets (e.g., equipment, used property) generates cash that can be used to fund the operations of the organization. Sources of money are not endless, but the EMS organization can identify creative methods for receiving financing.

As stated before, one of the goals of financial management is to identify the sources of funding, **allocate** the funds appropriately in order to accomplish the mission, and reach the goals of keeping the organization productive for future activities and avoiding losses that take away from the funding.

■ DEFINING RISK

Risk is a tricky concept. It means there is a **probability** or threat of damage, injury, **liability**, loss, or other negative occurrence, caused by external or internal vulnerabilities, and that may be neutralized through planned action. A **risk** is an uncertainty or an unknown. A person cannot know for certain if something will occur (probability), how (mode) it will occur, how often (**frequency**) it will occur, or how much damage will occur as a result (severity). One thing is for certain in every business— losses will occur. It is the astute manager who realizes this and prepares to reduce or **mitigate** the loss as much as possible.

■ THE RISK MANAGEMENT FUNCTION

Various functions under the management umbrella require the energy of the person in charge. The manager will either be directly or indirectly responsible for some activities, such as human resource management, purchasing, and finance. Risk management

crosses all of these areas because losses can occur in all of them.

Many people in management or decision-making positions focus their energy on ensuring that money is flowing into the organization to fund growth. Managers focus less on the money that is going out of the business in the form of losses. It is the function of management to work toward the organization's established goals by paying equal attention to both revenue and expenses. The organization is often hindered by what is not paid attention to. When discussing losses with managers, they will often remark, "Well, I don't know anything about that" or "That's what I pay insurance for." Risk management is not a subset of management—it is the essence of management.

> ### Side Bar
>
> According to research, best practice organizations treat the management of risks as a strategic responsibility—with visible CEO and CFO involvement—no matter what type of risk is being addressed.

Managing risk is a large part of what managers do. It is the process of making or implementing decisions that minimize the adverse effects of losses within the organization. No one wants to see personnel hurt, but in the EMS profession sustaining an injury is always a possibility. Sometimes, the injury is unavoidable. More often, however, losses due to an injury are avoidable or can easily be reduced. What about the loss that is not related to an injury per se but occurs due to a decision by an employee?

For example, there is an activity that is subjected to a loss that is performed daily in an EMS organization. It has a significant probability of occurring, has a high frequency of exposure, and when it does occur can be severe or **catastrophic**. If the EMS manager was told that the organization will sustain this loss and it will cost the organization in direct and indirect ways that include cash, reputation, morale, loss of employees, decrease in business, and potential legal action, would the manager attempt to avoid it? What resources would be invested in avoiding this event? Would the manager do anything to prevent this event?

Four functions of risk management impact the financial position of the organization or how the company recovers from a loss. These functions include risk management, risk control, loss control, and loss management.

RISK MANAGEMENT

Risk management is a process of proactive decision making that minimizes the adverse effects of unanticipated losses. It is the proactive efforts to minimize an exposure and avoid the loss. The key terms here are *proactive efforts* and *decision making*. Management in general is about decision making. Risk management specifically is about decision making to reduce losses. The first step, however, is to identify the hazard or potential loss and then actively put into action those steps that will reduce the occurrence.

RISK CONTROL

Risk control is a conscious effort or action (or decision not to act) that reduces the frequency, severity, or unpredictability of unforeseen losses. From a financial standpoint, the more frequent or more severe an event is, relative to a loss, the more that loss will cost the organization. For example, if two of your personnel sustain back injuries and they are both out of work for 6 weeks, the indirect and direct costs can exceed $40,000 per injury. If next year nothing is done to reduce the possibility of back injuries and the number of back injuries doubles, the cost will increase proportionally. As frequency

increases, cost increases. If the number of injuries during the following year stays the same but the personnel who are injured are out of work for 4 months, the severity has increased substantially and so has the cost of treating the injuries.

The key concept is that management has a choice: either to act or not to act. Management either makes a conscious effort or decision to do something, or it does not. In the preceding example, management did not address the injuries and did not attempt to change the causes of the injuries; thus, more employees sustained an injury. Risk control requires management to do something to avoid further loss. If management does nothing to eliminate the loss, then from an economic perspective, management should prepare to pay out of the operations budget for the losses.

LOSS CONTROL

When a loss occurs—whether due to an accident, employee injury, or administrative oversight—some degree of financial loss results. The premise for loss control kicks in after the occurrence and the immediate steps management takes to control the effects of the loss. For example, Main Street EMS has a partially paid staff, and the remaining hours are covered by volunteers. Main Street has a volunteer board of directors. The EMS manager is paid, as is the billing person/treasurer. Both the manager and treasurer have a long-standing affiliation with the organization as active running crew members and have served in numerous capacities over an extended time. They have gained the trust of the crew and the community.

The board of directors decided to conduct an independent audit of the financial position of the organization. The board had never previously conducted an independent audit. The board had not suspected that anything was wrong, but board members wanted to ensure that business practices were accurate and consistent.

The auditor conducted the assessment and reported some significant irregularities in tracking and disbursement of funds. Upon further investigation, upward of $100,000 was either missing or used to purchase items not earmarked for the EMS organization. The findings were reported to the local district attorney. Subsequently, the treasurer was found to have diverted funds into his personal accounts, and he bought personal property with monies allocated for purchasing organizational equipment.

Risk management would have recognized this as a possibility despite the overwhelming trust placed in the treasurer. Risk control would have determined that policies and procedures as well as checks and balances, would need to be instituted to avoid such an occurrence. Since it did occur and fallout is still occurring, management must now find a method to keep the organization functioning at the same level as before the event occurred. A review of all financial transactions is needed along with assurances that money is available to pay current and future obligations.

It should be obvious that the cost to recognize the possibility of an occurrence or loss and the institution of policies and procedures to protect the assets of the organization are minimal compared to what it takes to implement loss control and recover from the loss. EMS managers do not typically plan for recovery because they do not often identify the potential for losses, and they do not adequately prepare the organization financially for a loss.

LOSS MANAGEMENT

The concept of loss management requires the management team to attempt to return the organization to the pre-loss state. The loss has occurred, and the management team has tried to mitigate the short-term effects of the loss to the best of its ability. Once through this stage, the management team sets a course that will move the organization into a position that, financially, is similar to what it was before the loss occurred. However, the organization will never be exactly the same again. In fact, it may look very different. Management must seek to rebound from the situation and return the organization to a state as close as possible to the way it was.

Side Bar

Risk should be perceived as a set of potential outcomes that can be understood, measured, monitored, mitigated, and ultimately leveraged. The best-practice ERM program allows decision makers to make well-informed decisions about the inherent trade-offs between risks and rewards.—Mary Driscoll, senior research director for APQC

■ FINANCING RISK MANAGEMENT–

Financing risk requires the organization to develop internal and external sources of funding to pay for losses that occur during normal operations. Let's assume that the preceding example does occur. Risk financing is the activity that a manager will do to prepare the organization to return to pre-event state. Will the organization be the same after the event? The organization will change, sometimes significantly. There will be casualties. People may leave the organization, business may drop off, or people may reduce their donations. The manager should prepare the organization to withstand the consequences of a loss in advance—that is, before the loss occurs. In addition, if the manager is doing his job, he will be working to ensure that the loss never occurs at all.

LOSSES

Before going further in developing risk financing, let's discuss losses. A **loss** is anything that is of value that disappears as a result of an action or inaction, a decision or no decision, an activity or no activity. For example, if a spouse places a valuable ring in a safe, those who need to know where it is can find it quickly. The decision to protect the ring and the subsequent act of placing it in a safe reduce the possibility of the ring becoming lost. The value of the ring is maintained.

If the same spouse places the ring on a countertop and forgets about it, the possibility of the ring becoming lost—say, due to the cat jumping up and taking the ring and hiding it or playing with it—increases dramatically. The decision to place the ring on the counter and the lack of actively putting it away where it would be protected could potentially cause a loss. Although the ring would still have value, neither spouse can realize the value because it is lost.

Anything important will lose its value when a loss occurs. For example, the manager of an EMS unit is aware that certain male crew members make jokes about female crew members. These same male crew members talk disparagingly about females in general. The males make sexual innuendos about females and act as if EMS is just a male profession. A group of female crew members reports the activity to a supervisor and the supervisor remarks, "Oh, they are just carrying on. Lighten up. Get used to it. This is EMS!"

What is the potential loss? Maybe the females quit. Maybe they file a complaint with the state human relations board. Maybe they contact an attorney. Whether they have a case or not, the fact remains that the organization is facing enormous losses. These losses are divided into certain categories to illustrate the complexity of looking at loss potential in an organization. The losses include, but are not limited to the following:

Indirect financial loss	Direct financial loss
Reputation	Increased labor cost due to loss of staff if the female employees quit
Bad publicity	Defense cost to investigate and defend the organization
Decrease in morale	Increase in administrative costs
Inability to find qualified personnel	Loss of revenue due to potential inability to provide requested services due to decreased crew availability
	Loss of contracts
	Suspension of or termination of guilty personnel

It is better to avoid the loss because there is no way of knowing what the loss is going to cost the organization. By avoiding the loss, talking to the male crew members, conducting sexual harassment or diversity training for employees, and educating the supervisor on the correct method of handling a complaint will reduce the chance of the loss occurring. Is there a cost in prevention? Yes, but the cost will always be cheaper than paying the expense of the loss. Why?

The EMS manager can control the expense of prevention but can never control the cost of the consequences of the loss. EMS managers can research legal cases that describe the circumstances surrounding a case (in this example, a sexual harassment suit) and the subsequent monetary awards to realize how much money the EMS organization can potentially lose. This question often arises: "How can I, as the EMS manager, measure prevention in tangible, return on investment (ROI) terms?"

The investment in preventive activities is measured by what the loss possibility could be. If the EMS manager reduces severity, reduces the frequency, and eliminates known hazards or opportunities for a loss, the ROI is huge as compared to looking at situations where the loss occurred and the EMS organization had to pay out.

If the EMS manager talks with the male employees and puts them on notice that their behavior is unacceptable, there is potential for a loss. The male employees could simply quit. A void in the schedule would need to be filled, which could mean overtime. An increase in cost may be reflected in the need to train another person, and the manager may be seen as hard-nosed, thus morale may fall. These are unavoidable consequences, but they are certainly much more controllable than receiving a legal notice stating that the organization is being sued for sexual harassment, with the outcomes being certainly unpredictable and the fallout unknown. Similarly, by letting the offending male employees quit, the manager could be seen as having high moral character and being willing to ensure that the operations of the organization are of the highest ethical caliber. Successful recruitment of new members might improve, and the cost of retention might decrease—both viable possibilities.

By conducting proactive education, the offending male crew members would, hopefully, see that their behavior is not acceptable and would simply change their behavior, thus avoiding all possibility of a loss. Paying for education is necessary, but again the expense is considerably less than facing legal action.

> **Side Bar**
>
> The biggest risk in many organizations is simply not accepting the internal message that bad things might—and in fact will—occur.—Mary Driscoll, senior research director for APQC

INDIRECT COSTS

A cost that is not directly related to the production of a specific good or service but is indirectly related to a variety of goods or services is considered an indirect cost. Whereas this definition is more general to business and making money, the handling of indirect costs in finance is the same, whether the cost is associated to revenue-generating activities or expenses.

An example of an indirect cost incurred in the daily operations of an EMS organization would be allocating storage space for training equipment or medical supplies. Training and education are directly related to the response of an ambulance to an emergency call. EMS providers require ongoing training and need medical supplies to treat patients. However, the actual storage space for equipment or supplies is not directly related to any specific emergency call.

From a risk management perspective, an indirect cost of a loss would mean a potential decrease in productivity of the staff due to the loss. For example, if a patient was dropped by a crew while being seated on a wheelchair and carried up steps, as opposed to the crew using the proper equipment, the manager may see that crews are less motivated to perform their jobs or other duties around the building after the offending crew members are disciplined. The crew may spend more time talking about the loss while performing tasks, and the speed at which the tasks are completed may be slower and the quality of the task reduced. The crew may spend more time away from the building by driving the long way back after transporting a patient to the hospital.

The EMS manager should realize that many indirect costs are associated with normal activities as well as loss situations. They should also be aware that each situation may have many unique indirect costs associated with the loss.

DIRECT COSTS

In business, direct costs are directly related to producing specific goods or performing a specific service. From a business perspective, direct costs are associated with activities that are directly related to the actual activity of doing business. Purchasing of fuel for the ambulance is a direct cost of doing business. When a loss occurs, the time taken to investigate the incident is a direct cost. A person who investigates the incident, whether internal or external, has associated costs attached to his time. By conducting the investigation internally, the person must be reassigned from his normal duties to another function (which results in loss of production from normal duties) and his services allocated to another function. This person continues to receive pay, but technically the pay is allocated to another function, unless the EMS organization is large enough to employ a risk manager to conduct the investigation. Even in a sizable organization, however, investigating an incident takes the risk manager away from the primary responsibility of prevention and avoidance.

■ DETERMINING THE COST OF RISK FINANCING ──────────

The process of determining how to account for the financial implications of losses begins with the vision and mission of the organization. The leadership team must have the foresight to establish a vision and mission that not only encompass the organization's growth and development but also ensures the protection of its assets. By addressing both growth and protection, the leadership team is stating that both have equal standing and decision makers must have the knowledge and skill to look at both equally.

An organization can establish an aggressive mission of being the biggest and best EMS unit in a county, but if 40 cents of every dollar is spent on losses, the organization may deceive itself into believing it is reaching its goal by merely occupying more territory. By reducing that 40 cents to 10 cents, revenue gains can be anticipated. Let's assume the board changed the mission statement to reflect a protection clause and now the mission statement reads, "Main Street Ambulance seeks to be the responder of choice for emergent as well as nonemergent responses, while protecting the people and assets entrusted to it by the community." Suddenly, the management of Main Street Ambulance is held accountable for both growth and protection.

Once the risk management functions align with the mission, goals, and objectives of the organization—adding financial support to the priorities and implementing measurements to assess the activities—the organization positions itself for future success. Financial support can take many forms. Generally, it can be divided into dollars allocated for growth and dollars allocated for protection.

Financing risk should be given the same scrutiny as allocating money for projects that enhance operations or develop new programs. When determining what risk processes to finance, the manager must understand the goals of risk financing. According to the Insurance Institute of America, risk financing is a process for making and implementing choices that serve the objectives of an organization by providing funds to prevent or restore an organization's losses. Because this is a broad view of risk financing, the definition encompasses not only losses but activities that prevent the loss from occurring. As stated earlier, it is easier and less costly to identify and prevent a loss than it is to pay for and recover from a loss.

There are steps to make risk financing decisions that not only assist in determining how and where to start evaluating potential losses but also provide assistance in guiding managers in what questions to ask in order to begin eliminating the potential causes. One thing that is integral to these steps is understanding that any loss is not an uncommon problem but, rather, it is most often a symptom of greater issues within an organization. By identifying and attributing the monetary costs to a loss, the manager can further plan to reduce the costs associated with losses. To do this, he must look at the underlying causes. The dollar loss is directly related to the underlying cause.

For example, consider these questions again: *If the EMS manager was told that the organization will sustain this loss and it will cost the organization in direct and indirect ways that include cash, reputation, morale, loss of employees, decrease in business, and potential legal action, would the manager attempt to avoid it? What resources would be invested in avoiding this event? Would the manager do anything to prevent this event?* Then ask this: *What would an EMS manager do to avoid a situation that can potentially cost the EMS organization money in legal fees, loss of contracts, poor publicity, personnel injuries, and personnel leaving the organization, which may result in the inability to provide EMS services as a result of one incident?*

In this situation, management can calculate the average direct and indirect costs of the incident. Management can determine the direct cause of the incident, but in most cases, as previously stated, the incident is a symptom of greater potential losses and this one incident is an expression of deeper risk issues within the organization. Issues, if permitted to continue to exist, will cause greater financial challenges to the survival of the organization.

Consider this situation: A 23-year-old male was recently permitted to drive to emergency calls. He has been with the organization for 5 years, 3 as an attendant and 2 as a crew chief. He successfully passed his EMT schooling and, in fact, was one of the top five students in the class. He has earned the respect of his co-workers and has shown exceptional maturity in many situations. The crew is dispatched to a person struck by a car with CPR in progress. The call is 2½ miles from the building. Upon approach to an intersection of a four-lane highway divided by a double yellow line and controlled by directional signals, traffic is stopped in the driver's direction and the opposite lane. This young driver determines there is no oncoming traffic and moves the ambulance into the opposite lane of travel. As he nears the intersection, he determines that his lane and the opposing lane continue to have the red light. He approaches the intersection at 35 miles per hour, when a car coming from the right begins to accelerate through a green light and turns left directly into the ambulance. The driver of the car is a 67-year-old male. As the vehicles collide, the young driver is propelled against the window and sustains severe head injuries. The crew chief, in the passenger's seat, sustains critical injuries, including a life-changing spinal injury. The 67-year-old dies as a result of the crash.

Most EMS professionals have either heard of, have known of, or worse have been involved in a vehicle accident involving an ambulance or fire truck. Most often, management looks at the actual crash, investigates the circumstances, and then makes changes to prevent the situation from occurring again. Let's take a different approach. Let's compare the costs associated with the accident and the costs associated with prevention and determine from a business standpoint why the accident occurred and what could have been done to avoid it.

IDENTIFYING AND ANALYZING LOSS EXPOSURE

Identifying and analyzing potential losses is critical in the prevention process. When determining the effects of a particular loss, management must evaluate three things:

1. The degree to which a loss exists
2. How the loss would interfere with the organization's objectives
3. The relative frequency and severity of the potential loss

Question: Relative to driving, how often does the exposure happen?

Answer: Every time the ambulance leaves the building.

One of the most dangerous points in any emergency response is at an intersection. So the frequency of the exposure is essentially every intersection the driver crosses because each intersection is a potential accident and ultimate loss.

Question: If an accident did occur, how would the loss of the vehicle and/or personnel interfere with the organization's goals?

Answer: If the organization has one ambulance, the organization would have no means to respond. If the EMS organization has more than one vehicle, but the person who is injured runs 75% of all calls, then the impact would be fewer responses.

Identifying and analyzing loss is a function of risk management. Risk management is about prevention and avoidance. By identifying that intersections are an area for potential loss, the EMS manager can institute processes for responding through an intersection. Even with a process in place, an accident could occur. To avoid a substantial financial loss, the EMS manager could purchase insurance. Purchasing insurance is a risk financing strategy. Insurance is a risk control process. So, in dissecting the accident we have to determine the cause. In other words, we must identify the underlying reason it happened in order to prevent it, thus reducing the cost of doing business.

Did the young driver attend an emergency vehicle response course? Did the course simply review how to drive the ambulance, or was it more extensive, covering the issues surrounding driving, the physical laws of driving, methods for reducing the possibility of having an accident, and the state's laws relative to ambulance operations? If the young driver did

attend and pass the course, what is the culture of the organization? Was the young driver told that getting to the scene was most important? Does the culture of the organization communicate that speed is what is most important, or in business terms, does the organization have a "production" mentality?

All of these questions should be or could be asked to identify the potential loss exposure. If these questions are not addressed, and the culture remains unchanged, another loss of some type will occur.

A process for identifying and analyzing situations can be built to determine how to make risk financing decisions. Figure 10.1 shows, where management of an EMS organization can look for hazards by reviewing the objective and subjective activities of the organization. By looking at the culture and determining the extent the culture plays in losses, a manager can then look at the outcomes of culture by looking at what losses occur.

In looking at the organization's driving history and analyzing the culture, for example, management determines that for generations drivers were not only permitted to drive in excess of the speed limit but were encouraged in order to show the community that "We arrive in less than the national average of seven minutes." The number of accidents has steadily increased in frequency and severity, and the dollar losses associated with those accidents have also risen. Looking at the increase in the organization's fleet insurance premiums, one can see the relationship that culture plays in loss prevention.

Most often, however, EMS managers will not review the real reason behind a driving accident. Rather, they stop short of completing the entire investigation and most often blame it on the driver of the other vehicle or conclude it was simply an error of judgment on the part of the ambulance driver.

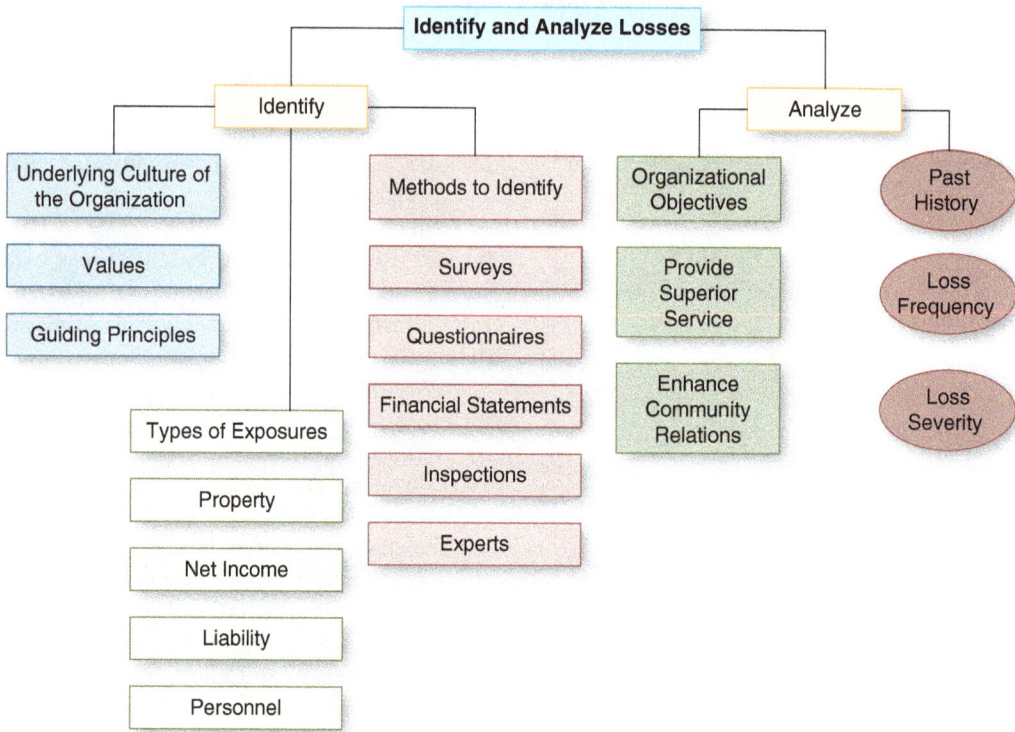

FIGURE 10.1 ■ Identifying and analyzing losses.

CULTURE OF THE ORGANIZATION

In an organization, everything starts and ends at the top with the person who sets the direction. The founder of the EMS organization, the current president of the board of directors, or the manager can all have a hand in developing and maintaining a positive culture. The culture of an organization has a direct effect on the cost of running the organization. An EMS organization that condones risk-taking behavior and encourages a production mentality will experience higher losses than an organization that establishes limits of acceptable behavior and realizes that more is not necessarily better.

The culture is the guiding light of the organization. The culture can be passed from one generation to another, and so can the costs associated with it. Changing a negative culture or culture that accepts losses can cost very little compared to the amount of money that can be lost by maintaining the status quo.

Managers can gauge the culture by examining what values guide the organization. Which behaviors are acceptable, and which are not? If management accepts crew members' comments that disparage others, the risk of discrimination, harassment, or malpractice legal action increases. At the end of the day, the manager should ask, "What is most important?"

TYPES OF EXPOSURE

Losses can occur in many parts of an EMS organization. When looking at exposure, evaluate the organization's potential for property, financial, liability, and personnel losses. These categories can be further divided into many areas that can cause losses to an organization.

Property

Look at the organization's building. Are there areas that are potential security breaches and invite theft? When an ambulance leaves the bay, are garage doors left open? Are floors permitted to remain wet, increasing the possibility for crews to slip? Are there tripping hazards? These are just a few examples of property loss that the manager can evaluate.

Revenue

Since every organization survives on its ability to generate revenue, protecting the revenue is an essential part of the manager's job function. Questions that help evaluate the financial aspect of the organization include these: Are all financial transactions formally tracked? Are systematic checks and balances in place for staff who will be handling organizational funds? Is a review of the finances done consistently, and does the organization routinely conduct independent audits? Does *independent* mean "the treasurer's brother-in-law"?

Liability

EMS organizations are exposed to liability in many areas from both internal and external sources. The technical definition of *liability* is "an obligation by an individual or company to pay a debt." In risk, a liability is a potential cost that could be paid for a wrong that occurs.

Internal Liabilities. The people within an EMS organization are exposed to many hazards that are potential liabilities for the organization. Sexual harassment was previously discussed, but inadequate employment procedures, work-related injuries, and discrimination are also potential liabilities. If one of the responsibilities of the crew is to wash the ambulance but there is no push to clean up the freestanding water, the possibility of an unsuspecting visitor or crew member falling can put the organization into a liability situation.

Similarly, if management hires an applicant but does not check his driving history, conduct a criminal background check, or evaluate the person's ability to do the job by conducting a post-offer, pre-employment functional capacity exam, the organization is potentially setting itself up for substantial losses.

External Liabilities. Since EMS interacts with the public, liabilities involving patients, families, and members of the community increase. As with most liabilities, the cause of a wrong can be reduced or eliminated. If the action or behavior of an EMS responder causes a victim to feel wronged, the wronged party generally seeks a resolution. When a question is raised by someone external to the organization against an action of a crew member, management often jumps to the defense of the organization, thus causing a defensive posturing. If the situation's severity is minor, an apology by the organization or offending crew will often satisfy the person seeking remediation. However, many interactions involving the public are not as easy to resolve because the action or behavior causing the liability is often steeped in tradition, ingrained behavior, or culture.

External liabilities can range from poor medical care and incomplete documentation to ambulance crashes and patient drops. When these occur, the EMS organization will often pay the person who has a legitimate claim. Reducing or eliminating the causes of these liabilities noticeably reduces the organization's financial loss.

Personnel

How has the organization reduced or eliminated the potential liability associated with people? Is the manager the only person who knows the inner workings of the organization? Does the manager share information or delegate responsibilities to others? What if the manager leaves unexpectedly? What will be done to recover the lost knowledge, and how can the organization recover? Does the organization rely on a small group of people to operate the organization? If any of these people perform illegal or questionable activities with organizational funds or equipment, what effect will these activities have on the organization's ability to continue to function?

The EMS manager should recognize the importance of maintaining control of organizational activities and define the role individuals play in the organization. Too much control by one or a few people may expose the organization to large losses if those key people leave or something unexpected happens to them. The opposite—many people having access to all the information—is also not appropri-

ate because the liability increases due to little or no control of confidential information. The EMS manager should understand that balance is needed in all activities. The organization incurs an associated cost when the balance is tilted one way or another.

Reducing personnel liability requires cross-training and delegating responsibilities to help minimize the effects of a key person leaving. If a small group of personnel is responsible for the majority of organizational decision making, building strong checks and balances can minimize losses that may occur. Developing committees to make decisions or encouraging the board of directors to become more involved may limit liability. The makeup of the board can also minimize the effect of small groups. If the board of directors is comprised of previous crew members or friends of the EMS organization, the potential for liability increases due to potentially less oversight and complacency.

Best Practice

This best practice is a summary of a story of how important relationships are and the impact they have on organizations. EMS organizations interact with people every day and each of the exchanges can result in positive or negative consequences. Described below are lessons learned about one contact.

One morning the administrator of a nursing home arrived at work to find the staff performing CPR on a resident. The patient was transported to the local hospital where she eventually died. The author went to the hospital and while standing at the nursing desk overheard a conversation with the charge nurse and the caller. The nurse, while still on the phone, began to discuss the call with the physi-

cian. The facility the author worked at was mentioned. The author introduced herself to the physician. She was handed the phone by the nurse and learned that the caller was a charge nurse at the facility. Another nurse at the facility had grabbed the chart of a patient with the same first and last name and contacted that family about the incident at the nursing home. They were on their way to the hospital. The deceased patient's family was still unaware of the death.

The administrator told the physician she would meet the arriving family in the lobby to explain the facility's mistake. Following the difficult but ultimately positive encounter, the administrator returned to the facility. When she entered the facility she saw the employee who had made the mistake waiting in the hallway. The nurse ran to the administrator and asked to written up. But instead of a disciplinary action, it was suggested that both families deserved a personal apology for her mistake. Having to face both families would be more difficult for her than any discipline.

During the investigation of the event, there was no doubt that such an incident would have opened the facility up to extensive liability. Such events raise the question of negligence and inadequate care, especially when an initial response

is defensive or full of denial. The author stated she was thankful they had a trusting relationship with both families prior to the event, and they forgave the staff. They also identified potential risk issues related to duplicate names—ranging from residents receiving other residents' mail to the increased risk for medication errors—and made necessary adjustments in the operations. By recognizing the errors the organization demonstrated accountability and showed respect by listening to suggestions, auditing operating procedures, and keeping vested parties informed of the progress.

■ RECOVERING FROM A LOSS

Many risk financing activities focus on ways to pay for recovery after a loss occurs. A major aspect of risk management, and ultimately the manager's job, is to prevent losses from occurring. Intuitively, if a loss never occurs, the organization is not required to pay for it, and the investment upfront is less costly than the payment afterward.

The challenge lies in determining what potential losses require review and assessment in order to determine the allocation of financial resources in order to prevent future losses. Each EMS organization is different, and each is going to have unique risk exposures. The place to start looking for exposures is the history of losses and payouts the organization has experienced. By reviewing the historical information, the EMS manager should be able to determine trends that will lead to initiating a plan of action. Gather information by looking at past insurance claims, direct payouts from operational funds, or payments for **deductibles**.

Once this information is collected, the EMS manager should look at the frequency of the losses as well as the severity. If during the investigation the EMS manager determines that the organization has very few claims or losses paid for, becoming complacent is not an option. The manager should look at this information and ask "What are we doing right?" and "How can we make it better?" The manager should look at industry trends to determine where others experience difficulty, and if exposure exists for the same or similar losses. Much of this information is available through an insurer.

It is then time to determine what possible future losses could affect the organization and allocate sufficient funding to reduce the possibility. For example, the organization has never had a severe vehicle accident but has had multiple incidents during which the ambulance was scratched, mirrors were removed, and dents from hitting stationary objects were incurred. So, frequency is high in this case and should be a warning sign that more training is necessary because it is only a matter of time until a significant accident occurs.

Making a decision on not only if training is needed but also on how much money is necessary to change behavior and decrease the frequency and avoid a serious accident is a critical management function. If the manager decided that training is not necessary, even though the evidence suggests otherwise, he must consider whether the organization is adequately prepared to finance the consequences of a significant loss.

ALTERNATIVE RISK FINANCING TECHNIQUES

There are three basic risk financing techniques: retention, transfer, and hybrid. As Figure 10.2 illustrates, the EMS manager has a few options available for funding losses. Each option has its own set of pros and cons.

Retention

When an organization decides to retain financing, it is saying "We can handle any cost associated with a loss." There are a few techniques that an organization can use to fund these losses. They include use of reserves, borrowing, and use of a wholly owned captive insurer.

With retention, the EMS manager must consider the level of the possibility of losses, the organization's culture regarding prevention, and the associated behaviors of each person affiliated with the organization, appropriate funding, and management's degree of tolerance for risk.

When the organization has a safety-first culture, and the history shows few or no financial losses, the organization may choose to retain the cost of any subsequent loss. In that case, one area that is important to consider is the availability of appropriate funding. The manager should look at the organization's financial reserves, cash flow, and ability to receive money if needed. By choosing to retain the cost of losses, management is gambling with the organization's money. There is no method to predict when a loss will occur or how severe the loss will be. Management must be certain that it can control the availability of funds sufficient to pay for any loss when funds are needed.

Using funds out of operations or savings for loss payment interrupts the organization's ability to continue to reach organizational goals. Net cash flow is the key to determining how efficiently the organization uses its funds. Often managers look at profit as an indicator of success. Net cash flow measures all productivity, not just operations, and is an indicator of how the organization uses its resources to fulfill its goals.

Loss retention may be necessary in some situations, such as loss of insurance or when purchasing insurance is extremely difficult

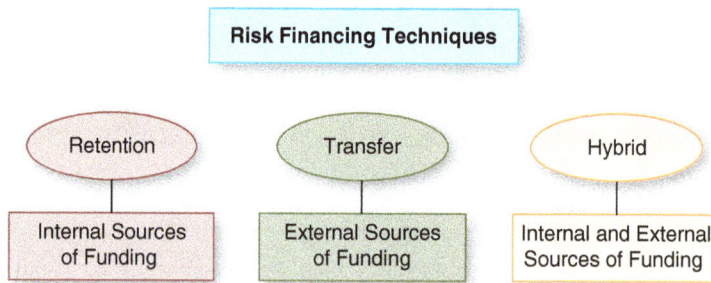

FIGURE 10.2 ■ Risk financing techniques.

due to past losses. In such a case, management must look at why losses are significant and change the underlying cause.

Transfer

Options for transferring the financial cost of a loss include insurance and contractual transfers of risk such as hold harmless agreements. These agreements are different from contracting or leases. A benefit of purchasing insurance is the ability to replace the uncertain cost of a loss with a more predictable outlay of cash for the insurance premium. Insurance is a safeguard against the uncertainty of the financial implications of a loss.

Each organization must determine its individual needs for transferring the cost of a loss. If the organization historically has had few losses and the culture focuses on prevention and training, management may purchase an insurance policy with a higher deductible, thus reducing the cash outlay for premiums.

On the other hand, if the organization sustains many small losses, it may choose to have a lower deductible and pay a higher premium. Every manager must review every unique circumstance and determine what risk financing program meets the organization's goals. EMS managers must refrain from focusing on short-term financial goals such as increasing profits or improving cash flow, especially if these measurements are used to determine salary. If the EMS manager decides to purchase low-level insurance coverage, operations increases cash flow, this decision improves the salary of key administrative people, and a significant loss occurs, the organization may not have the funds to recover.

Another careful consideration managers must attend to the question of why they are transferring the cost of losses to someone else. Risk control is preferable to risk financing. Risk control safeguards assets, thus reducing the need to finance a loss. If the organization does nothing to reduce losses, then purchasing insurance is not going to reduce the money spent on financing those losses. Insurance is a relatively costly source of loss financing unless the loss is very large and unpredictable.

Side Bar
Most EMS losses are predictable and preventable.

Areas to Consider for Coverage. Most people, when asked, do not understand the concept of insurance. As previously stated, insurance is available when an organization wishes to transfer the financial risk of a loss from the EMS organization to a company that is willing to absorb the loss for a predetermined cost. Generally, people think about purchasing insurance for cars or other personal property. Although it can be somewhat painful writing out a check to an insurance company without seeing any benefit, think of insurance as an invisible blanket of safety. If a car accident occurs or a tree falls onto the house and repairs are needed, suddenly that insurance policy is worth its weight in gold because the insured does not have to pay for the total loss. The deductible is paid, and the insurance company pays the rest. This discussion is an oversimplification, but the point remains the same: People are willing to pay to transfer the risk of financing to the insurance company.

In an EMS organization, the potential exposures for losses are great. For example, the ambulance building unintentionally burns to the ground. Seventy-five years of community service is now piled into a heap of smoking rubble. The loss is estimated at $4 million. The organization is able to return to a pre-fire state with a comprehensive insurance policy.

In this scenario, the EMS manager should have looked at purchasing more than fire insurance. He also should have preplanned how the EMS organization will continue to serve the public during the reconstruction phase. Appropriate loss control procedures would have had the EMS manager discussing with a neighboring EMS organization or an ambulance vendor how to borrow an ambulance or lease one.

What happens if the board of directors evaluates a problem and arrives at a solution but the decision is wrong, exposing the organization to public scrutiny and potential legal action? What protection exists for decisions? In this scenario, the EMS organization can purchase errors and omissions (E&O) coverage to protect the organization from the financial implications of a decision. The insurance coverage does not reduce the possibility of legal action, but the loss may be covered with the insurance company, up to the terms of the policy.

EMS managers often may feel pressured to buy insurance for everything. Of course, each item insured adds to the cost. The EMS manager must decide, based on potential, what clearly needs to be protected, what should be protected, what would be nice to be protected, and what the organization can absorb if it were not protected. Each of these decisions involves a risk. The EMS manager must determine the level of risk in order to accept coverage or reject it. Ultimately, it is the EMS manager who accepts responsibility for the decision, and any cost associated with a loss will be reflective of the decision.

Hybrid

A hybrid approach to risk financing may appeal to larger EMS organizations. This type of financing is often seen in the workers' compensation arena, where the EMS organization combines a high deductible with a captive risk program. When an organization retains a greater portion of the cost, it also maintains more control and has greater flexibility over the hazard reduction program and operational funding. The EMS organization has more

incentive to control losses because it directly benefits from reduced injuries.

Hybrid financing is not the same as a self-funded program; some call it self-insurance because the organization continues to retain the services of a licensed insurer. The deductibles in a hybrid are often very high; thus, the advantage for the EMS organization is the ability to develop initiatives that will reduce the financial losses for small claims and to maintain the protection of the insurer if, unfortunately, a sizable claim is incurred.

Many EMS organizations have an agreement with the local, municipal government to provide workers' compensation coverage. With this arrangement, the EMS manager may have no control over the costs associated with the premiums as they are not coming out of the EMS budget. However, as a steward of community funds, the EMS manager should remain diligent in preventing employee injuries and avoid complacency by believing the local government will pick up the cost. In his diligence, the EMS manager would determine if injuries were sustained while working and whether the municipality will absorb the costs, paying for any medical bills out of taxpayer funds. It is in the manager's best interest to prevent accidents from occurring. By believing that the municipality will provide the funds so the EMS organization does not have to worry about the costs, the EMS manager unknowingly establishes a culture in which injuries are acceptable. The big-picture view is as important as the organizational view. Any increase in EMS injuries directly or indirectly impacts the way the municipality conducts its business, and any increase in costs directly affects taxpayers.

■ FINANCING SAFETY ────────

Safety is a part of the risk management process. To review, risk management is avoidance and prevention. Risk management is the umbrella that protects the whole organization against losses. Safety is a concept that protects people against losses. Whereas many managers believe that safety and risk management are interchangeable concepts, they deal with separate areas of operations. They overlap in many situations, but they seek to control losses differently.

No one intentionally wants another person to sustain an injury. The implications of having a member of the public injured due to the unsafe actions of an EMS crew member or receiving a call that a crew member sustained an injury will turn an EMS manager's day into a bad one quickly. The goal in safety, as well as in risk management, is to avoid injuries to others as a result of EMS activities. Safety looks at how the organization evaluates hazards and reduces or eliminates the hazards with the intent to provide a healthy work environment.

When looking at safety issues, the manager should look around and question what areas have the potential for losses. Managers should look at the use of extension cords. Are they used to power electrical equipment, or do they extend across the floor and create a tripping hazard? Do office personnel leave file drawers open? When getting things off shelves, do employees reach above their heads and expose themselves to back injury? Managers can establish procedures that instruct crews to sweep the bays after washing ambulances in order to avoid standing water and a slipping hazard. Prior to lifting a patient of more than 160 pounds, crews would evaluate how the lift is performed and discuss proper methods of lifting or requesting help.

An important part of understanding the safety of a job is knowing which behaviors are harmful, so another evaluation could assess how patients are carried to the ambulance. For example, some crew members pile all the equipment onto the ambulance stretcher or sling it over their shoulder, potentially causing an injury. Knowing that this behavior is harmful would make a difference in their behavior and lower the risk of injury.

These examples of safety issues have cost organizations tens, if not hundreds, of thousands of dollars in legal action, employee injuries, and medical costs. By allocating money to educating staff, most of these situations are avoidable.

FINANCING TRAINING

As is also true regarding safety, the education of EMS staff is often a second thought when developing budgetary items. Most EMS managers allocate funding for staff to meet the minimal requirements of certification. The EMS manager must be assured that this level of education supports the mission of providing the best care to the community. The training budget should not only cover the basics but also should allow the opportunity for crew members to learn the newest concepts. It is often the belief of leadership that determines the value of further education. If the leader does not believe that a new concept is important, he will reject any attempt to implement the concept. A common refrain is "We have never done it that way before" or "What we learned when we were going through training has always worked for us."

The progressive manager will look at the newest concepts of patient care and determine the value that the new assessment tool or treatment option brings to the patient. Often these new ideas are learned at conferences, but in-house training by an expert can also expose crew members to new ideas.

If the decision is made to invest in education, it is the manager who should hold the attendees responsible for educating others. It is expensive to send a few people to a conference in another state. Once a decision like this is fulfilled, the representatives should return and conduct crew education.

Of course, any loss to an organization will cost money. When people leave an organization due to frustration or boredom or the perception that there are no opportunities, the organization must spend money to fill the vacancy. If a person who has worked for or volunteered for an organization for years, and the investment in training, development, and experience has now walked out the door due to poor management style, it will take a fixed amount of financial resources to hire a new person and educate them to the same level. Many real-life examples and research articles indicate that it is far more costly to recruit and train a new employee than it is to retain a good current employee (Avramidis, 2009; Bladen, 2010; MFGpeople.com, 2011).

The point is this: If the same people attend conferences, make all the decisions, or participate in all notable activities, other crew members may begin to feel less valued and seek employment elsewhere. This is not to say that everyone should attend or represent the organization as events occur, but management should actively determine the benefits of exposing others to various aspects of organizational life with the goal of developing crew members.

Another idea to consider is investing in the cost of sending one or more people to a conference or training seminar. Management should expect that the attendees will enroll in and attend courses that are pertinent to the EMS organization's growth. There is no value in paying a crew member to attend a high-angle rescue session if the organization does not participate in or have any high-angle rescues. It is not effective to pay for a 6-day conference if the crew members only attend three half days and sightsee the rest of the time. The manager and attendees must remember that the money spent on education is not theirs and has come from the community, the local government, or in payment for services rendered.

CHAPTER REVIEW

Summary

EMS activities, by their very nature, are hazardous. Employees are placed in situations that are neither planned nor expected. Most 9-1-1 responses or routine transports are completed without any injury or property damage. Most EMS organizations do not experience theft, embezzlement, discrimination cases, or management errors that become lawsuits. However, the possibility exists that any of these could occur at any time.

Allocating appropriate organizational funds to either retaining the loss or transferring the loss is the challenge of EMS managers. When retaining the loss, the manager must be able to determine where the money will come from and what operational programs may need to be curtailed in order to pay for the loss. A well-managed risk financing program tries to control the cost of financing by appropriately balancing risk retention with risk transfer. Simultaneously, the EMS manager determines the funding for risk management and loss reduction. It is this act of balancing the funding for increased business and revenue growth rather than funding programs that reduce or prevent losses that challenges most EMS managers. The direction most often chosen by managers is increased business and revenue growth since they are easier to control and understand. However, over time the sheer potential of financial loss that could occur overshadows the incremental gains of revenue growth. It is the wise and informed EMS manager who can properly balance both.

WHAT WOULD YOU DO? Reflection

As the EMS manager, you have many concerns. Ensuring that the other driver and your crew are medically cared for is the most important immediate priority. Reaching out to the families will also take precedence. Assisting with the investigation is a crucial aspect, and working with the insurance company on the initial claim is necessary. You also need to consider how the accident will affect the rest of the staff. You prepare to communicate the medical condition of the crew and the status of the investigation to the appropriate people. If it is possible that any of the patients will succumb to their injuries, you prepare for an in-depth investigation by OSHA, the district attorney, and the personal attorney of the other driver.

At no time do you alter or purge any records. You plan to review the organization's insurance coverage as well as review the current financial position of the organization. If it is determined that your driver was responsible for the accident, you know you will need to prepare for legal action, especially if there is a record that his driving was of concern.

Ensuring the organization's continuing ability to respond to EMS calls is essential. You plan to look at both staffing and equipment to prevent any lapse in service.

You plan to notify the board of directors as well as the corporation's attorney. When considering legal representation, you plan to include a person with expertise in defending EMS services against driving claims.

You plan to delegate some of these items because you will be extremely busy. You know you need a person who will be prepared for handling all aspects of the responsibility. Since much of your time will be spent on the accident, post-accident recovery, and organizational viability, delegating to another should include all aspects of the activities you are assigning. You want to avoid micro-managing operational decisions during this crisis because you know if you do that people will begin to lose faith in your ability to handle the situation. You will start to doubt your trust in your supervisors, and you may ultimately collapse under the strain.

Review Questions

1. What is risk financing?
2. How does risk financing relate to risk management and general management principles?
3. Explain how mode, frequency, severity, and probability affect the financial obligation of the organization.
4. Describe risk management in terms of finance.
5. Describe the four tenets of risk management.
6. What is a loss to the EMS organization, and how can losses be avoided?
7. Give an example of an indirect loss and a direct loss sustained by an EMS organization.

8. Name and describe the four types of exposures that can create a loss.
9. Name and describe the three types of risk financing.

10. What are the benefits and downside of insurance?
11. How do safety and education affect losses?

References

AQC. (2011). "Research on the Expanding Role of Enterprise Risk Management," quoting Mary Driscoll, APQC Senior Research Director. See the organization website.

Avramidis, M. (2009, February). "Retaining Employees." *Financial Planning*

Bladen, A. (2010, February 27). "Talent Management." *Leadership Excellence.*

Hawkes, R. (2001, January). "Retaining Employees Is Smart Marketing." *Vegetable Growers News*.

Head, G., M. Elliot, and J. Binn. (1996). *Essentials of Risk Financing*, 3rd ed. Malvern, PA: Insurance Institute.

MFGpeople.com. (2011, February 25). "The True Cost of Hiring vs. Retention Expense." See the organization website.

Omer, E. (2009, July 2). "It Costs How Much to Replace an Employee?" eZineArticles.com. See the organization website.

Reh, J. (2011, January). "What Good People Really Cost." See the About.com Management website.

Victor, L. R. (2006). "Managing and Mitigating Risk: An Administrator's View." *Long-Term Living, 55*(4), 57–59.

Key Terms

allocate To distribute according to a plan or set apart for a special purpose.

catastrophic Resulting in great loss and misfortune that brings physical or financial ruin.

deductibles Insurance policy clauses that relieve the insurer of responsibility to pay the initial loss up to a stated amount.

economics A branch of social science that deals with the production, distribution, consumption, and management of goods and services.

frequency The number of occurrences within a given time period.

insurance Financial assistance provided to ensure reimbursement for losses sustained under specified conditions.

liability An obligation of an entity arising from events, the settlement of which may result in the transfer of assets, provision of services, or other yielding of economic benefits in the future.

loss The act of losing something of value or an asset.

mitigate The act of lessening in severity or intensity.

probability Knowledge or belief that an event will occur or has occurred.

risk An uncertainty or an unknown.

severity Intensely or extremely bad or unpleasant in degree or quality.

CHAPTER 11

Auditing

Objectives

After reading this chapter, the students should be able to:

11.1 Define and discuss the purpose of auditing.

11.2 Describe the various aspects of the auditing process.

11.3 Explain what an auditor adds to the audit to ensure its accuracy.

11.4 Discuss the benefits of corporate governance and the value relative to the operations of the EMS organization.

11.5 Understand the effect which the Sarbanes-Oxley Act has on medical organizations that bill the government for services.

11.6 Briefly describe the Medicare and Medicaid programs and the audits generated for them.

11.7 Discuss why clinical audits serve as a risk reduction technique.

Overview

The purpose of this text is to introduce the concepts of finance to nonfinancial EMS managers. The chapters present valuable information to both new and experienced EMS leaders who may have varying degrees of experience, formal and informal. The goal is to stimulate thinking in order to change the way things are done, to avoid mistakes of the past, and to encourage future growth of EMS as a profession.

Key Terms

assertions	deficiencies	internal audit
assurance	deviation	mandatory
auditing	external audit	operational audit
bias	fidelity	opinion
compliance	fiduciary	unbiased
corporate governance	independent	verifiable

WHAT WOULD YOU DO?

You were recently promoted to the position of EMS director. During a staff meeting involving the management team, a discussion ensues related to some crew members acting unprofessionally, and questions arise about their skill level. You knew of these concerns from your supervisory experience, but the former director did not want to confront the issue. You are also informed by the billing coordinator that there seems to be a discrepancy between the income generated from operations and the amount of money shown on the financial report submitted by the treasurer. The treasurer's report is usually a verbal statement of the balances and a list of checks paid. You had noticed during a review of the financial books that the numbers just did not add up, but so far you have not had time to review the finances in depth.

Questions

1. How would you go about finding the discrepancies?
2. What tracking mechanisms are necessary to ensure that the recorded numbers equal the financial numbers?
3. What reports will help analyze the direction of the organization and ensure compliance with accounting standards?
4. How do you establish accountability for reporting activities that occur within the organization?
5. What checks and balances are assigned to administrative and supervisory staff for the work they oversee?
6. How can administrative and supervisory staff ensure that all activities are completed in a way to minimize loss, increase efficiency, and decrease liability?

■ INTRODUCTION

Operating an EMS organization is a multifaceted responsibility. The interdependency among many parties and their relationships, is of primary importance. Local citizens depend on the availability of highly trained, competent, and caring responders. The organization relies on an educated and motivated management team. Payers expect submitted bills to be accurate and timely. The municipality trusts the organization to operate in an efficient manner. The list of interrelationships is endless. One common denominator is the checks and balances between each relationship. For example, the checks and balances that exist between the patient and the responding crew members provide a means for addressing any

treatment issues that are perceived to be below a certain standard. Patient who are not satisfied with the care received should be able to notify the organization and report any **deficiencies**.

The relationship between the line staff and the management team depends on an objective board of directors that evaluates the effectiveness of the management staff. The board should question excess expenditures, trends of high turnover, and general operations, without attempting to micromanage the management team. Insurers should receive completed patient care reports that support any submission for reimbursement. The EMS organization should expect payment based on agreed-upon reimbursement terms without excess or unnecessary questions or denials.

■ CHECKS AND BALANCES

The complex process of checks and balances is necessary to ensure that the organization is running smoothly and that management is in control of running the organization. Without checks and balances, management can abuse the power of the position and use community resources indiscriminately. Boards of directors and municipal leaders depend on accurate, reliable, and objective information that gives an accurate picture of the financial status of the EMS organization and in turn provides a base to judge progress toward long-term goals. If the people who are using the information to make organizational, municipal, or system decisions lack confidence in the information, poor decisions are made and the system weakens. Fortunately, standards do exist for some of these operational activities. For example, accounting standards are defined by the Financial Accounting Standards Board (FASB) and the Governmental Accounting Standards Board (GASB).

Management should apply accounting principles and develop systems of internal controls that ensure that checks and balances are working. How do we know the process is truly working? **Auditing** provides the means to independently evaluate information and determine whether processes are meeting an agreed-upon standard.

EMS organizations generally define standard operating procedures, or standards, as in the phrase "They do not live up to our standard." A standard is a basis for comparison, a reference point against which other things are evaluated, or the ideal against which something can be judged. It is also described as conforming to or constituting a measurement or value (WordNetSearch, n.d.).

Most EMS professionals are aware of standards in a medical context. Responders use medical protocols as a basis to function. Standard operating *procedures* (SOPs) or

standard operating *guidelines* (SOGs) allow EMS professionals to make organized decisions for patient treatment. Though these terms are often interchanged, there is a difference between a guideline, a protocol, and a procedure.

Guidelines allow for variability in decision making. A guideline establishes a basic course of direction. For example, a guideline for purchasing might state, "When purchasing items over $500 but less than $1,000, identify three different vendors and purchase the product from the vendor that adds the greatest value." This is an umbrella statement and does not direct a specific course of action.

An example of a *protocol* in purchasing would read, "All purchases must be reviewed and signed off by the financial officer before any purchase." A *procedure* is different from guidelines and protocols because it lays out exactly how to perform an activity. For example, a procedure might read, "Before purchasing any item, the requester will complete form A and submit it to Operations. Operations will review the form and agree or disagree with the purchase. Upon agreement, return the form to the requester and then complete form B."

Guidelines, protocols, and procedures— were developed based on evidence or activities that support a predictable outcome. By developing guidelines, protocols, or procedures, we can develop an operational standard. By following a standard, management can determine how effectively operations are running or how well care and treatment are being delivered to each patient. In EMS, *standards* are expressions of the way things are normally done.

Problems that develop are traceable to determine if a **deviation** from an expected outcome exists, and if so, the process can then be corrected. Even if problems do not surface, a process must exist that ensures that all operational functions are intact and are working as expected. This is where auditing is beneficial.

In the EMS profession, auditing is an evaluation of a person, organization, system, process, or project. Performing audits assists in ascertaining the validity and reliability of information as well as in providing an assessment of a system's internal control. Auditing can take on very specific meanings, depending on the auditor or the specialty. In finance, for example, the auditing process attests to **assertions** made about economic actions and events within an organization.

■ THE INS AND OUTS OF AUDITING

An audit can be generated by an external agency with an interest in ensuring that a process is performed correctly. It also can come from a governmental agency, such as the Department of Health and Human Services, the Occupational Safety and Health Administration (OSHA), the Department of Labor, the U.S. Attorney General's office, or an accounting office that was hired by the EMS organization's board of directors.

Audits differ from simply tracking an activity or measuring success. When measuring the ongoing activities of a business, management may use techniques, such as the Balanced Scorecard, Statistical Process Control (SPC), or Six Sigma. In an audit, however, the information that is generated by business activities is evaluated and assessed. The thrust of an audit is to determine if current and past practices are moving the organization toward its goals, to determine if any deviation from performance expectations has occurred, or to identify any wrongdoing or deficiencies. Audits do not search for what is working, but if, during an audit, it is realized that a process works, that is reported.

■ AUDITING PROCESS

Auditing involves three processes: gathering evidence or information, evaluating the evidence against criteria, and communicating the evaluation's conclusions. As is the case for many organizational structures, the audit must take into consideration the audience that wants or needs the information. If the board of directors, municipal government, or other governing body is responsible for oversight of the EMS organization, requesting an audit of the financial statements is within its authority. Management is responsible for managing the organization, for safeguarding the assets entrusted to it, and for preparing any information that explains the financial position of the organization in a way that is easily reviewed or audited.

OBTAINING AND EVALUATING EVIDENCE

Auditing evaluates the evidence that confirms that a process is working correctly. The EMS management team decides what to audit—for example, the number of successful intubations versus unsuccessful intubations, purchasing green, or sustainable, items rather than the most inexpensive ones, driving speed relative to the nature of the call, whether work is being performed without proper pay, or determining if financial data are being recorded and presented correctly. Audits are not performed strictly to find fault. Audits are also conducted to ensure that the processes in place are complete and accurate. Conducting an audit, whether to ensure **compliance** or to determine any inaccuracies, is like being an investigator. All investigations start with obtaining evidence for evaluation. The person conducting the audit is expected to be **unbiased** and objective. Any findings from the auditor must be **verifiable** and show objectivity.

ASSERTIONS AND ESTABLISHED CRITERIA

An assertion is a statement about an action, event, performance, or condition over a specified period of time. Criteria must exist so that an impartial person can determine whether an assertion is appropriate. Organizations use GAAP to provide criteria for financial statements. The American College of Emergency Physicians (ACEP) provides criteria for medical care and treatment of prehospital patients by EMS. The National Fire Protection Agency (NFPA) provides criteria for EMS operations. Other organizations provide criteria for other types of audits.

Whether the audit is internal or external, a recognized standard must exist that provides a foundation upon which to evaluate the EMS organization. When a standard does not exist—for example, a management standard that addresses the activities of the EMS leadership team—the mission statement, organizational goals and objectives, or established policies and procedures may be used as the standard.

For a financial audit, the expectation is that management monitors the financial activities of the organization and prepares financially accurate reports. Since some organizations base financial reports on GAAP standards, the management team must present the information that portrays an accurate financial condition and represents the organization's legitimate activity. (*Note:* Not all financial statements are reported using GAAP. For small-budget and nonprofit organizations, accountants typically will use OCBOA [other comprehensive basis of accounting], usually on a tax basis or form-of-cash basis). For example, if on its financial statements management reports $5 million in inventory, management is asserting that the inventory exists, is complete, is owned, and is properly valued. The auditor would gather evidence to test the assertion by showing an inventory of $5 million.

It is important to differentiate internal and external financial audits. A CPA is required to submit an audit report when issuing an opinion. A letter from management that reports deficiencies with internal controls and processes will also accompany an external financial audit.

COMMUNICATING THE RESULTS

Communicating the results of the audit to the requester completes the process. The communication can look formal, like a report of the financial position, or less formal, like a review that consists of charts and a narrative. The audit report should delineate how a specific area or process performed during a set period of time. It shows who is responsible, summarizes the audit process, and presents an **opinion** of the results. As stated earlier, the auditor should present an unbiased assessment of the activities of the organization and should also have the freedom to comment constructively without the results becoming personal. Obviously, if the board of directors contracted an accounting firm to review the financial aspects of the organization, the auditor will return a report that will be viewed by the board. An audit report that presents a fair view of the financial position and does not contain any reservations is called an unqualified audit report. If the auditor expresses reservations about his findings, the audit report would explain the concerns. The most important point here is that the board and management should accept the information as an expert assessment because the report is delivered by a perceived expert.

The difference between an audit conducted by an outside expert and an **internal audit** conducted by a member of the EMS management team is the perceived objectivity or expertise of the person conducting the audit. If the management team commits the time, energy, and organizational resources to evaluate people or activities, it must support the findings even if the results are not well received or appear to suggest that significant improvements are needed.

If management exhibits any reluctance about initiating or accepting the results of an audit, it sends a distinct signal that will have a few unanticipated and undesirable consequences. The person conducting the audit views his activity as very important. If management is willing to place trust in the auditor's ability to look at the organization's functions and determine how the activity contributes to the organization's success, the auditor will perform the task with passion. If management indicates a reluctance to conduct the audit, the evaluator may approach his job with trepidation. If the results show that there is little oversight in the organization and that management is weak in its responsibilities, the auditor may minimize or disregard the findings.

Let's say the organization is concerned about the number of drivers who are exceeding the speed limit or driving through intersections without due regard for the safety of others. Management has received an increasing number of complaints by citizens (subjective information) and observes an increase in the number of accidents (objective information). Management delegates the task of conducting an audit to a member of the organization. The auditor is asked to evaluate crew members' driving habits, to submit a report on the findings, and to make suggestions for improvement.

The crew member (auditor) performs the audit and submits the report. Management can review the findings and determine if the results are a weakness in the organization, an opportunity for improvement, or unrepresentative of the actual activity. If the audit indicates an increase in accidents as a result of poor driving behavior, then management can choose between two actions: accept the

report, or not. By accepting the audit findings, management must feel that the auditor has conducted the investigation without **bias** and that the findings represent an objective view of the situation. If management rejects the results, management should determine if the cause of the rejection is based on the ability of the auditor, whether the findings have a bias, whether the findings are unsupported by the evidence, or whether they were rejected because management does not want to change the behavior.

Management should establish the parameters of an audit before it is initiated. If the report was rejected because the auditor did not conduct the investigation in the desired manner, management must determine if the fault lies with the auditor or with management for failing to clearly define the parameters. Internal results often are rejected, even if performed correctly, simply because the person conducting the audit is not perceived as an expert—in other words, "Crew members certainly cannot be knowledgeable about conducting an audit." The difference between accepting without question the results of an audit conducted by an outside firm and one conducted by internal personnel often comes down to the perceived expertise of the auditor.

Management should have a vested interest in making sure that an audit, whether internally conducted or externally generated, is accepted as long as the process is sound and the results can be replicated by another **independent** person.

NEED FOR UNBIASED REPORTING

Many people may have an opportunity to look at a financial audit. Such reports might be viewed by management, boards of directors, banks, governmental agencies, insurance companies, regulators, municipal leaders, and the court system. Knowing in advance who might use the audit results should guide the auditor in reporting results more appropriately. Audits are designed to detect weaknesses or differences between what is said and what is done. CPAs perform external financial audits to "obtain reasonable assurance about whether the financial statements are free of material misstatements" (Public Company Accounting Oversight Board, 1972).

To qualify for a loan, the EMS organization's assessment of its financial position must be acceptable to the lender. The lender relies on the financial statements to assess the risk of a loan. When financial information is accurate, the lender will feel better about granting the loan. Similarly, if the EMS organization is applying for a grant, the reviewers rely on the submitted financial statements to determine eligibility for funds. In some cases, it is possible for management to submit unaudited financial information and receive a loan or grant. In such a case, management could adjust the numbers to make it appear that the organization needs the money. In other words, in order to receive the loan or grant, management could alter its financial statements by changing the dollar amounts of revenue or expenses. Without an audited financial report, the grant writer or loan officer might award the money based on inaccurate information. Even an audit from a CPA does not guarantee that fraud or misstatement will be found; and even with an audited financial statement, monies may be loaned based on bad information.

> **Side Bar**
>
> A financial audit can determine whether or not the EMS organization prepares its financial statements according to GAAP. It does not attest to the absolute accuracy of the statements.

Outside organizations rely on accurate financial information to make financial decisions. These organizations need assurances that the information is accurate and portrays the financial position of the EMS organization. Managers may have information which they may not want to share that could ultimately impact the decision of the loan officer or grant reviewer. An independent audit can provide the assurance needed to the outside organization either that the organization's need for the money is legitimate or that the organization is not in a position to qualify for the money (perhaps it cannot pay it back).

As not getting funded may not be the expected or desired outcome, it is the best decision for the lender or the grant-making organization. In addition, if denied the loan or grant, it should be obvious that weaknesses might exist in the EMS organization and that the management team may need to reevaluate how certain activities are performed. The benefit of an audit is learning how to improve the organization's financial, as well as all other, processes.

■ ASSURANCE

Assurance creates confidence by reducing the risk of incorrect information. Banks or regulators make decisions because they believe they have reliable information. Management will make operational decisions based on internally generated reviews of processes. The auditor needs to exhibit certain attributes in order to provide assurance: subject matter knowledge, objectivity, the ability to adhere to preestablished and agreed-upon criteria, expertise in gathering and evaluating the information, and appropriate formatting of the presentation.

SUBJECT MATTER KNOWLEDGE

The auditor should have an appropriate level of expertise in the area being audited. The person conducting a review of the financial position should be an accountant and have knowledge of EMS organizations. The investigator of the driving habits of crews should have a background in risk management, the law, or insurance. Having an understanding of inventory control will help with auditing purchasing and supply management.

OBJECTIVITY

Providing information that is unbiased, objective, and independent of the desired outcome increases the believability of the results. Objectivity provides the assurances needed by the people who are reviewing the information and making decisions. From a financial perspective, the results of a review of the financial statements should be independent of any relationship with management. External organizations must have confidence that the auditor is not influenced by management and has no vested interest in the outcome. For example, the auditor should not have stock in a publicly held EMS company that he is reviewing, or the person who does the purchasing should not conduct an audit of the inventory.

ABILITY TO ADHERE TO PREESTABLISHED AND AGREED-UPON CRITERIA

Objectivity and the quality of the results improve when clear criteria exists concerning the process of the audit, the information for review, and the expectations of how the information will be presented. If an auditor makes it clear that he will use GAAP standards for the financial audit, management will know specifically what will be reviewed, reported, and discussed. Similarly, if management establishes the criteria for evaluating the driving habits of crew members and outlines the methodology for collecting the data, then, arguably, management should accept the results.

EXPERTISE IN GATHERING AND EVALUATING THE INFORMATION

Gathering information and evaluating the evidence require knowledge about how to

systematically collect information and analyze it to ensure statistical accuracy and reproducibility. The auditor should be technically competent in comprehensive EMS operations and in the area he is reviewing. A sound understanding of the basic elements of the intrinsic activity—whether it is financial, inventory, or clinical—is essential. Why is this understanding essential? One not-so-obvious reason is that one of the purposes of the audit is to prevent a subsequent loss. In other words, performing an audit identifies not only what the organization is doing right but identifies areas for improvement. The fundamental approach to risk management is avoidance and prevention.

An example of a business risk approach to an audit relative to a clinical scenario should be helpful. Assume that an EMS organization runs 25,000 calls. Of these calls, 40 percent are for advanced life support (ALS). Of the ALS calls, 3 percent require the provider to assess and subsequently determine if the patient requires intubation. The organization does not have a method for tracking the success rate of the intubation. It is unknown if the patient is successfully intubated on the first, second, or third attempt. What does this mean for the patient and the organization? One of the top four reasons that legal action is filed against an emergency provider is lack of proper airway control; management does not know for which case, out of the 300 intubations, legal action could be filed against the provider and the organization.

When a tracking method is in place, management has the ability to check on the success rate of intubations. Performing an audit would provide management with the information that identifies the strengths of this ALS skill or identifies whether additional training is required. By identifying the need for additional skills training, management reduces its overall risk of having legal action filed. Therefore, performing an audit of intubations is a risk management activity and a loss reduction strategy.

APPROPRIATE FORMATTING OF PRESENTED MATERIAL

The format is agreed upon prior to the audit. Once the audit is completed, the information is presented in a way that is understandable and readable.

The audit should identify all areas covered. Words that are unfamiliar to the reader are defined. The standards used to measure the results against are referenced. Overall, the presentation provides a way to find and pull out information easily.

▇ CORPORATE GOVERNANCE————

Many corporations—whether for profit or nonprofit, EMS/fire or manufacturing, stockholder or privately owned—have structures within which decisions are made. The direction of the organization is established by one person or many. In an EMS organization, someone must take responsibility for the overall direction of the entity. Simultaneously, and in concert with setting the direction, someone must also be held accountable for decisions that are made. This is the essence of corporate governance.

Corporate governance is described as a process by which the owners (or decision makers) exert control and require accountability for the resources entrusted to the organization. It is the board of directors, municipal leaders, or hospital administrators who provide the oversight of the organization's activities (Figure 11.1).

Figure 11.1 illustrates how a straightforward governance structure might look. Certainly, a municipal EMS organization may have the municipal directors between the community members and the board of directors, and possibly a layer or two between management and operations. A for-profit organization would replace community members with stockholders. The point is this: The board of directors and

Overview of Corporate Governance for Non-profit EMS Organization

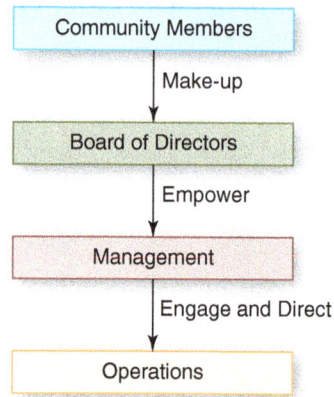

FIGURE 11.1 ▇ Overview of corporate governance for nonprofit EMS organizations.

management must answer to a group of people, whether the community or other stakeholders. Governance starts at the top. In this example, the community would expect the members of the board of directors to take responsibility for the activities of the organization and delegate the responsibility through management and, ultimately, operations.

In many organizations, the responsibility and/or accountability is never established or, at best, never discussed. In many EMS organizations, past or present crew members constitute the majority of the board. If the EMS organization has one or two community members on the board of directors, their numbers may be insufficient to make a difference, or they may not know the parameters of their role as board members. In other situations—for example, a hospital-based EMS unit—the board of directors is often concerned with a broader array of issues and cedes responsibility for operating the EMS unit to a hospital manager or director. In a municipally based unit, the municipal leaders may assign the responsibility for the EMS unit to the public safety director. In some cases, a supervisory committee accepts responsibility and delegates the accountability to a chief. There are numerous corporate governance structures. The overriding point is that someone must not only take responsibility for the activities of EMS operations, but also must be held accountable for the activities.

Many organizations in the United States have failed to develop a governance process, and history has revealed the consequences of these missteps. The reports surrounding these failures show a lack of governance that resulted in improper accounting and auditing activities.

Uninvolved governance can and does occur at all levels of an organization and in all types of organization. EMS organizations must strive to build a strong body of objective board members who are willing to question management and the reports generated as a result of organizational activity.

Best Practice

Dynamic Data, Inc. is a global high-technology, publicly traded corporation in the data networking industry. The company, founded in 1990, is headquartered in Nashua, New Hampshire and employs approximately 2,000 people, maintaining operations in ten countries. Management has a positive attitude about developing a reliable control environment and relies on the information generated from the accounting system to make management decisions. The company's board of directors has taken the view that it is management's job to set the direction for the firm and to formulate strategies. The Board has the power to conduct independent investigations of unethical behavior. The Board also pays close attention to monitoring the long-term financial performance of the firm. They closely examine management's ability to meet budgets and question all significant aggregate variances. The Board has also invested significant power in the Audit Committee to fulfill its charter. It is very supportive of the Audit Committee's role in ensuring sound financial reporting policies and a strong control environment for the firm. The Audit Committee (AC) of the firm has adopted a formal written charter that is similar to other firms in the industry. Further in accordance with the Sarbanes-Oxley Act, the AC also recommends the appointment/reappointment of the company's outside auditors.

Cohen, J. R., G. Krishnamoorthy, and A. M. Wright. (2005). Dynamic data: Corporate governance and auditors evaluation of accounting estimates. *Issues in Accounting Education 20*(1), 119–128. Accessed September 21, 2012, at http://aaajournals.org/doi/abs/10.2308/iace.2005.20.1.119

FIDELITY

When a person receives a position in an organization, he knowingly and unknowingly accepts responsibility for the activities of the position. One of the responsibilities is **fidelity**. In addition, all board directors, officers, and managers have the **fiduciary** responsibility to look after the finances of the organization. Fidelity is the observance of this duty. Fidelity is the trust that is placed in others to do what is right.

How many churches, community organizations, fire companies, EMS units, and small businesses fall victim to a trusted member of the organization who extorts or steals money from the organization that he serves? These crimes are reported in the local newspaper and are momentous news for a short time, but eventually disappear from the minds of most citizens. These criminal activities are no different from what the public hears about the Enrons and the AIGs of the world. The latter failures just happen to occur on a larger scale and affect many more people. The point is that, in all of these cases, there was no oversight of the management processes. People were given responsibility without accountability. This is not to say that people cannot or should not be trusted. In many organizations, especially EMS, it is the public, in whatever form, that provides resources for the organization to function. The public trusts that the resources will be used optimally, and that individuals who are responsible for making the decisions are making them for the right reasons. However, without accountability for those decisions, humans can feel they are above the rules and can use their positions for personal benefit. This is where an audit provides the checks and balances for any or part of any organization.

In another example, an EMS manager appoints an individual to supervise the maintenance aspect of the organization. The newly appointed person is eager and anxious to perform the duties with gusto. The organization does not have a formal purchasing system, so all purchases are made via a straightforward request to management. For the first few years, the maintenance supervisor goes through the chain of command and receives approval for the purchase of light bulbs, oil, belts, hoses, and so on. Eventually a trust is built between the manager and the maintenance supervisor. Over time, the maintenance supervisor begins to purchase items on his own and submits receipts for reimbursement. Over time, the maintenance supervisor begins to see how easy this is and buys a few extra quarts of oil, but uses them for his personal vehicle. Then he purchases an oil filter and some headlights and some car wax. He submits all of these personal purchases for reimbursement because, he asks, who is checking?

This scenario can continue with minimal losses to the organization or can become very big, depending on how involved the purchases become and how daring a person is. These reimbursements are business losses for the organization, and the community's resources are not utilized in the intended manner. With an audit process in place, it is reasonable to expect that the auditor would catch the activity in the early stages or, with the threat of an audit, avoid this situation completely.

Now magnify this same human weakness around money and one can quickly see how organizations without a formal governance process or auditing system can suddenly find themselves in serious financial trouble. Thus, people should be trusted to do what is right in any position held in the organization, but the organization should also maintain appropriate oversight.

THE SARBANES-OXLEY ACT OF 2002

The Sarbanes-Oxley Act of 2002 was enacted to address discrepancies in accounting practices in publicly held companies. This comprehensive legislation establishes a higher degree of oversight and accountability. For the EMS world the effects include, but are not limited to, requiring CEOs and CFOs to certify any financial statements and any disclosures in those statements, requiring companies to provide a comprehensive report on internal controls over financial reporting, and requiring their auditors to report on those controls. The law also requires that audit committees include at least one person who is a financial expert and disclose the name and characteristics of that individual. Characteristics include the person's role in that organization and his role in accountability, among other things.

Not every EMS organization will be subject to the requirements of this legislation, but EMS management is not absolved from the spirit of the bill. Corporate responsibility still requires EMS managers to implement a system of internal controls that ensure completeness and accuracy of business activities, whether financial, operational, or clinical in nature.

Another portion of the law requires management to certify the accuracy of the financial statements, and it specifies criminal penalties for materially misstated financial statements. Further, it requires management to implement a corporate code of conduct, including whistle-blowing provisions.

The impetus for performing audits—whether internally generated, externally contracted, or governmental agency initiated—is to ensure that organizational processes are accurate and that management looks at activities that can affect patient health, community assets, and taxpayer financial resources. An objective audit satisfies many of these goals.

TAXPAYER ASSETS

The Medicare and Medicaid programs were signed into law on July 30, 1965, by President Lyndon B. Johnson. The most significant legislative change to Medicare—the Medicare Modernization Act (MMA)—was signed into law by President George W. Bush on December 8, 2003. This legislation affects EMS organizations because in many cases most revenue is received through Medicare or Medicaid. Since much of EMS revenue comes from the federal or state government, understanding the history of these programs, payment structure, the expectations of these payers, and the audit process that seeks to ensure that taxpayer money is used correctly is essential. EMS managers must understand the audit process when receiving governmental reimbursement for services. The EMS manager must be familiar with the requirements in order to avoid any perception that the organization's business practices are fraudulent.

Medicare: A Health-Insurance Program

Medicare is a health insurance program that covers people age 65 or older, people under age 65 with certain disabilities, and people of all ages with end-stage renal disease (ESRD; permanent kidney failure requiring dialysis or a kidney transplant).

Medicare: Part A. **Medicare Part A is hospital insurance.** Most people do not pay a premium for Part A because they or their spouse already paid for it through their payroll taxes while working. Medicare Part A helps cover inpatient care in hospitals, including critical access hospitals, and skilled nursing facilities (not custodial or long-term care). It also helps cover hospice care and some home health care. Beneficiaries must meet certain conditions to get these benefits.

Medicare: Part B. **Medicare** Part B is medical insurance. Most people pay a monthly premium for Part B. Part B helps cover doctors' services and outpatient care. It also covers some other medical services that Part A does not cover, such as some of the services of physical and occupational therapists, and some home health care. Part B helps pay for these covered services and supplies when they are medically necessary.

EMS organizations fall under the Part B portion of Medicare as a result of the addition in 1997 of Section 1834 to the Social Security Act. This addition mandated the "implementation of a national fee schedule for ambulance services furnished as a benefit under Medicare Part B. The fee schedule applies to all ambulance services, including volunteer, municipal, private, independent, and institutional providers, i.e., hospitals, critical access hospitals (except when it is the only ambulance service within 35 miles), and skilled nursing facilities" (California Department of Industrial Relations, 2011).

Section 1834 also requires **mandatory** assignment for all ambulance services. Ambulance providers and suppliers must accept the Medicare allowed charge as payment in full and not bill or collect from the beneficiary any amount other than any unmet Part B deductible and the Part B coinsurance amounts (California Department of Industrial Relations, 2011).

On March 23, 2010, President Barack Obama signed the Patient Protection and Affordable Care Act (PPACA) into law. PPACA Sections 3105 and 10311 apply to certain ambulance payment provisions. The PPACA extends 3 percent increases in the ambulance fee schedule for covered ground ambulance transports that originated in rural areas and 2 percent increases for covered ground ambulance transports that originate in urban areas. The new law uniformly extends the provision for air ambulance services provided in any area that was designated as a rural area for purposes of making payments under the ambulance fee schedule.

TYPES OF AUDITS

The Deficit Reduction Act (DRA) became law on February 8, 2006. The DRA seeks to control spending on federal entitlement programs such as Medicare and Medicaid to decrease the federal deficit. More specifically, the DRA seeks to accomplish this goal, in part, by reducing Medicare and Medicaid fraud, waste, and abuse.

The EMS manager should become familiar with a few types of audits. The first is the Medicaid Integrity Program (MIP) audit. The MIP employs a joint federal/state strategy to assist states in reducing fraud and abuse in the Medicaid program through provider audits, data mining, and provider education. MIP audits are going after an estimated $32.7 billion of overpayments.

The Centers for Medicare and Medicaid Services (CMS) has identified four objectives of MIP audits to ensure that paid claims were for services actually provided and properly documented, for services billed using correct

procedure codes, for covered services, and paid according to federal and state policies, rules, and regulations.

Under MIP, CMS hires private contractors, known as Medicaid Integrity Contractors (MICs), to perform one of three functions: review provider claims to identify high-risk areas and potential vulnerabilities of the state Medicaid program as well as potential audit targets; conduct post-payment audits of providers through a combination of field audits and desk reviews, and identify overpayments by Medicaid; and educate EMS responders by providing training materials and conducting provider workforce education.

Audits are conducted according to *Yellow Book* standards. The *Yellow Book* is a publication of the U.S. Government Accountability Office (GAO), which provides standards for audits of government organizations, activities, and programs. MIP auditors are not involved in the collection of overpayments and do not receive contingency compensation (unlike auditors under the Recovery Audit Contractor Program).

The Recovery Audit Contractor (RAC) Program is another type of CMS audit. RACs focus on fee-for-service Medicare providers such as hospitals, ambulatory surgery centers, physicians, and skilled nursing facilities. RACs review claims on a post-payment basis and are only able to look at claims submitted within the 3 prior years.

There are technical differences between the MIP and the RAC programs. These differences include that the RAC program has a single contractor for each region that manages audits and recovery determinations, with appeals handled at the federal level; RAC contractors are paid on a contingency basis whereas MICs are paid a fee; and RAC programs involve only fee-for-service organizations. These are a few examples of how external agencies affect daily operations of health care organizations. Whether the EMS organization submits bills that are subject to scrutiny under MIP, RAC, or any other payment structure, management must ensure that the process is performed correctly; otherwise the organization will be subject to intense investigation.

REASONS FOR AN AUDIT

EMS managers should understand what may trigger an audit. Generally, utilization patterns that fall outside the norm in a given region may trigger interest. This is why establishing a program that evaluates the activities of the entire organization is so important. Areas that may also increase the risk for an audit include the following:

- *Incomplete documentation.* CMS's objective is to ensure that services were actually provided and properly documented. Incomplete documentation will raise questions about whether services were actually provided, and will result in negative treatment for improper documentation.
- *Conflicting documentation.* Similarly, documentation that is inconsistent or even conflicting will tend to call into question the validity of services provided, and will result in negative treatment for improper documentation.
- *Improper coding.* Coding is a complex task and if improperly done can call into question claims for services actually provided. The task is made more complicated since subjectivity can enter into coding decisions. In these circumstances, inadvertent errors can easily become part of the patient record.
- *Providing services that may compromise the quality of care.*
- *Billing for services not provided.*
- *Violating patient privacy.* Federal and state laws provide limitations and prohibitions on the disclosure of certain patient health information. Some states have privacy and confidentiality laws and regulations that are complex, and at points more stringent than federal law. MIP

contractors may issue very broad requests for patient health information. To avoid potential liability, a responding provider should take care not to disclose patient information protected under either federal or applicable state law without that patient's consent.
- *Duplicate billing.*
- *Providing services not medically necessary.*
- *Excessive payments and up-coding for higher reimbursement of billed procedures.*
- *Payments for unapproved transportation services.*
- *Providing false certifications in the claims process.*

Having a compliance plan in place and following it are also critical activities for EMS organizations of any size or type. The plan should establish a process for routine monitoring, internal audits, and educating employees when problems are identified through an audit. The compliance plan can prevent errors, or at least act as a safeguard for the organization. When errors are identified and corrected through education, a formal audit may be avoided.

Also important is a contingency plan that establishes the process to follow when an audit is triggered. A point person should coordinate all audit communications, as well as assign responsibility for reviewing records, documentation, and audit results (Roop, 2010).

EMS managers should develop a strategy for contacting consultants and attorneys for advice in the event of a repayment demand. This plan should include the advisors and the criteria to guide decisions regarding appeals. For both large and small EMS organizations, having an outside auditor available for guidance is essential to ensure that the correct processes are followed.

Receiving Notification

The audit MIC sends to providers selected for an audit a notification letter detailing the claims and records in question. Each state determines how far back audit MICs can go when reviewing claims and the length of time an EMS provider has to produce the requested records in the formats specified. The audit MIC will also schedule an entrance conference with the EMS provider to discuss the scope of the audit. On completion of the audit, the audit MIC presents preliminary findings to the provider in an exit conference, during which the provider has an opportunity to comment or provide additional information (Roop, 2010).

When an EMS organization receives a request for information as a result of an audit, management should prepare its response carefully. Because of the risks presented by MIP audits, the potential privacy issues involved, and the costs of appeal, providers should carefully and comprehensively respond to MIP auditors' requests, preferably with assistance from experts in privacy and coding, and not simply turn over documents and wait for the MIP contractor's decision. Some actions to consider before turning over any documents include the following:

* Identifying those documents and records that the auditor has the lawful authority to request, and not assuming that the auditor's request is wholly proper
* Identifying those documents that are subject to additional protections or exclusions under applicable privacy laws and resolving any disclosure issues regarding those documents (e.g., determining the "minimum necessary" information to disclose)
* Considering having the requested documents reviewed by someone with expertise in billing and coding, and carefully comparing requested medical records with billing records

■ LABOR AUDITS

Another example of an area with audit potential is the work performed by staff. Managers know employees must be paid for the time they work while performing the essential functions of their job. If the organization schedules for 12-hour shifts, employees are paid for those hours. If an employee works more hours than scheduled, he is customarily paid a premium for the additional hours.

What happens if an employee conducts work-related business outside of his scheduled shift or, after clocking out, travels to another business to pick up supplies? Does the employee receive pay for this activity? Every state has laws that deal with these gray areas. The point is that managers cannot make arbitrary determinations on such issues, especially if a law covers the issue. EMS managers must become familiar with and maintain their knowledge of labor law. If decisions are made and an audit determines that those decisions were incorrect, the organization will be liable for the financial consequences related to correcting the mistake.

Another question that arises when hiring is whether the potential employee is required to submit proof of citizenship or the ability to work in the United States when asked on an employment questionnaire "Are you a citizen of the United States?" or "Are you able to legally work in the United States?" Or does management/human resources simply accept a "yes" answer from the applicant as true and correct? Should each employer require proof of citizenship or eligibility to work? These areas might have to undergo the scrutiny of an audit.

■ COMPLIANCE AND ORGANIZATIONAL AUDITS

A compliance audit ensures that EMS activities comply with relevant laws and regulations. An **operational audit** explores the effectiveness and efficiency of the EMS organization's activities while seeking to reduce the risks related to the activities. When performing an operational audit, the auditor may include a variety of criteria other than monetary measures, such as the percentage of calls not responded to in less than 2 minutes or the percentage of dollars spent on salaries. It is the responsibility of the auditor to determine appropriate measures on the basis of experience and insight into the functions of the EMS organization. Typically, performance is measured against prior periods, industry standards, other operational units, or budgeted activity.

CLINICAL AUDITS

EMS organizations exist to provide prehospital health care to the community. The expectation is that the patient will not be harmed when receiving that care. However, in many cases the EMS provider did not provide the appropriate and necessary health care, and ultimately the patient sustained greater injury or died. Subsequently, the provider and the organization are forced to endure legal action and subsequent liability. The question is, can these situations be avoided? In most cases, the answer is "yes."

To reiterate, one of the main responsibilities of EMS management is to operate the organization to satisfy the best interests of the community. The concept of best interest requires management to use community assets appropriately and to ensure that the care the public receives is proper. From a risk management perspective, EMS leadership must determine areas of potential or actual loss and seek to eliminate or prevent the loss. When performing these functions, management must evaluate that all actions and activities are performed properly. From a financial perspective, any care that is inappropriate will cost the organization in direct and indirect losses. Billing for care not received can initiate an audit. Providing inappropriate or negligent care can cause a legal suit.

Let's look at this in reverse. A legal claim is brought against Main Street Ambulance and crew members A and B for improper treatment resulting in the death of patient M. The legal action states that the crew failed to recognize that patient M had an airway problem. When the problem was recognized, providers A and B were unable to correct the problem and the patient sustained further injury, resulting in patient M's death. How can an EMS organization prevent or reduce the effects of this legal action?

First, we have to understand that when an adverse outcome occurs, the families want answers, especially if they perceive that something was done incorrectly. Due to being in a business where unfavorable outcomes can occur, every organization should be prepared for legal action. There is a vast difference, however, in an outcome that could not be prevented or avoided and one that should never have happened. This is where clinical audits help.

Main Street Ambulance hires many students who graduate from the local EMS school as EMTs and paramedics. Many of the new hires complete their clinical requirement at Main Street Ambulance. Once a new provider is hired, he is required to participate in an orientation that covers the history of the organization, reviews equipment, and explains the organization's policies and procedures. The new provider is assessed for medical knowledge and clinical abilities. Each year, every provider attends a 1-day clinical verification test on airway management, spinal immobilization, and splinting techniques. Above and beyond that, there is very little, if any, review of the provider's skill level.

It should be evident where potential problem exists. The management of Main Street Ambulance does not have an evaluation tool to track how well providers function between annual competencies. The organization may know if provider A responded to and attempted 32 intubations in 1 year because the calls are documented. However, the organization may not know how successful this provider is because the patient care reports are not reviewed. What if the provider has a success rate of only 32 percent for intubations? It should be apparent that this rate of "expertise" raises the possibility of risk relative to failing to adequately control a patient's airway. For each level of risk, a financial cost is borne by the organization.

By developing a systematic method for evaluating provider skills or medical knowledge, the EMS manager can reduce the possibility of unexpected losses. One may argue that insurance is purchased to cover losses. Still, without conducting audits to determine the potential exposure, EMS managers may purchase a lower limit of coverage that will not adequately cover a substantial loss. By auditing the provider's skill, EMS managers identify areas of provider weakness, and they also determine the degree of potential risk. Once the level of weakness is identified additional, training can be used to raise the degree of competency and lessen the degree of risk, thus reducing the costs associated with the risk.

From a financial standpoint, the organization must invest in the auditing of all personnel in order to avoid a loss when something goes wrong. Allocating financial resources is always cheaper before an incident occurs than after.

EMS organizations often do not understand the value of allocating funds to training, auditing, or risk-reduction strategies because there is no perceptible return or noticeable gain.

When an organization purchases an ambulance stretcher, the stretcher is real; it can be touched and used, so it has demonstrable value. When an organization invests valuable financial resources on auditing, some people believe this is intrusive and that they are being watched or questioned about their ability. Providers often feel that spending money on reviews or redundant training is a waste of time. Why? If an event never occurs, a provider cannot say with 100 percent certainty that came about as a direct result of the training or the audit.

If the organization invests $10,000 per year on auditing activities and avoids a $2.5 million lawsuit, the organization's resources were appropriately utilized. Many frontline providers do not understand the concepts of prevention and avoidance. They simply know that the organization has never been the defendant in any legal action, and they feel their time is wasted by attending the same training each year or attending meetings that review the results of an internal audit. The organization's leadership is responsible for communicating to everyone on staff the importance and need for auditing and training.

CHAPTER REVIEW

Summary

Every EMS organization's management team has responsibility to the community to ensure that staff members conduct themselves in a professional manner, and that the delivery of care is of the highest quality. The management team also has the responsibility to properly use the resources given to the EMS organization. One of the methods of ensuring that these two goals are met is auditing the activities of the organization. Through the audit process, managers learn what strengths the organization possesses, and they are able to determine which weaknesses need correcting.

When conducting an audit of organizational processes, management should establish criteria by which the auditor gathers information, analyzes it, and communicates the findings. The auditor must be familiar with the area to be reviewed and should know how to conduct the audit, how to look at the information, and how to communicate the results without bias.

Audits are conducted to investigate internal concerns or in response to an external agency that questions organizational activity. Labor, safety, and medical billing are a few of the many areas that might be the target of an **external audit**. The difference between internal and external audits is that internal audits are conducted by someone with connections to the company being audited, while external audits are conducted by someone who is independent of the company being audited. Internal audits are conducted to examine clinical activities or organizational processes. Management must have a high degree of faith in the results of an audit if the audit was conducted scientifically and the results are reproducible. If management rejects results that make the organization or management "look bad," then management must accept responsibility for financial losses that result from this decision. Furthermore, management should be held accountable for all losses under the prevailing system of corporate governance.

Audits are valuable management tools and can be used to identify areas where the organization is meeting or exceeding its goals. An audit can also identify areas in need of improvement. In the hands of a skillful manager, an audit can reduce financial loss and propel the EMS organization closer to achieving its goals.

WHAT WOULD YOU DO? Reflection

In your new position, you have many areas that need attention. Establishing priorities is essential. You delegate to others some of the areas that require your attention. In order to determine if the financial area is strong, you request an audit of the books that focuses on the current method of tracking and reporting the finances. By contracting an outside firm, you hope to gain confidence about the overall financial health of the organization. However, you know that if the results report any weakness in how the finances are tracked and reported, you begin to correct this with your treasurer. If the results indicate that the finances are inaccurate, you plan to make the relevant adjustments so that you can start with accurate information.

The personnel issues may require an audit of crew skills. By assigning a person who is objective to the duty of conducting skills verification, you hope to learn about the competency of all crew members. By establishing a baseline for skill proficiency, you can then evaluate the crew members who are under question and address any weaknesses. Further, you instruct the training team to initiate a review of all charts and establish a method to track the skills you deem to be high-risk procedures. Once this list and tracking method are finalized, and prior to the initiation of the program, you plan to present it to the crew. You will be prepared for any feedback, both positive and negative.

As for the lack of professionalism, you make it known that any action perceived as unprofessional must be documented in writing by whoever observed it and that the supervisors responsible for the crew must investigate the actions to determine the validity of the complaint.

By establishing baseline criteria and expectations of behavior and skill level, you are setting expectations for the associates within the organization. You are also proactively reducing the potential exposure to future losses by developing an audit program for both finance and clinical operations.

Review Questions

1. Describe why checks and balances are essential for managers.
2. What financial standards exist that guide the EMS manager and ensure the accuracy of financial reports?
3. Explain the differences between a process, a procedure, a guideline, and a standard.
4. Discuss the pros and cons of an internal and external audit.
5. What are the main purposes of an audit?
6. Name the parts of an audit process, and explain each one.
7. Why is it important for the auditor to be unbiased? What attributes must the auditor exhibit in order to establish credibility?
8. Describe the corporate governance structure, and discuss the value of developing this level of accountability.
9. Describe the federal programs associated with governmental audits.
10. What events might prompt a government audit?
11. Describe the risk management benefits of clinical audits.

References

Arens, Alvin A. (1997). *Auditing: An Integrated Approach*, 7th ed. Upper Saddle River, NJ: Prentice Hall.

Burke, J., and A. Dalessio. (1998, November–December). "Highlights of SAS No. 82 for the Internal Auditor," *Internal Auditing* pp. 40–44.

California Department of Industrial Relations. (2011). "Ambulance Fee Schedule Public Use Files." See the organization website.

Cohen, J. R., G. Krishnamoorthy, and A. M. Wright. (2005). Dynamic data: Corporate governance and auditors evaluation of accounting estimates. *Issues in Accounting Education* 20(1), 119–128. See the organization website.

Helms, M., ed. (2009). *Encyclopedia of Management*, 6th ed. Detroit: Gale, pp. 501–504

Pepper Hamilton LLP. (2009, June 16). "Medicaid Providers Face New Risks Under MIP." *White Collar and Corporate Investigations Newsletter.* See the organization website.

Public Company Accounting Oversight Board. (1972, November). "Au Section 110. Responsibilities and Functions of the Independent Auditor." See the organization website.

Rittenberg, L., and B. Schwieger. (2005). *Audits: Concepts for a Changing Environment*, 5th ed. Cincinnati, OH: South-Western.

Roop, E. (2010, March 1). "Medicaid Integrity Program Promises New Headaches." See For The Record Magazine website.

WordNetSearch.com. (n.d.) Princeton University. See the organization website.

Key Terms

assertions Statements about an action, event, performance, or condition over a specified period of time.

assurance Confidence that financial statements are reliable and the organization has met regulatory requirements.

auditing A systematic process of objectively obtaining and evaluating evidence regarding assertions about organizational activities and communicating the results to interested parties.

bias A partiality that prevents objective consideration of an issue or situation.

compliance Conformity; acting according to certain accepted standards.

corporate governance A process by which the owners or decision makers control and require accountability for the resources entrusted to the organization.

deficiencies Noncompliance; substantiated allegations of violations of federal and/or state laws or regulations.

deviation The difference between an observed value and the expected value of a variable or function.

external audit An audit conducted by an individual that is independent of the company being audited.

fidelity The observance of promises or duties by a person to another.

fiduciary A legal or ethical relationship of confidence or trust between two or more parties.

independent Being objective and unbiased while performing professional services.

internal audit An independent and objective examination of organizational activities designed to add value and improve organizational governance, risk management, and operational processes.

mandatory Obligatory; required or commanded by authority.

operational audit A systematic appraisal of an organization's operations to determine whether those operations are being conducted in an efficient manner and whether constructive recommendations can be made.

opinion A formal decision that includes a detailed explanation of the legal principles involved.

unbiased Indifferent; characterized by a lack of partiality.

verifiable Confirmable; capable of being tested (verified or falsified) by experiment or observation.

Appendix

TABLE A ■ A Present Value of Annuity (PVA) is a numerical representation of the current value of a specific dollar amount when paid at a future period.

Present Value of Annuity

n/i	0.01	0.02	0.03	0.04	0.05	0.06	0.07	0.08	0.09	0.10	0.11	0.12
1	0.990	0.980	0.971	0.962	0.952	0.943	0.935	0.926	0.917	0.909	0.901	0.893
2	1.970	1.942	1.913	1.886	1.859	1.833	1.808	1.783	1.759	1.736	1.713	1.690
3	2.941	2.884	2.829	2.775	2.723	2.673	2.624	2.577	2.531	2.487	2.444	2.402
4	3.902	3.808	3.717	3.630	3.546	3.465	3.387	3.312	3.240	3.170	3.102	3.037
5	4.853	4.713	4.580	4.452	4.329	4.212	4.100	3.993	3.890	3.791	3.696	3.605
6	5.795	5.601	5.417	5.242	5.076	4.917	4.767	4.623	4.486	4.355	4.231	4.111
7	6.728	6.472	6.230	6.002	5.786	5.582	5.389	5.206	5.033	4.868	4.712	4.564
8	7.652	7.325	7.020	6.733	6.463	6.210	5.971	5.747	5.535	5.335	5.146	4.968
9	8.566	8.162	7.786	7.435	7.108	6.802	6.515	6.247	5.995	5.759	5.537	5.328
10	9.471	8.983	8.530	8.111	7.722	7.360	7.024	6.710	6.418	6.145	5.889	5.650
11	10.368	9.787	9.253	8.760	8.306	7.887	7.499	7.139	6.805	6.495	6.207	5.938
12	11.255	10.575	9.954	9.385	8.863	8.384	7.943	7.536	7.161	6.814	6.492	6.194
13	12.134	11.348	10.635	9.986	9.394	8.853	8.358	7.904	7.487	7.103	6.750	6.424
14	13.004	12.106	11.296	10.563	9.899	9.295	8.745	8.244	7.786	7.367	6.982	6.628
15	13.865	12.849	11.938	11.118	10.380	9.712	9.108	8.559	8.061	7.606	7.191	6.811
16	14.718	13.578	12.561	11.652	10.838	10.106	9.447	8.851	8.313	7.824	7.379	6.974
17	15.562	14.292	13.166	12.166	11.274	10.477	9.763	9.122	8.544	8.022	7.549	7.120
18	16.398	14.992	13.754	12.659	11.690	10.828	10.059	9.372	8.756	8.201	7.702	7.250
19	17.226	15.679	14.324	13.134	12.085	11.158	10.336	9.604	8.950	8.365	7.839	7.366
20	18.046	16.351	14.878	13.590	12.462	11.470	10.594	9.818	9.129	8.514	7.963	7.469
21	18.857	17.011	15.415	14.029	12.821	11.764	10.836	10.017	9.292	8.649	8.075	7.562
22	19.660	17.658	15.937	14.451	13.163	12.042	11.061	10.201	9.442	8.772	8.176	7.645
23	20.456	18.292	16.444	14.857	13.489	12.303	11.272	10.371	9.580	8.883	8.266	7.718
24	21.243	18.914	16.936	15.247	13.799	12.550	11.469	10.529	9.707	8.985	8.348	7.784
25	22.023	19.524	17.413	15.622	14.094	12.783	11.654	10.675	9.823	9.077	8.422	7.843
26	22.795	20.121	17.877	15.983	14.375	13.003	11.826	10.810	9.929	9.161	8.488	7.896
27	23.560	20.707	18.327	16.330	14.643	13.211	11.987	10.935	10.027	9.237	8.548	7.943
28	24.316	21.281	18.764	16.663	14.898	13.406	12.137	11.051	10.116	9.307	8.602	7.984
29	25.066	21.844	19.188	16.984	15.141	13.591	12.278	11.158	10.198	9.370	8.650	8.022
30	25.808	22.397	19.600	17.292	15.372	13.765	12.409	11.258	10.274	9.427	8.694	8.055

TABLE B ■ The Future Values of Annuity (FVA) represents the value of a payment at a specified period in the future.

Future Values of Annuity

n/i	0.01	0.02	0.03	0.04	0.05	0.06	0.07	0.08	0.09	0.10	0.11	0.12
1	1.010	1.020	1.030	1.040	1.050	1.060	1.070	1.080	1.090	1.100	1.110	1.120
2	1.020	1.040	1.061	1.082	1.103	1.124	1.145	1.166	1.188	1.210	1.232	1.254
3	1.030	1.061	1.093	1.125	1.158	1.191	1.225	1.260	1.295	1.331	1.368	1.405
4	1.041	1.082	1.126	1.170	1.216	1.262	1.311	1.360	1.412	1.464	1.518	1.574
5	1.051	1.104	1.159	1.217	1.276	1.338	1.403	1.469	1.539	1.611	1.685	1.762
6	1.062	1.126	1.194	1.265	1.340	1.419	1.501	1.587	1.677	1.722	1.870	1.974
7	1.072	1.149	1.230	1.316	1.407	1.504	1.606	1.714	1.828	1.949	2.076	2.211
8	1.083	1.172	1.267	1.369	1.477	1.594	1.718	1.851	1.993	2.144	2.305	2.476
9	1.094	1.195	1.305	1.423	1.551	1.689	1.838	1.999	2.172	2.358	2.558	2.773
10	1.105	1.219	1.344	1.480	1.629	1.791	1.967	2.159	2.367	2.594	2.839	3.106
11	1.116	1.243	1.384	1.539	1.710	1.898	2.105	2.332	2.580	2.853	3.152	3.479
12	1.127	1.268	1.426	1.601	1.796	2.012	2.252	2.518	2.813	3.138	3.498	3.896
13	1.138	1.294	1.469	1.665	1.886	2.133	2.410	2.720	3.066	3.452	3.883	4.363
14	1.149	1.319	1.513	1.732	1.980	2.261	2.579	2.937	3.342	3.798	4.310	4.887
15	1.161	1.346	1.558	1.801	2.079	2.397	2.759	3.172	3.642	4.177	4.785	5.474
16	1.173	1.373	1.605	1.873	2.183	2.540	2.952	3.426	3.970	4.595	5.311	6.130
17	1.184	1.400	1.653	1.948	2.294	2.693	3.159	3.700	4.328	5.054	5.895	6.866
18	1.196	1.428	1.702	2.026	2.407	2.854	3.380	3.996	4.717	5.560	6.544	7.690
19	1.208	1.457	1.754	2.107	2.527	3.026	3.617	4.316	5.142	6.116	7.263	8.613
20	1.220	1.486	1.806	2.191	2.653	3.207	3.870	4.661	5.604	6.728	8.062	9.646
21	1.232	1.516	1.860	2.279	2.786	3.400	4.141	5.034	6.109	7.400	8.949	10.804
22	1.245	1.546	1.916	2.370	2.925	3.604	4.430	5.437	6.659	8.140	9.934	12.100
23	1.257	1.577	1.974	2.465	3.072	3.820	4.741	5.871	7.258	8.954	11.026	13.552
24	1.270	1.608	2.033	2.563	3.225	4.049	5.072	6.341	7.911	9.850	12.239	15.179
25	1.282	1.641	2.094	2.666	3.386	4.292	5.427	6.848	8.623	10.835	13.586	17.000
26	1.295	1.673	2.157	2.772	3.556	4.549	5.807	7.396	9.399	11.918	15.080	19.040
27	1.308	1.707	2.221	2.883	3.733	4.822	6.214	7.988	10.245	13.110	16.739	21.325
28	1.321	1.741	2.288	2.999	3.920	5.112	6.649	8.627	11.167	14.421	18.580	23.884
29	1.335	1.776	2.357	3.119	4.116	5.418	7.114	9.317	12.172	15.863	20.624	26.750
30	1.348	1.811	2.427	3.243	4.322	5.743	7.612	10.063	13.268	17.449	22.892	29.960

TABLE C ■ Future Values Interest Table (FVI) represents the value of an asset at a specific date.

Future Values Interest

n/i	0.01	0.02	0.03	0.04	0.05	0.06	0.07	0.08	0.09	0.10	0.11	0.12
1	1.000	1.000	1.000	1.000	1.000	1.000	1.000	1.000	1.000	1.000	1.000	1.000
2	2.010	2.202	2.030	2.040	2.050	2.060	2.070	2.080	2.090	2.100	2.110	2.120
3	3.030	3.060	3.091	3.122	3.153	3.184	3.215	3.246	3.278	3.310	3.342	3.374
4	4.060	4.122	4.184	4.246	4.310	4.375	4.440	4.506	4.573	4.641	4.710	4.779
5	5.101	5.204	5.309	5.416	5.526	5.637	5.751	5.867	5.985	6.105	6.228	6.353
6	6.152	6.308	6.468	6.633	6.802	6.975	7.153	7.336	7.523	7.716	7.913	8.115
7	7.214	7.434	7.662	7.898	8.142	8.394	8.654	8.923	9.200	9.487	9.783	10.089
8	8.286	8.583	8.892	9.214	9.549	9.897	10.260	10.637	11.029	11.436	11.859	12.300
9	9.369	9.755	10.159	10.583	11.027	11.491	11.978	12.488	13.021	13.580	14.164	14.776
10	10.462	10.950	11.464	12.006	12.578	13.181	13.817	14.487	15.193	15.937	16.722	17.549
11	11.567	12.169	12.808	13.486	14.207	14.972	15.784	16.646	17.560	18.531	19.561	20.655
12	12.683	13.412	14.192	15.026	15.917	16.870	17.889	18.977	20.141	21.384	22.713	28.029
13	13.809	14.680	15.618	16.627	17.713	18.882	20.141	21.495	22.953	24.523	26.212	28.029
14	14.947	15.974	17.086	18.292	19.599	21.015	22.551	24.215	26.019	27.975	30.095	32.393
15	16.097	17.293	18.599	20.024	21.579	23.276	25.129	27.152	29.361	31.773	34.405	37.280
16	17.258	18.639	20.157	21.825	23.658	25.673	27.888	30.324	33.003	35.950	39.190	42.753
17	18.430	20.012	21.762	23.698	25.840	28.213	30.840	33.750	36.974	40.545	44.501	48.884
18	19.615	21.412	23.414	26.645	28.132	30.906	33.999	37.450	41.301	45.599	50.396	55.750
19	20.811	22.841	25.117	27.671	30.539	33.760	37.379	41.446	46.019	51.159	56.940	63.440
20	22.019	24.297	26.870	29.778	33.066	36.786	40.996	45.762	51.160	57.275	64.203	72.052
21	23.239	25.783	28.677	31.969	35.719	39.993	44.865	50.423	56.765	64.003	72.265	81.699
22	24.472	27.299	30.537	34.248	38.505	43.392	49.006	55.547	62.873	71.403	81.214	92.503
23	25.716	28.845	32.453	36.618	41.430	46.996	53.436	60.893	69.532	79.543	91.148	104.603
24	26.974	30.422	34.427	39.083	44.502	50.816	58.177	66.765	76.790	88.497	102.174	118.155
25	28.243	32.030	36.459	41.646	47.727	54.864	63.249	73.106	84.701	98.347	114.413	133.334
26	29.526	33.671	38.553	44.312	51.113	59.156	68.677	79.955	93.324	109.182	127.999	150.334
27	30.821	35.344	40.710	47.084	54.669	63.706	74.484	87.351	102.723	121.100	143.079	169.374
28	32.129	37.051	42.931	49.968	58.403	68.528	80.698	95.339	112.968	134.210	159.817	190.699
29	33.450	38.792	45.219	52.966	62.323	73.640	87.347	103.966	124.136	148.631	178.397	214.583
30	34.785	40.568	47.575	56.085	66.439	79.058	94.461	113.283	136.308	164.494	199.021	241.333

TABLE D ■ Present Value table (PV) represents the discounted value of one dollar if invested now for payment at a future time.

Present Value of $1 at period X

n/i	0.01	0.02	0.03	0.04	0.05	0.06	0.07	0.08	0.09	0.10	0.11	0.12	0.14	0.16	0.18	0.20	0.22	0.24	0.26	0.28	0.30
1	0.990	0.980	0.971	0.962	0.952	0.943	0.935	0.926	0.917	0.909	0.901	0.893	0.877	0.862	0.847	0.833	0.82	0.806	0.794	0.781	0.769
2	1.970	1.942	1.913	1.886	1.859	1.833	1.808	1.783	1.759	1.736	1.713	1.690	1.647	1.605	1.566	1.528	1.492	1.457	1.424	1.392	1.361
3	2.941	2.884	2.829	2.775	2.723	2.673	2.624	2.577	2.531	2.487	2.444	2.402	2.322	2.246	2.174	2.106	2.042	1.981	1.923	1.868	1.816
4	3.902	3.808	3.717	3.630	3.546	3.465	3.387	3.312	3.240	3.170	3.102	3.037	2.914	2.798	2.690	2.589	2.494	2.404	2.320	2.241	2.166
5	4.853	4.713	4.580	4.452	4.329	4.212	4.100	3.993	3.890	3.791	3.696	3.605	3.433	3.274	3.127	2.991	2.864	2.745	2.635	2.532	2.436
6	5.795	5.601	5.417	5.242	5.076	4.917	4.767	4.623	4.486	4.355	4.231	4.111	3.889	3.685	3.498	3.326	3.167	3.020	2.885	2.759	2.643
7	6.728	6.472	6.230	6.002	5.786	5.582	5.389	5.206	5.033	4.868	4.712	4.564	4.289	4.039	3.812	3.605	3.416	3.242	3.083	2.937	2.802
8	7.652	7.325	7.020	6.733	6.463	6.210	5.971	5.747	5.535	5.335	5.146	4.968	4.639	4.344	4.078	3.837	3.619	3.421	3.241	3.076	2.925
9	8.566	8.162	7.786	7.435	7.108	6.802	6.515	6.247	5.995	5.759	5.537	5.328	4.946	4.607	4.303	4.031	3.786	3.566	3.366	3.184	3.019
10	9.471	8.983	8.530	8.111	7.722	7.360	7.024	6.710	6.418	6.145	5.889	5.650	5.216	4.833	4.494	4.192	3.923	3.682	3.465	3.269	3.092
11	10.368	9.787	9.253	8.760	8.306	7.887	7.499	7.139	6.805	6.495	6.207	5.938	5.453	5.029	4.656	4.327	4.035	3.776	3.544	3.335	3.147
12	11.255	10.575	9.954	9.385	8.863	8.384	7.943	7.536	7.161	6.814	6.492	6.194	5.660	5.197	4.793	4.439	4.127	3.851	3.606	3.387	3.190
13	12.134	11.348	10.635	9.986	9.394	8.853	8.358	7.904	7.487	7.103	6.750	6.424	5.842	5.342	4.910	4.533	4.203	3.912	3.656	3.427	3.223
14	13.004	12.106	11.296	10.563	9.899	9.295	8.745	8.244	7.786	7.367	6.982	6.628	6.002	5.468	5.008	4.611	4.265	3.962	3.695	3.459	3.249
15	13.865	12.849	11.938	11.118	10.380	9.712	9.108	8.559	8.061	7.606	7.191	6.811	6.142	5.575	5.092	4.675	4.315	4.001	3.726	3.483	3.268
16	14.718	13.578	12.561	11.652	10.838	10.106	9.447	8.851	8.313	7.824	7.379	6.974	6.265	5.669	5.162	4.730	4.357	4.033	3.751	3.503	3.283
17	15.562	14.292	13.166	12.166	11.274	10.477	9.763	9.122	8.544	8.022	7.549	7.120	6.373	5.749	5.222	4.775	4.391	4.059	3.771	3.518	3.295
18	16.398	14.992	13.754	12.659	11.690	10.828	10.059	9.372	8.756	8.201	7.702	7.250	6.467	5.818	5.273	4.812	4.419	4.080	3.786	3.529	3.304
19	17.226	15.679	14.324	13.134	12.085	11.158	10.336	9.604	8.950	8.365	7.839	7.366	6.550	5.877	5.316	4.844	4.442	4.097	3.799	3.539	3.311
20	18.046	16.351	14.878	13.590	12.462	11.470	10.594	9.818	9.129	8.514	7.963	7.469	6.623	5.929	5.353	4.870	4.460	4.110	3.808	3.546	3.316
21	18.857	17.011	15.415	14.029	12.821	11.764	10.836	10.017	9.292	8.649	8.075	7.562	6.687	5.973	5.384	4.891	4.476	4.212	3.816	3.551	3.320
22	19.660	17.658	15.937	14.451	13.163	12.042	11.061	10.201	9.442	8.772	8.176	7.645	6.743	6.011	5.410	4.909	4.488	4.130	3.822	3.556	3.323
23	20.456	18.292	16.444	14.857	13.489	12.303	11.272	10.371	9.580	8.883	8.266	7.718	6.792	6.044	5.432	4.925	4.499	4.137	3.827	3.559	3.325
24	21.243	18.914	16.936	15.247	13.799	12.550	11.469	10.529	9.707	8.985	8.348	7.784	6.835	6.073	5.451	4.937	4.507	4.143	3.831	3.562	3.327
25	22.023	19.524	17.413	15.622	14.094	12.783	11.654	10.675	9.823	9.077	8.422	7.843	6.873	6.097	5.467	4.948	4.514	4.147	3.834	3.564	3.329
26	22.795	20.121	17.877	15.983	14.375	13.003	11.826	10.810	9.929	9.161	8.488	7.896	6.906	6.118	5.480	4.956	4.520	4.151	3.837	3.566	3.330
27	23.560	20.707	18.327	16.330	14.643	13.211	11.987	10.935	10.027	9.237	8.548	7.943	6.935	6.136	5.492	4.964	4.524	4.154	3.839	3.567	3.331
28	24.316	21.281	18.764	16.663	14.898	13.406	12.137	11.051	10.116	9.307	8.602	7.984	6.961	6.152	5.502	4.970	4.528	4.157	3.840	3.568	3.331
29	25.066	21.844	19.188	16.984	15.141	13.591	12.278	11.158	10.198	9.370	8.650	8.022	6.983	6.166	5.510	4.975	4.531	4.159	3.841	3.569	3.332
30	25.808	22.397	19.600	17.292	15.372	13.765	12.409	11.258	10.274	9.427	8.694	8.055	7.003	6.177	5.517	4.979	4.534	4.160	3.842	3.569	3.332

Glossary

account balances The amount of money in an account equal to the net of credit and debits at that point in time for that account; the equality of debit and credit totals in an account.

accounting conventions Methods or procedures used by accounting practitioners that are based on custom (past practices) and are subject to change as new developments arise.

accounting equation In nonprofits the accounting equation will read TA = TL.

accounting period Is a recording of the financial transactions pertaining only to a specific period that are considered when preparing accounts for that period.

accrual The most commonly used accounting method, which reports income when earned and expenses when incurred. The term *accrual* refers to any individual entry recording revenue or expense in the absence of a cash transaction.

accrual concept Takes into account when a transaction occurs and not when the cash is received or paid out.

accrued expense An expense that is incurred, but not yet paid for, during a given accounting period.

allocate To distribute according to a plan or set apart for a special purpose.

allocation The assignment of assets to expense as well as the assignment of liabilities to revenue over a time frame. It is also apportionment or assignment of income or expense for various purposes.

amortization The gradual elimination of liability, such as a mortgage, in regular payments over a specified period of time.

analysis An investigation of the component parts of a whole and their relations in making up the whole.

annual report Contains basic information on both the financial and operational activities both from the preceding year's operations.

annuity An annuity can be defined as a contract that provides an income stream in return for an initial payment. It is also income from a capital investment paid in a series of regular payments, usually payable at specified time intervals. Or it is an amount paid at regular intervals for a set period of time. Mortgage payments are a form of an annuity paid to the lender.

assertions A positive statement that is unsupported by fact or proof.

assets A resource with economic value that an individual or corporation owns or controls with the expectation that it will provide future benefit.

assurance Confidence that financial statements are reliable and the organization has met regulatory requirements.

astute Having or showing shrewdness and discernment.

audit A professional auditor's examination and verification of a company's financial and accounting records and supporting documents.

auditing A systematic process of objectively obtaining and evaluating evidence regarding assertions about organizational activities and communicating the results to interested parties.

balance sheet The report that tracks the assets and the liabilities and ownership of the organization.

Balanced Scorecard A metric that gives managers a more balanced view or organizational performance.

beneficiary In insurance, the person or (more rarely) organization that receives money from the insurance company when the insured event occurs.

bias An individual's prejudice or position held on a subject at the expense of considering other alternatives or options.

bilateral contract A contract in which each party is both promisor and promisee.

bonds A debt investment in which an investor loans money to an entity that borrows the funds for a defined period of time at a fixed interest rate. Bonds are used by companies; municipalities; and state, U.S., and foreign governments to finance a variety of projects and activities. Bonds are commonly referred to as fixed-income securities and are one of the three main asset classes, along with stocks and cash equivalents.

breach The failure to perform a contractual obligation.

breakeven analysis A calculation of the approximate revenue volume required to just cover costs, below which production would be unprofitable and above which it would be profitable. Breakeven analysis focuses on the relationship between fixed costs, variable costs, and profit.

budget Inclusive list of proposed expenditures and expected receipts of any person, enterprise, or government for a specified period, usually 1 year.

capital budget The planning process used to determine whether an organization's long-term investments are worth pursuing.

carrying costs Financial and operational expense associated with operational activity. This can also be thought of as the opportunity cost of unproductive assets, the expense incurred by ownership.

cash budget An estimation of the cash inflows and outflows. Used to assess if an organization has sufficient cash resources to operate and determine if access cash is accumulating in unproductive accounts.

cash flow Actual net cash, as opposed to net income, that flows into a company during a specified period and allows the organization to provide services.

cash flow cycle Way in which actual cash flows into or out of the organization during predetermined periods.

cash flow statement Examines the flow of funds within the entity and between the entity and suppliers of capital.

catastrophic Resulting in great loss and misfortune that brings physical or financial ruin.

cause A reason for an action or response.

claims A legal action to obtain money in accordance with an insurance policy.

clean claim A PCR that is complete and free of errors.

coherence The quality or state of cohering, especially a logical, orderly, and aesthetically consistent relationship of parts.

co-insurance A form of medical cost sharing in a health insurance plan that requires an insured person to pay a stated percentage of medical expenses after the deductible amount, if any, was paid.

committed costs Money that is already spent on such things as long-term investments, mortgages, and equipment.

competitive Comparative concept of the ability and performance of a firm, subsector, or country to sell and supply goods and/or services in a given market.

competitive edge The ability of an organization to utilize its resources and services more effectively than others do, thereby outperforming them. This means they must stay ahead in four areas: being responsive to customers, innovation, quality, and efficiency.

compliance Conformity; acting according to certain accepted standards.

conformity Action in accordance with some specified standard or authority.

congruency The quality of agreeing; being suitable and appropriate; the state of being congruent.

consistency concept An accounting method used the same way every time.

control chart A graph with limit lines that is used to detect changes in a process from the graphed data that are collected.

controlling Authority or ability to manage or direct.

coordinating Determining the timing of activities so they mesh properly.

co-payment A form of medical cost sharing in a health insurance plan that requires an insured person to pay a fixed dollar amount when a medical service is received.

corporate governance A process by which the owners or decision makers control and require accountability for the resources entrusted to the organization.

cost basis An asset's value is recorded in the organization's financial books they should be actual cost paid.

cost behavior Examination of specific variable costs to determine their response to changes in business activity (production) or business volume.

cost-benefit analysis (CBA) An analysis that evaluates the cost-effectiveness of a project or policy.

cost center A unit for which costs are accumulated. It can be a designated department that incurs costs in an effort to carry out the purposes of the organization.

cost of risk Measurement of the total cost related to the risk management function.

credibility Perception of trustworthiness an individual imparts to other people.

current assets A balance sheet account that represents the value of all assets that are expected to be converted into cash within one year in the normal course of business. Current assets include cash, accounts receivable, inventory, marketable securities, prepaid expenses, and other liquid assets that can be readily converted to cash.

current liabilities A company's debts or obligations that are due within one year. Current liabilities appear on the company's balance sheet and include short term debt, accounts payable, accrued liabilities, and other debts.

current ratio A financial ratio that measures whether or not a firm has enough resources to pay its debts over the next 12 months.

customary charges Amounts a provider normally charges the majority of patients for particular medical services.

data points Items of factual information derived from measurement or research.

deductible Amount of money the insured must pay before an insurer pays its contractual share.

deductive A form of reasoning in which conclusions are formulated about particulars from general or universal premises.

deferred expense Refers to an item that will initially be recorded as an asset but is expected to become an expense over time and/or through the normal operations of the business. Sometimes called prepaid expenses.

deficiencies Noncompliance; substantiated allegations of violations of federal and/or state laws or regulations.

delegating Committing or entrusting to another or giving or committing (duties, powers, etc.) to another as agent or representative.

demand The desire to purchase goods and services.

demand theory Explains the relationship between consumer demand for goods and services and their prices.

department A specialized division of a large organization.

depreciation A noncash decrease in value of an asset due to obsolescence, wear and tear, age, or use.

deviation The difference between an observed value and the expected value of a variable or function.

diagnosis-related groups (DRGs) A system of classifications for identification of services that medical provider offers.

discretionary costs A cost that management uses and can be easily changed such as advertising, repairs, and training.

dissemination Circulation: causing to become widely known; spreading information.

disseminator The manager who provides tools for others to make decisions.

economic efficiency How well a system generates the maximum desired output with a given set of inputs and available technology.

economic ordering quantity The optimum quantity of goods for which, if orders are placed, the aggregate order placing cost and the aggregate inventory carrying cost will be equal and economical.

economics The branch of social science that deals with the production and distribution and consumption of goods and services and their management.

effect Consequence that follows an action. The change in an outcome that results from an intervention.

efficiency Competency in performance.

engineered costs Have a direct and clear relationship with output.

entitlement The right granted by law or contract (especially a right to benefits).

entity Accounting records that reflects the financial activities of a specific business.

equilibrium The condition of a system in which competing influences are balanced, resulting in no net change.

ethical Being in accordance with the accepted principles of right and wrong that govern the conduct of a profession.

ethics A branch of philosophy that seeks to address questions about morality—that is, about concepts such as good and bad, right and wrong, justice, and virtue; the standards that govern the conduct of a person, especially a member of a profession.

expenditures Money paid out; an amount spent

external audit An audit conducted by an individual that is independent of the company being audited.

fidelity The observance of promises or duties by a person to another.

fiduciary A legal or ethical relationship of confidence or trust between two or more parties.

fixed assets A long-term tangible piece of property that a firm owns and uses in the production of its income and is not expected to be consumed or converted into cash any sooner than at least one year's time.

fixed costs Costs that do not vary depending on production or sales levels, such as rent, property tax, insurance, or interest expense.

flow Process by which inputs and outputs move in an organization.

forecasting A planning tool that helps management to cope with the uncertainty of the future.

fraud A false representation of a matter of fact that deceives and is intended to deceive another so that the individual will act on it.

frequency The number of occurrences within a given time period.

full disclosure The financial statements and their notes (footnotes) that contain all pertinent data relevant to the activities of the entity.

future value The value of an asset or cash at a specified date in the future that is equivalent in value to a specified sum today.

Generally Accepted Accounting Principles (GAAP) The standard framework of guidelines for financial accounting.

going concern An organization for which accounts are being prepared is solvent and viable, and will continue to be in business in the foreseeable future.

hypothesis A proposal intended to explain certain facts or observations.

income statement A summary of a management's performance as reflected in the profitability (or lack of it) of an organization over a certain period. It itemizes the revenues and expenses of past that led to the current profit or loss, and indicates what may be done to improve the results.

independent Being objective and unbiased while performing professional services.

inductive Of reasoning; proceeding from particular facts to a general conclusion.

insurance Financial assistance provided to ensure reimbursement for losses sustained under specified conditions.

integrity Steadfast adherence to a strict moral or ethical code.

interest The percentage or rate charged by a lender to use borrowed money.

internal audit An independent and objective examination of organizational activities designed to add value and improve organizational governance, risk management, and operational processes.

inventory control A means of supervising the organizational supplies, storage of inventory, and accessibility of clinical items in order to ensure that an adequate supply is available for responders.

investments In finance, investments are purchases of financial products or other items of value with an expectation of favorable future returns. In general terms, investment means the use of money in the hope of making more money. In business, investment is the purchase by a producer of a physical good, such as durable equipment or inventory, in the hope of improving future business.

k The nominal or stated rate of interest on any given security.

k* The real risk-free rate of interest. It is the rate that would exist in a riskless security if zero inflation were expected.

k$_{RF}$ The nominal risk-free rate of interest. This is the stated interest rate on a security that is free of default risk.

leading (commanding) The process by which a person influences others to accomplish an objective and directs the organization in a way that makes it more cohesive and coherent.

liability An obligation of an entity arising from events, the settlement of which may result in the transfer of assets, provision of services, or other yielding of economic benefits in the future.

long-term liabilities Obligations payable at a future period more than 12 months away from today or the date of the balance sheet.

loss The act of losing something of value or an asset.

macroeconomics The study of the sum total of economic activity, dealing with the issues of growth, inflation, and unemployment and with national economic policies relating to these issues.

managerial accounting The process of identifying, measuring, analyzing, interpreting, and communicating information for the pursuit of an organization's goals.

mandatory Obligatory; required or commanded by authority.

marginal costs Additional cost associated with producing one more unit of output.

marginalism Changes in the quantity used of a good or of a service, as opposed to some notion of the overall significance of that class of good or service, or of some total quantity thereof.

market value Inventory valued either at cost or the market value (whichever is lower).

master budget The comprehensive budget plan encompassing all the individual budgets related to the operations of an organization.

matching Transactions that affect both revenues and expenses in the same accounting period.

material breach Occurs when the non-faulted party is discharged from further obligations under the contract.

materiality Events that should be fully disclosed if they make a significant difference in the finances of an organization.

microeconomics The branch of economics that studies the economy of consumers, households, or individual firms.

mitigate The act of lessening in severity or intensity.

monitor The act of observing something (and sometimes keeping a record of it).

moral Concerned with principles of right and wrong or conforming to standards of behavior and character based on those principles.

net income Income after all revenues and expenses have been accounted for; also known as the bottom line.

net present value (NPV) Today's value of future costs and benefits.

net working capital The difference between current assets and current liabilities.

observations What is seen or viewed.

operating expenses Rent, gas/electricity, wages, and so on.

operational audit A systematic appraisal of an organization's operations to determine whether those operations are being conducted in an efficient manner and whether constructive recommendations can be made.

opinion A belief or conclusion held with confidence but not substantiated by positive knowledge or proof.

opinion A formal decision that includes a detailed explanation of the legal principles involved.

opportunity cost The return that may be realized by the next best alternative.

organizations Groups of people who work together; a social arrangement that pursues collective goals.

organizing Assembling required resources to attain organizational objectives.

outcomes A final product or end result, consequence, or issue.

output The act of production or manufacture.

overhead Refers to the ongoing expense of operating a business.

payback method Method to evaluate an investment project.

planning Establishing goals and objectives to pursue during a future period; the process of setting goals, developing strategies, and outlining tasks and schedules to accomplish the goals of an organization.

preferred Preference refers to the set of assumptions relating to a real or imagined "choice" between alternatives and the possibility of rank-ordering these alternatives, based on the degree of happiness, satisfaction, gratification, enjoyment, or utility.

prepaid expenses Payments made for goods or services that will be received or used in the future.

present value The current value of an asset or cash.

pro forma statement Hypothetical financial statement showing assets and liabilities, or income and expenses that may be recognized in the future. Pro forma statements also can illustrate projected earnings if a company were to merge with another or sell off part of its operations.

proactive Acting in advance to deal with an expected change or difficulty. Being proactive is about being anticipatory and taking charge of situations.

probability Knowledge or belief that an event will occur or has occurred.

procurement A method by which the process of assessing the need for products or services, the evaluation of purchases for appropriateness, and the ongoing tracking of all products purchased occurs.

prudence concept Revenue and profits are recorded on the balance sheet only when they are realized.

purchasing To obtain in exchange for money or its equivalent; buy.

qualified To specify as a condition or requirement in a contract or agreement; in other words, meeting requirements.

quick ratio Measures the ability of a company to use its near cash or quick assets; current assets less inventory divided by current liabilities.

ratios Proportion; the relationship between things (or parts of things) with respect to their comparative quantity, magnitude, or degree.

reform Make changes for improvement in order to remove abuse and injustices.

reimbursement Pay back for some expense incurred.

relative value units (RVUs) Used to calculate compensation for medical providers using a set formula that is tied to various services.

relevant How pertinent, connected, or applicable something is to a given matter.

resource dependency theory For a manager or organization to survive, it must not become dependent on others.

risk An uncertainty or an unknown.

Securities and Exchange Commission (SEC) An independent agency which holds primary responsibility for enforcing the federal securities laws and regulating the securities industry.

self-pay A patient or guarantor responsible for the balance owed; a self-pay account.

sensitivity testing A series of tests of a strategy to find out how its performance changes with changes in the assumptions made. It is also the systematic investigation of the effects on outcomes of changes in assumptions.

severity Intensely or extremely bad or unpleasant in degree or quality.

spreadsheet A program used for managing, analyzing, and presenting information. Spreadsheets allow information to be sorted or displayed in a chart or graph for calculations to be performed on data.

standardization The condition in which a standard has been successfully established.

standards Written definition, limit, or rule, approved and monitored for compliance by an authoritative agency or professional or recognized body as a minimum acceptable benchmark.

statistical process control (SPC) The use of statistical techniques and tools to measure an ongoing process for change or stability.

stewardship The conducting, supervising, or managing of something, especially the careful and responsible management of something entrusted to one's care.

stock Refers to wealth in monetary (dollars) or other forms (buildings, land, accounts receivable) available to owners at a given point in time.

strategy A plan of action designed to achieve a particular goal.

supplemental insurance A private health insurance coverage that may be purchased to supplement or fill gaps in health plan coverage.

supply The amount of goods or services a business provides.

sustainability The ability to achieve and sustain an impact for as long as there is a need for its intervention. It can also mean the ongoing process of achieving development or redevelopment that does not undermine its physical or social systems of support.

systematic Of or pertaining to a system; consisting in a system; methodical; formed with regular connection and adaptation or subordination of parts to each other, and to the design of the whole.

tangible assets Physical assets represents property, plant and equipment.

theory An unproven conjecture; an expectation of what should happen, barring unforeseen circumstances. A coherent statement or set of statements that attempts to explain observed phenomena.

time breach No time for performance is stated or implied in the contract, but the performance was not completed within a reasonable amount of time.

toleration To refrain from intervening, to allow one to participate or function.

total assets All current assets, fixed assets, and other assets.

total liabilities All current liabilities and long-term debt.

trends Tendencies; general direction(s) in which something tends to move. Gradual change(s) in a condition, output, or process moving in a certain direction over time.

unbiased Indifferent; characterized by a lack of partiality.

uncertainty In finance, uncertainty usually refers to risk or volatility.

unilateral contract A relatively simple form for a contract, such as a purchase order.

uninsured Not covered by insurance.

unit A unique entity or thing that is a function of a whole and is used to value or compare against something different.

validity Describes how well a particular assessment method actually measures the outcome it is intended to measure.

variable costs Expenses that change in proportion to the activity of a business.

variance The difference between a budgeted, planned, or standard amount and the actual amount incurred/sold; variances can be computed for both costs and revenues.

verifiable Confirmable; capable of being tested (verified or falsified) by experiment or observation.

waiver The act of intentionally relinquishing or abandoning a known right, claim, or privilege; *also,* the legal instrument evidencing such an act.

working capital policy The organization's basic policies regarding the target level for cash in each category of current assets and how current assets will be financed.

working capital A financial metric that is a measure of current assets of a business that exceeds its liabilities and can be applied to its operation.

Index

www.ingramcontent.com/pod-product-compliance
Lightning Source LLC
Chambersburg PA
CBHW080934220326
41598CB00034B/5779